KU-259-072

THE BLUE GUIDES

Austria
Belgium and Luxembourg
China
Cyprus
Czechoslovakia
Denmark
Egypt

FRANCE
France
Paris and Versailles
Burgundy
Normandy
Corsica

GREECE
Greece
Athens and environs
Crete

HOLLAND
Holland
Amsterdam

Hungary

ITALY
Northern Italy
Southern Italy
Florence
Rome and environs
Venice
Tuscany
Umbria
Sicily

Jerusalem
Malta and Gozo

Moscow and Leningrad
Morocco
Portugal

SPAIN
Spain
Barcelona

Switzerland

TURKEY
Turkey: the Aegean
  and Mediterranean Coasts
Istanbul

UK
England
Ireland
Scotland
Wales
London
Museums and Galleries
  of London
Oxford and Cambridge
Gardens of England
Literary Britain and Ireland
Victorian Architecture in Britain
Churches and Chapels
  of Northern Engalnd
Churches and Chapels
  of Southern England
Channel Islands

USA
New York
Boston and Cambridge

Yugoslavia

*The Bull's Head Rhyton from the Little Palace at Knossós
(Herakleion Museum, Gallery IV)*

BLUE GUIDE

Crete

Pat Cameron

Atlas, maps and plans by John Flower

A & C Black
London

WW Norton
New York

Sixth edition 1993

Published by A & C Black (Publishers) Limited
35 Bedford Row, London WC1R 4JH

© A & C Black (Publishers) Limited 1993

ISBN   0–7136–3588–6

A CIP catalogue record for this book
is available from the British Library

Published in the United States of America by
W W Norton & Company, Inc
500 Fifth Avenue, New York, NY 10110

Published simultaneously in Canada by
Penguin Books Canada Limited,
2801 John Street, Markham, Ontario L3R 1B4

ISBN   0–393–30969–X

Please write in with your comments, suggestions and corrections. Writers of the best letters will be awarded a free Blue Guide of their choice.

Pat Cameron is an MA of Oxford University where she read English Language and Literature at Somerville College. In 1979, after gaining the London University Diploma in Archaeology, she joined the staff of the British School at Athens to catalogue material in the School's Stratigraphical Museum at Knossós. She lived for five years on Crete working on this project and had time to acquire a detailed knowledge of the island to which she now regularly returns.

Printed and bound in Great Britain by
Butler & Tanner Ltd, Frome and London

PREFACE

The first edition of *Blue Guide Crete* appeared in 1974 as an expanded version of the existing chapter covering the island in *Blue Guide Greece*. It was brought up to date twice in six years, but eventually a major revision became necessary. After the untimely death of the Guide's previous author, Stuart Rossiter, I was asked to undertake this task. The fourth edition, published in 1986, was revised and substantially expanded for a fifth in 1988.

As this sixth edition is ready for publication I find myself increasingly aware of my indebtedness along the way to an often unacknowledged host of experts in one field or another. Without their suggestions and guidelines, and their generous sharing of specialised knowledge, this book could not have been written.

I continue to be grateful to Dr Hector Catling, Director of the British School at Athens, who allowed me to make a start on the Guide whilst I was still on the staff of the School, and then encouraged and advised me on many occasions. Vronwy Hankey gave me the initial confidence to undertake the revision, and has shown unfailing patience in allowing me to discuss problems. In the beginning the archaeology in the book owed much to Sandy MacGillivray who found himself the most accessible authority when questions arose; he was unstinting in his willingness to expound and explain. However, the conclusions I have reached are my own responsibility.

I regret that I cannot name individually all the members of the British School who have aided me in both academic and practical ways. I owe a great debt to the sum total of their friendly efforts. Ann Brown's travels on Crete in pursuit of her own projects have produced generous quantities of information and ideas for me.

I should also like to thank Cheli Duran and Eléni Faragoulitákis-Kouvídes who explained many aspects of Cretan life and language; their meticulous scrutiny led to many corrections and improvements of my first version, as did Kerin Hope's kindness in reading the medieval section of the island's history. Carol Lister contributed a valuable paragraph of geological information. For this edition I have had particular help on Crete from Mrs Kalokairinoú of the Herákleion Historical Museum, Mrs Khronáki of the Service for Byzantine Antiqutities and from C. Macdonald at Knossós.

The National Tourist Organisation of Greece gave practical help from their offices in London as well as in Herákleion and Khaniá; this help included arranging for me a complimentary flight to Crete on Olympic Airways.

I am grateful to all who provided or allowed me to use photographs, especially W. Müller and P.W. Warren, the Visitors of the Ashmolean Museum in Oxford, the Committee of the British School at Athens, and the Archaeological and Byzantine Services of Crete.

At each stage John Flower has contributed plans and patiently corrected maps. David Smyth helped me with the basis for a new plan of the surroundings of the Palace of Knossós which was taken from his own large-scale plan for the 1981 Archaeological Survey of the Knossós Area (Hood and Smyth).

Among the many authorities and written sources I have drawn on I would like to acknowledge in particular the work of G. Cadogan,

P. Callaghan, N. Coldstream, S. Hood, A. Makridákis, I. Sanders, S. Spanákis, P. Warren and D. Wilson, some of whom kindly helped with specific problems in their own field. Further sources are listed in the Bibliography, especially early travellers such as the scholar Robert Pashley, the naval surveyor Captain (later Admiral) T.A.B. Spratt in the 19C, and the Italian Guiseppe Gerola whose treatise (1905–32) on the island's Venetian monuments laid the foundations of research in this field. The most recent addition, 'Kreta' by Gallas, Wessel and Borboudákis is likely to remain the definitive work on the churches of Byzantine Crete for many years to come.

During work on my first edition I received invaluable help with the final preparation of the manuscript from my brother, Christopher Cruise. Since then Emma Bullard and Mary Laing have read the revised and expanded text and made many improvements to it. My original editor, Tom Neville, was extraordinarily patient about a revision which turned out to be much more radical than he had bargained for. I am also grateful to Gemma Davies and Judy Tither now responsible for Blue Guides at A and C Black for their support and help with this new edition. By all these people, at various stages, I have been saved from a large number of errors and obscurities. To reduce the number still further I have had the benefit of many letters from readers, and all further suggestions will be welcomed.

A Note on Blue Guides

The Blue Guide series began in 1915 when Muirhead Guide-Books Limited published 'Blue Guide London and its Environs'. Finlay and James Muirhead already had extensive experience of guidebook publishing: before the First World War they had been the editors of the English editions of the German Baedekers, and by 1915 they had acquired the copyright of most of the famous 'Red' Handbooks from John Murray.

An agreement made with the French publishing house Hachette et Cie in 1917 led to the translation of Muirhead's London guide, which became the first 'Guide Bleu'—Hachette had previously published the blue-covered 'Guides Joannes'. Subsequently, Hachette's 'Guide Bleu Paris et ses Environs' was adapted and published in London by Muirhead. The collaboration between the two publishing houses continued until 1933.

In 1933 Ernest Benn Limited took over the Blue Guides, appointing Russell Muirhead, Finlay Muirhead's son, editor in 1934. The Muirhead's connection with the Blue Guides ended in 1963 when Stuart Rossiter, who had been working on the Guides since 1954, became house editor, revising and compiling several of the books himself.

The Blue Guides are now published by A & C Black, who acquired Ernest Benn in 1984, so continuing the tradition of guidebook publishing which began in 1826 with 'Black's Economical Tourist of Scotland'. The Blue Guide series continues to grow: there are now 50 titles in print with revised editions appearing regularly and many new Blue Guides in preparation.

'Blue Guides' is a registered trade mark.

CONTENTS

8 *CONTENTS*

MAPS AND PLANS

Maps

Plans

EXPLANATIONS

Type. The main routes are described in large type. Smaller type is used for branch-routes and excursions, for historical and preliminary paragraphs, and (generally speaking) for descriptions of minor importance.

Asterisks (*, **) indicate points of special interest or excellence.

Distances are given cumulatively in kilometres (the total once in miles) from the starting-point of the route or sub-route. An attempt has been made to give road distances as accurately as possible; detours are not included in the total. Sometimes the route distances start from a junction on the bypass of a large town rather than from its centre; this is noted in the text. New kilometre posts are installed on main routes, and figures given in the Guide conform to the new system where possible.

Walking distances have been indicated as an approximate time allowance. A Cretan asked a walking distance will always give the answer as a walking *time*, which takes account of the terrain along the way.

Abbreviations. In addition to generally accepted and self-explanatory abbreviations, the following occur in this Guide:

Ay. = Ayios, Ayía, Ayii, Ayiés (Saint or Saints)
c = circa
C = century
Dr(s) = drachma(s)
EOT (NTOG) = Ελληνικός Οργανισμός Τουρισμού (National Tourist Organisation of Greece)
ΚΤΕΛ (KTEL) = Κοινόν Ταμείον Εισπράξεων Λεωφορείων (Joint Pool of Bus Owners)
ΛΕΩΦ. = Leophóros (Avenue)
OTE = Οργανισμός Τηλεπικοινωνιών Ελλάδος (Telecommunications Organisation of Greece)
Plat. = Plateía (Square)
Rte = route

Transliteration and stress accents. The chief guiding principle has been to help the reader, with or without a classical education, to pronounce the Greek words in the text, especially the place-names, in a manner recognisable to a modern Greek speaker. Absolute consistency in transliterating is difficult for a number of reasons, but especially because some well-known words already have an accepted spelling in the English language, for example Herakleion and Zeus. Moreover, pedantically strict consistency sometimes produces unnecessarily ugly words without assisting pronunciation.

The transliteration of place-names on signposts does not always follow the system used in this Guide. The transition of modern Greek from *katharévousa* (or formal) to a *demotikí* (colloquial) form, most conspicuous in the grammatical endings, is nearly complete, but a process of simplification continues and many spelling variations will still be encountered: Knossós and Knosós, Lassíthi and Lasíthi.

In addition, *all* place-names decline like other nouns; this often produces a change of stress as well as of inflection. Some places have their more modern spoken form in the accusative, for example Zákro, though they appear offically on maps and signposts in the nominative, Zákros.

Street names are usually in the genitive: literally Street of 25 August, Square of Freedom. As in English, a church may be referred to by the name of its saint in the nominative or the genitive. This is particularly noticeable in Greek in the case of monasteries: Moní Arkadíou, the monastery of Arkádi.

The written accents of modern Greek are in the process of being drastically simplified, but because correct stress is vital to the understanding of the spoken word, the transliterated versions in the text have been given an acute accent to indicate the stress. The names of Classical sites have been stressed as in modern Greek to help the tourist enquiring for them. Upper case characters are not accented, so in unmarked words starting with a vowel (Ayios, Embaros) the initial syllable carries the stress.

CRETE

The island of Crete, in Greek Κρήτη (Kríti), the Candia of the Venetians, has a particular character which clearly distinguishes it from all other Mediterranean islands. Crete's history has always been influenced by its geographical position at a crossroads of sea-routes between Europe, the Levant and North Africa. The island was the cradle of the Minoan civilisation, the first civilisation to emerge in what is now Europe. The Dorian city-states of the Iron Age were submerged in the Roman Empire, and Roman rulers were succeeded in due course by Arabs, and then by the forces—both military and cultural—of Byzantium, of Venice and of the Ottoman Empire. Crete became politically united with Greece only at the beginning of this century.

The island is by far the largest in the Greek archipelago, and its territory includes the most southerly point in Europe; on Latitude 35.007 it is farther south than Algiers or Tunis. As the southern boundary of the Aegean basin it forms the major link in a chain of smaller islands stretching through Kýthera to the Peloponnesian mainland of Greece, and through Kásos and Kárpathos to Rhodes and Turkey, while to the south the coast of Africa is only 300km away. In length 250km, nearly 60km at its widest point but only 12km at its narrowest, Crete is dominated by its great mountain backbone; in the west the White Mountains (Levká Ori, 2453m), in the centre, the massif of Mount Ida (Psilorítis, 2456m), towards the east the Lasíthi mountains (Díkte, 2148m), and at the eastern end, beyond the narrow isthmus of Ierápetra, the Siteía range. The mountains are composed of folded rocks, ranging in age from Late Palaeozoic to Early Tertiary. These hard crystalline limestones, phyllite, schist, and occasional altered igneous rocks (such as serpentinite) were placed in their present position by Alpine earth movements. In contrast to the upland areas, the low-lying ground is formed of Late Tertiary sediments, notably cream-coloured limestones, sands, clays and gypsum, deposited after the main mountain-forming episode.

The mountains slope gently to the north and very steeply to the southern coast, and therefore habitation has concentrated on the north coast around and behind the great bays of Kastélli, Khaniá, Soúda, Réthymnon, Herákleion, Mirabéllo and Siteía. By contrast the southern coast cannot support much of a population and there is only one sizeable town, Ierápetra. The fertile Mesará plain, watered by the Ieropótamos and Anapodáris, is the only cultivable area of any size in the south, but terraced hillsides and the hothouses along the coastal strip often make good use of less propitious land. An interesting geographical feature is the incidence of high upland plains enclosed by a ring of mountains, such as the Lasíthi plain, that of Nída on Mount Ida and the Omalós in the White Mountains.

Crete enjoys a typical Mediterranean climate with long hot dry summers. The winter rain, often torrential, falls as snow in the mountains, but there is also an extensive frost-free coastal zone. This climate favours the island's two main crops, the olive and the vine; it is also suitable for the fig, almond, pomegranate, carob tree and quince, all of which can be found growing wild. (The Latin name of the quince is derived from Kydonía, one of Crete's ancient cities.) Melons and apricots are traditionally successful, and there are extensive citrus groves especially in the north-west coastal belt. Along the south coast, which enjoys relatively high winter temperatures, serried ranks of practical but unsightly plastic hothouses supply vegetables year-round for the Athens markets. The number of banana groves is increasing, and there are projects for kiwi fruit and avacado pears. The upland plains, especially Lasíthi, grow potatoes, onions and apples, also some cereals, though Crete is no longer the granary it was under Roman and Venetian rule.

About 20 per cent of the island's population of a little over 500,000 lives and works in Herákleion, which is the fifth largest city in Greece, and has the highest per capita income in the whole country. The profits from tourism are chiefly responsible for this prosperity, but Greece's membership of the European Community has led to an increasing variety of investment from abroad.

In the villages much of the traditional work is still concerned with the vines and the olives, both labour-intensive operations at certain seasons of year; since Minoan times olive oil has been an important source of Cretan wealth, alongside the vast number of sheep and goats that graze the mountain pastures. An accepted way to raise money, for a daughter's dowry or to build a new house, has been to serve a spell 'on the ships' in Greece's merchant navy. Money also returns to the island from Greek communities overseas.

The climate and a geographical position close to Asia are responsible for Crete's astonishing variety of wild plants and flowers. The many hundreds of known species include over 130 peculiar to the island. Botanists will not need to be reminded of the specialised flora of Crete's mountains, gorges and coasts, and many guided botanical tours are arranged from all parts of the world. However, the visitor with a more general interest can also scarcely fail to be delighted by the island's wild flowers. Many varieties of orchid and ophrys appear in the spring. Sheets of *Anenome coronaria* at the beginning of the year are followed by *Ranunculus asiaticus*, most noticeable in a shining buttercup yellow. In damp ground under trees and bushes *Cyclamen creticum* flourishes. At the edge of the melting snow on Ida or the Omalós plain are the predictable belts of Crete's special crocus, *C. sieberi var. sieberi*, often mixed with *Chionodoxa cretica*. In their season there are wild iris and scented narcissus, lupin, gladiolus and the idiosyncratic Cretan tulip. There are asphodels and mandragora or mandrake familiar from literature. In late spring the fields turn yellow with *Chrysanthemum coronaria*, and the hillsides are coloured by pink and white varieties of cistus. When the first oleanders flower in dried-up stream-beds, or along the verges of the roads, it is a sign that spring is over. There are autumn flowers too, as growth starts again in October after the first rains, but they are less profuse and conspicuous, a more specialised interest.

Crete's original forest cover has been exploited since Minoan times, but until the 16C cypress trees still covered the slopes of Mount Ida. The forests declined drastically during the Turkish occupation, and nowadays herds of goats still cause damage which discourages regeneration. Large areas have been reduced to a scrub known elsewhere in the Mediterranean region as 'macchie' or 'garigue', and in Greece as 'phrygana'. The typical vegetation can be uncomfortably spiny, but the all-pervading scent of herbs such as sage, thyme and origano will provide ample compensation, and the undergrowth shelters a great many members of the orchid family. Unfortunately the main archaeological sites are now sprayed with herbicides to protect architectural features from invasive roots and weed cover. But many of the less well-known sites to which this Guide points have not been affected, and moreover are legally protected from cultivation and grazing, so that they make ideal refuges for all manner of plant life.

Among the wild animals now found are the Cretan ibex (known locally as the kri-kri or the agrími, a word used in Greek for any wild animal), badger, wild cat, marten and weasel. The agrími, *Capra aegagrus cretensis*, often depicted in Minoan art, survives in the wild in very limited numbers in the remoter regions of the White Mountains, and is also protected in various reserves on off-shore islands along the north coast. Butterfly experts will be on the lookout in spring for the Eastern Festoon, known only from western Crete, the Cretan Argus on the slopes of Mount Ida, and the Cretan Grayling. Reptiles are less widespread than on the mainland, though the viper is known. Scorpions are not uncommon and there is a dangerous species of poisonous spider, the rogalída, though as it lives in underground burrows this is rarely seen.

Ornithologists come to Crete to observe the varied bird life especially during the spring migration. Some spectacular birds of passage are egrets, hoopoes, bee-eaters and golden orioles, also large flocks of red-footed falcons. Among the resident bird population specialists watch for Bonelli's eagle, Eleonora's falcon, and the bearded vulture or lammergeier, now a species threatened with extinction, though the Greek government has made a welcome start on protection measures. The uninitiated visitor is likely to notice other huge vultures (usually the griffon vulture), eagles, buzzards and various falcons including perhaps the swift peregrine. A flash of vivid blue, and a voice unmistakeable once heard is the blue rock thrush. A melancholy drawn-out note, rhythmically repeated at intervals, comes from the Scops owl; it is a characteristic sound of the Cretan dusk.

The Cretan authorities are very aware of the tourist potential of the island's climate and natural beauty combined with the interest in its antiquities, both at the archaeological sites and displayed as masterpieces in the museum collections. Large hotels continue to be built along the north coast and even remote areas are equipped to receive visitors. The greatly improved road system offers easy access to all the main tourist objectives.

The Bronze Age Minoan civilisation will be the primary interest for the majority of readers of this Guide, but many later antiquities are also rewarding in a variety of ways. The hilltop sites have great appeal for keen walkers and nature lovers even if little has yet been excavated and only the quantity of stone hints at former occupation. Crete's surviving monasteries, though often sorely depleted as religious institutions, are now on the tourist circuit; despite much restoration made necessary by their turbulent history they retain architectural surprises, and they remain for the most part havens of tranquillity. Sunday may prove the exception for then they are popular objectives for the traditional Cretan Εκδρομή or 'outing'.

At the beginning of this century the Italian scholar Guiseppe Gerola listed 809 Byzantine churches with fresco paintings on Crete, and perhaps as many as 600 still remain in sufficiently good condition to be studied by experts. The Service for Byzantine Antiquities is engaged in an admirable programme of conservation. Specialists in this field will already be aware of what they seek on the island, but for the uninitiated a number of the better-preserved and more easily accessible frescoed churches and chapels are recommended in the itineraries. In other circumstances an exhibition of these paintings would attract widespread attention. No such exhibition could match the beauty of their native setting.

HISTORICAL BACKGROUND TO CRETAN ANTIQUITIES

Neolithic Period (c 6000–3500 BC). The earliest settlers of Crete arrived by sea from the east or south, perhaps from Anatolia (Asia Minor). Their economy was based on farming, with domesticated animals and cultivated crops, and they spun and wove cloth. They lived in villages in the open, sometimes on low hills as at Knossós and Phaistós, and sometimes for part of the year in caves. They built simple rectangular houses, at first entirely of sun-dried mudbrick and later of mudbrick on a stone socle. Their burial places, frequently in caves or rock shelters, were outside the settlements, which suggests a relatively advanced culture. Cave sanctuaries evidently played an important part all through the Neolithic period. The first inhabitants of Knossós seem to have been at an aceramic stage of development, but this was short-lived and Neolithic pottery reached a high standard in the dark geometric burnished wares, sometimes with incised decoration of simple geometric patterns filled with white paste. Other characteristic artefacts were stone and bone tools, bone arrowheads, obsidian blades, stone vessels and maceheads. There are female figurines in both stone and clay, often of pronounced steatopygous shapes. By the end of the fourth millenium BC, settlement had spread throughout Crete, and as far as some relatively remote off-shore islands.

The Bronze Age (3500–1100 BC). Sir Arthur Evans characterised the Cretan Bronze Age as Minoan, after the legendary King Minos. He identified Early, Middle and Late Minoan periods (EM, MM, LM), and gave each period three sub-divisions (EMI, EMII, EMIII and so on). In some cases these periods were further refined to reflect archaeological evidence (eg LMIA and LMIB, even LMIIIA1 and LMIIIA2), but usually these sub-divisions can be ignored by the layman.

Evans based this system on stratigraphy and changes in pottery styles recognised during his excavations at the Palace of Knossós and correlated with work at other sites on Crete. The system has certain limitations, especially in eastern Crete where the pottery styles may be more conservative than at Knossós, but by and large nearly a century of archaeological study has confirmed rather than refuted Evans's original interpretation.

More recently the eminent Greek archaeologist N. Pláton proposed a system of chronology based on major events in the time-span of the Minoan palaces. Pláton divided the Bronze Age into four periods: Prepalatial (the approximate equivalent of Evans's Early Minoan), Protopalatial (the period of the Old Palaces), Neopalatial (the period of the New Palaces) and Postpalatial. The majority of Minoan sites were destroyed at the end of LMI. However the Palace of Knossós was re-occupied after that LMI destruction and there is increasing evidence (not yet well understood) for use as late as the 13C, so the so-called Postpalatial dates may be open to confusion.

Both these systems, which are not incompatible (see simplified chronological chart p 18), are attempts to establish a relative chronology or intelligible sequence within the Bronze Age of Crete. For an absolute chronology, or calender dates, archaeologists beginning with Evans's painstakingly built up correlations with the world outside Crete, especially Egypt, using foreign artefacts excavated in a reliable context on the island, and Cretan artefacts similarly found abroad. Absolute dating of the Egyptian sequence was possible because its hieroglyphic script had been deciphered in 1822. The scientific method of Radiocarbon dating (despite an error factor at the time of the Minoan palaces of about 100 years) has provided a valuable complementary system for correlation with what are in effect historical dates from Egypt, and the opportunity to confirm or challenge them.

Further study of pottery styles and inter-disciplinary discussion has led and is still leading to revised interpretations, especially in the realm of absolute dates, and it should be understood that this is a continuing process. Archaeological discoveries, in Egypt as well as Crete, are now evaluated in the light of increasingly sophisticated scientific evidence to refine the relative chronology of the Minoan civilisation as well as its correlation with the rest of the Aegean world.

The Prepalatial Period (3500–1900 BC), EMI–III and MMI. The transition from Neolithic to Early Minoan c 3500 BC resulted from a gradual infiltration of new settlers, again probably from the East, bringing with them the technique of copper-working. Many new settlements date from this time. The EMI period is marked by several innovations in pottery technique and style. The pottery is hand-made, but it is much more skilfully fired, and there are distinctive new shapes such as the beak-spouted jug. Pýrgos ware (named after the cave site near Nírou Kháni excavated in 1918) includes tall pedestalled chalices, and their patterned surface is achieved by burnishing. The earliest painted decoration on pottery also dates from this period. Ayios Onoúphrios ware has patterns composed of narrow stripes of red or brown on a buff or cream ground; these groups of stripes are arranged in a variety of designs, sometimes intersecting for a cross-hatched effect. Burial in caves continued, but the first built tombs are recorded; there was a primitive 'tholos' near Krási on the route up to Lasíthi, and a huge cemetery of pit graves at Ayía Photiá in eastern Crete. At Pýrgos (see above) the first known interments in clay coffins or 'larnakes' were discovered.

The circular tombs of the Mesará plain begin to appear during EMII. Tombs of this type, which occur elsewhere on Crete but less frequently, are large communal graves, stone-built and free-standing, with a single low entrance always facing east. They were in use for many generations during the second half of the third millenium, and some continued during the following period contemporary with the Old Palaces. The term 'tholos' (indicating a circular domed shape), which is often applied to these tombs, may be misleading, for it is thought unlikely that, in the case of the larger ones at least, they would have been vaulted in stone.

The monochrome and painted pottery styles of EMI continued their development into EMII, but this period marked the appearance of the mottled red, orange and black ware named after the site of Vasilikí, where it was first found. The striking effect over the entire surface of the vase was achieved by a combination of uneven firing and the use of several different-coloured slips on the same vessel.

Two sites of this period have been thoroughly excavated. Mýrtos (Phournoú Koriphí) on the south coast is a close-knit settlement with defined living areas, kitchens, store-rooms and workrooms, but without separately defined houses. At Vasilikí in eastern Crete the settlement plan suggests a less communal social structure. The quality of the architecture of the so-called 'House on the Hill' at this site has long been recognised; important features were the paving of a West Court, and internal walls finished with hard red-painted plaster. Recent study has revealed that this building is not one but two houses, both dated within the second half of EMII. Vasilikí is said to foreshadow the mode of life of the palace civilisation of the next millenium. A more centralised society was encouraging specialised craftsmen who produced the bronze daggers, gold jewellery, ivory carving, seals and stone vases, often of superb refinement, which are known from the tombs of this Prepalatial period. Foreign contact increased and with it foreign influence; a Minoan colony was founded on Kýthera, an island off the southern Peloponnese.

The Old Palace or Protopalatial Period, MMIB–MMII. This period, conventionally dated 1900–1700 BC (but see discussion under Neopalatial period below) is marked by the development of the palaces at Knossós, Phaistós and Mállia. There is fuller evidence of town life on the main sites, and individual villas have been identified, for example at Mállia. Peak sanctuaries, as on Mount Júktas above Knossós and Petsophás above Palaíkastro, began to play an important part in Minoan religious life. The Early Minoan tombs continued in use, but in many places a new method of burial was introduced with the body placed in a clay storage jar (pithos), as at the cemetery at Pakhyámmos near Gourniá.

In the palaces the EMIII/MMI style of pottery with white spiral decoration on a dark ground was succeeded by exquisite thin-walled polychrome vases, known as Kamáres ware, made possible by the introduction to the potters' workshops of the fast wheel. Great strides were made in all forms of metalwork; bronzesmiths mastered elaborate castings in two-piece moulds, and understood the lost-wax (*cire perdue*) process. Some of their best work was reserved for the daggers, other weapons and tools exemplified in finds of this period from the Mesará tombs. The superb jewellery on display in the Herákleion Museum includes examples of the goldsmiths' work, showing a free use of granulation and filigree techniques, with decorative patterns in minute grains of gold, or designs using fine gold threads. The art of the seal engraver also developed rapidly; though soft stones continued to be used and earlier shapes survived, harder stones appear in new shapes, with more vigorous and life-like designs. Remains of a sealcutter's workshop were found at Mállia, including tools and unfinished seals, while a deposit of nearly 7000 sealings at Phaistós greatly enlarged the corpus of known designs. The so-called Hieroglyphic Deposit at Knossós (sealings, labels and tablets) testifies to the connection between seals and writing.

Foreign contacts were wide; Egyptian scarabs appear in Crete and MMII pottery in Cyprus, Egypt and the Near East, while both pottery and stone vases have been found on the Greek mainland and in the islands. At the end of MMII a great catastrophe left the palaces in ruins. The damage was almost certainly caused by earthquakes, and the huge blocks hurled from the south façade at Knossós into Evans's 'House of the Fallen Blocks' are evidence of the strength of the upheaval.

The New Palace or Neopalatial Period (1700–1450 BC), MMIII–LMI. (The background to the controversy over the conventional dates of the LMI period is discussed below.) After the MMII disaster the palaces were rebuilt, and to this period belong most of the elaborate Minoan buildings whose remains are now visible, including the mansions that surround the palaces, and the large houses elsewhere across the island. Fresco paintings decorated the walls of major rooms; efficient plumbing and drainage systems were installed. The extensive areas filled with huge storage jars bear witness both to the economic prosperity of the age and to the sophisticated redistribution system on which its economy was based.

Foreign contacts were wide-ranging. Crete exercised a profound influence on the mainland of Greece at least from the beginning of the LMI period onwards, and indelibly stamped its character on what came to be called Mycenaean culture. Influence on the Cycladic Islands was even more profound; it is suggested that there were Minoan colonies on some of them, for example Kéa and Mélos, and the clearest example yet excavated of a provincial Minoan town is the Akrotíri site on Théra (Santorini). Strong influence, if not actual settlement, has been noted on Rhodes and Kos, while sites in Asia Minor (e.g. Miletus and Troy) were well within the Minoan trading orbit. Further afield Minoan products reached the Lipari islands in the west and Cyprus, the Levant and Egypt to the east. At this point Crete commanded apparently unlimited supplies of copper and tin (copper ingots found at Ayía Triáda and Zákros, Palatial hoards of bronze vessels at Knossós, Mállia and Týlissos). There is debate concerning the source of these metals; scientific research now suggests much copper may have come from deposits in the Lávrion area in Attica, and only a small quantity from the much better-known source in Cyprus. The source of tin, a vital constituent of bronze, is even more uncertain; Cornwall, Bohemia and Sinai have all been suggested.

It is a mark of the prosperity of the times that decorated pottery was no longer the leading artistic medium (despite the excellence of the so-called 'Marine style'). The innovative artists may have turned to fresco painting, and craftsmen were working in stone (vasemakers, gemcutters) or metal (weapons as well as vessels). Pottery ornament and shape, in many cases both based on metalwork, became highly repetitive, in marked contrast to the great diversity of the earlier polychrome Kamáres ware. Technically, however, the best pottery of the New Palace period is excellent.

The Minoans had developed a cursive syllabic script (Linear A) to write a language which (despite limited progress and continuing studies) is not yet deciphered to general satisfaction. Still the most useful analogy is with a picture-book without text. A proportion of its signs are derived from the hieroglyphic script used from EM times and influenced by contemporary Near Eastern writing, but the majority are probably of local origin. The development seems to have taken place within the Minoan culture (though doubtless with a degree of external inspiration) and evidently to satisfy the new record-keeping needs of the emerging palace economy. The script is found on sun-dried tablets, interpreted as administrative records, but also on artefacts such as libation tables and ladles, miniature double axes, rings or pins in precious metals, various pottery including large clay pithoi, as well as the potter's wheel. A significant mumber of these artefacts come from sacred caves or peak sanctuaries and it seems probable that in those cases the inscriptions have a religious connotation. Linear A writing has been recognised at more than a dozen sites, but by far the greatest number of finds so far come from Ayía Triáda and Khaniá.

The decline of the Minoan civilisation is not yet as well understood as its development. The end of LMI is marked by a horizon of major destruction by fire recognised in all four palaces and in Minoan excavations right

Dates BC	Minoan periods	Palace sequence
3500	Early Minoan I-III	Prepalatial Crete
2000	Middle Minoan I	
	II	Protopalatial Crete Period of the Old Palaces
	III	
1600	Late Minoan I — A/B —	Neopalatial Crete Period of the New Palaces
	II	Postpalatial Crete except at Knossos
1100	III	

Chronological outline for the Cretan Bronze Age

across Crete. Many attempts have been made to link this (LMIB) destruction with the volcanic eruption which is known to have destroyed the island of Théra (Santorini) and its settlements. However the evidence emerging from the detailed exploration of the Minoan town at Akrotíri on Théra, buried beneath layers of pumice, and especially the study of its pottery, establishes beyond any doubt that the eruption occurred not at the end of LMIB but well before the end of the LMIA period. Crete cannot have been unaware of this catastrophe only 150km to the north, but some other explanation must be sought for the widespread destruction on the island more than 50 years later, and the type of damage then is consistent with warlike activity rather than destruction by natural causes such as earthquake or tidal wave.

With the relative dating on a more secure basis, there has been new thinking about **absolute dates**. Despite extensive fine tuning to accord with the increasing refinements of radiocarbon dating, the original chronological outline of Evans and his contemporaries has, until recently, remained broadly accepted. This early work, correlating the evidence from the palaces with historic dates derived from Egypt, placed the LMIB destruction and thus the beginning of the end of Minoan civilisation at around 1450 BC, and under this conventional chronology the Théra catastrophe would have occurred only a few years before 1500 BC.

However during the last decade a formidable body of interested scientists, from the disciplines of geology and seismology among others, has added a new dimension to the researches of Aegean and Egyptian archaeologists. In 1989 at their third international congress ('Thera and the Aegean World III') proposals for the date of the great volcanic eruption ranged as far back as 1675 BC, with strong arguments advocating 1628. The new dating techniques now make use of evidence from ice and lake bed cores as well as dendrochronology. The evidence is not yet conclusive, but greater precision is keenly awaited, especially in conjunction with radiocarbon results, and may be expected to affect many of the conventionally accepted dates for second millenium Minoan Crete.

Archaeologists also look towards Egypt where new information from a current excavation at Tell el-Dab'a (ancient Avaris) in the Nile Delta may corroborate or refute the scientists' theories.

The End of the Neopalatial Period at Knossós, LMII–LMIIIA1. For reasons imperfectly understood, Knossós was less affected by the LMIB destruction than other sites. Its damage was soon repaired and its life continued for several generations, apparently under the direction of Mycenaean Greeks who were either responsible for or took advantage of the events that had brought low the rest of Crete. At this period archives in the Linear B (Mycenaean Greek) script which had supplanted Linear A show clearly that Knossós was the administrative centre of the island.

Sometime early in LMIIIA there is evidence of yet another major destruction, but (contrary to earlier thinking) it is increasingly apparent that at least parts of the palace continued to be used into LMIIIB (13C).

The Postpalatial Period; last years of the Bronze Age LMIIIA2–LMIIIC. After the widespread destruction at the end of LMI many sites were never reoccupied. In this category are the settlement at Mókhlos and the large villas at Nírou Kháni, Sklavókambos and Vathýpetro. In some cases of reoccupation on a reduced scale during LMIII, individual

Linear B tablet from Knossós

houses or rooms were cleared and re-used, but there were also substantial new buildings as at Ayía Triáda and Týlissos. Occasionally new settlements were established, for instance at Khóndros near Viánnos. The town at Khaniá flourished (with vases imported from Cyprus indicating foreign contacts) and it seems to have become a main centre of power on the island.

Shrines from this Postpalatial period have been found; characteristic furnishings include snake tubes and clay female figurines with raised arms and cylindrical skirts. Examples noted in the text are at Knossós, Gourniá, Ayía Triáda and Mitrópolis near Górtyn. A new and distinct method of burial was introduced, with rectangular painted clay chests (larnakes) placed in chamber tombs.

The epics of Homer, written down about 700 BC, set events which can be dated as contemporary with the LMIIIB period against the background of an heroic age. Unfortunately, tantalising hints of life in prehistoric times have to be accepted in part as the romantic embroidery of succeeding generations of story-tellers, and not as a completely reliable account of that period.

The Early Iron Age (1100–c 650 BC). Geometric and Orientalising Periods. The Subminoan period of transition was a troubled time, and there was a movement of population to inaccessible mountain refuge sites such as Karphí above Lasíthi. Knowledge about this period is still relatively slight, but two things are noticeable: there is some continuity of cult from the Late Bronze Age to the Iron Age, as shown by deposits of objects in sacred caves, notably the Idaian Cave on Mount Ida and the Diktaian cave above Psykhró; moreover a number of Iron Age settlements have traces of LMIII occupation. Górtyn, Praisós, and Vrókastro are examples. A rich cemetery at Priniás in central Crete was in continuous use from Late Minoan times to the Greco-Roman period.

In retrospect it can be seen that a new era was beginning. The cultural traits of the Minoan and Mycenaean civilisations lost their dominance, and gradually the elements emerged which would shape Crete in the Hellenic world. Increasing familiarity with the technique of working iron, and its potential strength as opposed to bronze for agricultural tools and for weapons, were a basis for future economic development.

During the disturbed conditions early in the millenium the Dorians, a tribe of Greek speakers distinguished by their dialect, had begun to infiltrate from the Peloponnese. Their arrival at Knossós is marked by an abrupt break in tomb usage as well as in the non-Minoan features of the new Subminoan pottery. Late Minoan chamber tombs were methodically cleared before receiving the new burials. There was some local variation in burial practices across the island, but from the 10C cremation became the common rite, the urn containing the ashes often being placed in a rock-cut or stone-built family tomb which remained in use for several generations.

The Dorians gradually spread throughout the island and to their tradition of social institutions is credited the emergence of the 'polis' or city-state. Homer (Odyssey, XIX, 177) speaks of a mixed population, including Dorians and Eteocretans. The latter adhered to Minoan traditions, and inscriptions show that their language was prehellenic. At Praisós and Dréros an apparently peaceful assimilation can be traced.

The detailed chronology of this period is still based on pottery sequences largely built up from cremation urns (pithoi) and the vases which accompanied them as grave gifts (see Herákleion Museum, Galleries XI and XII). The pottery decoration of the Geometric period was based on increasingly elaborate arrangements of linear patterns and precise concentric circles. One Knossian workshop incorporated into its designs a range of fan-tailed birds with raised wing, and though Mycenaean pictorial decoration virtually disappeared there are rare but important portrayals of figures, such as the divinity known as the Mistress of Animals.

From around 850 BC there is evidence for intensification of foreign contacts, and pottery styles began to reflect influences from the eastern shores of the Mediterranean. There grew up on Crete one of the earliest Orientalising cultures of the Aegean. Once again the island's geographical position on a trade route from the Levant to the Central Mediterranean was an important factor in shaping its cultural development.

This oriental influence is strikingly demonstrated in the metalwork of the period and especially in the new figured relief work on beaten bronze for the votive shields from the Sanctuary of Zeus in the Idaian cave; these remarkable pieces, some of which are exhibited in the Herákleion Museum, are attributed to a guild of itinerant craftsmen from the Near East. The same technique is used for spectacular jewellery (Gallery XII in the same museum) from a tomb at Teké within the Knossós North Cemetery, and it has been plausibly argued that this was the goldsmiths' family tomb. The characteristic burial urns of the fully developed Orientalising period were decorated with appropriate motifs in vivid polychrome of red and blue on a white ground.

This period saw the rise of the 'polis' or city-state. The island was divided among a great number of these small city-states, each built in an easily defendable position usually on a hill-top with a water supply and agricultural land available nearby. Territory was jealously guarded and feuds were common. The cities were ruled by the Kosmoi, a body numbering less than ten, elected annually as administrators and, if necessary, as leaders in war. By the mid 8C Dréros had an agorá (or city-centre) and beside it a small temple, a sanctuary of Apollo Delphinios. In the following century an oath administered to the young men of Dréros lays down an exacting code of behaviour, with the civic virtue of loyalty to the 'polis' already pre-eminent.

In the late 7C archaeologists recognise an emphatic full stop in the Cretan record. All Early Iron Age cemeteries were suddenly abandoned; burial in chamber tombs ceased and with this the diversity of grave gifts which had contributed significant evidence about the societies of the Geometric and Orientalising period. Round about 750 BC a semitic script was adopted for the Greek language and from this time inscriptions, as the earliest recorded history, are a useful aid to archaeological interpretation.

The Archaic, Classical and Hellenistic Periods (c 650–67 BC). The Daidalic style of sculpture, named after the legendary craftsman Daidalos, may have originated in Crete, and it played a seminal part in the development of Archaic Greek sculpture. Daidalic figures adopt Egyptian conventions, such as the rigidly frontal posture and wig-like hair. A bust from Eléftherna and the goddesses from above the transom of the Priniás Temple A doorway (both in Herákleion Museum, Gallery XIX) are good representative examples, as are the terracottas from Oloús and Siteía in the museums at Siteía and Ayios Nikólaos.

Politically Crete remained somewhat detached from the mainstream of Greek history, from the impact of the Persian Wars and the short-lived brilliance of 5C Athens. The conservative and aristocratic pattern of Doric society continued to prevail.

Despite this detachment the conquests of Alexander the Great of Macedon, and the imperial aspirations of his successors, brought new prosperity to the island. The warlike character and traditional bravery of the Cretans became a marketable commodity; they were in demand as mercenaries, and payment for their services enriched the island. Piracy was a well-documented source of income.

On a wider scale the extensive trade patterns of the Hellenistic world in the wake of Alexander's conquests gave added importance to control of the sea routes. On the island the petty wars and fluctuating alliances continued, as Knossós, Lýttos, Górtyn and Kydonía (Khaniá) gradually emerged as the main contenders for supremacy. But the rivalry was complicated by the involvement of foreign powers exploiting their influence on Crete in their own power struggle for control of the Aegean. Against a background of Macedonian expansionism, the Spartans intrigued in West Crete, the Egyptians gave garrison support to Itanos, Rhodes cultivated Oloús, and Eumenes of Pergamon contracted an alliance with 13 of the city-states. Gradually Rome became involved in Crete, first as a peacemaker between warring city-states, and then to reduce the menace of piracy from bases on the island.

The Greek mainland became part of the Roman Empire in the mid 2C BC. There was an abortive expedition against Crete in 71 BC, and two years later Q. Caecilius Metellus (later Creticus) invaded with three legions. It took him nearly three years to subdue the island.

The Roman and First Byzantine Periods (67 BC–AD 824). With its capital at Górtyn, Crete became, with Cyrene in North Africa, part of a joint praetorian province. It was administered by a proconsul who governed with a Provincial Council and a system of magistrates again known as Kosmoi. Knossós was made a Roman colony at a date still disputed, but not later than 27 BC. The island lay on the route which linked Rome with her Empire in the east. It shared the Eastern Mediterranean culture transmitted along the trade routes and enjoyed from the conquest until the 7C AD an unusual period of peace and prosperity, which was reflected in large, spread out settlements in low-lying or coastal areas such as Górtyn, Knossós or Ierápytna (Ierápetra). Significantly, Lató on its almost impregnable hill near Kritsá gave way in importance to Lató pros Kamára at modern Ayios Nikólaos on the Bay of Mirabéllo. The settlement pattern came to include isolated villas and farms unknown in warlike Hellenistic times. Many sites such as Mókhlos were inhabited for the first time since the Bronze Age. It speaks volumes for the skill of the Roman Empire's colonial administration that, for perhaps the only time in Crete's history, foreign rule was not accompanied by a perpetual state of rebellion.

After AD 330 historians refer variously to a Late Roman or Early Byzantine period. The triumph of Christianity and the foundation of Constantinople by the Emperor Constantine the Great mark the beginning of the Byzantine era in Greece. With the division of the Roman Empire in 395, it was natural for Crete to become part of the eastern sphere of influence, looking to the new imperial capital on the Bosphorus, a bright beacon of European civilisation during the centuries when the Western Empire was in decline.

The architects of the earliest churches on Crete followed the prevailing practice by adopting the form of the basilica, a standard Roman public edifice divided into three aisles by interior colonnades; one or three apses were added at the east end to form the sanctuary, while at the west end a portico (narthex) extended across the whole width of the building. The sites of some 70 of these churches are known or suspected, and the great majority are attributed to the mid 5–mid 6C. The best preserved, and architecturally the most sophisticated is Ayios Títos at Górtyn, but many other basilica sites have been excavated, for example at Pánormos on the north coast, Vizári in the Amári valley and high in the hills above Gouledi003ná, south of Réthymnon; the church at Vizári is interesting because it dates from the late 8C, not long before the Arab conquest.

The Arab Occupation (824–961). During the 7C the decline of the Roman

Empire affected the security of the eastern Mediterranean, and in 674 the main Arab fleet wintered on Crete. From then on the island was under constant threat from Arab raiders based in North Africa, and there are indications at a number of sites of renewed attempts at fortification. But in 824 a band of Arab adventurers (originally from Spain, but by then based on Alexandria in Egypt) captured the island and held it, against several relief expeditions from Constantinople, until 961. Sicily also was lost to Christendom at this time.

The Arabs laid waste the capital city of Górtyn (which never recovered its grandeur), ravaged the whole island and destroyed every one of its basilica churches. There is little positive evidence of Arab occupation apart from a scattering of their coinage. The major exception is the foundation, on the site of the modern city of Herákleion, of Rabdh el Khandak for a while the slave-trading capital of the eastern Mediterranean.

The Second Byzantine Period (961–1204). Eventually in 961 Nikephóros Phokás recaptured Rabdh el Khandak, and the Arabs left Crete. When Cyprus too was seized by Phokás (965) Byzantine control of the sea allowed regular communication between Crete and 'the City', as Constantinople was known to the Greek world. With the island restored to Byzantium, the main task was to reinvigorate the much-depleted Christian community. The monk Nikon the Repenter led a band of missionary clergy to the island. Many basilica churches were built or rebuilt some to serve as episcopal churches. Early in the 11C Ayios Ioánnis Xénos, St. John the 'Stranger', also called Ermítis (the hermit), who came from a village on the edge of the Asteroúsia Mountains, was celebrated as an evangelist all over western Crete, and is still revered today.

The castle of Témenos (Rte 3D) is all that remains of an abortive attempt to move the capital to a less vulnerable position inland, and the administrative centre was re-established on the ruins of Rabdh el Khandak, thereafter Khándakas. In the twelfth century it was thought necessary to strengthen the Christian ruling class, and the tradition is that 12 noble families, the Arkhontópouli ('aristocrats') were sent out to Crete from Constantinople. Their names, such as Kallérgis, Skordílis, Khortákis, have been influential throughout subsequent Cretan history. Many of the small churches and chapels that these families built on their estates survive today, in some cases gloriously redecorated in the following centuries. Gradually prosperity seems to have returned, based on an agricultural economy rather than piracy. This, Crete's second Byzantine period, was to last until 1204.

The death of the Emperor Basil II (1025) is usually taken as the zenith of the Byzantine Empire. With benefit of hindsight the next 400 years can be seen to have been a period of slow but inevitable decline. The Great Schism of 1054 effected the final break between Rome and Constantinople. The Crusades, which began as a movement to rescue Christianity's holy places from the Moslems, ended in a thinly-veiled power struggle between the forces of the West. Venice, originally a vassal of the Byzantine Empire, became first an independent ally and then an implacable foe. In 1081 the Emperor Alexius I made trading concessions to Venice which were eventually to result in her commercial dominance in the eastern Mediterranean, but these concessions also caused much bitterness, which came to a head with the 'Massacre of the Latins' at Constantinople (1182). In 1204 Venice succeeded in diverting the Fourth

Crusade to Constantinople in order to put the young Alexius IV on the imperial throne. But his failure to fulfil his promises to Venice led to the sack of Constantinople not by Moslems, but by the forces of Christendom.

The Venetian Period (1204–1669). In the subsequent division of the Empire, Crete was apportioned to Boniface of Montferrat who, prefering mainland territory, sold the island to Venice reputedly for 1000 silver marks. Meanwhile, rival forces from Genoa landed on the island under the command of the notorious pirate, Enrico Pescatore, and, often with Cretan support, fortified isolated settlements from Canea (Khaniá) to the Castle of Mirabéllo (Ayios Nikólaos). But Venice was not to be trifled with. In 1210 a Venetian Governor, Giacomo Tiepolo, was appointed Doge of Candia, as Khándakas, and indeed the whole island came to be known. This was Venice's first formally constituted overseas colony, with the Doge serving (as for the Republic itself, but only for a two-year term) with a Signoria and a Great Council. The Republic's new acquisition produced grain, wood for shipbuilding, oil, hides and wine; but more importantly it had an unequalled strategic position for trade with the Levant. Harbours and dockyards were a priority.

Venice set about imposing a feudal administration with Venetian colonists as the ruling class. Castles were built, or strengthened, to control the countryside. But 'La Serenissima' found herself running up against the implacably independent character of the native Cretans, and the inevitable conflict became a tale of ferocious revolts and harsh repression. The new taxes and labour obligations were a heavy burden. By 1363 even the Venetian nobility on Crete was divided. One faction, incensed by excessive demands from Venice, went so far as to declare the short-lived Republic of St. Titus. The rebellion was eventually crushed by an expedition sent from Venice, and punitive measures were applied. The plateau of Lasíthi (Rte 6), a refuge for the rebels, was forcibly depopulated and cultivation and pasturing were banned.

Throughout this period of oppression, Cretan links with a regenerated Constantinople were cemented by a common language and the doctrines of eastern Christendom. The Venetians imported their own ecclesiastical hierarchy, and built many Latin monasteries; 376 were recorded by the 16C. Pope Alexander V (1409/10) was born in the Mirabéllo district, and educated by the Franciscans in Candia before he set out for Italy. The Orthodox clergy, at first ordained outside the island, were officially subject to Latin bishops, but there was little active proselytising by Venetian Catholics. The Cretan ruling families continued to build and decorate their small (Orthodox) churches and chapels, the survivors of which are so moving today.

The Italian scholar Giuseppe Gerola, in his great work on Venetian architecture, 'Monumenti Veneti nell'Isola di Creta', published in 1905, listed more than 800 frescoed churches on Crete (the majority 14–15C). A remarkable concentration of 600 or so still retain at least fragments for specialist study. The wall paintings are strongly conservative; against a background of foreign occupation and uncertain economic conditions they scrupulously preserve the hagiographic traditions of Byzantine art. Orthodoxy was a very strong thread in the fabric of Cretan nationalism.

Gradually an uneasy co-existence was established between Venetians and Cretans, and by the 15C there was a degree of intermarriage (sometimes with adoption of the Orthodox faith) and much less overt hostility.

The church at Arkádi

With the capture of Constantinople by the Turks (1453), Crete became an important staging-post for Greeks fleeing to the West, and the manuscripts and works of art brought with them gave a new impetus to Byzantine culture on the island. The larger monasteries (Arkádi, Goniá, Ayía Triáda, Angárathos) became centres of Greek learning and built up great libraries. In the 16C the college in Herákleion attached to Ayía Aikateríni, a daughter foundation of the important Orthodox monastery on Mount Sinai, was renowned for fostering both Greek scholarship and religious art. Fresco painting continued, but Crete also produced many notable icon painters, the greatest of them being Mikhaíl Damaskinós, several of whose works hang today in the Ayía Aikateríni icon collection. Some of these artists left Crete to work abroad, among them Doménico Theotokópoulos, who moved to Venice probably in 1567, was in Rome in 1570 as a disciple of Titian, and then went on to Toledo in Spain, where he became famous as El Greco. As a result of a recent purchase one of his paintings has returned to the island and is now on display in Herákleion's Historical Museum.

Travel between Crete and Venice was a natural progess, and with it the transmission of the elements of Byzantine thought and art that nourished the Italian Renaissance. Members of the Cretan community in the mother-city contributed to the renewed interest in this learning. Márkos Mousoúros published Greek authors at the Aldine printing press, one of the earliest (1492) examples of this new and influential Venetian technology.

Poetry and drama flourished on the island during the 16th and 17th centuries. One enormously long heroic poem, the 'Erotókritos' by Vinzétzos Kornáros, remains popular today, as much for its use of the Cretan vernacular as for its romantic sentiments. It is read, sung and quoted wherever Cretans gather.

The discovery of the sea-route to the Far East around the Cape of Good Hope diminished the importance of the Mediterranean trade-route on which Venice's wealth and prestige depended. As Venetian power gradually declined, the Ottoman Turks pressed westward. They landed on Crete in 1645 and two years later laid siege to Candia. The city held out for 22 years, making this one of the longest and most heroic sieges in history. Help from the Christian world came too little and too late, and in 1669 this last bastion of Christendom in the eastern Mediterranean fell into Turkish hands.

The Turkish Occupation (1669–1898). This time the overlords came not from a different rite within the Christian church, but from a different faith. The island was divided into three Pashaliks, and was ruled from Herákleion, known after the long siege as Megálo Kástro, the great fortress. The 'Sublime Porte' was not at first particularly destructive, but was totally indifferent to the economic conditions of the countryside, thereby causing great hardship and deprivation. The Turkish administrators favoured urban life both for safety and because it better suited their traditions; and their mosques (without exception converted churches), fountains, and a few houses preserved in the towns along the north coast are the only visible reminders of this foreign occupation of more than 200 years.

There was ruthless discrimination against Christians, especially insofar as taxation and property were concerned; survival frequently depended on compromise, and tactical conversions to Mohammedanism were understandably frequent. There was a sharp contrast between the vulnerable lowland districts and the remote and inaccessible mountain areas where sporadic rebellion and scheming in the cause of independence became a way of life. Unfortunately the lowlanders often had to endure the reprisals when the warriors withdrew to their mountain strongholds.

In 1770 a major revolt was led by the legendary Daskaloyiánnis from the proudly independent Sphakiá district of western Crete; he was encouraged by the Russians, as part of a diversionary move to further their own strategy on the mainland. The revolt collapsed, its leader surrendered and was executed, and Sphakiá suffered accordingly.

Throughout the island, leadership was provided, often covertly and in dangerous circumstances, by the monasteries. Their efforts were directed not only to protecting the Orthodox church but also to preserving through education the cultural tradition of Hellenism, with the ultimate aim being Cretan independence.

On the wider scene Crete once again became a pawn in international power politics, this time in the world of the 'Great Powers' of post-Napoleonic Europe, at that time Britain, France, Italy and Russia. The Revolt of 1821, triggered by the outbreak of the Greek War of Independence, was crushed with Egyptian help, and when, in 1832, the Greek state was established it did not include Crete, which had to undergo the humiliation of ten years of Egyptian rule.

The Greek throne was given to Prince Otto of Wittelsbach and placed under the protection of Britain, Russia and France; but this attempt to establish stable constitutional government was unsuccessful, and in 1862 Otto was deposed. A Danish Prince became King George I of the Hellenes, a hint of concession to the idea of a broader-based Greek state. In Crete the renewed outcry for 'enosis', union with Greece, resulted in the uprising of 1866, when the women and children killed in the battle for the Arkádi monastery attracted world-wide sympathy for Crete's plight.

Greece's attention was taken up with problems on her northern frontiers, and her relationship with the Great Powers was often strained to the point of hostility. Uprisings continued on Crete until 1898 when the Powers finally took the opportunity of peace negotiations between Greece and the Ottoman Empire over mainland territory to impose a settlement on the island. Crete was granted autonomous status under Ottoman suzerainty, and a High Commissioner was appointed, in the person of Prince George, second son of the Greek king, who governed from Khaniá.

In a further crisis in 1906 Prince George resigned. His eight years of rule had brought 'enosis' no closer, and he was faced with the rebel Cretan Assembly, constituted as a rival government pledged to this union with Greece. One of its leaders was Elefthérios Venizélos. Born in Khaniá in 1864 (but technically a Greek subject) he had been prominent as a young man in the struggle for the island's independence, and now was an influential member of the Assembly which first raised the Greek flag on Crete, on the hill of Prophítis Ilías on the Akrotíri overlooking Khaniá. The crisis was temporarily resolved, with the appointment of the veteran Alexander Zaimis as High Commissioner, but two years later Venizélos was called to Athens in a climate of nationalist rebellion, and after a revision of the constitution he became Prime Minister of Greece for the first of many times.

In 1913 'enosis' was at long last achieved. At the Treaty of Bucharest, which ended the Balkan Wars, Greek sovereignty over Crete was accepted and amid scenes of wild rejoicing the island finally became an integral part of the Greek nation.

Modern History (from 1913). An understanding of the early part of this turbulent period is inextricably involved with the decline of the Ottoman Empire, which led in due course to the emergence of modern Turkey, and with Greece's struggle to come to terms with her northern neighbours in a multilateral conflict among the evolving Balkan states.

Political consciousness is essential to the Greek character, as is still evident in the passionate arguments of day-to-day conversation, so that despite physical isolation from the zones of conflict Crete was much involved after 1913 in the decisions and events unfolding in Athens. For much of this period constitutional issues were in one way or another crucial, with the uneasy relationship between monarchy and elected government often at the heart of the matter.

The Cretan-born statesman Elefthérios Venizélos was a force in national politics and a central figure in this constitutional controversy for a quarter of a century. Venizélos came to be respected as a master of diplomacy abroad, and as a leader with the strength of an exceptional command over public opinion at home.

During the 1914–18 war, his convictions, which led him to favour the cause of the western allies, often put him at loggerheads with King Constantine I whose wife was the sister of the German Kaiser. In September 1916 matters came to a head, and from his native Khaniá Venizélos issued a proclamation which led to his establishing a rival government in the mainland city of Salonika (Thessaloníki). After nine months of negotiations, the king left the country and was succeeded by his second son, Prince Alexander. In Athens Venizélos recalled the parliament which the king had dissolved in December 1915, and received an overwhelming vote of confidence after a speech lasting nearly nine hours. The country entered the war on the allied side and played a part in the eventual victory.

Between 1920 and 1922 Greece was involved in a disastrous campaign of expansionism on the mainland of Turkey for which Venizélos did not escape all blame. The political motives included the ancient 'Megáli Idéa', the reconstitution of the Byzantine Empire with its capital at Constantinople. The trauma of defeat and the sack of Smyrna, the Greek city on the coast of Asia Minor, by Turkish forces under Mustapha Kemal is still a painful memory in Crete today. The ensuing exchange of populations under the Treaty of Lausanne (1923) brought more than a million refugees to Greece. A considerable proportion of them (including some Armenian families) were resettled on Crete, taking over the redistributed property of Turks who had remained behind when their army departed in 1898. The upheaval caused much hardship on both sides, but in modern times it has resulted in a homogeneous population spared any risk of the tensions suffered by Cyprus.

Constitutional questions continued to dominate Greek politics; for a period the country became a republic. Venizélos was in and out of office as leader of the Liberal party, but his lasting achievements at this time were in the field of foreign affairs. In 1932 in a climate dominated by the insoluble problems and hardship of the years of world-wide economic depression, and faced with bitter opposition to measures which were seen as an attempt to restrict the freedom of the press, Venizélos was forced to resign. The following year he survived an assassination attempt, and then in a mood of frustration at the failure of the Republic he retired to Crete. In 1935, after a last unsuccessful republican coup, he fled into exile; condemned to death in his absence, he was pardoned under an amnesty declared by King George II after the restoration of the monarchy, but died in France in 1936. He is buried on the Akrotíri outside Khaniá.

The new figure at the centre of Greek politics was the fervent monarchist, General Metáxas; his solution for constitutional stalemate was to persuade the King to dissolve Parliament (the Chamber did not sit again for ten years), and himself to assume power as a dictator. However he foresaw that war in Europe was inevitable, and he has been given due share of the credit for the fact that Greece, alone among the countries of south-east Europe, was in a position effectively to resist aggression when it came.

Mussolini occupied Albania on Easter Monday 1939, and the threat posed by a fascist power on Greece's border led to a British and French guarantee of Greek territorial sovereignty. Metáxas reaffirmed neutrality early in August 1940. On 27 October he attended an evening reception at the Italian legation in Athens, but early next day the Italian Minister conveyed to him an ultimatum which he rejected with the single word 'No'. This legendary gesture of defiance is proudly commemorated by a national holiday ('Oxi' day) on 28 October each year. Mussolini's troops were even at the time of the ultimatum already invading Greece, which became the only country voluntarily to enter the war on the Allied side during that period when Britain stood alone against the Axis powers.

The Greek army drove back the Italians to a position of stalemate in the mountainous terrain of Albania, but the balance was to be altered by Hitler's decision to enter Greece to protect the southern flank of his planned Russian front.

Metáxas died unexpectedly at the end of January 1941. In March Greece accepted reinforcement by a small expeditionary force composed of British, Australian and New Zealand troops, and a frontline was established in northern Greece, but the combined forces were unable to halt Hitler's invasion, and despite Greece's proclaimed determination to fight to the last, the campaign became a series of rearguard actions. In mid April the Prime Minister committed suicide; the King turned to a Cretan, Emmanuel Tsouderós, and it was to Crete that the inevitable evacuation was to be directed.

The Battle of Crete. The withdrawal of the expeditionary force from the mainland of Greece took place during the last week of April and the first week of May 1941. King George was evacuated with his Government and Prime Minister Tsouderós. He stayed briefly at the Villa Ariadne at Knossós and was then established at Khaniá. The island was defended from sea-borne invasion by the British Mediterranean Fleet.

As the campaign on the mainland ran into difficulties during 1940, Churchill had continually insisted on the strategic importance of holding Crete, but the resources of General Wavell, C-in-C Middle East, were greatly overstretched and it was not feasible to create the fortress of Churchill's vision.

The terrain of the likely battlefield presented particular problems. All the main harbours, including the huge anchorage of Soúda Bay, were on the north coast and exposed to enemy aircraft. The more protected fishing ports on the south coast were useless for supply purposes because of the inadequacy of the roads across the island; the one from Soúda over to Sphakiá had not been completed even though it stopped only some six kilometres short of the Libyan Sea. There were airfields at Herákleion and at Máleme, west of Khaniá (at that time the capital of the island), and a landing-strip between them at Réthymnon, all on the narrow north coast plain that rendered communications and troop movement by day very difficult.

Historians writing with the benefit of hindsight have been critical of the lack of preparation or of any defined policy at this time; there had been six changes of command on the island in the six months before 30 April, when Wavell appointed the eminent New Zealander General Bernard Freyberg VC as C-in-C.

Hitler's principal objective was to use Crete as an air base against British forces in the eastern Mediterranean. His commander was General Student (of XI Air Corps), whose strength included a crack assault regiment of glider-borne storm troopers, a parachute division, a specialised mountain division and groups of the dreaded Stuka dive bombers. The Luftwaffe, flying from rapidly constructed forward bases in the Peloponnese and the Aegean islands, had undisputed command of the air.

Freyberg's garrison consisted of 32,000 British, Australian and New Zealand troops (including 21,000 of the expeditionary force who had been evacuated from the mainland), and 11,000 well-trained but lightly-armed Greek troops. The Cretan division, to its lasting chagrin, had been cut off on the Albanian front. It proved impossible to operate planes from the exposed airfields, so the force was severely handicapped by lack of air cover.

General Freyberg's Creforce headquarters was located to the north-east of Khaniá in the Soúda sector. West of Khaniá was the New Zealand Division, with some Greek support including a unit out along the coast at Kastélli. The New Zealanders were thus responsible for the defence of the vital airfield at Máleme; this was dominated by their command position at the end of a ridge running out from the White Mountains, named Hill 107.

In the centre of the line, in the area around Réthymnon, were four Australian and two Greek battalions. The Herákleion sector was held by three British, two Australian and three Greek battalions, the airport being defended by a British force.

The airborne invasion began on 20 May. The landings concentrated as expected on the airfields and the main towns of the north coast. In the Máleme area the Germans established a toehold west of the river Tavronítis and south of Kolymbári. A detachment of parachutists attempted to land in the broad valley (nick-named Prison Valley) running south towards the Omalós and the White Mountains; their aim was to converge with the forces on the coast road to advance on Khaniá, but at the end of the first day most of the German troops in this sector were disorganised and not responding to central control. The assault, using gliders, on the Akrotíri failed entirely, and thus the threat from the rear to Khaniá and Freyberg's headquarters did not materialise.

The Réthymnon airstrip, important to the Germans for a flanking movement to capture the anchorage of Soúda, was successfully defended, despite a heavy imbalance of troops and firepower, by the Australians. Around the Herákleion airfield the Germans were in considerable disarray, and in the town their initial success had developed into heavy street-fighting with the civilian population, which led to a position of stalemate.

The first wave of landings met much stronger resistance than had been expected by German Intelligence, which had also underestimated the hostile reaction of the local Cretan population. The invading forces suffered heavy losses which were particularly critical in their command structure. It is generally agreed that this first assault was very nearly defeated, that General Student's eventual success was by a narrow margin, and that at the end of the first day the outcome hung in the balance.

However what turned out to be the crucial battle had developed to the south and west of Máleme, centred on the New Zealand position on Hill 107. With hindsight it can be seen that the position of the German assault forces was exceedingly precarious. However in the confusion of battle, which was compounded by an almost total breakdown in communications due to a shortage of vital wireless sets, essential defence reinforcements did not become available in time. On the evening of the first day of the assault, the commanding height had to be evacuated, leaving the vital airfield undefended, and thus the fragile balance altered. Most historians agree that at this point the battle for Crete was lost and won.

German forces were quick to exploit the situation, and to use the airfield to bring in troops and vital supplies. A counter-attack, organised on the second day, was carried out during that night, 21–22 May, but despite the valiant efforts of the Maori battalion, Máleme airfield remained in enemy hands. On the fourth day of the battle German fighter planes began operating from its runway.

At sea the German invasion fleet was routed on 21 and 22 May, but with appalling losses to the Royal Navy. Throughout the battle the Navy was operating in waters which could only be reached through narrow straits (c 50–60km), guarded to the west by the island of Kýthera, and to the east by Kásos and Kárpathos, all in enemy hands. Once into the Cretan Sea, as the Greeks call this area south of Théra (Santorini), ships were in reach of the network of bomber airfields that crowded the islands of the Aegean. Over three days Admiral Cunningham lost two cruisers and four destroyers, and had a battleship, two cruisers and four destroyers severely damaged.

On land the Máleme position had been given up, and the weary Australian and New Zealand troops fought a series of brave rearguard actions as they fell back on Khaniá. On 26 May, with the Luftwaffe fighters at Máleme within a 20km range, Khaniá and the Soúda sector were plainly indefensible, and early next day the order reached their garrisons for the long withdrawal south across the island to Sphakiá, a coast-to-coast distance of c 40km.

The retreat along this route over the eastern flank of the White Mountains was only possible at all because of the heroic obstinacy of a Greek regiment cut off at the south end of 'Prison Valley', in the area of the Alikianós river-crossing (on the modern road up to the Omalós plateau). For two days (24–25 May) these troops, reinforced by gendarmerie and civilians, held up crack German mountain troops who otherwise, in an outflanking move by the Mesklá and Kerítis valley route, would have cut the Sphakiá road, the only possible line of retreat for Freyberg's army. (King George and his ministers had been escorted down the Gorge of Samariá to embark at Ayiá Rouméli.)

The shambles of this march over the mountains, by Stýlos, across the upland plain of Askýphou and down the precipitous Nímbros gorge, has been described in many records, including Freyberg's own official report. However, the column was successfully protected against constant enemy harassment by relays of rearguard troops. Some 12,000 men were involved in the retreat, and during the nights of 28–31 May the Navy evacuated about three-quarters of them from the beach at Khóra Sphakíon. The author Evelyn Waugh, who took part in the retreat, gives a vivid account of it in the second volume of his war trilogy, as—from the New Zealand viewpoint—does Geoffrey Cox (see Bibliography).

At Réthymnon the Australians denied the Germans the use of the airstrip for the whole course of the battle, until they were at last overwhelmed on 31 May. From the port of Herákleion the Royal Navy evacuated the garrison by sea through the perilous Kásos strait on the night of the 28–29, with horrific loss of men and ships; the episode symbolises the courage with which this campaign was fought. The bald figures at its conclusion were: 18,000 evacuated, 12,000 taken prisoner, 2000 killed.

A considerable number of men who had not been evacuated were hidden by the Cretans until they could later be helped to escape from the island. There are many accounts of the Resistance movement that developed during the German occupation of Crete. The guerilla warfare, coordinated by Allied undercover agents and supplied from North Africa, affected German morale, and tied down units increasingly needed on other fronts. The civilian population suffered appallingly in the inevitable acts of retribution. One extraordinary account of the Resistance, *The Cretan Runner*, is especially recommended because its author who was part of the movement is himself Cretan. Available in translation (see Bibliography) this book throws light not only on the progress of the guerilla war, and on the involvement of idiosyncratic foreigners as seen through native eyes, but incidentally on many essentials of the Cretan character.

The month of May 1991 marked the 50th anniversary of the Battle of Crete. Moving celebrations and reunions took place on the island. The anniversary also saw the publication of a comprehensive account 'Crete: the Battle and the Resistance' by Antony Beevor. His book follows the story on land, at sea and in the air, with material from both sides engaged in the conflict, and from the fall of Greece through to the end of the war in Crete. He was able to draw on the authoritative published accounts and on previously secret Military Intelligence reports, but the book also benefitted from the first-hand recollections of a wide variety of the original participants. Along the way the story of the dedicated and often heroic involvement of Cretans is sympathetically told.

GLOSSARY

ABACUS, a flat block crowning the capital of a column.

AGORA, public square or market-place.

ASHLAR, square-cut stone in regular courses of masonry.

ASKOS, a vase shape derived from the traditional form of a wineskin, equipped with handle and small opening for pouring; often in the shape of an animal or bird.

ATRIUM, forecourt of a Roman house or basilica.

AYIOS, AYIA (f.), AYII (m.pl.), AYIES (f.pl.) Saint(s).

BASILICA, originally a Roman building used for civil administration; in Christian architecture, a three-aisled church (with apse or apses but without transepts) where the nave was divided from the side-aisles by columns which supported the raised roof (clerestory) of the centre portion.

BEMA, the chancel in a Greek Orthodox church.

BRECCIA, a conglomerate rock.

CELLA, central portion of a temple, enclosed within solid walls.

DEMOTIC, the vernacular Greek language, as opposed to KATHAREVOUSA, formal academic Greek.

DIMARKHEION, town-hall.

EXEDRA, semi-circular (sometimes rectangular) recess with seats.

FAIENCE, in antiquity, the product of fusing granular quartz or sand with an alkali, which was then coated with an alkaline glaze.

FIBULA, pin to fasten clothing, ornamental as well as practical.

FRESCO, painting executed on wet plaster.

GYPSUM, an easily worked white to pinkish-buff limestone.

HORNS OF CONSECRATION, stylised bull's horns, associated with Minoan shrines.

ICONOSTASIS, screen adorned with icons in Orthodox church separating the sanctuary from the main body of the church.

KALDERIMI, a paved road dating from before the era of the motor vehicle.

KERNOS, cult vessel with a number of small receptacles.

KOULOURA, Greek word meaning round and hollow, hence a pit.

KRATER, large two-handled bowl used for mixing wine and water, associated with ceremonial drinking.

LARNAX, LARNAKES (pl.), clay coffin(s).

LEKYTHOS, one-handled vase with narrow ovoid body and tall narrow neck.

LUSTRAL BASIN, small sunken room in Minoan architecture associated with purification and cleansing.

MEGARON, in Greek, an imposing hall. The Mycenaean megaron was rectangular with a central hearth, and a single entrance through the porch at one end.

MELTEMI, the prevailing north wind of summer in the Aegean.

NARTHEX, a shallow porch extending the width of a church, derived from the basilica plan.

NOMARKHEION, centre of provincial administration (for the Nome or province).

OBSIDIAN, a natural glass occurring in restricted volcanic areas.

ODEION, concert-hall, usually in the shape of a Greek theatre, but roofed.

OINOCHOE, a one-handled wine jug distinguished by narrow neck with round or trefoil mouth.

ORTHOSTAT, large stone slab set vertically.

PANAYIA, the All-Holy Virgin.

PANTOKRATOR, Christ, the Ruler of all things, portrayed in the act of blessing, while also holding a bible; usually a half-figure in the painted decoration of the dome of a Byzantine church.

PERISTYLE, colonnaded court resembling a cloister.

PHYLAX, or PHYLAKAS, guardian, here of antiquities.

PITHOS, PITHOI (pl.), large pottery jar(s) for the storage of oil, wine, grain, etc.; such vessels were also used for inhumation burial. A smaller version, usually decorated, held the ashes after a cremation.

PLATYTERA, representation of the Virgin and Child as a symbol of the Incarnation.

PRONAOS, porch in front of the cella of a temple.

PROPYLON, or PROPYLAEUM, gateway of architectural importance. Plural form, PROPYLAEA, for a multiple entrance.

PROTOME, three-dimensional representation of the head and forepart of an animal, or head and upper part of human body, usually as applied decoration.

PRYTANEION, the assembly hall of the ruling council of a Greek city-state.

PYXIS, small lidded box in pottery, stone, ivory, etc.

RHYTON, vessel designed for the pouring of libations; often a tapering shape with hole at tip, but sometimes in human or animal form.

SCARAB, beetle-shaped seal.

STEATOPYGOUS, fat-buttocked.

STIRRUP JAR, jar with a blocked central mouth, three stirrup handles connected to the false neck and a spout added to the shoulder.

STOA, porch or portico not attached to a larger building.

TEMENOS, a sacred precinct.

THOLOS, circular vaulted building.

SELECTED BIBLIOGRAPHY

Art, Archaeology, Myth and History. K. Branigan, *The Tombs of the Mesara*; A. Brown, *Arthur Evans and the Palace of Minos*; G. Cadogan, *Palaces of Minoan Crete*; J. Chadwick, *Linear B and Related Scripts*; R. Clogg, *A Short History of Modern Greece*; C. Daváras, *Guide to Cretan Antiquities*; Sir A. Evans, *The Palace of Minos*; R. Graves, *The Greek Myths*; R. Higgins, *Minoan and Mycenaean Art*; S. Hood, *The Arts in Prehistoric Greece, The Home of the Heroes, The Aegean before the Greeks, The Minoans*; R.W. Hutchinson, *Prehistoric Crete*; K. Kalokýris, *The Byzantine Wall-paintings of Crete*; S. Marinátos and M. Hirmer, *Crete and Mycenae*; ed. J.W and E.E. Myers and G. Cadogan, *Aerial Atlas of Ancient Crete*; J.J. Norwich *A History of Venice*; J.D.S. Pendlebury, *The Archaeology of Crete*; N. Pláton, *Zakros*; N. Psilakis, *The Monasteries of Crete*; M. Ventris and J. Chadwick, *The Decipherment of Linear B*; P. Warren and V. Hankey, *Aegean Bronze Age Chronology*; R.F. Willetts, *Cretan Cults and Festivals, Ancient Crete: A Social History, Everyday Life in Ancient Crete*; C.M. Woodhouse, *Modern Greece: A Short History*.

General. A. Beevor, *Crete: the Battle and the Resistance;* C. Buckley, *Greece and Crete 1941*; A. Clark, *The Fall of Crete*; G. Cox, *A Tale of Two Battles*; X. Fielding, *The Stronghold*; A. Hopkins, *Crete—its Past, Present and People*; A. Huxley and W. Taylor, *Flowers of Greece and the Aegean*; N. Kazantzákis, *Zorba the Greek, Report to Greco, Freedom and Death, The Odyssey: A Modern Sequel, Christ Recrucified*; E. Lear, *The Cretan Journal*; M. Llewellyn Smith, *The Great Island*; R. Pashley, *Travels in Crete*; G. Psychoundákis (trans. P. Leigh Fermor), *The Cretan Runner*; D. Powell, *The Villa Ariadne*; I. Stewart, *The Struggle for Crete*; E. Waugh, *Diaries, Officers and Gentlemen*.

Some of these books are out of print, but should be obtainable from libraries. A number may be bought locally from bookshops or museums on Crete. In case of difficulty, consult *Zeno's Bookshop*, 6 Denmark Street, London WC2H 8LP (off Charing Cross Road); tel. 071 836 2522, or the *Hellenic Book Service, 91 Fortess Road, London NW5 1AG; tel. 071 267 9499.*

PRACTICAL INFORMATION

Tourist Offices

Preliminary information may be obtained, in person or by post (free), from the National Tourist Organisation of Greece (NTOG), 4 Conduit Street, London, W1R ODJ (tel. 071 734 5997; fax 287 1369), open 9.30–17.30 (Friday 16.30); closed Saturdays. The New York office is at 645 Fifth Avenue, Olympic Tower, New York, NY 10022 (tel. 212 4215 777). The organisation does not recommend hotels, nor make travel arrangements.

The London office publishes a useful list of tour operators specialising in travel to Greece, with an indexed entry for Crete which covers destination, type of holiday and the UK airports from which charter flights now operate to Herákleion or Khaniá. There is no need for a stark choice between an all-inclusive 'package' holiday based on one resort hotel, and totally independent travel bookings. Most travel agents offer arrangements which combine the financial advantages of group travel with itineraries tailored to individual requirements; a growing number of smaller specialists offer an individual service. Villa holidays in self-catering apartments are widely available and increasingly popular.

Formalities and Currency

Passports are necessary for all British travellers entering Greece; a Visitor's Passport is valid. Permission to stay is granted in the first instance only for three months. Greece is a full member of the European Community which may affect the regulations.

Money. The monetary unit is the drachma (Δράχμα), abbreviated to Δρχ or Drs. There are coins of 1, 2, 5, 10, 20, 50, 100 and 200 drachmas, and notes of 100, 500, 1000 and 5000. Currency regulations no longer present a problem to the average tourist visiting Crete for a holiday from within the European Community, but if there are special circumstances consult your bank. It is obviously good policy to arrive on the island with sufficient Greek currency for the first two or three days.

Customs Regulations. For travellers coming from EC member-states the usual regulations limit the value of goods which may be imported duty free (details obtainable from the NTOG, or at airport of departure). Drug regulations should be strictly observed, including a new (total) ban on codeine. In practice bona fide holiday-makers will have no trouble from the Customs authorities. (If you travel from mainland Greece all formalities will be attended to at the point of entry to Greece.)

Personal Health Insurance is strongly recommended.

Getting to Crete

By Air. Olympic Airways maintains scheduled services from Athens airport (Ellinikó West) to both Herákleion and Khaniá: peak summer service Athens–Herákleion, c eight flights a day, and to Khaniá, c five flights, in both cases offering connections to and from major cities in Europe and the USA. On scheduled services from abroad via Athens, there are advantages in travelling Olympic on both legs of the journey. You avoid the necessity to change terminals at Athens airport, and in the event of a missed connection, the airline is responsible for your onward journey (not necessarily the case when two airlines are involved). This is particularly important when leaving an island where strong winds can affect schedules.

From Herákleion Olympic Airways flies to Rhodes, Mýkonos, Santorini (Théra), Páros and Thessaloníki. A small airport was opened at Siteía in 1984; it presently operates only to Rhodes via Kásos and Kárpathos.

On all Olympic Airways flights, travellers are advised to pay careful attention to instructions about the reconfirmation of return flights.

Charter flights are the only direct flights to Crete from outside Greece. They are primarily intended for complete package holidays, but, especially out of season, surplus seats are sometimes available (with a nominal charge for accommodation), and any travel agent specialising in departures to Crete will be aware of these possibilities. Cheap flights to Crete are often advertised in the daily and Sunday newspapers.

By Sea. There is a *car ferry service* nightly all the year round between Piraeus (port of Athens) and Herákleion (12 hours), also between Piraeus and Soúda for Khaniá (11 hours). To Herákleion there are two sailings run by rival companies, Minoan Lines and ANEK (departures 18.30 and 19.00 respectively). For Khaniá, ANEK has a sailing every night (at 19.00), and Minoan Lines one on alternate nights (but some years only during the summer season) departing Piraeus on Monday, Wednesday and Friday at 18.30 and returning the following night at the same departure time. Réthymnon now has a direct service using the Arkádi bought by public subscription and operated by the new Rethymniáki line. The ferry leaves Piraeus on Monday, Wednesday and Friday at 19.15, returning the following night; there is also a daytime sailing on Sundays departing from Piraeus at 08.00.

For main booking offices on Crete, see the relevant sections of town information. Boat tickets are widely available at agencies throughout the island.

Accommodation on the ferries is priced in five classes: de Luxe, First, Second, Tourist and Deck. The ships are not uniform and facilities vary slightly. Prices also vary according to route and even direction because of harbour dues. In recent years a berth in a First Class cabin with private shower and toilet has remained comparable with the Athens–Herákleion air fare. The basic deck-class ticket covers travel in Pullman-type seats, or out on the decks in summer, and costs roughly the equivalent of £15. Ticket prices do not include meals, but all ships have a restaurant (restricted to First and Second Class passengers) and a cafeteria. In high season it is essential to book if you bring a car or want a cabin. At peak times, such as August weekends or festivals, there may be extra services by day.

Direct ferry services to Crete from abroad: for some time the Italian Adriatica Line has run a regular car and passenger service Venice–Piraeus–Herákleion–Alexandria all year except mid January to mid March and more recently Marlines began to operate a similar weekly service (July–September) on the Ancona–Patras–Herákleion–Rhodes–Limassol route. There can be no guarantee that these services will continue to operate, but if they are of interest it is worth making enquiries (from the NTOG in London) about them or any similar new arrangements.

Domestic ferry schedules around the Aegean (except for the above direct services) are liable to alter from year to year, and the new programme is not announced much before Easter, so it is essential to make careful enquiries at a tourist information office or a travel agent. For many years a weekly boat on the Piraeus–Rhodes route has called at Ayios Nikólaos and Siteía. Also Kísamos (Kastélli-Kisámou) in western Crete is linked by a service to the island Kýthera, and mainland harbours along the south-east coast of the Peloponnese (on a route terminating at Piraeus). For shipping agents on the island see the information section under the appropriate town.

Importation of Motor Vehicles. Consult well in advance the London office of the NTOG which issues a leaflet of explicit instructions. See also *Blue Guide Greece*. Membership of the AA or RAC is an advantage, for in case of breakdown it ensures free assistance from the Greek equivalent ELPA (ΕΛΠΑ).

Travelling on Crete

Motoring. The majority of visitors touring Crete by car use rented vehicles. The fly-drive arrangement, with a hire car waiting at the airport on arrival, is extremely popular, or the rental can be arranged for a selected period later in the holiday. Cars, jeeps, motor cycles and scooters may be hired from agencies in all the main towns, in the large hotels and at the airports. A local arrangement is convenient when the vehicle is only required for occasional expeditions, but the rate per day will be higher than when the cost of car hire is part of a package arranged abroad. (In either case the rate, including any optional insurance costs, is subject to 18 per cent V.A.T.) Hertz provides a reliable service; it has more than a dozen agents across the island, including desks at both airports. Head office: 44, Odós 25 Avgoústou, Herákleion, tel. (081) 229 802. (Other firms may be less expensive but the condition of their cars and their emergency service are not always as good. Note that under some circumstances Hertz insurance can cover damage to tyres which many policies exclude.)

All car hire firms require a full driving licence; most stipulate that it must have been held for at least one year. Some firms require the driver to have reached the age of 23; others set the limit at 21 provided the rental is backed by a credit card, which is in any case the best way to handle the necessary deposit. For motor bike and scooter hire the age limit is 19. In all cases it is wise to check that you have *full comprehensive insurance*.

Most *petrol stations* close on weekdays at 19.00 (Saturdays 15.00) and work a rota system for evening and Sunday opening. The relative scarcity of filling stations across the south of the island makes it advisable to leave the north coast with a full tank.

Roads. There has been steady improvement in the general condition of the island's road system. All main roads, and those to the most popular tourist objectives, now have an asphalt surface, and work continues annually (primarily for the benefit of isolated communities) on country roads in remote rural areas. Non-asphalt surfaces are generally noted in the text, though this information is likely to become out-of-date, but driven with reasonable caution hard-packed dirt roads need present no problems. Except on the north coast highway (New Road) between Khaniá and Ayios Nikólaos, distances may be deceptive and you need to allow time for gradients and winding roads. Roads to the south have tended to radiate in the natural historical pattern from the north coast capitals of the four nomes or provinces, but the recently completed section of the south coast road across the Mesará plain now provides an easy route between the central region around the Palace of Phaistós and the coast of south-eastern Crete.

It is customary to use the horn on blind corners. In the mountains, rock falls are a hazard, and subsidence or the torrential winter rains may produce unexpected pot-holes or gaps at the edge of the road. However, upkeep is generally good (except in the villages where the cost is often a burdensome charge on the inhabitants), and the road system is now more than adequate for exploring to the remotest parts of the island.

Signposts have been greatly improved in recent years in conjunction with a new system of kilometre posts along the main routes. There are duplicate signs, 50m apart, on all the main roads, the second one helpfully transliterating the Greek alphabet. (The result does not always match exactly the transliteration used in this Guide.) On minor roads the convention is to sign the chief destination once, and then to signpost the turnings off the road without repeating the original destination. It is assumed that you continue straight ahead unless directed otherwise.

Country Bus travel on the island is efficient and inexpensive. Long-distance buses run to schedule fairly frequently between the four nome capitals (Khaniá, Réthymnon, Herákleion and Ayios Nikólaos—see information sections). Because these services are operated (as they are throughout Greece) by Joint Pools of Bus Owners, KTEL, journeys via Herákleion may involve a change of bus station. Within each nome there are services between the provincial capital and the chief towns of the eparchies (districts). Villages without a formal bus service nearly always have a communal taxi with comparable prices (marked ΑΓΟΡΑΙΟΝ) which acts in lieu of a bus. Tickets for inter-nome destinations are sold at an office designated ΠΡΑΚΤΟΡΕΙΟΝ (praktoreíon) in the bus station, and those for destinations within the nome are sold on the bus. Retain all tickets until the journey is completed; inspectors are not uncommon. At country stops, hail the bus in a clear fashion; it will not halt automatically.

Within the nome, timetables are naturally designed for the needs of villagers: for shopping in town, hospital visiting, for the school day. They are therefore often not particularly convenient for tourist excursions from the town, but sometimes a taxi may bridge the gap to the nearest long-distance route. Note that Sunday bus schedules are usually reduced. Summer (mid April to mid October) and winter schedules differ markedly, so early or late season holiday-makers should check in advance especially carefully, at the bus station itself if possible.

Taxis are easily available (and relatively cheap) in the main towns, and one will be found on request in almost any village on the island (see below). A taxi is sometimes invaluable to supplement an awkward bus schedule. Hire by the day may be arranged, but both itinerary and price should be agreed beforehand. The rates to all main towns from Herákleion airport are clearly displayed in the arrival hall.

Walking. Crete offers many advantages to walkers, not least the chance to escape from the tourist scene to experience the natural beauty of the island, and to catch a glimpse of a traditional way of life which is altering fast while still retaining its own distinct character. The physical scale of the island is such that the scenery varies strikingly within the range of one day's walk. People in rural areas are friendly and helpful out of a tradition of hospitality to strangers which has not been eroded, as it sometimes has in the tourist resorts, by sheer weight of numbers. Local transport is generous with lifts.

The remote mountain areas are relatively unpopulated, and are only suitable for experienced walkers who will know how to take sensible precautions. Consult the Greek Alpine Club in Herákleion or Khaniá (see town information sections), or in case of difficulty the NTOG.

Many of the better-known walks described in this Guide, for example along the south flank of the White Mountains or to archaeological sites such as Lissós or the Kamáres cave, are waymarked with intermittent splashes of paint. Here, obviously, you will find other foreigners. However, if desired, it should also be possible to pick up hints and suggestions in the chapters of route descriptions in order to get right off the beaten track into the Cretan countryside.

Crete's modern road system dates from the period since the end of the Second World War. Realignments have been required for motor traffic, but the age-old routes between villages remain, and are still used as footpaths. The roughly paved trackway or 'kalderími' is usually thought of as a Turkish road, and some were indeed built by the Turks to help control a rebellious countryside, but they often follow the line of the earlier Venetian or even Roman roads.

Large-scale maps are not easily available for detailed planning; on cross-country routes suggested in this Guide it is a matter of studying the lie of the land on the road map, perhaps in conjunction with the footpath map now being issued (see below), and then asking for directions to the next village, antiquity or church. It is important to accent names correctly.

Maps may be obtained by post from Stanfords, 12–14 Long Acre, London, WC2E 9LP (tel. 071 836 1321). Telephone orders are accepted with Access or Barclaycard. Probably the best road map (1:200,000) is published by Freytag and Berndt as sheet 14 of their series covering Greece; clearly presented and conscientiously updated, it includes much useful tourist information, including large-scale town plans. Nelles issues an alternative, Crete (to the same scale), on which a number of country roads and tracks are indicated, which together with helpful contour information may appeal to walkers. The system it uses for folding makes it particu-

larly convenient to handle. A specialised map for walkers is being prepared by Harms Verlag; it concentrates on the footpath system (in five
sheets at 1:80,000) but does not yet cover the whole island.

Coastal Boats. There is a well-established boat service operating to
schedule on a route along the south coast between Khóra Sphakíon and
Palaiókhora (details given in Rtes 15 and 18). Its primary function is to
transport from Ayiá Rouméli the great numbers of people who now walk
down the Gorge of Samariá to the Libyan Sea, but it offers many other
opportunities to explore parts of this coast which are not accessible by
road. The boats also serve the island of Gávdos.

Various examples of local initiative are noted in the following text, e.g.
boats from Kolymbári to the Diktýnnaion sanctuary. Others may be
expected as a response to the needs of tourism, but the position changes
from year to year. It is sometimes possible to arrange to hire a boat pri-
vately (for example from Ayios Nikólaos or Mókhlos to visit the island of
Pseíra) but with considerations such as the cost of fuel and the potential
profit from the alternative of a day's fishing, this has become a relatively
expensive business.

Accommodation and Food

Hotels on Crete are inspected annually and graded in six categories; de
Luxe to Class E. The NTOG issues a leaflet listing all establishments of
Class C and above, with category and telephone numbers (but not prices);
it is an indispensable aid for anyone planning to travel around the island
using this type of accommodation. (Make sure you are given the current
one.) Occasionally in the route descriptions below, the existence of a
hotel is mentioned where it might be useful in an out-of-the-way location. To avoid disappointment the official list should be consulted before
firm plans are made. (The great majority of resort hotels are closed from
the end of October to mid March—apply to the NTOG for a separate list
of the few that remain open.)

The independent traveller will not be surprised that here, as elsewhere
around the Mediterranean, many hotels near popular beaches are geared
(especially in the high season) to package tours and block bookings from
agencies abroad, rather than to the unexpected overnight guest.

Prices are fixed by the Greek Hotel Association, and notice of the
approved rate, inclusive of service and taxes, is displayed in the room.
There may be surcharges for short stays (less than three nights) and
during the high season (July and August). A small reduction (20 per cent)
can be expected for single occupancy of a double room if no single is
available.

A chart showing hotel price ranges for the current year is available at
all NTOG offices. Other accommodation (such as pensions, rooms for rent
and self-catering apartments) is also regularly inspected and graded.

In general two levels of prices apply on Crete. Whereas simple food
and accommodation (above all in rural areas) are still relatively cheap by
European standards, charges for the smarter holiday accommodation and
luxury goods in the tourist resorts are not necessarily lower than at comparable resorts anywhere else around the Mediterranean.

Whether in the main towns or at beach resorts, the *accommodation* offered by de Luxe and Class A hotels is likewise comparable with that of their counterparts elsewhere. They have private bath (or shower), balconies, room service, and a full range of tourist facilities. Demi-pension terms are usually obligatory. Class B hotels are thus classified because of limitations of space, number of public rooms and room service. Class C hotels can be expected to provide simple, clean bedrooms, sometimes with balconies, almost always with private shower/w.c. Frequently they have no restaurant, and thus no compulsory demi-pension terms, which frees their guests to enjoy a meal in the local taverna.

Classes D and E (rare) are for the adventurous traveller, prepared to put up with spartan conditions in pursuit of economy or a bed in a chosen location. Out-of-reach of a tourist information office, tourist police in the local police station will be able to give advice.

A time-honoured and characteristic feature of touring on Crete is the ubiquitous *Rent Room*. In place of the traditional hospitality in family homes, inexpensive rooms are available for a single night or a longer period. (Allow the equivalent of £5–10 per night for a double room, depending on location and the time of year.) Often these rooms are in purpose-built modern houses, with private (if eccentric) facilities, and a communal fridge and simple kitchen where food may be kept and prepared. It is customary to make a thorough inspection before coming to a decision, and a negative one will be respected. Out-of-season, and depending on local circumstances, bargaining may lead to a mutually satisfactory reduction in the officially regulated price. Rent rooms are mentioned in the text at a few chosen points, but a large proportion of villages on the island can provide a room of some description. The English phrase is familiar, but in case of difficulty ask for 'ενα δωμάτιο' (ena domátio, a room).

Self-catering villas and apartments (sometimes now advertised as studios) have greatly increased in popularity over the last few years. As with all other accommodation their grades and prices, too, are regulated by the authorities—in case of difficulty consult NTOG or Tourist Police. It is becoming easier (especially out of season) to arrange a rental locally, either direct to the owner or manager, or through the agents recommended for organised travel under town information. However the majority of properties are still contracted on an annual basis to agencies abroad, and are obtainable only as part of a holiday package which includes flight costs. The NTOG in London can supply a list of such agencies. For high-season rentals enquiries should be made well in advance.

Youth Hostels. The Greek Youth Hostel Association (4 Odós Dragatsianoú, Athens) is affiliated to the International Youth Hostels Federation. The number of hostels on Crete tends to vary from year to year but they are usually to be found in all the main north coast towns, including Siteía, also in Ierápetra and near Plakiás on the south coast. The NTOG compiles a list.

Camping on Crete is officially restricted to recognised camping sites. A current list with telephone numbers is available at all NTOG offices; in 1992 there were over a dozen such sites, all by or near the sea.

Restaurants. Hotel menus on Crete usually keep to a bland international cuisine with only an occasional touch of local colour, more noticeable in the name of the dish than in its flavour. Formal restaurants (ΕΣΤΙΑΤΟΡΙΑ; estiatória) are rare on the island and restricted to the main centres.

Instead there is the Tavérna (TABEPNA), often family-owned and run, and characterised by a relaxed, friendly atmosphere and a strongly conservative, uncompromisingly Greek cuisine. In summer the tables are likely to be outdoors. The dishes vary according to season, using local produce when it is plentiful and keeping prices down accordingly. Cretan produce has a deservedly good reputation; even in the smart markets of Athens the cry 'fresh from Crete' is a recommendation. Most tavernas have their own inexpensive 'house' wine (χυμά, khimá). (Traditionally this is ordered not by the litre or half litre, but by the equivalent kilo—ena kiló, ena misó kiló.)

In towns and tourist resorts a menu may be displayed near the entrance. By law this must give for each dish first the basic price and then the final charge, which includes taxes and service (15 per cent). It is customary (especially in the case of foreigners) to leave a little extra in recognition of friendly service unless you are looked after by the owner himself. Traditionally tips left on the bill plate are for the waiter, and those on the table for the mikrós or wine boy (if there is one) who has done the fetching and carrying.

A ΨΗΤΑΡΙΑ (psitariá) generally provides meat (and chicken) roasted on the spit, or charcoal-grills each order. A take-away counter is a traditional part of the service (often limited to evenings only) with queues forming in the late evening and especially at weekends. Visitors with self-catering accommodation should ask for a recommendation in their neighbourhood.

A ΖΑΧΑΡΟΠΛΑΣΤΕΙΟΝ (zakharoplasteíon) or patisserie, sells pastries and confectionery, ice-creams, coffee and drinks of all sorts; for the younger generation these are replacing the traditional Greek kapheneíon (see below). Larger establishments in the towns may serve light meals, but in general their prices are not cheap.

Snacks are easy to find in all the main centres, where places selling pizza and hamburgers probably now outnumber those offering the traditional 'souvláki', little pieces of meat grilled on a wooden skewer, or 'tirópitta', a flaky-pastry cheese pie.

The traditional Greek café (ΚΑΦΕΝΕΙΟΝ) of the villages is an austere establishment usually thronged with male patrons for whom it is both a local club and political forum. Casual customers generally feel more comfortable at the tables outside. The kapheneíon serves Greek coffee, bottled soft drinks, ice-creams, and alcoholic drinks such as rakí or koniák (Greek brandy).

An ΕΞΟΧΙΚΟΝ ΚΕΝΤΡΟΝ (Exokhikón Kéntron), a 'rural centre', combines the functions of café and taverna out in the countryside or at the beach.

Food and Drink. The favourite Greek aperitif is *oúzo*, a strong aniseed-flavoured drink made from the residue left when grapes have been pressed for wine. Traditionally it is served with *mezédes*, snacks consisting of anything from a slice of cheese or tomato or an olive to pieces of salami sausage or grilled octopus. In Crete oúzo is often replaced by *rakí* (also called tzikoudiá), a stronger distillation without aniseed flavouring. Beer and lager (both locally brewed and imported) are very popular.

Cretan wine (κρασί, krasí) can be excellent. Retsína, the resinated white wine particularly characteristic of the Attica region of mainland Greece, is now bottled on the island (and is still very cheap) but there is also a large variety of unresinated table wines, white (άσπρο, áspro), red (μαύρο, mávro, literally black), or rosé (κόκκινο, kókkino, literally red). At grander restaurants (and in most supermarkets) the principal mainland varieties (Cambás, Demestiká) are available, but the local bottlings are just as good and cheaper. Minós, Górtys and Lató are widely known. Relative newcomers, recommended, are Logádo and Olympiás. The Arkhánes cooperative ranks high (and has won awards) in assessments of Greek wines. Most 'house' wine in jugs is 'kókkino', the characteristically brownish rosé of Crete.

The best Greek 'champagne' comes from Rhodes.

Tavernas which serve meals both at midday and in the evening (and, especially in the towns, not quite all do) usually cook their prepared dishes (étimo fayetó, literally 'ready food') at lunchtime. Depending on the size of the establishment there may be from two to a dozen dishes ready for inspection, with a choice of meat dishes, stuffed vegetables, and pulses such as beans, lentils, or chick-peas cooked as a cross between a soup and a vegetable stew. It is possible to order grilled meat and fried potatoes, or an omelet and salad, but the traditional lunchtime dishes are prepared in advance. In the evening these dishes may still be available, but only rarely will they have been cooked afresh. If in doubt it may be wise to avoid them.

A Cretan party starts the evening meal with a variety of hors d'oeuvres (orektiká) for communal tasting, including a large mixed ('Greek') salad with olives and féta cheese. The dishes to be shared are set on the table with knives and forks and bread, but no individual plates unless these are specially requested. The subsequent orders of grilled meat or fish, or a house speciality such as 'stiffádo' (stew), may arrive in haphazard fashion as they are ready from the stove or the charcoal grill.

To cope with large numbers of foreign visitors tavernas in the most popular tourist resorts sometimes now resort to refrigerated cabinets displaying sample dishes; establishments which expect tourists naturally translate the menus for their benefit and most waiters anyway speak a little English. However the correct way to order a taverna meal is still to go to the kitchen to inspect the food, and in the traditional taverna you will be respected and helped if you indicate that you understand this. Even in the larger restaurants in Herákleion and Khaniá Cretans (or one or two of the party) will expect to visit the kitchen or serving counter to see and discuss what is offered.

There are many specialist fish tavernas around the coast of Crete. If you are going to eat fish a choice will be shown you from the ice, and then your selection will be weighed to ascertain the eventual charge on the bill. At this point you are still free to change your mind in any way. (Note that prawns, a popular choice with tourists, are in season only October–May. In summer they will be frozen.)

The traditional taverna did not serve a dessert course or coffee; for delicious pastries or ice-cream one moved on to linger in the Zakharoplastéion. However, in places frequented by tourists, fresh fruit, ice-creams and coffee are now often available to end a taverna meal. Greek coffee is served on the grounds in small cups. It is traditionally very sweet but can be ordered 'medium' or without sugar (see end of Menu). Instant coffee (referred to as Nescafé) is also available, but more expensive.

The MENU below describes some of the more widely available dishes. The choice of fish and vegetables depends to some extent on the season.

ΟΡΕΚΤΙΚΑ (orektiká), Hors d'oeuvres
Ταραμοσαλάτα (taramosaláta), smoked cod's roe paté
Ντολμαδάκια (dolmadákia), stuffed vine leaves served cold, or hot with egg-and-lemon sauce
Ελιές (eliés), olives
Τζατζίκι (tzatzíki), yoghurt flavoured with grated cucumber and garlic
Κολοκυθάκια τηγανιτά (kolokithákia tiganitá), fried baby marrows
Σαγανάκι κεφαλοτύρι (saganáki kefalotíri), fried cheese
Μελιτζανοσαλάτα (melidzanosaláta), aubergine salad
Γίγαντες (yígantes), butter beans in oil and lemon dressing
Καλαμαράκια (kalamarákia), fried baby squid
Μαρίδες (marídes), whitebait
Σκορδαλιά (skordaliá), garlic dip
Σαλιγκάρια (salingária), snails (a Lenten speciality)

ΣΟΥΠΕΣ (soupés), Soups
Σούπα αυγολέμονο (soúpa avgholémono), egg and lemon soup
Ψαρόσουπα (psarósoupa), fish soup
Φακές (fakés), lentil soup
Φασόλια (fasólia), haricot bean soup
Ρεβίθια (revíthia), chick-pea soup

ΖΥΜΑΡΙΚΑ (zimariká) ΚΑΙ ΡΙΖΙ (rízi), Pasta and Rice dishes
Πιλάφι (piláfi), plain rice pilaf
Μακαρόνια (makarónia), spaghetti, με σάλτσα (me sáltsa) with sauce, με σάλτσα και τυρί (me sáltsa ke tirí) with sauce and cheese
Παστίτσιο (pastítsio), macaroni baked with meat and bechamel sauce

ΨΑΡΙΑ (psária), Fish
Φαγκρί (fangrí), sea bream, and Λιθρίνι (lithríni), red bream
Ξιφίας (ksifías), swordfish
Μπαρμπούνια (barboúnia), red mullet
Γαρίδες (garídes), prawns
Κταπόδι (ktapódi), octopus

ΑΥΓΑ (avgá), Eggs Βραστά (vrastá) boiled, Αυγά μάτια (avgá mátia) fried
Ομελέτα (omeléta), omelet, ζαμπόν (jambón), with ham; πατάτες (patátes), with fried potato

ΕΝΤΡΑΔΕΣ (entrádes), Entrées
Μουσακά (mousaká), layers of aubergine, minced beef, and cheese, covered with bechamel sauce and baked in the oven
Αρνάκι φασολάκια (arnáki fasolákia), lamb with beans
Ψητό κοτόπουλο (psitó kotópoulo), roast chicken
Στιφάδο (stifádo), rich beef stew with onions
Τζουτζουκάκια (tkákia), meat balls in tomato sauce

ΣΧΑΡΑΣ (skháras), Grills
Σουβλάκι (-ια) souvláki (-ia), kebab(s) of pork (occasionally lamb)
Μπριζόλες χοιρινές (brizóles khirinés), pork chops
Μπριζόλα μοσχαρίσια (brizóla moskharísia) veal chop
Παϊδάκια αρνί (paîdákia arní), lamb cutlets (or chops)
Φιλέτο (filéto), steak
Κοκορέτσι (kokorétsi), lamb's liver, kidney, sweetbreads and heart, sliced and wrapped in intestines, then cooked on the spit
Κεφτέδες σχάρας (keftédes skháras), grilled meat balls

ΛΑΧΑΝΙΚΑ ΚΑΙ ΣΑΛΑΤΕΣ (lakhaniká ke salátes), Vegetable dishes and Salads
Γεμιστές ντομάτες (yemistés domátes), stuffed tomatoes
Γεμιστές πιπεριές (yemistés piperiés), stuffed peppers
Παπουτσάκια (papoutsákia), stuffed aubergines with cheese (literally, 'little shoes')
Μπριάμ (briám), mixed vegetables stewed in olive oil
Αγκινάρες (angináres), artichokes

Αλα πολίτα (ala políta), artichokes with potatoes, carrots, onions, and sometimes broad beans, flavoured with dill
Χόρτα (khórta), green vegetables, including wild greens
Φασολάκια φρέσκα (fasolákia fréska), green beans
Κουκιά (koukiá), broad beans
Χωριατική σαλάτα (khoriatikí saláta), mixed ('Greek') salad, literally village or country salad, with olives and féta cheese
Σαλάτα ντομάτες (saláta domátes), tomato salad
Αγγούρι (angoúri), cucumber
Μαρούλι (maroúli), lettuce
Λάχανο (lákhano), cabbage
Παντζάρια (pandzária), beetroot
Κρεμμύδι (kremídi), onion
Πατάτες τηγανιτές (patátes tiganités), fried potatoes (chips)

ΤΥΡΙΑ (tiriá), Cheeses
Φέτα (féta), soft white goat's milk cheese
Μησύθρα (misíthra), unsalted soft cheese made from sheep's milk, known in western Crete as ανθότιρος (anthótiros)
Γραβιέρα (graviéra), Gruyère-type hard cheese

ΓΛΥΚΑ (gliká), Sweets
Μπακλαβά (baklavá), layered pastry filled with honey and nuts
Καταίφι (kataífi), pastry shredded and filled with sweetened nuts
Γαλακτομπούρεκο (galaktoboúreko), pastry filled with vanilla custard
Ρυζόγαλο (rizógalo), creamy rice pudding

MISCELLANEOUS
Γιαούρτι (yiaoúrti), yoghurt, με μέλι (me méli), with honey
Ψωμί (psomí), bread
Βούτυρο (voútiro), butter
Αλάτι (aláti), salt
Πιπέρι (pipéri), pepper
Μουστάρδα (moustárda), mustard
Λάδι (ládi), oil
Ξύδι (xídi), vinegar
Ζάχαρι (zákhari), sugar
Νερό (neró), water, παγωμένο (pagoméno), iced
Παγωτό (pagotó), ice cream
Λεμόνι (lemóni), a lemon
Λεμονάδα (lemonáda), lemonade
Πορτοκαλάδα (portokaláda), orangeade
Πεπόνι (pepóni), melon
Καρπούζι (karpoúzi), water melon

ΕΛΛΗΝΙΚΟΣ ΚΑΦΕΣ (ellinikós kafés), Greek coffee (served on the grounds)
γλυκός (glikós), sweet; μέτριος (métrios), medium sweet; σκέτος (skétos), without sugar; διπλός (diplós) a double, a large cup

General Information

Tourist Information. The National Tourist Organisation of Greece or NTOG (in Greek EOT, Ellinikós Organismós Tourismoú; pron. Ay-ót) maintains regional offices in Herákleion and in Khaniá. Municipal Information offices are a relatively new and very useful development; at present they are in operation in Réthymnon, Ayios Nikólaos, Ierápetra and Siteía but others may follow. For addresses and telephone numbers consult the information section for the appropriate town.

The Tourist Police service is in the process of being replaced as a separate organisation by members of the ordinary police force who staff information desks in police stations.

Banking Hours. At present Monday–Friday 08.00–14.00. In high season, at tourist centres such as Ayios Nikólaos, one foreign exchange till may reopen at 17.30.

These bank opening hours are now supplemented by the convenient Currency Exchange service operated by the Post Office—see below.

Postal Services. The main post offices (ΤΑΧΥΔΡΟΜΕΙΟΝ; takhydromeíon) in both Herákleion and Khaniá are open for normal postal business Monday–Friday 07.30–19.30; in other towns and the larger villages the hours are Monday–Friday 07.30–14.00. Subsidiary post offices in temporary caravan accommodation are now common in popular tourist areas. Their weekday opening hours are as above (according to location) but conveniently they are also open (same hours) on Saturdays, and usually on Sundays as well (09.00–18.00 in the main centres, reduced hours elsewhere). Staff generally speak some English. Letter-boxes (ΓΡΑΜΜΑ-ΤΟΚΙΒΩΤΙΟ) and the post office caravans are painted yellow. Postage stamps, γραμματόσημα (grammatósima), can be bought at kiosks and at many shops which sell postcards, but a small premium is charged for the convenience.

Correspondence marked 'Poste Restante' (to be called for) may be addressed to any post office and is handed to the addressee on proof of identity (passport preferable). A fee is charged. The surname of the addressee, especially the capital letter, should be clearly written.

Parcels are not delivered in Greece. They must be collected from a Parcels Office, where they are subject to handling fees, full customs charges, and often to delay. On the island the bus companies operate an efficient parcels service between their own booking-halls.

The Post Office now operates a *Currency Exchange* for both cheques and foreign money, on a par with the banking system. In conventional post offices (Monday–Friday) the hours are 08.00–13.30 but the caravans offer this service whenever they are open. The extensive network of post offices in villages across the island and the extra opening hours in the bigger cities and tourist areas make this a particularly welcome innovation.

Telephones. The Greek telephone and telegraph services are maintained by a public corporation, Οργανισμός Τηλεπικοινωνιών Ελλάδος (OTE, always referred to by its acronym pronounced O-táy). All large towns have a central office of the company, with call-boxes and arrangements for making domestic and international calls. The calls are metered, and payment is made to the cashier at the end, with no need for correct change. The same metering system works for the many instruments available to the public at kiosks (períptera, see below) and in cafés, bars, hotels etc. throughout the island. OTE offices in the cities are open 07.00–23.00. Most villages have a (signed) OTE centre, usually the local kapheneíon; in some cases opening hours may be restricted.

Coin-operated call-boxes are gradually increasing in number.

Area Codes on the island:
Herákleion 081
Khaniá 0821
Réthymnon 0831
Ayios Nikólaos 0841
Siteía 0843
Kísamos (Kastélli Kisámou) 0822
Ierápetra 0842

For the UK dial 0044 and drop the first 0 of the British area code. For the USA dial 001. Transferred-charge calls can be arranged through the operator (domestic 132, international 161).

Telegrams are most easily sent from OTE centres; English is accepted.

Seasons. Summer on Crete is generally dry and warm without extremes at sea level; July and August temperatures are to some extent moderated by the often strong prevailing north wind (the meltémi), but anyone planning a walking holiday would be well advised to avoid these months. Though the sea is usually warm enough for swimming (especially on the south coast) from mid April to November, beach life in full swing can only be relied on from mid May to late September. Amounts of rain or snow (mostly between December and March) vary widely throughout the island, being heavy in the central mountainous areas. The wild flowers are at their best from February to May, but at least until the end of April the weather is uncertain.

As a guide, the following table gives average air and sea temperatures (Celsius) in the Herákleion region.

	Air	Sea		Air	Sea
Jan.	12.3	17.1	**July**	26.4	24.2
Feb.	12.5	16.2	**Aug.**	26.4	24.8
March	13.8	16.9	**Sept.**	23.6	24.4
April	16.8	17.9	**Oct.**	20.3	22.5
May	20.4	20.0	**Nov.**	17.2	19.6
June	24.4	22.3	**Dec.**	13.9	17.4

Use of Time. Holidays from the travel agent's brochure may be chosen for a variety of reasons other than convenient access to the island's antiquities, but with improved road conditions you can visit the Herákleion museum and the Palace of Knossós in one long day from a base almost anywhere on Crete. The determined touring motorist can see the greater part of the island in two weeks. Two-centre holidays are gaining in popularity, and from comfortable hotels on the coast they can offer the chance to explore both ends of the island at a more leisurely pace; however it helps to be aware that the notorious built-up strip of north coast given over to packaged beach holidays runs (with only a few honourable and usually expensive exceptions) from Herákleion to Mállia.

It is hoped that by following the routes of this book selectively, readers will be able to adapt the suggested itineraries to their particular interests. At the planning stage it is worth considering the possibility of using Khaniá airport in order to start and end a holiday in the relatively unspoilt tranquillity of western Crete, to prepare for the more strenuous demands of Herákleion and the major archaeological sites. The Minoan Palaces and the majority of the other important Minoan excavations are located in the central and eastern parts of the island.

Museums and Archaeological Sites. Ancient remains of any significance are usually signposted and the sites are enclosed, though in the case of minor sites not necessarily locked. It has to be accepted that the position may change from year to year. Admission charges are levied only at museums (both state-run and private institutions) and at the major and most frequently visited sites.

Opening hours are liable to alter slightly each year, and it is impossible to give accurate information ahead of the annual (early spring) announcement. Moreover, the hours differ according to season, and are not uniform at sites of varying importance throughout the island. Generally, however, there are two set periods: the 'summer' season runs from mid March to mid October and 'winter' hours are considerably reduced. State museums, but not necessarily sites, are closed on Tuesdays—except for the Herákleion Archaeological Museum which closes on MONDAYS. In the text, 1992 summer opening hours are given as a rough guide, but readers are urged to CHECK on arrival on the island, either in person or by telephone at the nearest tourist information office.

It should be expected that both museums and guarded archaeological sites will be *closed* on 1 January, 25 March, Good Friday afternoon, Easter Sunday, and Christmas Day. Note that Sunday opening hours apply to other public holidays and festivals, in particular: Shrove Monday (the beginning of the Orthodox Lent), Easter Saturday and Monday, 1 May, 15 August, 28 October, Christmas Eve and New Year's Eve, and 6 January (Epiphany). To avoid disappointment visitors on the island for the Greek Easter weekend should make particularly careful enquiries about the opening arrangements for the current year, which, at the start of a new season, are often a matter of dispute until the eleventh hour.

In general *photography* (hand cameras only) is free on archaeological sites, and in museums is permitted (save where unpublished material is on display) on purchase of a second ticket for the camera. ΑΠΑΓΟΡΕΥΕ-ΤΑΙ (apagorévetai) means forbidden. Standard fees (not cheap) are chargeable for using tripods, etc., and a permit may be required. Consult the NTOG.

If *directions* to sites are needed beyond the detailed instructions given in the text, the following phrases may be useful: yiá or pros (towards) ta arkhaía (ancient things), to kástro (any fortified height), tis anaskaphés (excavations), to phroúrio (medieval castle), to tápho (tomb). Ask for a church by its saint's name.

A great many of the frescoed churches are nowadays kept locked. As far as possible, advice is given in the Guide about the whereabouts of the key (to kleidí), but if the arrangement has been changed local help is often forthcoming. There is increasing interest in these churches, and the Service for Byzantine Antiquities is keen to make them more easily accessible. However it has to be faced that the search for a key can be a time-consuming business, and is not always successful.

In Orthodox churches women are not permitted to enter the sanctuary.

The majority of *monasteries* now close their gates during the afternoon (usually 14.00–17.00). Owing to the decline of monastic communities, as well as the ever-increasing number of visitors, most of them no longer offer over-night accommodation. Decorous dress is always requested; exact rules are not laid down, but shorts are particularly disliked.

Public Holidays. Official public holidays in Greece are: New Year's Day;

6 January (Epiphany); Kathará Deftéra ('Clean Monday', the Orthodox Shrove Day at the beginning of Lent); 25 March (Independence Day); 1 May (exodus to the countryside to pick wild flowers); Orthodox Good Friday, Easter Sunday and Monday, also Ascension Day; 15 August (Feast of the Assumption of the Virgin); 28 October ('Okhi' day; see below); Christmas Day; and 26 December.

Carnival after a three week period of festivities reaches its peak on the last Sunday before Lent with processions and student revels; on Clean Monday families take to the countryside and fly kites. Procession of shrouded bier on Good Friday (Epitáphios) and the burning of Judas in the churchyard; at midnight preceding Easter Sunday the 'Khristós anésti' (Christ is risen) celebration, with ceremonial lighting of the Paschal Candle during mass, and the release of fireworks in front of churches; the roasting of Paschal lambs and cracking of red Easter eggs on the morning of Easter Day.

Okhi Day, commemorating the Greek 'no' (όχι) to the Italian ultimatum of 1940 (see section on Modern History), is celebrated with remembrance services and military processions.

Additional *local celebrations*: in Asi Goniá the sheep-shearing festival on St. George's day (23 April unless this falls in Holy Week); in Khaniá there are festivities in late May (Anniversary of Battle of Crete); in Sphakiá on 26 May and in Ierápetra on 3 October (both for Anniversary of 1821 revolution); at the Arkádi monastery 8–9 November commemorating the heroic episode there during the 1866 revolt; and in Herákleion on 11 November, the feast of her patron saint (Ayios Minás).

Calendar and Time: all movable festivals are governed by the fixing of Easter according to the Orthodox calendar. Greece uses Eastern European Time (in summer 3 hours ahead of GMT, in winter 2 hours). Note also that π.μ. (p.m.) = English a.m. and m.m. (m.m.) = English p.m.

Shops are open on summer weekdays 08.00–13.00 (most categories of food shop 13.30), also Tuesday, Thursday and Friday, 17.00–20.00 (winter 16.00–19.30). On Monday, Wednesday and Saturday they do not reopen, but the morning session is extended to 14.00 (Saturday 15.00). Tourist 'souvenir' shops, and food shops in designated 'tourist areas' may remain open all day, including Sundays. The regulations are exceedingly complicated; butchers in particular keep different hours—enquire locally. Chemists take turns to offer a 24-hour service; the rota is posted on the shop door.

Tourists on a self-catering holiday or shopping for picnic lunches will have no difficulty in finding a supermarket (accented supermárket) selling all basic requirements; opening hours are usually as for food shops above, with extended hours in the main resorts.

The ΠΕΡΙΠΤΕΡΟ, or pavement kiosk, developed from a French model, is a characteristic feature of Greek urban life. Selling newspapers, postcards and stationery, stamps, cigarettes, chocolate, toilet articles, film, etc., kiosks are open for about 18 hours a day.

Language. A knowledge of ancient Greek is a useful basis, but no substitute, for the study of modern Greek. Apart from the unfamiliarity of modern pronunciation, many of the commonest words (e.g. water, wine, fish) no longer come from the same roots. Those who know no language but English can get along quite comfortably anywhere on the main tourist routes. A knowledge of at least the Greek alphabet is highly desirable, however, since street names, bus destination plates, etc., may otherwise be puzzling. A phrase book such as the 'Penguin Greek Phrase Book' can be very helpful.

The Greek alphabet now as in later classical times comprises 24 letters:

A α, B β, Γ γ, Δ δ, E ε, Z ζ, H η, Θ θ, I ι, K κ, Λ λ, M μ, N ν, Ξ ξ, O o, Π π, P ρ, Σ σ ς, T τ, Y υ, Φ φ, X χ, Ψ ψ, Ω ω.

Vowels. There are five basic vowel sounds in Greek to which even combinations written as dipthongs conform: α is pronounced very short, ε and αι as e in egg (when accented more open, as in the first e in there); η, ι, υ, ει, οι, υι have the sound of ea in eat; o, ω as the o in dot; ου as English oo in pool. The combinations αυ and ευ are pronounced av and ev when followed by loud consonants, af and ef before mute consonants.

Consonants are pronounced roughly as their English equivalents with the following exceptions: β = v; γ is hard and guttural, before a and o like the English g in hag, before other vowels approaching the y in your; γγ and γκ are usually equivalent to ng; δ = th as in this; θ as th in think; before an i sound λ resembles the lli sound in million; ξ has its full value always, as in ex-king; ρ is always rolled; σ (ς) is always hard, never like z; τ is pronounced half way between t and d; φ = ph or f; χ, akin to the Scottish ch as in loch, a guttural h; ψ = ps as in lips. The English sound b is represented by the Greek double consonant μπ, d by ντ. All Greek words of two syllables or more have one accent which serves to show the stressed syllable. In the termination ον the n sound is disappearing in speech and the ν is often omitted in writing.

The above are the equivalents commonly given for the Greek language, but in fact the pronunciation of the Cretan dialect is considerably softer than that of mainland Greece. In Αγιος, for example, the γ is nearer to 'j' than to the transliterated 'y' of this Guide or the alternative 'gh' of signposts, and χ approaches the 'ch' of church, or even 'sh', rather than the 'ch' in loch.

For *transliteration* in this volume see Contents page for Explanations.

Manners and Customs. Travellers may like to pay attention to the more formal conventions of Cretans and indeed all Greek people. The handshake at meeting and parting is usual and enquiry after the health taken seriously. The correct reply to καλώς ωρίσατε (kalós orísate; welcome) is καλώς σας βρίκαμε (kalós sas vríkame; glad to see you). To the enquiry τι κάνετε (ti kánete; how do you do?) or πως είστε (pos íste; how are you?) the reply should be καλά ευχαριστώ, και σείς (kalá efkharistó, ke sis; well thank you, and you?), or έτσι και έτσι, και σεις (étsi ke étsi, ke sis; so-so, and you?). General greetings are χαίρετε (khérete; greetings), or less formally γιά σας (ya sas; hello). Στο καλό (sto kaló; keep well, the equivalent of godspeed) is used when bidding farewell to one who leaves, not when one is leaving oneself. Περαστικά (perastiká) is a useful word of comfort in time of illness, meaning 'may things improve'.

It is still customary to greet shopkeepers, the company in kapheneíons, etc., with καλημέρα (kaliméra; good day) or καλησπέρα (kalispéra; good evening). Σας παρακαλώ (sas parakaló; please) is used when asking for a favour or for information, but not when ordering something which is to be paid for, when θα ήθελα (tha íthela; I should like) is more appropriate. The Greek for yes is ναι (né) or, more formally, μάλιστα (málista); for no, όχι (ókhi).

When drinking in company glasses are often touched with the toast, εις υγεία σας (your health) which is generally shortened in speech to the familiar yásas, or, to a single individual, yásou (to you), or yámas (to us).

In direct contrast to English custom, personal questions showing interest in a stranger's life, politics, and money are the basis of conversation in Greece, and travellers should not be offended at being asked in the most direct way about their movements, family, occupation, salary, and politics.

The 'Volta', a structured evening stroll, is universal throughout Crete. Fasting is taken seriously in Lent, and is rigorous in Holy Week.

Equipment. Binoculars greatly enhance the pleasure of travel on Crete. A pocket compass can be of help in understanding inland site plans and directions. A torch is useful, especially for frescoed churches or caves. Basic picnic equipment does double duty on Rent Room terraces. Protection from the sun is clearly necessary, but anyone on a touring holiday in the early part of the year (March–April) should remember that in the mountains the weather may still be wet, and, at least at night, distinctly chilly. Cretan hillside undergrowth is remarkably spiny, and even in summer heat the protection of trousers and sensible shoes may be preferred. Mosquito repellent is advisable; small electrical devices (very efficient) are available locally in town chemists and all supermarkets.

Electricity. The voltage on Crete is 220v and the current is AC.

Newspapers. Foreign-language newspapers are obtainable in the main towns and resort hotels but (because flown in) are expensive. The London papers are on sale the day after publication.

Weights and Measures. The French metric system of weights and measures, adopted in Greece in 1958, is used with the terms substantially unaltered. Thus κιλό (kiló, pl. kilá), misó kiló (half kilo), grammária (grams), etc. Some liquids are measured by weight, not in litres.

Antiquities. The regulations to protect Greece's heritage are strictly and comprehensively enforced; even picking up sherds on an ancient site is prohibited. Except with special permission, it is forbidden to export antiquities and works of art (dated before 1830) which have been obtained (whether bought or found) in Greece. If a traveller's luggage contains antiquities not covered by an export permit (supplied with bona fide purchases) the articles are liable to be confiscated and prosecution may follow. Note that the use of metal detectors is prohibited throughout Greece.

I   HERAKLEION AND CENTRAL CRETE

1   Herákleion

HERAKLEION or **IRAKLIO(N)** (in Greek ΗΡΑΚΛΕΙΟ), medieval *Candia*, lies midway along the north coast of Crete, and since 1971 has been the island's administrative capital. With two night-ferries all the year round from Piraeus (the port of Athens), and the principal airport of the island nearby, Herákleion is still for many tourists their introduction to Crete, and its vibrant modernity is often a surprise. Its population of 102,000 makes it the fifth largest city in Greece, and its per capita income is the highest in the whole country.

The city has often been damaged by earthquake—the last major one in 1926—and historically it suffered from pirate raids, foreign occupation, internal conflict, and in 1941 the full horror of modern warfare. The 1941 bombing of Herákleion is strikingly illustrated by photographs in the Historical Museum. In recent years the understandable urge to modernise overnight—made possible by the advent of comparative affluence—has very often resulted in piecemeal redevelopment, usually in aesthetically unpleasing reinforced concrete. But the medieval street plan endures, the Venetian fortifications have been well restored, and other traces of the architectural past do survive to illuminate the island's history. The proximity of the Minoan Palace of Knossós and the unique contents of the Archaeological Museum continue to make Herákleion one of the most important tourist objectives of the Aegean.

Tourist Information Office (NTOG or in Greek EOT): 1 Odós Xanthoudídou, off Plateía Eleftherías, opposite the entrance to the Archaeological Museum (see town plan at end of book). Opening hours: summer weekdays 07.30–15.00 (Saturdays and Sundays CLOSED). Tel. (81) 228 225; ask for Information.

Tourist Police: Leophóros Dikaiosíni, near the market street in the centre of town.

Airport: 4km east of the city on the Old Road; for details of services turn to Practical Information—Getting to Crete.

Taxis from the rank at the airport are prepared to go anywhere on the island. Prices to the most popular destinations are listed inside the terminal building (domestic arrivals) so that the fare can be agreed in advance.

For the town centre the No. 1 bus (see below) now operates with an improved schedule to and from the airport to replace the Olympic Airways shuttle service which has been discontinued.

Leaving the airport by car you join (in less than 1km) the Old Road from eastern Crete which leads directly (another 3km) to the centre of Herákleion, Plateía Eleftherías. At 3km, through the suburb of *Néa Alikarnássos*, an alternative (newly- upgraded) ring-road is well signed, right for the waterfront and (nearer the centre) left for Knossós.

For the north coast highway (New Road), bypassing Herákleion to other destinations, join the Old Road as above, follow it less than 1km over the first main crossroads (traffic lights), and take the next left, an insignificant one-way street recently signposted only from the direction of the city. Very shortly there is a right turn, then a left bend, and the highway is in sight.

Car Hire: turn to Practical Information—Travelling on Crete.

Ferry boats from Piraeus dock at the east quay (see plan) where there is a comfortable café. Taxis meet the boats. Buses for town (and Knossós—No. 2) outside the dock gates, or 200m west, beside the long-distance bus stations.

Two companies operate the ferry services (turn to Practical Information—Getting to Crete). The *Minoan Lines* office is at 78 Odós 25 Avgoústou, opposite Ayios Títos (tel. (81) 229 602); the *ANEK* line is on the other side of the same street, nearer the harbour (tel. (81) 222 481).

Accommodation is plentiful at all price levels. There are four Class A hotels in the city. There are beach hotels in both directions, at Amoudára beach (to the west) and at Amnisós (east), both within 15 minutes of the centre by car (also served by town buses), but for a short visit without private transport, it may be more convenient to stay within the city walls. There is a cluster of comfortable modern Class C hotels, most without restaurant, in a central position above the Venetian harbour. They are on or near Odós Epimenídou, a one-way street running east from Odós 25 Avgoústou. For cheaper accommodation consult the Tourist Information Office.

Youth Hostel: 24 Odós Khándaka.

Swimming and beach facilities: see Rtes 3A, 5 and 11A for recommended beaches within easy reach of the city.

The Greek Alpine Club runs a refuge hut on Mount Ida. For information from the Herákleion office telephone (81) 227 609.

Tour Agencies: *Candia Tours*, 51 Odós Epimenídou (near the Lató Hotel), tel. (81) 226 168; *Creta Travel*, 22 Odós Epimenídou, tel. (81) 227 002; *Adamis Tours*, 23 Odós 25 Avgoústou, tel. (81) 283 820; *Zeus of Crete*, 1 Odós Víronas tel. (81) 229 473 and also a desk at the airport. These and many others arrange guided tours to the main archaeological sites, to the Gorge of Samariá and a number of other places of interest or natural beauty. Several *shipping agents* have offices in Odós 25 Avgoústou, and most lines are handled by Kavi Club, 2 Papalexandroú, in the little square next to the NTOG. See also Ferry Services above. (If in need of further assistance or if telephone numbers have changed, apply to NTOG.)

There are one-day cruises to the islands of Théra (Santorini) and Ios subject to weather conditions; in midsummer, when the 'meltémi' wind blows most strongly, it is not always possible to land on Santorini.

National Bank of Greece: Odós 25 Avgoústou near Ayios Títos, and also in Plateía Kornárou opposite the top end of the market street.

Post Offices: main office in Plateía Daskaloyiánni, open for all mailing business Monday–Friday 07.30–19.30. Foreign Exchange for cheques and currency operates here, mornings only till 13.30. Subsidiary offices in caravans have been established in El Greco (Theotokopoúlou) Park and beside the bus stations on the harbour: open for all services, including Exchange, 08.00–20.00 daily except Sunday 09.00–18.00.

OTE (telephone company): head office in El Greco Park open 07.00–23.00. (Area code 081.)

Public Lavatories: in El Greco Park, and in the public gardens on the edge of Plateía

Eleftherías, opposite the Venizélos statue and behind the Nikephóros Phokás memorial. Also, for visitors to the Archaeological Museum, next to the garden café.

Car Parking is strictly controlled in the town centre, 08.00–20.00 (except Sundays), and central Herákleion is no place for apprehensive drivers in unfamiliar vehicles. There is a municipal car park (token charge per half-day payable straightaway after parking) in the moat, just outside the New Gate on the right when entering the town (see plan); this is recommended for the Archaeological Museum. At the other end of town, parking has traditionally been unrestricted near the seafront beyond the Historical Museum (c 10 minutes on foot to the centre).

Buses on town routes are blue. Tickets must be bought in advance from kiosks found near all the principal stops. Most useful bus routes are:
No. 1 ΣΤΡΑΤΩΝΕΣ east to the airport terminal and every 30 minutes in summer to the Amnisós beaches. Bus stop in the middle of Plateía Eleftherías.
No. 2 ΚΝΩΣΟΣ every 20 minutes from the harbour (near the long-distance bus stations—see plan), with convenient boarding points in Plateía Venizélou (Morosini fountain) and Odós 1821. On the return route, the bus stops in Plateía Eleftherías, for the Archaeological Museum, and then descends by the ramparts directly to the harbour.
No. 6 for the beaches and hotels west of the city, also for Camping Herákleion. (Not all buses on this route run to the end of the line; look for signs on windscreen or check with the driver). Bus stop outside the cinema in Plateía Eleftherías.

Country or long-distance buses are green. Because separate companies operate the various routes there are several bus stations around the city, all under the umbrella of ΚΤΕΛ, the bus owners' association. Current telephone numbers of the bus stations are available from NTOG.
I. The main bus station serving eastern Crete is east of the roundabout (towards the quay for the Athens ferries, see plan) at the bottom of ΛΕΩΦ. ΔΟΥΚΑΣ ΜΠΩΦΟΡ (Doúkas Bófor). For routes to: Mállia, Ayios Nikólaos and Siteía, the plateau of Lasíthi, and Ierápetra via Ayios Nikólaos— via Viánnos see iv. below. Also for buses to Arkhánes.
II. The bus station for north coast routes west to Réthymnon and Khaniá is on the same open area near the harbour, adjacent to the main station above. It also runs one service a day through to Ayía Galíni via Réthymnon and Spíli.
III. The bus station outside the Khaniá Gate, 150m down the side street to the right, is for routes to the south-west: Górtyn, the Palace of Phaistós, Mátala, Ayía Galíni; Zarós and Kamáres; Léndas. Also (separate office) for Phódele, Týlissos and Anóyia.
IV. Oasis bus station, under the walls outside the New Gate (not on plan), serves Viánnos, for Arví and Mýrtos on the south coast, and on by this route to Ierápetra. Also other destinations to the south-east within the province of Herákleion, such as Thrapsanó and the Kastélli Pediádas region.

Rocca al Mare, the Venetian fortress built to guard the harbour of Candia (Herákleion)

British Consulate: 16, Odós Papalexandroú, in the little square next to the NTOG (tel. (81) 224 012).

General Hospital: Apollónion, between Odós Alber and Odós Márkou Mousoúrou—across the main road in front of the cathedral (Ayios Minás) and one block towards Plateía Kornárou and the market street.

History. In the Neolithic period there was at least one settlement on the high ground above the Kaíratos stream-bed, on the east side of what is now Herákleion. Here the modern suburb of Póros lies on the site of a Minoan harbour town and cemetery. By Roman times 'Heraclium' was the harbour of Knossós (Strabo, X, 476, 7). With the Saracen conquest, in AD 824, the town was renamed 'Rabdh el Khandak', literally translated 'the Castle of the ditch' referring to a great moat dug around it; the Arab settlement became a centre of piracy and the principal slave market of the Mediterranean. After a number of abortive attempts to liberate the island, the army of Nikephóros Phokás, including Russian, Slav and Scandinavian mercenaries, laid siege to the town, and the Byzantine general is renowned for demoralising the defenders by catapulting over the walls the heads of his Moslem prisoners. After 10 months and much bloodshed, Crete was once again part of Christendom. During this second Byzantine period the city (now known as Khándakas) extended to what today are Khándakas and Daídalos streets.

When the Venetians eventually took control of Crete (1210—see Historical Background p 25) they made the city their capital, calling it (and the island) Candia. The city became the seat of government for the Duke and his councillors, and was laid out accordingly by Venetian architects, with a ducal palace across the piazza from the church of their patron saint, St. Mark. To encourage the development of the city, both the new Venetian nobility and the Greek aristocracy were obliged to build houses and to live here for part of the year. At first the new building adapted to the existing Byzantine fortifications but as the city flourished the enceinte was no longer adequate. The impressive defences that still stand today, a 3km star-shaped circuit of walls, bastions and fortified gates, were built over a long period (14C–17C), with an important phase of construction after 1538 under the supervision of Michele Sanmicheli (architect of the Palazzo Grimani in Venice). Candia is documented in the Republic's archives as a major city of the empire. From the early years of the Venetian occupation the great fortress, Rocca al Mare, guarded the harbour which became one of the leading seaports of the eastern Mediterranean, vital for the control of the trade-route to the Levant which underpinned Venice's extraordinary wealth and prosperity.

But in due course the power of Venice declined. In 1648 the ascendant Ottoman Empire began the great siege of the city of Candia which was to last more than 21 years, making it one of the longest in history. The Turkish camp lay 4km to the south on the hill of Fortétsa from which their cannon bombarded the town. During the siege it is calculated that the Venetians and their allies lost 30,000 men, the Turks 118,000. The city was the last bastion of Christendom in the eastern Mediterranean, but the Christian world only watched and waited. Eventually, in 1668, Louis XIV sent a relief force under the Duc de Beaufort. An heroic but ill-judged sortie resulted in the defeat of Beaufort's force, and the French withdrew. On 5 September 1669 the Venetian commander, Francesco Morosini, at last accepted the inevitable defeat; he negotiated the surrender of the city and the Venetians were allowed to sail away from Crete unharmed.

The Turks chose to rule the island from Khaniá, and Morosini's city, deservedly known as Megálo Kástro, the Great Fortress, became the seat of a Pashalik. The city reverted to the name Herákleion after Turkish rule ended in 1898. Though Khaniá was then the capital of independent Crete, Herákleion grew rapidly to become the chief commercial centre. Because of this pre-eminence, and a central position, the administrative capital was transferred here in 1971.

A. The Town

One way to orientate yourself in Herákleion is to find the central crossroads with traffic lights at the downhill end of the city's traditional market street (agorá); officially this crossroads is ΠΛΑΤ. ΝΙΚ. ΦΩΚΑ (Plateía Nikephórou Phoká). (See town plan at end of this book or on most good maps of Crete). On foot during shopping hours you will encounter here the bustle and traffic typical of commercial Herákleion.

With the stalls of the market street behind you, and slightly right, you will be looking north in the direction of the sea, into ΟΔΟΣ 25 ΑΥΓΟΥΣΤΟΥ (Odós 25 Avgoústou) which runs down to the harbour. Along it you will find banks, shipping offices and travel agents, but now you can glimpse (50m north of the crossroads) the Plateía Venizélou where pavement cafés offer a shady respite around the Morosini fountain—see below. To your left is Leophóros Kalokairinoú (ΛΕΩΦ. ΚΑΛΟΚΑΙΡΙΝΟΥ), which passes near the cathedral and ends at the Khaniá Gate, the western exit from town. Immediately behind you is Odós 1821 (ΟΔΟΣ 1821), on the bus route to Knossós. Continuing anti-clockwise, next is the market street, ΟΔΟΣ 1866 on maps, and finally, right, Leophóros Dikaiosíni (ΛΕΩΦ. ΔΙΚΑΙΟΣΙΝΗ).

Along Dikaiosínis, on the right-hand side and past the *Tourist Police*, is the NOMAPXEION (Nomarkheíon), the administrative and legal headquarters of the province (nome) of Herákleion. The offices occupy restored Turkish buildings on the site of Venetian barracks. The elegant marble *portal* of the central block, sent from Italy in 1409 by the Cretan pope, Alexander V, originally graced the Franciscan monastery which stood on the present site of the Archaeological Museum.

Just beyond this are steps, right, past the *statue of Ioánnis Daskaloyiánnis* (an 18C revolutionary leader from Sphakiá), to the plateía of the same name now paved as a pedestrian precinct (tavernas and bars). On one side is the central *Post Office*.

Dikaiosínis ends in ΠΛΑΤ. ΕΛΕΥΘΕΡΙΑΣ (Plateía Eleftherías), a noble name in the Greek language, the Square of Freedom. The *Archaeological Museum* (see below) is in the near left-hand corner of the square.

A short distance from the central crossroads near the market (see above) is the paved Plateía Venizélou (ΠΛΑΤ. ΒΕΝΙΖΕΛΟΥ) readily identified by its Morosini fountain. The square has become a focus for tourists, with cafés open from breakfast-time on and bookstalls selling foreign newspapers. There are the usual souvenir shops, and one or two just out of the square specialise in antique items. Be prepared to bargain.

This area around the Plateía Venizélou was the centre of the Venetian city, and once the site of the Ducal Palace. The *fountain* was built in 1628 by order of the Venetian governor Francesco Morosini the elder, and was supplied by an aqueduct from Mount Júktas, 15km away. It was originally completed by a marble statue of Neptune, but this was demolished during the Turkish occupation. The lions are 14C work, probably from an earlier fountain elsewhere. Below the basins are delightful marine scenes in relief.

Across the road from the fountain stands the restored Venetian church of *Áyios Márkos*, now a hall for concerts, lectures and exhibitions; forthcoming events are advertised in the portico.

A triple-transept basilica was built here in 1239, damaged by earthquake in 1303 and again (after restoration) in 1508. There was a campanile at the south-west corner and during the Great Siege (1648–69) the bells played their part in rallying the population. During the Turkish period the church became a mosque, and the campanile was replaced by a *minaret*; the lower part can still be seen to the right of the façade.

Walking downhill, on the main street, Odós 25 Avgoústou, heading towards the harbour, you can see (left) a public garden planted with orange trees; this is Párko Theotokopoúlou (ΠΑΡΚΟ ΘΕΟΤΟΚΟ-ΠΟΥΛΟΥ) known to most foreigners as El Greco Park. There is a *post office* cabin here, and on the west side of the gardens the head office of the *telephone company* (OTE).

The Morosini fountain during the period of Turkish rule (from Gerola, Monumenti Veneti nell'Isola di Creta, 1905–32)

On the right of the main street is the reconstructed Venetian **loggia**, a careful copy of the original arcaded design (1626) which provided an elegant meeting-place for the Venetian nobility. Adjoining the loggia, the restored Venetian *armoury* has become the City Hall or ΔIMAPXEION (Dimarkheíon). Set in its north wall is a relief from the Sangredo fountain (1602) which originally decorated the north-west corner of the loggia; Sangredo was one of the Dukes of Crete. The sadly defaced female figure is believed to represent Crete, holding in her left hand a shield and in her right a club. In mythology the nymph Crete was the mother of Pasiphae (wife of Mínos) who gave birth to the Minotaur.

Behind the loggia, set back from Odós 25 Avgoústou in a tree-lined square, is the church of Ayios Títos. Titus was the friend and companion of St. Paul who consecrated him the first Bishop of Crete. The original Byzantine church, which had been converted into a mosque, was destroyed by earthquake in 1856. However, the mosque was rebuilt, and this, rededicated to Ayios Títos, is substantially what you see today. A revered reliquary containing the saint's skull, which had been carried away to the safety of Christendom by the defeated Venetians at the end of the Great Siege in 1669, was returned to this church in 1966.

The road ends at the *Inner Harbour*, a busy scene of fishing boats and yachts. The harbour is guarded by the **Venetian fortress** 'Rocca al Mare' or in Turkish 'Koúles'—open to the public during the summer 08.30–15.00, closed Mondays. Entrance charge.

The original castle dated from the first years of the Venetian occupation, but it was destroyed by earthquake in 1303. The building was completely reconstructed in 1523 as the inscription over the northern gate bears witness. The restored interior with 26 chambers is an impressive example of its kind. A ramp leads to the upper level which in summer becomes on open-air theatre. There is a commanding view from the battlements.

On the external walls are three high-relief carvings of the *Lion of St. Mark*; the best preserved is the one to seaward. The walk out along the mole is recommended.

On the esplanade to the west of the harbour, the ruined walls of the Venetian cathedral of St. Peter hide the 19C neo-classical building (with striking new glass and aluminium extension) housing the *Historical Museum* (see Rte 1C below). A walk in this area could include (along Odós Delimárkhou) the fountain of Antonio Priuli built by the Venetians during the Great Siege (1666) in response to the Turkish destruction of Morosini's aquaduct. The influence of Palladian architecture is noted in the design based on the Corinthian temple 'in antis' with pillars and columns supporting a pediment flanked by brackets in the form of decorated volutes. A Latin inscription commemorated Priuli; the tablet above was added by the Turks.

Just across the road along the Inner Harbour are the partially restored 16C **arsenals**, remains of the great dockyard which was begun soon after the Venetians took over the island. The arsenals now stand as two groups of echoing arcades. Here, on what was then a sloping shore, the Venetians built or repaired their ships, each vault holding one galley.

There is a pleasantly situated café beside the yacht moorings on the east quay of the Inner Harbour. Behind it are the Port Authority offices, and nearby on the Outer Harbour, the berths used by cruise liners. (Two *bus stations*—one serving eastern Crete, the other destinations west to Khánia—are just inland of these quays.) Beyond, further to the east, lie the regular Athens ferry boats, and further still, through the Customs barrier, the docks for international shipping. The dual carriageway alongside these docks, improved as a ring-road leading out to the airport, has become the scene of a dynamic new market, especially active on Saturdays.

From the roundabout east of the arsenals ΛΕΩΦ. ΔΟΥΚΑΣ ΜΠΩΦΟΡ (Doúkas Bófor, i.e. Beaufort) sweeps up along the rampart to Plateía Eleftherías. At the entrance to the square the Archaeological Museum is to the right. On the left stood the St. George's Gate (1565); a Turkish fountain has been set in the restored city wall. Here the *Old Road* to eastern Crete descends through the ramparts.

Opposite the museum entrance around the corner, is the *Tourist Information Office* (NTOG, in Greek EOT). In the big square you can walk left along the rampart, enjoying a fine view over the harbour, to the huge *statue of Elefthérios Venizélos* (1864–1936), the respected national statesman and one of the architects of modern Greece, who was a native of Crete (see p 28). Across the road from the statue are public gardens; at the far (south) end of them there is a good view of the Vituri Bastion and moated walls.

Plateía Eleftherías used to be the most popular outdoor café of Herákleion, but it has now more or less succumbed to the city's ever-growing motor traffic. To complete a circular tour you could walk down Dikaiosínis, but recommended is the pedestrian precinct, parallel and one block nearer the sea, ΟΔΟΣ ΔΑΙΔΑΛΟΥ (Odós Daidálou), which will bring you out exactly opposite the Morosini fountain.

A visit to the lively *market street* in the centre of town is a traditional feature of Herákleion life. Side streets specialise in blacksmiths' work, and near the top is the fish market. At the uphill end of the street the *Bembo fountain* (1588) is composed of antique fragments, including a headless statue which the architect Zuanne Bembo brought from Ierápetra (Greco-Roman Ierápytna) in south-eastern Crete. The fountain stands behind a polygonal kiosk, itself adapted from a Turkish fountain, and now in use as a café, convenient for a pause to observe the market scene. You may still notice men of the older generation dressed for a day in town in the traditional Cretan costume of breeches or baggy trousers, tall leather boots, cummerbund and the 'mavromándilo', a long black scarf knotted round the head. In the old days this was the prized symbol of manhood.

Across the open space of ΠΛΑΤ. ΚΟΡΝΑΡΟΥ (Plateía Kornárou) is the massive modern sculpture entitled 'Erotókritos and Aretoúsa'. It was commissioned by the Municipality from the Cretan Ioánnis Parmekéllis.

To the right the main road would lead (past a taxi rank and ΟΔΟΣ Μ. ΜΟΥΣΟΥΡΟΥ (Odós M. Mousoúrou) for the new hospital, the Apollónion) to the modern cathedral of Ayios Minás, and the *Icon Collection* housed in the medieval church of Ayía Aikateríni (see Rte 1D below).

ΟΔΟΣ ΕΒΑΝΣ (Odós Evans) continues ahead, slightly left from the market, to pass through the walls at the reconstructed Jesus Gate (now the Kainoúria Pórta or New Gate). The walls are over 40m thick at this point.

Outside the gate (right, not shown on plan) is the entrance to the outdoor theatre which in July and August is the venue for many concerts and other events brought to Crete from the Athens Festival. In the shadow of the wall (the Jesus Bastion) there is a pleasant shaded café. The large municipal *car park* uses the moat on the other (left) side of the New Gate.

Inside the gate ΟΔΟΣ ΝΙΚ. ΠΛΑΣΤΗΡΑ (Odós Nikoláou Plastíra) leads west (less than 5 minutes) to the Martinengo Bastion and the *tomb* of Níkos Kazantzákis, the eminent Cretan author of, among many other works, *Zorba The Greek* and *Freedom and Death*. He died in Germany in 1957. The inscription on the memorial here quotes one of Kazantzákis's more famous lines: 'I hope for nothing. I fear nothing. I am free'. (Kazantzákis Museum under Rte 3C.)

B.   The Archaeological Museum

The **Archaeological Museum**, at one corner of Plateía Eleftherías, houses a vast collection of material, amassed since 1883, from the Neolithic to Roman periods of Cretan history. The Bronze Age exhibits are particularly outstanding and are very well displayed. Few Minoan artefacts have found their way from Crete to museums elsewhere in the world, so the collection here may justifiably be called unique. Many people will want to make more than one visit, ideally before and after exploring some of the sites where the objects were found.

Open (summer): 08.00–19.00, except Sunday 09.00–19.00. Closed Monday. Admission fee. Check opening hours in advance if possible, or on arrival in town (especially for public holidays). During the winter season the museum closes at 15.00.

The museum building (1937–40), designed on functional anti-seismic principles rather than aesthetic ones, provides 20 galleries on two floors, but so great is the appeal of its exhibits that in high season overcrowding is sometimes a problem. Air conditioning was installed throughout the museum in 1988. A more recent addition is a coffee shop (with toilets) on the terrace behind the main building.

The museum stands on the site of the Latin monastery of St. Francis which dominated this hill, and the skyline of Herákleion, during the Venetian period. An excavation in the garden of the entrance courtyard during 1984, under the auspices of the director of Byzantine Antiquities (M. Borboudákis), revealed part of the foundations of the friars' church, which proved to have been destroyed by Turkish bombardment during the Great Siege (1648–69).

The museum's Bronze Age collection is well labelled. The case numbering of the ground floor rooms has in the past been based strictly on the principle that you start on the right of the doorway as you enter, continue round the wall anti-clockwise and then follow an anti-clockwise spiral for the central cases, ending down the middle of the room. This system did not easily accommodate new discoveries, nor were the present numbers of visitors envisaged when the layout was designed.

After completion of the recent lengthy, and inevitably disruptive, programme of building work to install air conditioning, the museum staff has taken advantage of the opportunity to reorganise some of the exhibits. The position of cases within the gallery may be altered, though individual contents and case reference numbers almost always remain as before; in particular the most spectacular exhibits, which attract the guided tours, are likely to be found at the far end of each room where a gathering for a lecture is less of an obstruction to other museum visitors. It is hoped that careful attention to case numbers will enable the reader to understand the display.
  The **conventional chronology** for the second millenium BC has here been retained. Refinements suggested by recent research are discussed under Historical Background on p 18.

Gallery I. Neolithic and Early Minoan (Prepalatial) Period (c 5000–2000 BC). Cases 1 and 2 contain Neolithic and Sub-Neolithic pottery, violin-shaped and steatopygous idols, and bone and stone implements from Knossós, the cave of Eileíthyia near Amnisós, Phaistós and other sites. The hand-made pottery was decorated by rippling or burnishing, or with incised geometric patterns filled with a white chalky paste.

Case 3 illustrates from burial caves the various styles of 'Sub-Neolithic' or Early Minoan I (3000–2600 BC) with grey wares and pattern-burnished vases from Pártira (Central Crete) and Pýrgos (on the coast to the east of Herákleion), and red-on-buff painted wares from the cave of Kyparíssi near Prophítis Ilías. Note the tall pattern-burnished cups as well as the rounded bases typical of some EMI vases.

Case 4 is devoted to Early Minoan vases from the great circular tombs at Lebéna, on the coast south of the Mesará plain: EMI red-on-buff and white-on-red wares in a great profusion of shapes. Also from Lebéna (Case 5) are jewellery, figurines and bronze daggers which illustrate the character of the society that built these communal tombs of the Mesará.

Case 6 contains the distinctive EMII Vasilikí mottled ware, in characteristic shapes such as beak-spouted jugs and horizontally spouted 'teapots'; these are from Vasilikí itself (upper shelves) and other east Cretan sites (bottom shelf).

In Case 7 the finest of the early stone vases (EMII–III) come from the cemetery on the off-shore island of Mókhlos; the banded marbles and limestones are remarkably well adapted to the shapes of the vases. Breccia, chlorite and polished green serpentine, and black and creamy steatite are also used. The vases were made by hand, the inside being cut out with a reed or copper drill and an abrasive powder. A large chlorite pyxis (from Marónia) is incised with two registers of running spiral. The pyxis lid with dog handle (Mókhlos) and the nearly complete pyxis beside it (from Zákros) are clearly by the same hand. Case 8 displays EMIII vases from Vasilikí and Mókhlos. A style of pottery with white decoration on a dark ground (black or brown) now replaces the Vasilikí mottled ware but many of the earlier shapes continue.

Case 9 contains vases from various Mesará tombs, including 'Barbotine' ware with pinched relief decoration, and a bronze basin from Kalathianá in the Asteroúsia mountains to the south of the Mesará plain. Case 10 has EM–MMI vases, in both clay and stone, from Palaíkastro in eastern Crete. Note the flat-bottomed boat, also the four-wheeled cart, among the earliest (c 2000 BC) evidence for wheeled transport on the island.

In the centre: Case 16, Early and Middle Minoan I sealstones, many from the Mesará tombs, notably the ivory cylinders with designs cut at each end. See also 1098, the Babylonian haematite cylinder of the period of Hammurabi, from Tomb B at Plátanos, and 2260, the 14-sided seal with hieroglyphic symbols from Arkhánes. In Case 12, vessels and figurines from Mesará tombs; a •bull, with tiny acrobats clinging to the horns, and the bird-shaped vases from Koumása are libation vases. Case 13 contains marble and ivory figurines, also chiefly from Mesará tombs, but also from the palace sites and the cave of Trapéza above the Lasíthi plain. The figurines are in the Cycladic style; a few were imported but the majority locally made.

Case 14 shows flat, leaf-shaped daggers and the longer (later) ones with a central mid-rib; most are of copper or bronze, the exceptions silver. In Case 15, clay figurines, including bulls, a bird and an 'agrími' (the Cretan ibex), again from the Mesará tombs. Among fine stone vases are 'bird's nest bowls', and vases known as 'kernoi', with multiple receptacles thought to have been used for offerings.

In the central Cases 17 and 18A are displayed elegant gold, rock crystal, and cornelian necklaces and other jewellery, from Mókhlos, the Mesará tombs, and the remarkable, more recently excavated, Arkhánes cemetery (Phourní). The *necklace in Case 18A combines gold, ivory and faience; with it are other outstanding examples of the Minoan ivory-carver's art.

Gallery II. Minoan Old Palace or Protopalatial Period (MMIB–II, c 1900–1700 BC), also some Prepalatial material. This room is devoted mainly to finds from Knossós and Mállia. In Case 19 are the earliest vases from the Mállia Palace and cemeteries, and from Khrysólakkos which many archaeologists now regard as a sanctuary site rather than a cemetery. There is some mottled Vasilikí ware, also stone vases and moulds for double axes; note the mother-goddess figure and a table for offerings. (The much-illustrated gold bee pendant from Khrysólakkos is in Gallery VII.) Case 20 contains MMI pottery, and some figurines, from the rectangular burial enclosures at Goúrnes, on the coast east of Herákleion, including a group of enigmatic bell-shaped objects usually referred to as 'sheep-bells'. Case 21 contains a wide variety of votive offerings from peak sanctuaries (Kóphinas, Traóstalos and Týlissos). In the corner, a pithos burial from the slopes of Aílias, overlooking Knossós, shows a typical method of interment at this period.

Case 21A and the adjacent (free-standing) addition (? 21B) display material from the recent excavations at the peak sanctuary on Mount Júktas, south of Knossós. There are tables for offerings, bronze double axes, figurines, a display of jewellery and miniature objects including a gold scorpion pendant, and stone seals.

Wall Cases 22 and 23 contain pottery from houses below the West Court of Knossós, then fine polychrome Middle Minoan II vases in the distinctive Kamáres style from Knossós. The faience 'sheep-bell', the only one known in this material, comes from Póros, one of the harbours of Knossós. Between these cases are clay burial chests (larnakes) and in the corner a large, elaborately decorated, pithos.

Case 24 contains MMI figurines, in characteristic pose, chiefly from the peak sanctuary of Petsophás, above Palaíkastro at the eastern end of Crete. Note the elaborate head-dresses of the female figures and the daggers worn in their belts by the males. There are also three figurines from the (Prepalatial) oval building at Khamaízi near Siteía. The clay models are identified as *shrines on account of the doves perched on pillars (Knossós), or the sacral horns on the roof.

The central case nearest the entrance (25) displays the polychrome faience *plaques found in the Palace of Knossós and known as the Town Mosaic; they are models of Minoan house façades, sometimes three storeys high. This case also contains tablets, labels and bars in the MM hieroglyphic script, which is still not fully deciphered though the numerical signs are clear. The gold-hilted dagger is from Mállia; it is shown with gold bands and bronze figurines from the peak sanctuary at Traóstalos near Zákros.

Case 26 contains examples of pottery from Mállia, including tripod incense burners, as well as bronze cauldrons. The central case (29) displays large vessels from Knossós; note the pithos decorated with palm trees.

Gallery III. Minoan Old Palace or Protopalatial Period (MMIB–II, c 1900–1700 BC). This room is chiefly devoted to the astonishing collection of *vases and related material found in the Old Palace (excavators' First Palace) levels at Phaistós.

The characteristic polychrome pottery was excavated for the first time at the Kamáres cave on Mount Ida (overlooking the palace), and took its name from the site. Many of the Kamáres ware vases from the Palace of Phaistós (along with those from Knossós in the previous room) show a remarkable harmony between the design of the decoration and the shape of the vessel, the patterns being brilliantly adapted to the form of the vase. One fine example out of many is the Kamáres ware jug prominent in Case 34. Popular shapes are bridge-spouted jars and several forms of cup, often thin-walled and with carinated (angular) profiles imitating metal shapes. Some of the smaller vases are known as 'eggshell ware' because of the incredible thinness of the pottery.

Noteworthy among the larger vessels are a tall vase with attached white flowers, and a fruitstand or bowl with toothed hanging rim and elaborately painted interior (both in Case 43). Case 32A shows objects of everyday use. Case 40 has examples of eggshell ware, but also demonstrates the wide variety of sealings in use at Phaistós. The archive, found in an MMII deposit, consisted of over 6500 seal impressions employing nearly 300 distinct motifs, the majority of them abstract designs. This may have been an inventory of the seals in use, early in the development of palatial organisation, to secure ownership of or access to property.

Case 42 displays the contents of a shrine from a room bordering the West Court at Phaistós. The great red-burnished clay libation table is decorated with a border of incised bulls and spiral motif.

The Phaistós Disk (Herákleion Museum, Gallery III)

In Case 41 is the renowned *Phaistós Disk, hand-made from clay and stamped in a spiral with characters in an unknown script. The signs, which are thought to constitute some form of syllabic writing, are framed and divided up by incised lines; the inscription runs from the outside to the centre. The disk was found in a MMIII (17C BC) context.

Among the collection of pithoi free-standing in this room is one (displayed on a pedestal) with relief decoration of a bull.

Gallery IV. Neopalatial Period (MMIII–LMI, 1700–1450 BC). Finds from the Palaces of Knossós, Phaistós and Mállia. Case 44 contains material from Knossós with examples of the Minoan Linear A script, which is incised on an amphora shoulder and on two silver pins, and written in cuttlefish ink inside two cups.

In Case 45 there is Knossós pottery with spiral decoration, and also the 'Lily Vases', the white painted lilies originally on a dull lilac-brown ground. An interesting conical rhyton decorated with horns of consecration is from the Royal Tomb. 7741 was perhaps a lantern; 7742 was for unwinding balls of wool.

Case 46 contains material associated with the worship of the Sacred Snake; in Minoan times this was a prominent domestic cult associated with the concepts of immortality and reincarnation, and the tubes have been interpreted as snake containers or shelters, with cups for milk. *Vase in the shape of a honeycomb encircled by a snake.

On the opposite wall, in Case 47, are bronze utensils, and terracotta and stone objects from the Palace of Mállia. *Brown schist sceptre, one end a leopard, the other an axe. Case 48: exhibit from houses of the Minoan town at Mállia.

The finds (Case 49) from the final destruction of the Palace of Phaistós in LMIB were not very plentiful, but notice the clay goddess, bare-breasted above a bell skirt, and a rhyton decorated (in the Marine style) with argonauts, also the graceful *jug with an all-over pattern of grasses.

This gallery contains some of the most widely known examples of Minoan art. Case 56 displays the skilfully restored ivory *acrobat, perhaps a bull-leaper (compare the fresco panel illustrated on p 82), and fragments of similar figures; there were traces of at least a partial covering of gold leaf.

Also individually displayed, in Case 51, is the **Bull's Head Rhyton which was found in the Little Palace of Knossós. The rhyton, with holes in the crown of the head and mouth through which sacred libations were poured, is carved from serpentine, with the eyes inlaid with jasper and rock crystal, and the nostrils outlined in white tridacna shell; the horns (restored) were of gilded wood. Note the double axe incised between the eyes.

Much of the material exhibited in this gallery comes from the two sunken stone cists in a small room near the Tripartite Shrine in the Palace of Knossós, which were named by Evans the Temple Repositories. The smaller objects from these treasure chests sealed at the end of MMIII are displayed in Case 50; they include the two faience figurines of the *'Snake Goddess', argonauts, flying fish and other decorative plaques (also of faience), banded limestone and marble libation vases, a rock crystal rosette for inlay, and painted shells. (Other vases from the Temple Repositories will be seen in cases 54, 55 and 58.) Beside Case 50, in Case 57, is the remarkable *gaming board found in a corridor at Knossós and dated c 1600 BC; the ivory frame is inlaid with rock crystal, faience, lapis lazuli, and gold and silver leaf.

The Snake Goddess, a faience figurine from the Temple Repositories of Knossós (Herákleion Museum, Gallery IV)

Case 52 contains ceremonial swords and other weapons of Middle Minoan date from Mállia. One *sword, nearly a metre long, has a pommel of rock crystal on an ivory hilt. Another, of rapier type, has a bone pommel, and on an encircling *disk of gold leaf an acrobat is displaying his skill (see drawing). Other finds in this case include stone vase fragments with relief decoration from Knossós and Phaistós and miniature work in ivory, rock crystal, and faience. One fragment of a relief preserves a scene which is interpreted as a procession of worshippers at a peak sanctuary and the offering of baskets of flowers.

A splendid series of bronzes from houses at Knossós is displayed in Case 53. These include a large saw, a tripod cauldron and bowls with chased decoration of leaves round the rims.

Case 54 contains the large vases from the Temple Repositories, including a 'bird jug', an import from the island of Mélos in the Cyclades; the birds decorating the jug have been shown to be a type of partridge. In Case 55, on one side there are bronze plates from scales, and lead and stone weights from various sites, and on the other faience reliefs from the Temple Repositories including a *cow suckling her calf—also a marble cross. In Case 58 are the stone ritual vessels from the Temple Repositories. These are chiefly rhytons, in alabaster, banded limestones and other variegated stones.

From the Central Treasury at Knossós came the *Lioness Head Rhyton made of a translucent marble-like limestone; this has Case 59 to itself. In three corners of this room are large stone vases of serpentine from Knossós.

Gallery V. The Final Palace Period at Knossós (LMII–IIIA, 1450–1380 BC). Around the walls is a series of Palace style amphoras, some from the palace itself, others from the Little Palace and the Royal Villa. It is noticeable that a formal element has entered the decoration, in contrast to the naturalism of the LMI vases. On the right near the doorway is a giant (unfinished) stone amphora with a decoration of shallow-relief spirals which was found in the Lapidary's Workshop in the palace; the material is banded tufa.

Case 60 contains material from the debris of the LMIB destruction of houses along the Knossós Royal Road. In Case 61 there are vases and architectural fragments from the palace, including stone friezes with split rosettes (popular in LMII) and spirals in relief. Two bronze figures of worshippers are noteworthy, also a large stone jug in banded limestone and a ewer of breccia imitating basketwork. With these are clay vases from the Little Palace and silver vessels from the South House.

On the end wall Case 70A displays a clay *model of a Minoan house, an important find from Arkhánes. This model, indicating both timber and stone construction, demonstrates many features typical of Minoan architecture: a main room with a supporting pillar, small windows for maximum insulation against both heat and cold, a little court serving as a light-well, a flexible pier-and-door partition arrangement with recesses for folding doors, and a stepped ledge on the roof-terrace.

Case 62 exhibits several fine large stone vases and lamps from Knossós made from a reddish marble, antico rosso, imported from the southern Peloponnese. Note also the pyramidal standard weight, of porphyry. Above are Egyptian finds from Knossós, including an alabaster lid with a cartouche of the Hyksos king Khyan, a large Predynastic or early Dynastic bowl, a carinated bowl (4th Dynasty) of diorite beside a Minoan obsidian imitation, and the lower half only of a diorite statuette of an Egyptian, perhaps an ambassador, named User (12th or early 13th Dynasty). As evidence of datable contact with Egypt, these pieces have played their part in establishing the chronology of Minoan Crete.

In the corner is a model of the LMI Royal Villa which stood on the slope above the Kaíratos stream and was connected to the palace by a paved road.

Case 63A contains vases and figurines from the grand house adjoining the Little Palace at Knossós, which Evans named the 'Unexplored Mansion'; the building was subjected to detailed excavation 1967–73. The small clay goddess clothed in a tight, mesh-patterned bodice above flounced skirt, her arms stretched forward, had apparently fallen from a shrine on an upper floor. In the same case is a *pyxis (complete with lid) with bird decoration; the oval shape is most unusual. Three goblets are of 'Ephyraean' type—short-stemmed goblets, with simple decoration of a single motif such as a rosette or an argonaut on each side of the vessel. From the same excavation came the basket vase decorated with skeuomorphic patterns; the clay for this shape was wheel-thrown and the sides were then squeezed before the handles were attached.

In Wall Case 64 are clay and stone vases (and clay horns of consecration) from the destruction debris of the palace and therefore crucial to a chronological assessment of that destruction. On this wall is a picture of the Tripartite Shrine (reconstructed) beside the Central Court at Knossós—a watercolour painting by the gifted draughtsman to Evans's excavation, the late Piet de Jong.

The central cases were in process of rearrangement at the time of revision but they may be expected to contain a display of exquisite Late Minoan sealstones and an exhibit of various styles of pottery decoration with examples of the Floral and Marine styles, also the use of bird motifs. Two Palace style octopus amphoras are contrasted with another, earlier and noticeably more naturalistic, of LMIB date.

Stone vases from the palace include a ewer of breccia imitating basketwork and the big flat gypsum alabastrons found in the Throne Room. Evans conjectured that the alabastrons played a part in some ritual during the last moments before the LMIIIA destruction of the palace, a ritual perhaps designed to avert that catastrophe.

Case 69 holds an important collection of tablets (and some other artefacts) showing inscriptions in Linear A, the still-undeciphered script of the Minoans; inscriptions have now been discovered at more than a dozen sites. The Linear B tablets, from the Knossós archive, are in an early form of Greek. Clay tablets were preserved by chance, baked hard in the fires which destroyed these sites.

Case 70 contains fine examples of Minoan ivory carving, from the houses beside the Royal Road at Knossós and from Arkhánes. Also from Arkhánes are the bronze figure of a worshipper and a stone fragment with relief of a captive bull. Another group of grave gifts comprises jewellery from a tomb at Póros, one of the harbours of Knossós (now a suburb of Herákleion).

From Póros too came a jug (near the door) with unusual decoration, painted but also in relief, in the Marine style.

Gallery VI. Neopalatial and Postpalatial Cemeteries at Knossós, Arkhánes and Phaistós.

Case 71 contains Late Minoan vases from the tholos tomb at Kamilári (south-west of Phaistós) in use for several centuries from MMI. Three important clay models came from this tomb: one is interpreted as a *shrine, with two pairs of seated divinities (or perhaps revered dead), and worshippers placing offerings before them; the second appears to be a banquet for the dead, the religious element emphasised by doves and horns of consecration; the third shows a ring of male dancers also in a ritual setting denoted by horns of consecration. The bird alabastron, decorated in a lively style, is dated to LMIIIA.

In Case 72 is material from the Temple Tomb at Knossós and the Royal Tomb at Isópata. From the latter (top shelf) came the splendid series of Egyptian 18th Dynasty alabaster *vases and an Old Kingdom bowl in porphyry. Clay and stone vases from the Knossian cemeteries of Mávro Spélio and Zápher Papoúra follow in Case 73, with a 'Kourotrophos' figurine, perhaps a goddess with child; then Case 74 for finds from a chamber tomb in the rich cemetery at Katsambás, one of the harbours of Knossós. Also from this tomb group, in Case 79A (between the two doors, or perhaps, temporarily, just inside the previous gallery) is a remarkable ivory *pyxis carved with a bull-catching scene akin to that on the gold cups from Vápheio (Athens, National Archaeological Museum).

On the end wall is Case 75 with bronze vessels and utensils from the Tomb of the Tripod Hearth at Zápher Papoúra, and (above) comparable objects from a tholos tomb at Arkhánes. Case 75A exhibits a ritual horse-burial, exactly as it was found; the horse had been sacrificed and dismembered.

The Wall Cases 76 and 77 display clay and stone vases from the Knossós cemeteries including Isópata, the Tomb of the Double Axes, and the LMII Warrior Graves excavated on the site of the Venizéleion hospital. A tomb at Ayios Ioánnis, north of Knossós, contained the ribbon-handled gold cup with embossed band of double running spirals (77). The associated bronze weapons from the Mycenaean Warrior Graves are nearby in Case 84; see also the bronze helmet with cheek pieces in Case 85.

In Case 78, from the Zápher Papoúra cemetery, is a reconstructed boar's-tusk *helmet of a type described by Homer.

The ivory pyxis from Katsambás (79A) has been noted above with Case 74. The remaining wall case (79) contains stone lamps and vases including some of Egyptian alabaster, as well as imported 18th Dynasty alabastrons, clay vases (notice the bird alabastrons), a rhyton fashioned from a triton shell, and a glass bottle, all from the LMIII cemetery at Kalývia near Phaistós.

Case 80 dislays a libation jug with stylised argonauts and spiked decoration from a chamber tomb at Katsambás. Case 81: miniature work, jewellery, ivory toilet articles and also weapons from the cemeteries at Knossós, Katsambás and Arkhánes. Case 82 contains amphoras from the Royal Tomb at Isópata, also large stone vessels from the Katsambás cemetery, including an Egyptian alabaster vase with a cartouche of Thutmosis III (1504–1450 BC), the great king of the 18th Dynasty, and a LMII *amphora decorated with four boar's tusk helmets similar to the reconstructed one on display in Case 78. Opposite, in Case 83, are large vases from the Palace at Knossós.

Cases 86 and 87 contain jewellery and ivory toilet articles from the Phaistós and Knossós cemeteries, and from various other tombs including Kamilári; among these exhibits (see also 81 and 88) are many of the finest achievements of the Cretan goldsmiths. Particularly admired (in Case 87) are the gold *ring from Isópata, showing an ecstatic dance with goddess and worshippers on a flower-filled ground, and earrings in the shape of bulls' heads, using the granulation technique. Case 88 displays finds from tholos tombs at Arkhánes: *jewellery, a bronze mirror with an ivory handle, and a pyxis lid in ivory with figure-of-eight shield handles.

Gallery VII. Neopalatial Settlements and Sacred Caves of Central and South Crete (MMIII–LMI, c 1600–1450 BC).

The first objects on the right are large bronze *double axes on restored poles and painted bases; these come from the villa at Nírou Kháni on the coast east of Herákleion. This building contained many other cult objects such as a quantity of painted plaster tripod tables (more than 40 found) and the stone horns of consecration on the right-hand wall.

The three huge bronze cauldrons by the doorway were found in one of the Týlissos villas. Other large vessels exhibited between the cases include a stone basin with spout from Ayía Triáda.

Case 89 displays figurines, vases and stone lamps from Nírou Kháni and Týlissos, including a rhyton of dark-grey imported obsidian, extremely difficult to carve because of its hardness and liability to fracture. Among the bronze figurines of young male worshippers in the typical saluting position is a rare portrayal (from Týlissos) of an older man whose waist is released from the constriction of the customary tight belt.

Individually displayed in this room and considered among the finest examples of the Minoan stonecarvers' art are the three serpentine vases carved with relief scenes, all from Ayía Triáda: the *Chieftain Cup (95) portrays a Minoan official receiving tribute of animal hides; the much-restored *Boxer Rhyton (96) has scenes of boxing and wrestling matches, and, in the second zone from the top, of bull sports. Only the upper half of the *Harvester Vase (94) is preserved: the shoulder is carved with a procession of youths, the leader carrying a long rod, the rest pitchforks and scythes; they are accompanied by four singers, one playing the sistrum. He, like the figure in Case 89 (above), has a dispensation from the usual tight belt. All three vases are believed to be products of a Knossós workshop.

In Case 90 are vases from the villas at Amnisós, Sklavókambos and Vathýpetro. Notice the fine bridge-spouted jug with zig-zag patterns and the stone conical rhyton from Sklavókambos. The stone lamps and large cup (second and lower shelves) are from Vathýpetro, the vases and head on the upper shelf from Amnisós. Beside this case, a throne from Póros made out of stone imitates a wooden prototype.

On the opposite side of the room, Case 93 displays material from Ayía Triáda, including an alabastron in the Marine style and a jug with the double-axe and sacred knot motifs; note the carbonised beans, barley, millet, and figs. In Case 92 are bronze figurines, both human and animal, also knives, daggers and double axes; most come from the votive deposits in the Diktaian cave, but some are included from other cave sanctuaries at Patsós and Skoteinó (saluting figures). Case 91 contains bronze double axes from a votive deposit found in the sacred cave at Arkalokhóri in central Crete. One of the central cases (97) exhibits the magnficent bronze swords and other weapons from the same cave, also bronze figurines and ivory pins and inlays from Týlissos and Nírou Kháni.

In Case 102 are human and animal votive figurines in bronze from Ayía Triáda, stone vases including a beautiful dolium shell of white-spotted obsidian, and a Hittite sphinx. Case 100 shows bronze tools, utensils and jewellery, all from that same site, two potter's wheels from Vathýpetro and seals from various sites.

In Case 99, on the wall between the two doorways, are copper talents or 'ox-hide' ingots (weight c 40kg), with incised signs, and copper hammers from Ayía Triáda.

Case 101 displays outstanding examples of gold and silver jewellery from central and eastern Crete. There are several examples with granulation. Here also is one of the great treasures of Minoan art, the gold *pendant of MMI date from the Khrysólakkos funerary precinct at Mállia. It consists of two conjoined bees (or wasps or hornets) around a golden ball with a smaller ball within, covered with granulation.

Gallery VIII. The Zákros Room. Finds mainly from the palace, but also from the houses in the Minoan town above it. (From palace where not otherwise specified.) Period: almost entirely Neopalatial (1700–1450 BC) and principally from the last (LMIB) phase of the New Palace immediately preceding its final destruction by fire.

Case 104: vases with unusual figure-of-eight handles. Case 105 contains pottery, and stone and bronze utensils. The bronze incense burner has chased decoration of ivy leaves (see adjacent drawing).

On the opposite wall, Case 106 displays rhytons in both conical and piriform shapes, also an elegant 'fruit-stand' with spiral and ivy-leaf decoration. Case 107 has further examples of vases from the palace. Case 108: *cup with double-axe decoration, stone horns of consecration and a stone capital from a votive column. The conical cup containing olives was retrieved from one of the palace wells; the olives at first appeared perfectly preserved, but then shrivelled after only a few minutes of exposure to air.

In Case 109 is an exquisite rock crystal *rhyton with a handle of crystal beads stained green by the bronze wire on which they are threaded. The exhibit is a tribute to the skill and dedication of the museum's conservation staff who restored this extraordinary work of art from more than 300 tiny fragments.

Case 110 contains material from the houses in the town. There are many vases in the LMIB Marine style in the Zákros Room, but here (middle shelf) a *rhyton decorated with shells, tritons, seaweed, rocks and starfish is a particularly fine example. See also the amphora to the right of the doorway to Gallery IX.

Case 111 displays the *Peak Sanctuary Rhyton, a superb piece of Minoan stone-carving, and valuable evidence for an understanding of Minoan cult practices. It depicts in relief a mountain shrine hallowed by the double axe, and with wild goats, birds and plants (drawing on wall). The material is chlorite, turned brown in parts from the effect of fire; a few traces survive of the gold leaf which once covered it.

Case 112 contains bronze weapons and tools from the palace including a sword with gold rivets, and a ceremonial *double axe with duplicated blades and decoration of stylised lilies (see drawing on wall). In Case 113 are bronze talents, and a complete elephant tusk found in the palace storerooms. It, also, is discoloured by burning in the great fire that destroyed the palace. In the same case (above) is fine pottery including an elegant *jug in the by now familiar Marine style, decorated with argonauts.

Case 114, bridge-spouted jugs and fine stone rhytons. Case 118, further stone vases, also stone hammers and three faience animal-head rhytons. The stone vases in these two cases (114 and 118), mostly from the unplundered Treasury of the Shrine, are the finest collection of such vessels yet known from the Minoan civilisation. They comprise: conical and fluted rhytons of Egyptian alabaster and polychrome banded limestones, one also of lapis Lacedaemonius (114) (a stone imported from the only known source near Sparta); a group of chalices including examples in gabbro, white-spotted obsidian (118) and polychrome limestones; two Old Kingdom Egyptian vases in porphyritic rock (118) adapted for use by the Minoans, one with the addition of bridge-spout and the other with bronze handles; several individual vases made of Egyptian alabaster and an 18th Dynasty imported alabastron; also a large multiple vase with high curving handles, made of polychrome banded limestone (also in 118).

Case 115 has bronze objects from the palace: large two-handled saws, two inlay plates decorated with papyrus flowers, and a circular strip, a vase mounting, with double axes.

A Marine style flask from Palaíkastro (Herákleion Museum, Gallery IX)

Case 116 displays a chlorite bull's head *rhyton; it is smaller than that from Knossós but of equally fine workmanship.

In Case 117 is miniature work from the palace and from houses in the town: ivory double axes and a *butterfly, all discoloured by fire in the final destruction; also a faience *rhyton in the shape of an argonaut.

Freestanding in this room are several large painted vases, and five coarse pithoi. The central one (on the end wall) has an inscription in Linear A, including the sign for wine. It comes from the villa just outside Ano Zákros, and was found beside a wine press which can now be seen in the Siteía Museum.

Gallery IX. Neopalatial Settlements of East Crete (MMIII–LMI, c 1700–1450 BC). Cases 119 and 120 on the right are devoted, in the main, to Palaíkastro. The first contains stone vases and lamps, one of antico rosso with ivy scrolls on the columns. Notice also a clay bull rhyton and bronze figurines, the large one from Praisós. Case 120, at the end of this wall, has three fine LMIB vases including an octopus *flask and a jug with papyrus decoration, also two feline heads in clay, and an eight-vesseled kernos.

Between these two cases, Case 161 displays finds from the 1970s' excavations on the Pýrgos site at Mýrtos. There are clay and stone vessels and utensils, seals and a bronze dagger. Unique is a thin-walled vase with fluted rim which contains a cluster of miniatures of the same shape.

The adjacent central case (125) has Marine style rhytons, a gabbro rhyton and two stone libation tables from Palaíkastro.

In Case 121 (on the opposite wall) is a series of LMI vases from Gourniá; note the unusual double vase, also a small bull's head rhyton, and a bronze figurine. The nearest free-standing case (126) also has finds from Gourniá; there are many rhytons including a fluted stone example in antico rosso, and several very large limestone lamps. Case 127 contains a collection of bronze tools and weapons, from Gourniá and other sites in central and eastern Crete. In the centre of the room (128A) the Marine style stirrup vase from Gourniá has a case to itself.

Case 129, towards the back of the room, has material from Mókhlos, an islet off the coast east of Gourniá; the exhibits include clay vases, bull rhytons, a stone lamp with foliate band decoration, and bronze vessels including a cup with ivyleaf decoration, closely similar in shape to the gold cups from Vápheio in the National Archaeological Museum in Athens.

In Case 122 (on the wall by the door) are clay and stone vases and lamps from the island of Pseíra, with a magnificent rhyton of breccia and a *basket vase decorated with double axes. The remaining wall case (123) contains clay votive figurines, both human and animal, from the MM–LMI sanctuary at Piskoképhalo near Siteía. The beetles are *Rhinoceros oryctes*; sometimes they have climbed on the human figures who presumably seek protection from them.

In the two remaining central cases are: (124) clay sealings from Knossós, Ayía Triáda, Zákros and Sklavókambos, (one from Knossós showing two figures with a hieroglyphic inscription, perhaps a title, beside them), together with small objects, notably ivories and inlays, from Palaíkastro and other sites in eastern Crete; (128) a magnificent collection of Late Minoan *sealstones in agate, carnelian, chalcedony, jasper, lapis Lacedaemonius, lapis lazuli, rock crystal, and other stones,

The Poppy Goddess, a terracotta figurine from Gázi
(Herákleion Museum, Gallery X)

from various sites. The main seal shapes are the lentoid, amygdaloid (almond) and flattened cylinder. Particularly noteworthy are Nos 165–69 from the Knossós Warrior Graves, 165–80 from the Kalývia cemetery near Phaistós, as well as those in lapis lazuli from Knossós.

Around the room are several large vases from eastern Crete including burial pithoi from the cemetery on the Pakhyámmos beach near Gourniá.

Gallery X. Postpalatial Period (LMIII, 1350–1100 BC). The decline of the Minoan culture is reflected in the remains from the Postpalatial age; it is noticeable that vase-painting has lost its vitality, and fine carving in stone no longer occurs. Wall Case 130 (with 131) exhibits pottery from Phinikiá, Katsambás, Phaistós, Gourniá and also from the houses of the LMIII reoccupation in the ruins of the Palace of Knossós. Popular shapes are the tall-stemmed kylix, tankard, ladle, krater, and stirrup vase. The earlier LM patterns, such as the octopus, have now become stylised, but the use of bird motifs in decoration from the first part of LMIII is of interest. See also Case 132 with pottery from the LMIII settlement at Palaíkastro, including the group of figures dancing round a musician playing the lyre.

The single wall case (133) contains large clay 'goddess' idols with raised arms from a shrine excavated at Gázi, on the western outskirts of Herákleion. The central figure has a head-dress of poppies.

Case 134 (with 136) displays (above) material from LMIII chamber tombs at Stamníi and Episkopí Pediádas, south east of Herákleion (unusual serpentine vase with five receptacles), and (below) material from Episkopí near Ierápetra, and the rich LMIII cemetery at Mouliariá in eastern Crete. From this Episkopí come several fine squat stirrup vases, and from Mouliariá a large flask decorated with concentric circles, also Close style stirrup vases with octopus patterns.

In Case 135 are figurines and other cult objects from the domestic shrine of the Minoan villa or farm at Mitrópolis near Górtyn.

Case 137 displays groups of grave gifts from tombs at Amnisós (Kárteros), Goúrnes and Pakhyámmos; the imported glass bottle is from Amnisós and the limestone horns of consecration from Póros, now an eastern suburb of Herákleion. Case 138 contains terracotta objects including 'psi' figurines and mounted horses.

The central cases exhibit the following objects: (139) bead necklaces, mostly of glass paste, some of semi-precious stones, from tombs at Goúrnes, Episkopí and Stamníi (Pediáda), also Mílatos near Mállia, together with stone moulds for ornaments; (140) furnishings from LMIII shrines at Knossós (Shrine of the Double Axes), Phaistós and Gourniá, with clay huts from the first two sites; (141) large vases, especially kraters, from Mouliariá (one with the earliest Cretan rendering of a warrior on horseback), Phaistós and Knossós; (142) contents of shrines from Gourniá, Priniás (Subminoan), Koumása in the Mesará and Kaló Khorió (the head of a large idol); (143) clay idols, animal and human, from sanctuaries at Ayía Triáda (notice especially the *figure on a swing) and the cave of Hermes in the gorge of Patsós on the way up to the Amári valley; (144) tools and weapons of all kinds in bronze, the main series from the two LMIIIC tombs at Mouliariá.

Gallery XI. Subminoan, Protogeometric and Early Geometric Period (1100–800 BC). The wall cases on the right contain Protogeometric and Geometric material from sites in central and eastern Crete. It is immediately apparent from the new pottery shapes and the decoration of geometric motifs that great changes were occurring on the island. During the period of the Cretan Geometric style, burial rites altered from inhumation, the habit of the Minoans and still prevalent in LMIII, to the practice of cremation; this became the rule until the end of the Late Orientalising period (c 630 BC), except in the east of Crete where the older tradition sometimes persisted. The ashes were buried in large clay vases, occasionally in a bronze vessel; the most usual pottery shape eventually became the more-or-less spherical pithos, though many variations occur and are well represented here and in the next room.

Case 145 contains vases from Phaistós (upper shelf) and from the large cemetery at Kourtés, including a kernos in the form of a ring with human figures as well as receptacles. Note the rhyton in the shape of a bird (ie. duck askos); there are several of these vessels in the following cases, each with individual character both in conformation and in the indication of plumage. Case 146 exhibits finds from Vrókastro and Kavoúsi on the Bay of Mirabéllo, including a pair of open-work basket vases (the kalathos shape), a hydria (three-handled vessel for carrying water) decorated with a chariot scene, a horse figurine and a bronze tripod. In Case 147 are Geometric vases and bronze figurines from these and other sites in central and eastern Crete: Psykhró (the Diktaian cave), Ayía Triáda, Ayios Sýllas, Amnisós, Kavoúsi, and Vrókastro.

In the nearby central case (154) are clay vases and ritual objects, including little clay huts, from the earlier LMIIIC mountain refuge settlement at Karphí above Lasíthi.

The large model of a house sanctuary was found in a Protogeometric tomb at Teké, part of the Knossós North Cemetery; interesting features are the interior ledge, small high-set square windows, chimney, ventilation holes, and flat roof with course of stones near the edge, also the painted decoration on the walls and door. (Further important material from this tomb is shown in the next gallery.)

From the shrine at Karphí (see above) come the large clay goddess idols with birds perched in their headdresses (exhibited on the end wall, in Case 148). The feet are made separately and fitted into the aperture in the cylindrical skirt. With these, from the same site, is a peculiar rhyton in the form of a charioteer drawn by bulls, of which only the heads are represented.

In Wall Case 149 is material from the cave sanctuary of Eileíthyia, goddess of childbirth, at Inatos (Tsoútsouros) on the south coast; the votive offerings include clay figures embracing (some in coital positions) and women pregnant or giving birth. Note the model boats, also the bull figurines and many double axes in the Minoan tradition. Further important finds from this site are also on show in Case 158 near the doors (see below).

Between Cases 149 and 150 stands a majestic lidded pithos, one of the grandest examples of the new cremation urns.

Case 150 and the central Cases 155, 156 and 157 contain a series of vases from Protogeometric and Geometric tombs of the Knossós North Cemetary (Teké). Typical vase-shapes displayed in 150 are: the oinochoe (jug) in a variety of shapes and sizes including trefoil-mouthed juglets; the hydria; on the top shelf the skyphos and bell-skyphos (two-handled drinking vessels); various cups. The pithos is represented with and without a defined neck.

In Case 155 there are two bell-kraters with figured scenes. On one a deer hunt is depicted. The other has two lions attacking a man, and on the reverse side facing sphinxes, with to right a water bird; this vase too had been used as a cinerary urn before the pithos shape became customary. Note the bird askos here.

Case 156 contains an imposing pedestalled krater. (Another very large one, decorated with Maltese cross in concentric circles, stands beside Case 151.) Case 157 shows a globular pithos between two belly-handled amphoras, all elaborately decorated with zones of typical motifs: rosettes and chequers, hatched meander, and filled concentric circles.

In Case 151 are finds from the rich tombs at Siderospiliá (Priniás), where a sheet-gold ornament with swastikas and a 'star of David' pendant make to the anachronistic eye a strange juxtaposition. The grave gifts included clay figurines of humans, in the Daidalic style, and of horses; the pair of galloping horses were probably harnessed to a cart, with the wheels shown being part of the same model. The bronze bit from a bridle was found on the skull of a horse skeleton in a burial of ritual significance within this cemetery.

The remaining central case on this side (158) has further material from the Inatos cave, including an ivory figurine of a naked goddess, faience goddesses, scarabs, necklaces and other jewellery. The scarabs have been dated to the Saitic period in Egypt.

Case 153 (opposite) exhibits metalwork: iron and bronze tools, weapons, utensils, pins, fibulae and tweezers from various sites including Knossós, Kourtés, Kavoúsi, Vrókastro, Arkádes and Praisós. With the spread of the new skill in smelting at the necessary high temperatures, bronze was gradually replaced by iron for the manufacture of tools and weapons, though the former continued in use for figurines, bowls and ornamented pieces such as shields; unfortunately iron objects of this age on Crete are rarely well-preserved.

Gallery XII. Late Geometric and Orientalising Periods (8–7C BC), also finds (covering a long period) from the Sanctuary of Hermes Dendrites at Sými, on the south slopes of Mount Díkte near Viánnos. In this room is a large series of cremation urns from tombs in the Knossós area, especially from a group near Fortétsa (now recognised as part of the Knossós North Cemetery), and also from the Arkádes cemetery near Aphráti in central Crete. Note the distinctive polychrome decoration of the Orientalising vases, with curvilinear patterns of lotuses and rosettes. Some smaller vases from Fortétsa show Protocorinthian influence (Case 162); Crete was in touch not only with the East, but with many parts of the Greek world.

Five cases exclusively display finds, mostly pottery, from the Knossós cemetery, while the Knossós jewellery and precious objects are shown beside comparable pieces from other sites on the island.

Case 159 exhibits cremation vases and gifts for the dead from Fortétsa. On the lower shelf is a bell krater with on one side facing wild goats, the Cretan agrími, and on the other a scene of boats; this early example of a vase used for a cremation burial dates from a tomb of the Protogeometric period when realistic decoration was practically unknown. The grave gifts found in it included a faience ring with a quasi-hieroglyphic design on the bezel. In contrast, above in the same case, are three polychrome Orientalising pithoi with looped feet and elaborate lids, and two examples of the lekythos with decoration of concentric circles.

Turn next to the free-standing Case 165, which displays a further three Orientalising urns, these from the tholos tomb (Khanniále Teké) which yielded the rich treasure on display in the central case in this gallery (see below). The pyxis is from the Fortétsa cemetery. Note also the bird askos with tail in the form of a hydria (also two small hydrias in this case), and the olpe (tall jug) with scale pattern and animal frieze which includes griffins.

Cases 166 and 167 both continue the exhibits from the Knossós cemetery. In the first, note the panels of birds in the painted decoration on the vases and their lids; one design shows a smaller bird carried on the parent's wing. In 167 are six polychrome pithoi, some with lids knobbed in the shape of miniature pots. One has a pair of human figures on the shoulder panel. There are also two lekythoi (with elongated slender neck) of the so-called Praisós type.

Wall Case 162 exhibits some of the finest clay, bronze and faience objects from these same tombs, each selected for outstanding quality. As well as exquisite small vases which include a feeding bottle and a double flask, there are unusual pieces in the form of birds and monkeys, a double horse, and trees with birds perched in their branches. One lid has Zeus before a cauldron, with birds; in one hand he holds an eagle and in the other a thunderbolt.

Cases 163 and 168 contain material from the important cemetery of Arkádes. Characteristic of this pottery are the straight-sided tub vases favoured at this site for cremation burials, the floral and plant decorative motifs influenced by eastern traditions, and the scenes of human or mythical figures incorporated in the decoration as early as the first half of the 7C BC. (The human figures often recall the style of Daidalic terracotta figurines of this period.) In Case 168 a chain of spirals terminates in feline heads (compare the pithos in the corner on the back wall). Plastic affixes are added to the vases, as on the cauldron (dinos) with griffins.

In the same case is a vessel painted in added white with a bearded man controlling a long-legged horse, another early example (mid 7C) of man and horse depicted together. On a similar vase is a winged male figure between two sphinxes. Orientalising influence is again reflected in a scene on a situla or bucket, where the Mistress of Animals (derived from the eastern 'Potnia theron') holds aloft the tree of life between two tall birds. On the lower shelf are two vessels, one bronze the other clay, which still contain the charred bones buried in them; in each was a single aryballos, a gift for the deceased.

Case 163 has more finds from the Arkádes cemetery: a lyre player, owl figurines, an anthropomorphic hydria, a crouching lion with a dish between its paws (said to be a clay imitation of eastern faience figures) and a cylindrical cremation vessel with a grieving woman one of a pair of mourners. Notable is the oinochoe with, depicted on its neck, two figures interpreted (on slender evidence) as Theseus and Ariadne.

In the two cases (169 and 164), opposite the giant pithoi with relief decoration, there is a display of metalwork from the Knossós cemetery, and also from other sites such as the great cave sanctuary on Mount Ida. In 169 are fragments of cast bronze which once decorated tripod cauldrons; one of the better-preserved scenes shows a couple in a boat propelled by oarsmen, and it has been suggested that this too may refer to the abduction of Ariadne. The ring-handles come from tripod cauldrons. On the other side of the case are: an embossed bronze quiver with sphinxes and the 'Master of Animals' between lions, from Fortétsa; two 'mitrae' (body armour) with representations of a chariot; and a pair of bronze greaves from Kavóusi.

Case 164 has a bronze girdle from Fortétsa, on which three divinities in a sanctuary are protected from a chariot attack by a file of archers.

In the central case (170) is a magnificent collection of 9–7C *jewellery, much of it from a single tomb at Teké, in the Knossós cemetery. This tholos tomb, originally constructed in the Bronze Age, was cleared out for re-use under the new rites at the height of the Protogeometric period (PGB), and remained in use until Early Orientalising times; the jewellery was found in two small plain Orientalising vases sunk into the ground just inside the tomb doorway. The treasure includes: a gold pendant with crystal and amber inlays on a plaited gold chain with snake's head terminals; a second gold pendant fashioned as a crescent ending in human heads and framing birds—strip cloissons on the crescent originally held inlays—and both it and the birds are delicately enhanced by use of the granulation technique; a gold band showing a hero subduing a lion, each panel impressed from the same matrix; a necklace of rock-crystal beads of which the string-holes are lined with gold; and two silver pins, with gold bird heads, linked by a gold loop-in-loop chain. It has been proposed that the superb craftsmanship of this material points to a guild of metal-workers at Knossós whose origins lay in the Near East, and moreover that this tomb may have been their family vault.

In this same case is a series of gold, silver and electrum dumps. The near-uniformity of the gold bars looks deliberate, and they have been considered by some to be forerunners of Greek coinage. However, a more intriguing suggestion is that they were the stock-in-trade of the gold-smiths, their raw material in the form in which it was usually handled.

The case also contains other miniature gold-work from Knossós, and pieces from Arkádes and Praisós.

The five remaining cases in this gallery, starting with 160 (on the first wall), contain material from the recently excavated sanctuary at Sými near Viánnos. The votive offerings found at Sými range in date from the Minoan to the Hellenistic period. An inscription (3C AD) between the first two cases affirms the dedication to Hermes Dendrites.

In Case 160 the Minoan material includes bronze figurines of worshippers, stone vases and small altars, one with an inscription in Linear A. (See also the Minoan swords in Case 161C.) There are also offerings from the succeeding period of Mycenaean influence, and from the Early Iron Age, including a bronze figurine of a woman with spear and shield. Case 161 contains votive offerings from the later periods; note the figure of Hermes playing a lyre.

The offerings in Case 161A are in the form of open-work bronze sheets of great interest for their graphic details of the contemporary pilgrim's approach to the sanctuary.

Case 161B contains a further collection of material from the same site, mainly from the 8–5C BC: terracotta figurines and plaques, and, among the bronzes, miniature votive shields. Outstanding in Case 161C are three Minoan swords, two of them ivory-handled.

The huge relief pithoi between the doors date from Subminoan (nearest Gallery XI, from Priniás) to Archaic; the one with Orientalising motifs of sphinxes and leopard-headed spirals is from Lýttos, the others from Arkádes and Dréros.

The Gallery of the Sarcophagi (XIII). During the Bronze Age, burials were often in clay chests or larnakes. Those displayed here are of two periods: there are Middle Minoan tub-shaped examples, painted with abstract designs, from various sites including Vóri near Phaistós, and also LMIII rectangular chests on four feet, often with gabled lids. Usually the designs on these chests consist of degenerate octopuses or stylised flowers, but several examples here are more unusual; decorative elements include birds, fish, a boat (from Gázi), an animal suckling her young (Gourniá), and griffins with the sacred horns of consecration (Palaíkastro). Sometimes elliptical bathtubs with marine designs were used for burials, and examples can be seen with a plug-hole to let the water escape. From occasional remains of wood in tombs and the panelled form of the LMIII chests it is considered that this design was based on a wooden prototype.

In one corner of this room can be seen a burial, transported from an LMIIIA–B tomb at Sellópoulo, near Knossós. A second skeleton (nearer the exit) is from Arkhánes; note the bronze finger-ring.

The Gallery of the Sarcophagi breaks the strict chronological sequence followed so far in the museum. A natural progession would lead from the material of the Orientalising period in the previous room (XII) to the ground-floor Gallery XIX (opposite the far end of the bookstall) which contains some important Archaic sculptures and bronzes mentioned during the relevant site visits elsewhere in this Guide. However, stairs from Gallery XIII lead to the museum's UPPER FLOOR which houses the Minoan fresco display, as well as further Archaic exhibits and the Giamalákis collection, so it is convenient to leave the two remaining ground-floor rooms to the end of the visit.

Gallery XIV. Hall of the Frescoes. Here, and in Galleries XV and XVI, are displayed the Minoan frescoes. Only fragments of the original wall-paintings remain, much restored after the collapse of walls and sometimes discoloured by the fires which destroyed the buildings they decorated. However the scenes illustrate the religious and secular life of the Minoans, including (often in the incidental details) their appreciation of the natural world around them. The artists used the true fresco technique; the paint was applied to the plaster while this was still wet, though in some cases the area of the picture seems to have been prepared by impressing with a tool or with taut string. Sometimes the plaster was moulded, before painting, into figures in very low relief, to give a three-dimensional effect.

The surviving pieces are mostly from Knossós and Ayía Triáda; Amnisós, Nírou Kháni, Pseíra, and Týlissos also contribute examples. The paintings, with few exceptions, date from the Neopalatial Period (mainly LMI). Some from Knossós are LMII–IIIA, and the floor with marine scenes from the shrine at Ayía Triáda is now known to belong to the Postpalatial period.

First, on the left at the top of the stairs, is a fragment of a Bull Fresco from the Upper Hall of the Double Axes at Knossós. Next come the remains of the *Procession Fresco* with its best-preserved figure the *Cup-Bearer* (notice the seal worn as a jewel on his wrist); these frescoes adorned the Corridor of the Procession, the long ceremonial approach to the palace and the propylaea, a great gate where the scenes were arranged in two superimposed friezes. Between the doors is the *Griffin Fresco* from the palace Throne Room.

Beyond (18–24) are fragments from Ayía Triáda: a kneeling female figure, perhaps picking flowers; a seated goddess beside a building that is identified as a shrine by the horns of consecration; a cat stalking a pheasant in a landscape of rocks and plants—the cat arches its back to spring but the pheasant struts about, not suspecting danger; a fresco (very similar to one that appears on the sarcophagus in the centre of the room and probably painted by the same artist) showing a ritual procession bearing offerings and led by a musician playing a lyre; another procession, this time of women approaching a shrine; and a woman leading a deer towards an altar. At the end of the room is a frescoed plaster floor from the LMIII (Postpalatial) shrine at Ayía Triáda. It consists of a colourful marine scene showing dolphins, an octopus and small fishes. Beyond are the remains of another floor fresco with abstract motives, from the First Palace at Phaistós (18C BC).

Exhibited here is an elaborate model of the Palace of Knossós, built (in wood) by the late master-technician, Zakharías Kanákis. The reconstruction greatly assists in envisaging the layout, especially for the West Wing (facing the museum staircase) showing the Tripartite Shrine, and for the Hall of the Double Axes (King's Megaron) at the bottom of the Grand Staircase in the East Wing.

Moving to the opposite wall, all except the last two frescoes are from Knossós. First is the restored *Shield Fresco* from the Upper Hall of the Colonnades; the markings on the shields represent the dappled hides of the oxen or bulls from which real shields were made. The rosette spirals are a clue to the LMII date of this work. A similar shield fresco was found in the palace at Tiryns on the mainland and another, more recently, at Mycenae. Next comes the familiar figure known as the Priest King or Prince of the Lilies, wearing his plumed lily head-dress and collar of fleurs-de-lis and leading an animal, perhaps a griffin, for this theme is shown on sealstones. This interpretation has recently been challenged by the theory that the figure is a boxer.

The *Charging Bull* in stucco relief is from the portico above the North

The Bull-leaper fresco from Knossós (Herákleion Museum, Gallery XIV)

Entrance Passage, the *Ladies in Blue* from the East Wing of the palace and the Dolphins from the Queen's Megaron. There follow two colourful spiral frieze frescoes and then, from the Caravanserai on the south approach to the palace, the frieze of partridges and hoopoes. The coloured objects are probably stones rather than eggs. Next comes the *Bull-leaper Fresco*, the most vivid representation of bull-leaping in Minoan art. Red is the convention for male figures, white for female, and here we see both participating in this sport.

The last two frescoes on the wall are the graceful white and red Madonna lilies and irises from the LMI villa at Amnisós; such lilies are frequently seen today in Cretan gardens.

At this end of the hall there is a scale model of the Little Palace at Knossós, and a case contains fragments of a chariot and other pieces also from Knossós.

In the centre (Case 171) stands the stone **sarcophagus from Ayía Triáda (found in a LMIIIA context); it is carved from a single block of limestone, covered with a layer of plaster and painted, as with the wall-paintings, while the plaster was still damp. Both long sides portray funeral ceremonies: the one with processions of figures bearing offerings consists of two scenes, distinguished by background colour and the direction in which the figures are facing. On the left the female figure pouring the contents of a vase into a krater is conducting a purification rite for the deceased. The sacred surroundings are symbolised by double axes with birds perching on them. On the right the procession conveys gifts, including a model boat, towards a figure in front of a richly decorated building. This figure used to be interpreted as the spirit or personification of the

The Ayía Triáda painted sarcophagus (Herákleion Museum, Gallery XIV)

deceased in front of his tomb, but considering the similarity between the long robe and the kilts in the procession, it is now thought more likely to represent a priest in charge of the rite.

On the reverse, female figures are officiating at the sacrifice of a bull, to an accompaniment on a flute. Ritual significance is seen again in the double axe with bird, the tree and the altar with sacral horns.

On the ends are shown a procession (not well preserved), and chariots driven by pairs of females and drawn by horses and griffins.

Galleries XV and XVI open off the main fresco hall. All the pieces are from Knossós except where otherwise stated.

In **Gallery XV** is the *Miniature Fresco* from rooms west of the North Entrance Passage; crowds of spectators attend some ceremony, including a dance, while another part of the picture shows a tri-partite shrine with columns which have double axes attached. Next is the lady named by Evans's workmen *'La Parisienne'*; the sacral knot over her neck is taken to be evidence that she is a priestess. Beside her is the restored *Camp Stool Fresco* with priests and priestesses seated on stools holding chalices and goblets. 'La Parisienne' may have been associated with this group though she is on a larger scale. The Spiral Cornice Relief also came from the area near the North Entrance Passage. Next are displayed relief fragments of athletes taking part in bull sports, then two griffins tied to a column tail to tail. (There seems to have been a whole frieze of these in high relief antithetically grouped in the East Hall of the palace above the Corridor of the Bays.) The central case in this room contains fragments of miniature style frescoes from Knossós and Týlissos. The diagrammatic representation of a labyrinth, from Knossós, is a motif common at a later date than that city's coins.

In the next-door **Gallery XVI** further fragments from Knossós are displayed in the central case (174); these include the *Palanquin Fresco*, part of a bull-leaping scene, pieces of the Miniature Frescoes, shrines, and dress fragments. In the corner left of the entrance from the main hall is the original restoration of the *Saffron Gatherer fresco* when the main figure was thought to be a boy. Later it was determined that it was a blue monkey, as shown in N. Pláton's adjacent restoration. Next comes the *Captain of the Blacks*, from the area of the LMI House of the Frescoes, then a dancing girl from the Queen's Megaron, a tri-columnar shrine (this fragment was found in the West Magazines of the palace), and olive trees in relief, from the North Entrance Passage. On the opposite wall is first another olive tree in relief, then the *Blue Bird* and *Monkey Frescoes* from the House of the Frescoes; the vivid bird is a roller. These are followed by a scene of women or goddesses in stucco relief, with elaborate dresses, from the island of Pseíra, and finally a sacral knot from the LMI villa at Nírou Kháni, east of Herákleion.

In recent years, owing to staff shortages, the next two rooms have, unfortunately, often been closed to the public.

Gallery XVII (through XVIII). The *Giamalákis Collection. The collection formed over a period of 40 years by the late Dr S. Giamalákis, a surgeon of Herákleion, is now displayed in this room. There are many objects of outstanding interest but not all are necessarily from Crete: (175) Early and Middle Minoan pottery and a Cycladic 'frying-pan' with incised decoration; a steatopygous burnished Neolithic *figurine from Apáno Khorió near Ierápetra; (176) over 50 stone vases including some of banded marble similar to those from Mókhlos; a case (187) of Minoan and later seals; another (188) of non-Minoan seals, including cylinder seals and Sassanid bullas made of chalcedony; (178) a bronze figurine of a young man bearing a ram over his shoulders; (182) Archaic and Classical Greek terracottas and vases; (190) a bronze helmet from Axós; (191) gold objects from the *"Zákros Treasure'* which include a diadem with the Mistress of Animals, a cup and a bull's head; several bronzes, and in the same case some very fine Venetian jewellery.

Gallery XVIII. Archaic and Greco-Roman Antiquities. The exhibits in this room consist mainly of terracottas, bronzes and coins from the Archaic, Classical, Hellenistic, and Roman cities of the island. Cases 192–194 contain: 7C to Classical clay figurines, pottery and plaques from a votive deposit on the acropolis of Górtyn (also Case 200); several figures with wig-like hair are in the Daidalic style; one figure represents Athena brandishing her spear. In Case 206 the plaques include Bellerophon fighting the Chimaera, and Klytemnestra and Aegisthus killing Agamemnon, while others show Archaic naked or draped goddesses wearing high polos head-dresses. Case 195: from Arkádes is a Daidalic head-vase (6639); from Praisós a protome of a man with a diadem; from the sanctuary of Zeus Diktaios at Palaíkastro a Gorgoneion (4920); also exhibited are a plaque with a sphinx from Lýttos and several fragments of Archaic relief pithoi. Cases 196, 197, 203 and 207A contain fine bronzes from Axós, Dréros, the acropolis of Górtyn, the Idaian cave and Praisós. These include: mitrai (armour to protect the abdomen) from Axós, with chased decoration, one showing Pegasus, another a tripod cauldron between two lions, a third two contending athletes; a bronze corselet from Arkádes (197), a Gorgoneion and a Palladion from Dréros; numerous handle attachments from the Idaian cave; and miniature votive armour from the sanctuaries of Praisós and Górtyn. Small clay figurines of the Archaic period, human and animal, come from Amnisós, Týlissos, and the Idaian cave. In Case 198 are bronze objects of the Archaic period from Fortétsa, Axós, and the Idaian cave, including (from Axós) a splendid 'helmet with cheek pieces embossed with winged horses. A vase from Dréros, standing separately, is decorated with a wild goat and snakes in relief.

Case 205. The Classical and Hellenistic coins of Crete are mostly of bronze and silver. Rare gold coins from Lissós and Hyrtakína in southwest Crete are also shown here. There are coins based on the Attic tetradrachm with the names of Cretan archons. Greek silver coins of Athens, Aígina, Argos, Corinth, and Sikyon, and coins of Macedon and the Hellenistic monarchies are also shown. (The Roman coins of Crete are in the Study Collection.)

Case 199 is devoted to Greek black- and red-figure vases; these include a good red-figure lekythos from Kydonía (Khaniá), Classical lamps and terracottas, Attic and Boeotian vases. In cases 201 and 202, Hellenistic vases including several Gnathian examples with plant motifs on a light or dark ground, Hellenistic white marble pyxides, Greco-Roman bronzes, terracottas, lamps and glass vessels. Among these are Late Roman bronze and clay lamps with erotic relief scenes. There are also several small Greco-Roman heads in marble. Case 207, containing Classical, Hellenistic, and Roman jewellery and gems, includes a fine Victory, from Knossós, inspired by the Victory of Paionios at Olympia, ear-rings from Oloús, diadems and a series of gold and silver rings. Among the gems is one of onyx with a representation of a Centaur, another of chalcedony with Theseus and the Minotaur. Near the entrance is a life-size bronze 'statue of a boy in sandals and toga from Ierápetra. It is a most sensitive portrayal, dating from the 1C BC.

GROUND FLOOR. **Gallery XIX. Archaic Sculptures and Bronzes (700–550 BC)**. Above the entrance to this gallery (opposite the foot of the stairs near the bookstall) is a 7C Gorgoneion from Dréros. In the corner to the left there is a lion head in poros from Phaistós and then, below the frieze, two groups of Archaic sculpture in the Daidalic style, of a god with two goddesses, from the acropolis of Górtyn. Two funerary stelai, of a warrior and a lady spinning, are also from Górtyn. An eagle and a hawk on pedestals with Ionic volutes came from the sanctuary of Zeus Thénatas at Amnisós, and the torso of an Archaic kouros from Eléftherna.

The *frieze of horsemen high up on the left wall is part of the sculpture which decorated one of the two mid 7C temples at Priniás (ancient Rizenía). The seated goddesses from the doorway into the cella of one of the temples here frame the doorway to Gallery XX; their thrones are placed over a frieze of lions and deer, suggesting that the divinity may be the Cretan Britomartis (Artemis), Mistress of Animals.

In the central Case 207 are three bronze *statuettes (7C BC) made by the sphyrelaton technique (hammered on a wooden core and then pinned); they come from the sanctuary of Apollo Delphinios at Dréros and are believed to represent Apollo with his sister, Artemis, and his mother, Leto. Cases 208 and 209 contain the remarkable bronze *shields from the Idaian cave, which have lion's head bosses and repoussé decoration showing battle and hunting scenes, an eagle gripping a sphinx, and the Cretan goddess, the Mistress of Animals. The superb workmanship is attributed to Orientalising craftsmen who probably settled on Crete. Other shields are from Palaíkastro and Arkádes (Aphráti). A bronze tympanon from the Idaian cave shows Zeus between two Kourétes.

From Praisós (centre of the room) comes a crouching clay lion, c 600 BC. Behind the bronze statuettes are architectural fragments from the 6C temple of Zeus at Palaíkastro, including a terracotta 'sima', or waterspout, showing a stylised chariot scene with dog; also Archaic relief pithoi. Against the wall on the right of the entrance are lion's head waterspouts from the Palaíkastro temple, a head from Axós (mid-6C), a Roman copy of the Archaic Hymn to Zeus Diktaios from Palaíkastro, and a black stone stele from Dréros with a winged human figure holding a bird.

Gallery XX. Greco-Roman Sculptures. Only the most interesting or important pieces are listed here.

Left of the doorway are relief plaques and grave stelae, with statues from *Knossós*: 273. Roman youth wearing bulla and toga praetextata; 220. Portrait head of Homer; 315. Dionysos, with wreath of ivy; 46. Bacchus pouring from a wineskin (in alabaster). Two doorways of a Classical house, one with lion's mask mouldings. 5. Colossal statue of Hadrian with decorated corselet showing the she-wolf suckling Romulus and Remus and two Victories crowning Roma (this piece from Górtyn). 42. Torso of Aphrodite, probably a copy of a Praxitelean work. 8. (in front of Hadrian) Sarcophagus with inscription 'Polybos'. An orator harangues the dead; below are the symbols of the Eleusinian mysteries.

On the far wall. Statues from *Górtyn*, mostly Roman copies of earlier works. 342. Torso, copy of the Doryphoros of Polykleitos. 3. Good copy of winged Pothos (Desire) by Skopas. The figure, wings missing, leans against a tree trunk. 325. Aphrodite, copy of Alkamenes's Aphrodite in the Gardens. 159. Torso of Aphrodite, probably copy of a Praxitelean work. 43. Aphrodite kneeling in a bath, copy of a work by Doidalsas. 347. Copy of the Athena Parthenos of Pheidias, the cult statue of the Parthenon. 67, 65, 64, 66. 1C AD busts of the family of Augustus: Livia, Tiberius, Augustus, and Germanicus (?). 259, 260. Two Egyptian deities identified with Persephone, and Pluto with Cerberus; from the Temple of Isis and Serapis. 155. Fine head of Dionysos. 77. Head of Hera, copy of a Classical original. 326. Cult statue of Apollo Kitharoidos from the Temple of Apollo Pythios. 153. Pan playing the syrinx. 73. Over life-size head of the emperor Antoninus Pius (AD 131–61). 60. Bust of the emperor Septimius Severus (AD 193–211). 1. A bearded orator or philosopher with books at his feet, perhaps Herakleitos. 208. Artemis, indifferent copy of a Classical original. 350, 351. Hygieia, with the sacred snakes. 349. Aphrodite, copy of a Classical original.

On the right wall. Statues from *other Cretan cities.* 2. Female figure, probably Hestia, copy of a Classical original in the severe style, from Kísamos in western Crete. 334. Roman empress, probably Julia Domna, wife of Septimius Severus and mother of Caracalla, from Khersónisos. 387. The Mállia Sarcophagus (2C AD) 265, 266. Two figures from the Death of the children of Niobe at the hands of Apollo and Artemis, poor Roman copies, from Inatós. 74. Portrayal of a eunuch, from Lýttos. 317. Fine head of Trajan (AD 98–117), from Lýttos. 336. Good copy of a Praxitelean torso of Apollo or Hermes, unknown provenance. 230. Bust of Marcus Aurelius (AD 161–180), from Lýttos. 340. Bearded head, wearing a Persian helmet. In front of the cult statue of Apollo is a *mosaic floor,* 2C AD, from Knossós. It is by an artist named Apollinaris (see inscription) and shows Poseidon drawn by sea-horses, accompanied by tritons and dolphins.

South Side. Classical, Hellenistic, and Roman reliefs. 378. Funeral stele showing departure of dead man, imitating the 4C BC Attic type, from Herákleion. 363. Metope, late 5C BC from Knossós. It shows a labour of Hercules, who brings the Erymanthian boar to the terrified King Eurystheus who takes refuge in a large jar. 249, 12, 10, 9. Fragments of Greco-Roman relief sarcophagi: the first, from Khersónisos, shows Atlanta's hunt of the Kalydonian boar; the others, from Górtyn, scenes of combat and Bellerophon and Pegasus; other fragments from these cities show Eros and Tantalos. 145. Attic 4C BC funeral stele, showing a hunter, a notable piece, is from the Bay of Akhláda, Herákleion.

C. The Historical Museum

The *Historical and Ethnographic Museum of Crete* (near the seafront opposite the Xenía Hotel—see p 60) opened in 1953 in the spacious neo-classical family house of Andréas Kalokairinós, a notable benefactor of Herákleion. This was a substantial building, restored and redecorated in 1903, with Doric columns and friezes (preserved in the hall) of scenes from the Iliad and the Odyssey. With the help of the Kalokairinós bequest, a collection of major importance was built up by the Society for Cretan Historical Studies, and to increase the exhibition space a wing (in similar neo-classical style) was added at the west side of the house.

Recently it became possible to transform the corridor linking the old building and the wing into an elegant bridge executed in glass and aluminium to the design of the architect J. Pertselákis. This new space, on two levels, became fully operational in 1991, and as well as offering an exciting architectural contrast it has provided an opportunity for the museum to widen the range of its display and to strengthen its educational impact.

A first visit is very worthwhile as an agreeable way of assimilating a historical framework before touring the island, and the collection of maps and views displayed in the hall is highly recommended for their topographical interest. Major pieces in the museum are meticulously labelled in English as well as Greek, and all the new background information is duplicated in translation.

Opening hours: 09.00–17.00. Closed Sundays and public holidays. Entrance charge.

The *Entrance Hall* is hung with a collection of 17C maps and views of the island's cities, fortresses and harbours. The coloured engravings are by

Marco Boschini, official Venetian cartographer, and were published under the title 'Il regno tutto di Candia' (Venice, 1651). The two cannons are from Venetian galleys sunk in Herákleion harbour during the Great Siege (1648–69).

The formal visit is designed to begin in the *basement* (stairs at back of hall) where the museum preserves a collection of architectural fragments from Crete's heritage. The sculpture and inscriptions are the more valued on account of their scarcity, the result of an unremitting history of conquest, revolt and attendant destruction.

On the left at the bottom of the stairs a 16–17C double doorway is framed by a set of stone reliefs from the Latin monastery of St. Francis, which, until it was destroyed by Turkish cannons during the Great Siege, dominated the Venetian city of Candia from the hill where the Archaeological Museum now stands. On the far side of the doorway, high up, is a coat of arms with a lion and a Hebrew inscription; it belonged to a Jewish family living on Crete in the 16C. Between the windows stands an elegant 16–17C fountain from a Venetian nobleman's house in Candia.

Among a collection of coats of arms, one with castle, cross and griffin and an inscription in Latin and Armenian (13–14C) was carved on a tombstone from the former Armenian church in Candia. In the centre of the wall, a vigorous St. George medallion, in high relief, came from the St. George's—Lazzaretto—Gate (1565) in the ramparts. Along the opposite wall is part of the original frieze from the Venetian Loggia (1626), including some fine sculptures. The Loggia, which suffered severe damage during the Second World War, has been faithfully reconstructed (p 59).

A second double doorway of carved stone is a relic of the city towards the end of the Venetian period, c 1600. It leads to a small room of Byzantine exhibits: three stone well-heads carved with relief decoration, on the central one a hunting scene; the pulpit from the post-Arab reconstruction of the basilica of Ayios Títos at Górtyn; and a collection of capitals and impost blocks.

Across the corridor is a room of the Turkish period, with inscriptions, tombstones of governors and other notable citizens; the walls are hung with glazed porcelain tiles from an 18C mosque in the city. In the corridor wall-paintings from a Turkish house show the city of Herákleion, known to the Turks as Megálo Kástro, the great fortress, in an idealised landscape.

The corridor leads round to a new exhibit of fresco fragments rescued from derelict churches of the Byzantine period.

On the *ground floor* both main rooms can be entered from near the front door. Behind the ticket desk is the *Cretan historical collection*, throwing light on political and social history with exhibits ranging from Venetian armour to memorabilia of the Independent Cretan State (1898–1913) under two successive High Commissioners for the Great Powers—Prince George of Greece up to 1906 and then Alexander Zaimis. (The events of these years are the subject of a photographic archive, with detailed explanations, on display later in the visit in the new extension.)

Left of the doorway are documents from the Turkish period, including firmans relating to the position of the Christian church at that time; one is illustrated with a view of the Monastery of St. Catherine on Mount Sinai. There is also an intriguing satirical interpretation of Turkish rule over Crete.

Much of this room is given over to exhibits connected with the long and proud struggle for independence from foreign rule. There are portraits of the Cretan chieftains and a lithograph of the leaders of ten revolts between 1770 and 1897, also a fine collection of their intimidating weapons. Newspaper cuttings add contemporary comment from abroad, and there is one case of commemorative china. A screen of historic photographs develops this theme of support from abroad for the Cretan national cause.

Across the hall: the *Medieval collection* preserves many valuable ecclesiastical items from destroyed or abandoned Byzantine churches. Cases display rare copper vessels, crucifixes, candlesticks and other sacred objects dating from the Early Christian period, from the 6C basilica of Ayios Títos at Górtyn and from nearby Mitrópolis. Icons from Savathianá in the district of Malevísi include a magnificent 'Virgin as Fountain of Life' (1655). There is a carved wooden *lectern and a 17C ecclesiastical throne from the former monastery church of Valsamóneros on the south slopes of Mount Ida. In the archway, *embroidered vestments (17 and 18C) belonged to the former Asómatos monastery in the Amári valley; a pastoral staff is inlaid with ivory, tortoiseshell and mother-of-pearl.

Further exhibits include: glazed earthenware (16–17C); elaborate liturgical vessels in silver; a case of Byzantine and Venetian *jewellery; gold and bronze coins.

Outstanding is a group of *icons from the church of the Panayía Gouverniótissa at Potamiés on the road up to Lasíthi; also the church's painted sanctuary doors and part of the wooden iconostasis with high-quality carving (all late 16C). The technique is characteristic of the style known as the Cretan School, with the modelling of flesh achieved with dense highlights on dark brown underpaint.

Outside this room, at the back of the hall, is a reconstruction of a frescoed *Byzantine chapel*. The room beside it has been specially air-conditioned to house a painting (c 1570) by Doménico Theotokópoulos, known as El Greco, of the *Monastery of Saint Catherine on Mount Sinai. This recent purchase by the municipality of Herákleion has made possible, for the first time in very many years, the permanent exhibition of a work by the painter on the island of his birth.

The modern extension provides a bridge to the *West Wing*. In the new display space the tattered 1912 banner of a chieftain from Argyroúpolis (in the hills behind Réthymnon) proclaims 'Freedom or Death' and is hung among portraits of Cretan revolutionary leaders and contemporary documents; pride of place is given to Eleuthérios Venizélos who became an internationally respected statesman and served on a number of occasions (see p 28) as Prime Minister in Athens.

On this landing the Mouréllos photographic archive records (with clear and informative historical commentary) the events of the brief period of autonomy which preceded Crete's union with Greece in 1913.

On the far side of the landing a room (right) is designed to display copies of Byzantine fresco paintings (13–15C).

The main staircase leads up to the next level of the extension. One of the principal exhibits here draws attention to secular aspects of *Byzantine art*, including changes in medieval costume as revealed in the portraits of donors preserved among the church wall-paintings, many recorded early this century by G. Gerola working with archaeologists of the Italian Mission.

A case of items for sale contains books, cards or reproductions with a particular historical interest, and also a display of illustrations inspired by the works of the Cretan-born author N. Kazantzákis (and see below).

In the old West Wing the passage walls are lined with photographs taken during the *Battle of Crete* in 1941.

On the left a room is furnished as the study of *Níkos Kazantzákis* (1883–1957) with desk, library and other personal possessions from his home on the island of Aígina. Examples of paintings and engravings inspired by his books hang nearby on the 'bridge'.

Across the way a large room houses a fine collection of old *maps*, to which has been added a case of *stamps* of the Cretan State from the 19 and early 20C. Here is also material connected with the Cretan statesman *E. Tsouderós*, a native of Réthymnon, who became Prime Minister of Greece on 18 April 1941, after the German invasion of Macedonia and only days before the evacuation of the Allied forces to Crete. The dais is furnished as his study.

The *top floor* houses a superb collection of Cretan *textiles*, demonstrating the wide variety of weaving, needlework and crochet traditional on the island. The exhibits are informatively labelled highlighting the most important local variations. In the room left of the stairs (and on the left of the doorway) is a case of *embroidery in silk on linen including, from the former Asómatos monastery, an 18C skirt or cope border (No. 1292) with a design of mermaids, dragons and peacocks among flowers. At the far end of the room an 18C dowry *chest has painted and carved decoration, and is fitted with little jewel cases, with drawers and miniature chests. In the corner, note the embroidered velvet jackets from Sphakiá and Anóyia which complement the costumes displayed outside on the landing.

There the two Cretan female costumes contrast the styles of Kritsá and Anóyia, villages with strong weaving traditions, the first in eastern Crete above Ayios Nikólaos, and the second on the slopes of Mount Ida, a little to the west of Herákleion. Opposite the stairhead is a fine exhibition of crochet and needlework, also further weavings. A double room (right) is fitted out as a house interior c 1900 and contains the museum's *ethnographic collection*.

D.   The Icon Collection in Ayía Aikateríni

Open: Monday–Saturday 09.30–13.00, and Tuesday, Thursday and Saturday 17.00–19.00 (winter 16.00–18.00). Closed Sundays and public holidays. Entrance charge.

A collection of icons, old manuscripts and liturgical objects is housed in the former monastic church of *Ayía Aikateríni of Sinai*, across a plateía from the north-east corner of the modern cathedral of Ayios Minás. (The old church of Ayios Minás—the medieval predecessor—stands alongside the terrace at the cathedral's West Front.)

From Plateía Nikephórou Phoká, at the bottom of the market, a main shopping street, Leophóros Kalokairinoú (once the Venetian 'Via Imperiale'), runs west to the Khaniá, or Pantokrátor, Gate (built c 1570, now restored). A short distance along Kalokairinoú, the fifth lane to the

The Council of Nicaea, an icon by Mikhaíl Damaskinós (Ayía Aikateríni, Herákleion)

left leads into an area largely reserved for pedestrians and to Plateía Ayía Aikateríni.

The church dates from 1555, with 17C alterations. It was a dependency of the monastery of the same name on Mount Sinai, and in the 16 and 17C its college here became a renowned centre of the arts and learning, and played an important part both in preserving and disseminating Byzantine culture after the fall of Constantinople.

The first portable icons documented on Crete (1025) were brought to the island from Constantinople. There is evidence of painters travelling (in both directions) between Crete and Constantinople before the Byzantine capital fell to the Turks in 1453, but it is after this date that Crete's particular political and social circumstances (as a fervently Orthodox community within the Venetian Empire) gave the island a special importance in the field of icon painting. Production is known to have been organised in workshops staffed by large numbers of apprentices, and there are records of substantial orders to satisfy demand from Western Europe as well as from the remaining Hellenic world. The painters working on Crete at this time inherited the iconographical traditions and strict conservative technique of the style that was revived under the Palaiologan emperors (1261–1453), the last Christian rulers of Constantinople. However the Venetian regime on Crete facilitated contact with the large Greek community in Venice, and the Cretan painters were therefore open to the influence of the art of Renaissance Italy. There was in any case a demand at this time from members of the Latin church for icons 'in the Latin style'. The versatility of the 15–16C Cretan icon painters is conspicuous.

Only a small proportion of the icons of this period have survived, and very few indeed remain on Crete. It was not customary for artists to sign their work, but one who did so is Mikhaíl Damaskinós.

Damaskinós, an older contemporary of El Greco (see Historical Museum above), is recognised as one of the major icon painters of the period. He studied at Ayía Aikateríni and then, like so many other Cretan artists at that time, sought employment abroad. He is known to have worked in Venice 1577–82. Though many of his icons show the influence of Italian art, his most-admired paintings are those which adhere most strictly to the Byzantine tradition. Today his work is widely dispersed.

The six Damaskinós icons exhibited in this collection are paintings of his mature period (late 16C) after his return from Venice. They hung in the Vrondísi monastery on the south slopes of Ida until 1800, when they were brought for safety to Ayios Minás in Herákleion. Now they are displayed in the main body of the Ayía Aikateríni nave, scattered among other exhibits. The collection is not numbered, but counting from the left behind the ticket desk (i.e. starting on the west wall of the church) the Damaskinós icons are:

2. Η Προσκύνηση των Μάγων. The Adoration of the Magi, showing most clearly the influence of western art.

5. Ο Μυστικός Δείπνος. The Last Supper.

8. Η Θεοτόκος η Βάτος. The Virgin with the Burning Bush, showing Moses on Mount Horeb, and the bush which burned but was not consumed, a symbol of the virginity of the Mother of God.

9. Μη μου άπτου. 'Noli me tangere', Christ appearing to the Holy Women.

12. Η Οικουμενική Σύνοδος. The Ecumenical Council held at Nicaea (AD 325) at which the Emperor Constantine conferred with his bishops to settle the Aryan Controversy. This work was painted in 1591.

15. Η Θεία Λειτουργία. The Divine Liturgy, with Christ celebrating mass, in the midst of the encircling hosts of angels.

The church of *Ayios Matthéos* contains a number of interesting icons (including two narrow panels which were exhibited in London in the 1987 Royal Academy exhibition 'Byzantium to El Greco'). Ayios Symeós Theodókhos (Receiver of God), St. Simeon with the Christ child in his arms, conveys the message of the Presentation in the Temple. Ayios Ioánnis Prodrómos (the Baptist) is portrayed in the iconographical tradition of the Palaiologan style (wearing a sheepskin, and with one hand raised in the act of blessing, the other holding an open scroll); however, the wings are an innovation, and the scene lacks the traditional severed head. Both these icons, though unsigned, are now attributed to Damaskinós.

The church is less than 10 minutes on foot from Ayía Aikateríni. (Ask the guardian there about hours of opening.) Cross the paved plateía to the main road opposite the West Front of the cathedral. On the far side of the road a narrow street half-left (named after a bishop martyred in 1821) opens after 20m into ΟΔΟΣ ΤΑΞΙΑΡΧΟΥ ΜΑΡΚΟΠΟΥΛΟΥ (Odós Taxiárkhou Markopoúlou); the church of Ayios Matthéos is on the right of the street after 200m.

2 Knossós

The Minoan Palace of Knossós is 5km (3 miles) from the centre of Herákleion. The site is open seven days a week: for opening times and detailed tour of the palace see p 102 below.

Bus No. 2 (ΚΝΩΣΟΣ) leaves the harbour terminus near the main bus station (see Herákleion town plan) every 15 minutes; journey time 20–30 minutes. Convenient stops in town at Plateía Venizélou (Morosíni fountain) and in Odós 1821. The palace site is at the end of the line. Note that on the return route the bus stops in Plateía Eleftherías, convenient for the Archaeological Museum, before descending by the rampart directly to the harbour.

Coach excursions to the palace are available from agents in all tourist centres including Herákleion.

By car: leave Plateía Eleftherías with the public gardens on your right. The road is a dual-carriageway as far as the cemetery church (right) of Ayios Konstantínos. Here keep left and at the next fork bear left again. (Straight ahead at this fork would lead you on to the north coast highway.) Away to the left of the road was the site of the Royal Tomb at Isópata, destroyed in 1942. Soon you pass under the highway, just after a slip-road from it which is the best approach from other parts of the island. At 3.5km a road (signed Ayios Sýllas) diverges for Fortétsa, on a ridge (right) from which the Turks bombarded Herákleion during the Great Siege. Opposite this turning is the Science Faculty of the University of Crete.

In 1978 a rescue excavation in advance of this new building, undertaken by the British School at Athens for the Greek Archaeological Service, uncovered a cemetery of more than 300 tombs dating from the Subminoan to Early Christian times, though the richest burials were from the Geometric and Orientalising periods (see archaeology and history below). 150m beyond the Fortétsa turn and the university buildings is the Venizéleion hospital. LMII warrior graves excavated here in 1952 contained artefacts characteristic of the first Mycenaean influence at Knossós.

This whole area, which continued as the main burial ground of Knossós into historic times, is now known as the *Knossós North Cemetery*.

The road is entering the settlement area which spread out around the Palace of Knossós in the Bronze Age. The latest thinking envisages a densely occupied central zone, and then, since there is no evidence that the Minoan town was at any time surrounded by defence walls, a gradual merging of town with countryside, with the houses on the outskirts separated by gardens or cultivated ground. The area of intensive settlement at the most flourishing period of the Minoan civilisation was approximately 750,000m^2, a little smaller than that of medieval Candia (Herákleion), and though calculations differ wildly—Evans's being among the more extravagant—a conservative modern estimate puts the population of the Minoan town at about 12,000.

The road to Knossós also passes through the centre of the Roman city, which occupied roughly 1km² of the Bronze Age settlement area, between the modern hospital and the Palace of Knossós. At 400m beyond the hospital, just before a track, right, to a cemetery church, the road cuts through the presumed site of a Roman theatre. In the next field across (left of) the road, stones and column fragments lying among the vines have for many years indicated the probable site of the Roman civil basilica. Where the stone wall begins, on the right verge of the road, there are steps up to the excavated Hadrianic *Villa Dionysos*, so called because of the subjects portrayed on its high-quality 2C mosaic floors. The site has never been open to the public but there is now hope that this may change.

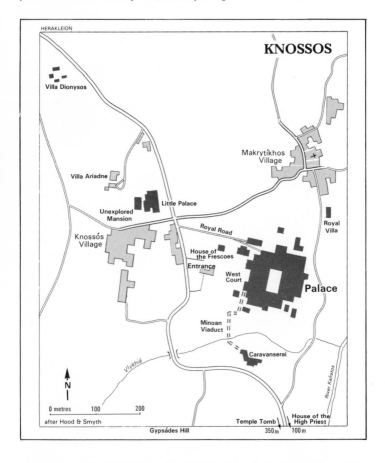

A major new study of the Roman town of Knossós was begun in 1991, under the auspices of the British School at Athens with close collaboration from the Greek Archaeological Service. Work began with a two-year geophysical survey which very soon confirmed the extensive nature of the remains, and will be followed, during the life of this edition of the Guide, by several seasons of excavation and academic analysis. A great deal of new light can be expected to be shed on historical times at Knossós.

At the end of the wall a short drive leads to the *Villa Ariadne*, built by Sir Arthur Evans as his dig-house. From 1926–52 the villa belonged to the British School but then, in a rearrangement of responsibility for the palace site, it became the property of the Greek government. The house sheltered King Paul of the Hellenes for a brief period after the evacuation from mainland Greece in 1941, and during the German occupation it was the residence of the Military Commandant.

At 5km, cafés and tavernas, car parks (free nearest the entrance), coaches and other paraphernalia of tourism mark the approach (see area plan) to *Knossós*.

In Greek *mythology* Knossós was renowned for the palace of King Minos, one of the three offspring of Zeus and Europa, who was married to Pasiphae, daughter of the nymph Crete. Central to the story was the Minotaur (half man, half bull), the monstrous result of Pasiphae's infatuation with a white bull sent by the god Poseidon. The Minotaur was incarcerated in the labyrinth built for Minos by his legendary architect Daidalos, and at regular intervals seven youths and seven maidens, tribute owed to Minos from Athens, were devoured by the monster. Eventually Theseus, son of the Athenian king Aegeus, determined to kill the Minotaur and volunteered as one of the seven youths. Minos's daughter Ariadne fell passionately in love with him; she gave him a sword and a ball of woollen thread to unwind so that, after the killing, he was able to retrace his steps out of the labyrinth. The lovers sailed triumphantly from Crete, departing from the harbour of Knossós, but Theseus soon abandoned Ariadne on the island of Náxos. His punishment was swift. On his return to Athens he neglected to hoist a white sail, the pre-arranged signal of success, and his father watching from the cliffs threw himself into the sea in despair. Thus the Aegean Sea got its name.

The **Palace of Knossós** with its surrounding town and cemeteries, was thoroughly explored at the beginning of this century thanks to the initiative of Sir Arthur Evans. After inconclusive probes had been made by the Cretan Mínos Kalokairinós in the 1880s, the site excited the imagination of Heinrich Schliemann (discoverer of ancient Troy), and he attempted to purchase the land with a view to excavating. Schliemann sensed the site's importance but failed to agree with the owner, and it was left to Evans to buy a large parcel of land and begin the great work (1900).

A major part of the site was exposed by 1906 but supplementary work, first with Duncan Mackenzie and later with J.D.S. Pendlebury, continued until the excavation of the Temple Tomb in 1924. The work is enshrined in Evans's massive four-volume *Palace of Minos*. Sir Arthur's interest in the site was transferred to the British School at Athens, which continued exploration on a small scale until 1939, and resumed a series of fruitful research excavations in 1951 under the leadership of M.S.F. Hood. Selective tests within the palace in 1987 aimed to clear up uncertainties about successive architectural phases, especially where Evans's original conclusions were a matter of dispute.

Archaeology and history. There was a Neolithic village here on a low hill on the bank of the River Kaíratos, which according to radiocarbon dates was founded by 6000 BC or even a little earlier. The first known phase of habitation seems to have pre-dated the use of pottery. Gradually through the Neolithic period the mound of occupation debris accumulated, so that by the beginning of the Bronze Age, c 3500 BC, the Neolithic strata were up to 7m deep.

Occupation continued through the Early Minoan period. The settlement expanded and the buildings became more substantial until in EMIII there is some evidence, on the same alignment but of less massive construction, for what may be a forerunner of the true Minoan palaces.

The first of these two palaces (known at Knossós as the Old Palace) was built at the end of MMI, and was destroyed by a mighty earthquake at the close of MMII. This covers Pláton's Protopalatial period. (See Historical Background—p 19—for current thinking on absolute or calender dates.) When foundations for the palace were being levelled, the top of the existing mound was in effect sliced off and much of the earlier material, which included demolished buildings, was dumped to raise and extend the north-west part of the site. From this unstratified Prepalatial material have come fragments of Predynastic and early Dynastic Egyptian stone vessels, important for demonstrating Minoan links with Egypt before the foundation of the palace. Evans suggested that the Old Palace began as a series of blocks, or 'insulae', with rounded corners. One such corner can be seen in the north wall of the Throne Room complex, but this hypothesis is not universally accepted.

Certainly by the close of MMII there was considerable architectural unity. The North Entrance Passage and the Throne Room had been constructed, as had the Royal Pottery Stores, the West Magazines (as Evans named this extensive storeroom complex), and the Magazines of the Giant Pithoi. A great cutting had been made on the east side of the site in which were rooms later remodelled into the Domestic Quarter.

After the earthquake destruction the palace was rebuilt during the following period, MMIII. The reconstructed remains visible today are largely of this, the New Palace. The Domestic Quarter took its final shape, the North Entrance Passage was narrowed and the North East Pillar Hall built on to it. The storage space in the West Magazines was increased by sinking rectangular cists or coffers into many of the storeroom floor spaces, as well as below the Long Corridor beside them. The capacity for storage and redistribution of commodities, and the administrative techniques to handle this operation, provided the economic basis for Minoan prosperity.

Towards the close of MMIII further destruction, also probably by earthquake, necessitated some rebuilding and restoration of the West Façade and South Propylaea, and at this time the West Porch was rebuilt.

At the same time there began the building of a series of great houses around the palace, such as the Royal Villa, the North-West Treasure House, the House of the Frescoes, the South House, the House of the Chancel Screen and the South-East House. The Temple Tomb belongs to this period, as does the Little Palace, and a fine mansion adjacent and connected to it by a bridge. This was left by Evans as the 'Unexplored Mansion', but it has since (1967–73) been comprehensively excavated by the British School (see below). This Neopalatial phase of building is mirrored in the excavated MMIII/LMI town and country houses spread across Crete.

The tantalising fragments of fresco decoration preserved in the Herákleion Museum mostly date from this period, which marked the artistic climax of the Minoan civilisation.

At the end of LMI there seems to have been a major break in the history of Knossós, contemporary with a horizon of fire destruction at excavated sites throughout Crete. Attempts to account for this destruction have sometimes included the consequences of volcanic activity on the island of Théra (Santorini) but it is now clear that this proposition is no longer tenable. (For further discussion see p 19.) Other explanations refer to internal warfare on Crete or conquest by invaders from the other great Bronze Age civilisation of the region, from Mycenae in the Peloponnese. At Knossós itself, however, there was a certain amount of damage but no wholesale fire destruction at this time, either of the palace or of the great dependent buildings. To the following LMII period belongs the Throne Room complex as it now appears, and the palace, and at least parts of the main dependent buildings, continued to be used (despite still further fire destruction in LMIIIA) through LMIIIB.

From the LMIIIA destruction debris came large numbers of clay tablets in the script known as Linear B, accidentally baked and thus preserved for posterity. In contrast to the Minoan Linear A language, which is not yet satisfactorily deciphered, this B script is an early form of Greek. Linear B tablets are well known from Pylos and Mycenae on the mainland, though apparently in later contexts (with Late

Helladic IIIB material). The Knossós tablets are concerned with the production and movement of commodities over a large area of the island, reflecting the organisational role of the palace at the time of the destruction.

The LMII period at Knossós saw a development in pottery decoration which has been called the Palace style. The naturalistic LMI vase painting, generally agreed to represent the epitome of Minoan art, is replaced by a strikingly formalised handling (often of the same motifs as before) in a style which is akin to mainland decoration of this period.

The combination of the Linear B tablets and this abrupt change in pottery decoration has led most archaeologists to accept that LMII–IIIA Knossós was inhabited by mainland Greeks, and became for a time the administrative centre of Mycenaean Crete.

Limited reoccupation in LMIIIB is attested by, for example, the Shrine of the Double Axes and the remains of massive walls along the South Front of the palace, as well as by evidence in the Little Palace and the 'Unexplored Mansion' a short distance away.

Near the staircase of the palace propylaea Evans found what he thought was a small Classical temple, but probably other evidence from the later history of the palace was swept aside in the enthusiastic haste to reach the prehistoric levels. Later remains lie thick all over the Knossós region, but it has been suggested that a tradition of sacred ground grew up around the palace site, possibly fostered by the myth of the Minotaur and the Labyrinth. This word may derive from the Greek 'labrys' meaning double axe. Both the bull and the labyrinth became standard symbols on the coins of later Knossós.

The *cemeteries* for the great settlement seem to have lain outside the inhabited area, on the hillsides that surround the site. Those so far known do not cover the entire Minoan history of Knossós for the earliest is a MMIA tomb on the acropolis hill to the west. Other MM graves were excavated in the opposite direction, on the Ailias slope to the east across the Kaíratos. As is the case with the rest of Crete, few LMI tombs have come to light, but rich LMII–LMIII graves have been excavated (from Evans's time on) to the north towards the coast: at Ayios Ioánnis, on the site of the general hospital (Venizéleion), at Zápher Papoúra and Sellópoulo. Some contained splendidly furnished burials of warriors, perhaps the Mycenaean successors of the Minoan rulers who vanished at the time of the LMI destruction of the palace. Similar but poorer groups of tombs have been found south of the settlement at various points on the Gypsádes hill. These scattered LM cemeteries might represent family burial plots on individual estates in the immediate vicinity of the town.

In the Early Iron Age there was settlement along the Royal Road (see area plan p 94) and the focus of the Geometric town seems to have moved to this locality, north and west of the palace. Recently a major excavation on the edge of the modern village, under the auspices of the British School (P. Warren), has resulted in a greatly improved understanding of the sequence of occupation.

However the best evidence so far for a flourishing settlement at this time comes from richly endowed burials of the Knossós North Cemetery (on the site now occupied by university and hospital buildings along the road from Herákleion—see above). For this, the main burial ground of the Early Iron Age, Late Minoan chamber tombs, conveniently available, were methodically cleared before re-use, a few receiving burials as early as the Subminoan period. Changes in burial practices—particularly the earliest (10C) cremations—and in the accompanying grave gifts are taken to indicate the arrival of Dorians from the mainland.

Among the finds a 10C bronze bowl, from one of a small group of Geometric tombs on the north edge of the cemetery is of special interest; it carries what is perhaps the earliest Phoenician inscription yet found in Greek lands (Herákleion Museum, Gallery XI, Case 155).

The richest tombs in the cemetery were from the Geometric and Orientalising periods, when grave offerings included quantities of pottery, many bronze and iron weapons and ornaments, a little gold jewellery, and luxury items of faience from the eastern Mediterranean region. Among the pottery, imports were identified from Athens, eastern Greece, the Cyclades and Cyprus.

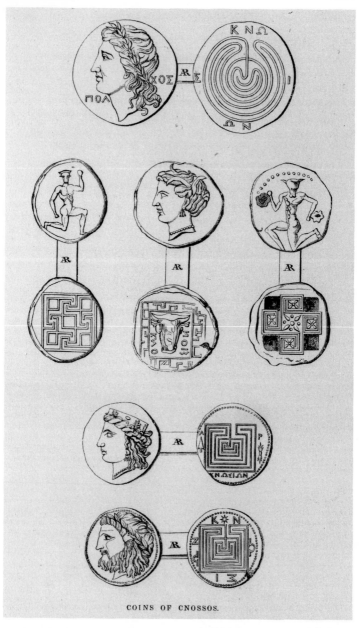

COINS OF CNOSSOS.

Coins of Greco-Roman Knossós (from Pashley, Travels in Crete, 1837)

Parts of the palace site became sanctuary areas. Near Evans's Classical temple there is now evidence for a possible hero cult dating from as early as the Proto-geometric period (10C BC). The Spring Chamber near the Minoan Caravanserai (see area plan) was frequented for cult purposes in the Subminoan period until votive offerings ceased when the water from the spring dried up. Finds including a goddess with raised arms and a hut-urn suggest that the Dorian newcomers did not prevent a revival of the Minoan vegetation cult.

On the lower slope of Gypsádes hill (just across the modern road from the Cara-vanserai), the Sanctuary of Demeter, goddess of the fruits of the earth, carried on the religious tradition and was an important place of worship from the late 8C down to the 2C AD. The sanctuary, with a huge deposit of terracottas, was exca-vated by the British School under N. Coldstream (1957–60); the dedication to Demeter was established by an inscription on an Early Hellenistic silver ring.

The use of chamber tombs, characteristic of the Geometric and Orientalising periods, ended abruptly around 600 BC. The vicissitudes of the period are not com-pletely understood, and Dorian Knossós may have suffered a temporary eclipse, but it certainly emerged as one of the leading Greco-Roman city-states, vying with Lýttos and Górtyn for domination of the centre of the island.

In the 3C BC Knossós was a member of the loose federation of Cretan cities known as the Koinon. The Greek city, like its Roman successor, lay to the north of the palace site, and there is no evidence that it ever resorted to defensive walls, as did many of its contemporaries.

The Roman Conquest (67 BC) must have been a mixed blessing for Knossós. The Pax Romana brought stability and prosperity to the island, but Knossós had to yield pride of place to its old rival Górtyn, now the capital city of Crete and Cyrenaica. Some 40 years after the conquest Knossós became the only Roman colony on Crete, with the title Colonia Julia Nobilis Cnossus, and this would have involved adjust-ment to a new ruling class. A new type of rock-cut chamber tomb with three side-niches for burials may have been introduced from Italy by the Roman colonists.

Until recently little of the Roman city had been excavated and almost nothing remains above ground, but now an archaeological survey in progress will lead to excavations so that radical improvements in the state of knowledge are to be expected. The usual large public buildings are recorded and an aqueduct bringing water from the hills to the south; also temples, including an Asklepieion, and many fine houses embellished with mosaic floors and statuary. The already excavated Villa Dionysos has pavements of a quality unusual on Crete.

Christian churches were built at Knossós. Two basilicas have been excavated to the north of the Roman city, one a large mortuary church (5C) and the other a martyrion (early 6C) built over Christian graves. The Bishop of Knossós was present at early Councils of the Church in 431, 451 and 787. As the threat of Arab raids increased, the city's undefended position near the sea probably contributed to a decline in importance. After the Arab Conquest in 824 fortified Rabdh el Khandak (modern Herakleion) became the principal settlement on the island and henceforth dominated the Knossós area.

Tour of the palace

Open daily: 08.00–18.00 (Saturdays, Sundays and holidays 08.30–15.00); winter 10.00–sunset. Charge for entry (and for photography with tripod equipment or video filming). Admission is only to the palace and the Minoan houses in the imme-diate vicinity. Outside the fence all the main dependent sites, the Little Palace, the Royal Villa, the Temple Tomb (see below) are closed to the public.

Evans's reconstructions at Knossós have sometimes provoked controversy among professional archaeologists, but they give the lay visitor an immediate impression of the extent and the lavish conception of Minoan palatial architecture. Ideally Knossós should be the first palace site a visitor explores, because its partial recon-struction helps towards understanding the excavations at Phaistós, Mállia, Zákros and Gourniá. Minoan palaces are laid out around a main Central Court (and usually with other subsidiary courts); they have rooms for ritual activity as well as state or reception rooms, also production areas, substantial storage facilities and a Linear A administrative archive. All these attributes will be identified during this tour.

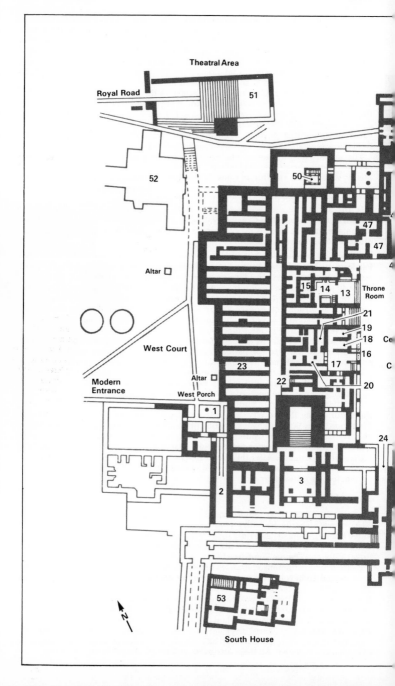

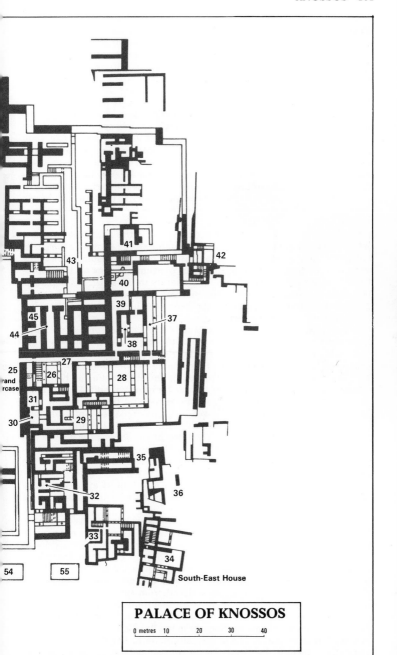

41
42
43
40
39
37
45
44
38
25
Grand
Staircase
27
26
28
31
30
29
35
32
36
33
34
South-East House
54
55

PALACE OF KNOSSOS

0 metres   10   20   30   40

The modern approach to the palace leads by a trellised path to the paved **West Court** (see main plan). The last stretch of the Minoan *ramp* is visible in the cutting to the right of the path. The bust of Sir Arthur Evans (the gift of the municipality of Herákleion) surveys his formidable achievement, and many visitors have felt that a nod of gratitude does not come amiss.

The paving of the West Court is crossed by *raised walks*, part original stone, part restored. The right hand walk directs you to the West Entrance. But notice first (left) three walled pits known from their circular shape as *kouloúras*; they were probably designed as granaries. When the court was extended at the end of the Old Palace period they were filled with rubbish including much broken pottery of high quality, and were paved over. At the bottom of the central pit you can see some remains of a house of MMIA date, the period immediately before the construction of the Old Palace, so this feature is one of the earliest (c 2000 BC) now visible on the site. A flight of steps leads down to the foundations of a room. Both the floor surfaces and the walls were found rendered with red plaster.

The Court runs up to the *West Façade*. Behind the *altar base*, a recess in the façade would have held a window in the storey above. The massive wall rests on a levelling course, and is faced with gypsum blocks now severely weathered. There are Minoan gypsum quarries on the appropriately named hill of Gypsádes immediately to the south of the palace. The signs of burning on the façade indicate that, at the time of the great fire that devastated the palace at the end of the LMIIIA period, the wind was from this southerly direction.

In the corner of the Court is the *West Entrance and Porch* (1 on plan), preserving the massive gypsum base of its single column, and an inner room with a red plaster floor. To the right (west) are the excavated remains of later houses. From the Porch, huge wooden doors opened into the *Corridor of the Procession Fresco* (2). The sockets for the doorposts remain, and between them is a small hole for a central bolt. The Corridor was paved with gypsum flagstones (the remaining fragments now very worn) which were flanked by blue schist set in red plaster. Unfortunately, part of this imposing processional way is lost owing to the erosion of the hillside here, but originally the Corridor of the Procession Fresco led south before turning left and left again, describing three sides of a rectangle to reach either the main ceremonial rooms of the palace, or the Central Court.

Where the coloured floor of the Corridor now falls away (at a modern flight of steps) the *South House* (53) can be seen in the valley below (details after palace tour).

Unable to follow the original route, you keep left to pass through a reconstructed doorway beside a restored column. The downward taper is a typical feature of Minoan architecture. One branch of the Corridor of the Procession Fresco would have turned left to enter the *South Propylaea* (3), a monumental roofed gateway supported by four huge columns. One corner has been restored and column bases indicate the ground plan. The fresco copy is a detail from the Procession Fresco, including the so-called 'Cup-bearer' (original fragments restored in Herákleion Museum, Gallery XIV). The figures strikingly resemble those of the Keftiu (Minoans) bearing offerings to the Pharoah on the walls of 18th Dynasty Egyptian tombs. The large restored *horns of consecration*, right, originally crowned the south façade of the palace. (There a second branch of the Corridor of the Procession Fresco turned left into the Central Court—see 24 on plan.)

From the 'Cup-bearer' fresco a monumental staircase ascends to the *Upper Propylaea* (4 on plan of Upper Floor). To the right was a small temple of the Classical period, but in the course of excavation this was removed. The staircase leads to Evans's 'Piano Nobile', where the grand state apartments and reception halls probably lay. Evans restored this Upper Floor on the evidence of architectural elements such as column bases, door jambs, paving slabs and steps, which had collapsed into the floor below. Moreover, the thickness of the walls of the lower storey helped to indicate where the upper walls should be. A *Porticoed Vestibule* leads to a *Tri-columnar Hall* (5), off which is a small room (6), Evans's *Central Treasury*; it was thought to have held a collection of important stone rhytons, including the Lioness Head Rhyton, and other ritual vessels (now exhibited in the Herákleion Museum) which were found in the debris below.

The *Upper Long Corridor* (7) ran north with rooms opening from it on both sides. In the reconstruction, a gap allows you to look down into the impressive *storeroom block* (8) below. The so-called 'Long Corridor of the Magazines' has 18 storerooms opening off it (22 and 23 on the main plan). The large jars, or pithoi, indicate the palace's storage capacity for such commodities as grain, oil and wine; the blackening of the gypsum slabs at the entrance to some of the storerooms is a reminder of how fiercely the oil must have burnt at the time of the destruction. For increased storage capacity during the life of the New Palace, cists or chests were sunk in the floor. The pyramidal stone stands in the Corridor would have held double axes on poles, as portrayed on the Ayía Triáda stone sarcophagus in Herákleion Museum, Gallery XIV.

From the columnar *Hall* (5) a staircase (11) leads down to the Central Court, but it is better to keep to the Upper Long Corridor (7). On the left was a large hall (9) with two central columns, opening north into a smaller hall with six columns. Opposite this, across the Corridor, is a series of rooms in one of which (10) are hung modern copies of some of the palace frescoes.

From the left inside the door:
1. Two panels of the Miniature Frescoes. Note the tripartite shrine portrayed on the upper panel.
2. The 'Ladies in Blue'.
3. The Bull-leaper.
4. The 'Captain of the Blacks'.
5, 6, 7 and 8 are from the 'House of the Frescoes': scenes from the Blue Monkey fresco and the much-illustrated 'Blue Bird'.

You are now above the Throne Room, and can look down into the Lustral Basin beside it. From the terrace outside, a small private staircase (12) descends (left) to the Central Court near the Throne Room complex of this *West Wing*. (The rounded corner, left at the bottom of the stairs, is one of the surviving elements of the Old Palace ground plan.)

The area for the **Central Court** was levelled at the time of the construction of the Old Palace in MMIB. The Court, c 50m by 25m and aligned north-north-east by south-south-west as at Phaistós and Mállia, was originally paved. A section of its drainage system is exposed under grilles in the north-west angle of the court, where you are now standing (see main plan). In this same area the excavators found an inscribed fragment of an

Egyptian diorite statuette; its Middle Kingdom date was one of the pieces of evidence that Evans used to establish the absolute chronology of Minoan Crete. The inscription gives the name of the figure represented as User, who must have been an eminent visitor to Knossós, possibly an ambassador from Egypt.

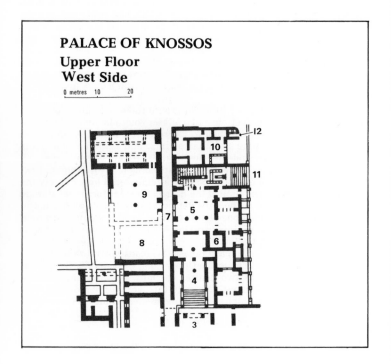

PALACE OF KNOSSOS
Upper Floor
West Side

0 metres   10   20

There is an Antechamber (13) in front of the Throne Room, with gypsum benches along two walls (and replica throne). The fine purple limestone basin was found in the passage immediately to the north. The *Throne Room* (14) is fenced off, but from the threshold you can see the original gypsum *throne* flanked by benches and guarded by painted griffins (remains of original fresco in Herákleion Museum, Gallery XIV). The floor is crazy paving bordered by regular gypsum flagstones. Opposite the throne is the *Lustral Basin* with steps leading down into it, seen already from the floor above. On the floor of the destroyed Throne Room Evans found overturned jars, and large flat gypsum alabastrons, evidence for him of a dramatic scene during the final moments of the palace. Behind the Throne Room was the small *Inner Sanctuary* (15).

Though Evans concentrated attention on the LMII remodelling of the Throne Room, recent research has recognised that its history goes back to the MMII Old Palace, and has tentatively distinguished four building phases which are likely to reflect changes in function. For Minoan times modern thinking emphasises the religious and cult aspects of this suite of rooms, even envisaging (from hints on Minoan seals and wall-paintings) an epiphany ritual with a priestess, robed in the inner sanctuary, appearing as goddess between the painted griffins. In the final reconstruction the lustral basin was filled in, and with other changes from a sacred to an administrative character in this area, it appears that the Throne Room may have become the megaron or hall of ceremonies of the Mycenaean ruler of Knossós.

Tripartite Shrine, Knossós. Reconstruction by M.A.S. Cameron from the Temple Grandstand Miniature Fresco

South from the Throne Room you pass the broad staircase (11) noted from the Upper Floor. In the Minoan building phase, the sanctity of this area of the West Wing was emphasised by a *Tripartite Shrine* (16) similar to the one portrayed on the Miniature Frescoes (original in the Herákleion Museum, copy already noticed here above Throne Room). Pairs of columns on the façade flanked a block supporting a single column, all shielding the sanctuary behind. On a gold ring from Arkhánes and a steatite vase from Zákros, as well as in fresco paintings, this type of shrine is shown to have a significant role in Minoan ceremonies. The particular one here in the Central Court had probably ceased to exist before the time of the LMIIIA destruction.

Next is the Lobby of the Stone Seat (17), referred to in its later phases as the *Room of the Column Bases*, which leads, right, to the Room of the Tall Pithos (18) and the *Temple Repositories* (19). Two large cists or stone chests with lids were sunk under the floor here in the early days of the New Palace. (The smaller box between them is a later addition.) Note the careful tight construction of the Repositories, suitable for precious objects, and peg holes indicating the interior fittings.

When this room was first excavated the chests were not found, and only when the floor began to sag the following year was their presence suspected. In the Repository nearer the Court Evans found the well-known faience figurines of the Snake Goddesses, with other furnishings of a shrine now on display with them in Herákleion Museum, Gallery IV. The other large chest had been robbed, but traces of gold leaf remained and Evans put forward the theory that its precious objects had been taken to the mainland, perhaps to find their way into the Mycenae shaft graves much of whose contents has long been considered to be of Cretan workmanship.

From the Lobby of the Stone Seat (17) you can look into the outer of the two Pillar Crypts (20). Double-axe incisions on the pillars reinforce religious significance, and troughs in the floor were thought to be for liquid offerings. Pillar crypts, dark and mysterious, seem to play an important part in Minoan ritual connected with shrines and sacred treasuries. (In the Vat Room (21) off the east—nearer—crypt Evans found a further small treasure hoard of MMIA date, c 2000 BC, which confirmed the early sanctity of this area.)

The gypsum-paved passage from (17) (Room of the Column Bases) along the south side of the crypts, is now closed off by a gate at its far end, but it was originally designed to afford and perhaps control access from the Central Court into the main Storeroom Block (22 and 23)—already noticed from above. (Evans's 'Long Corridor of the Magazines' can be seen through the locked gate.)

For the Minoans the architectural evidence shows that this access was clearly associated with one of the most sacred areas of the palace. From the later Mycenaean times the Linear B archive found at the Court end of the Corridor (i.e. 17 on plan) deals with the arrival and despatch of olive oil, and begins to build up a picture of different priorities and an emphasis on administrative functions in this important area. Other deposits of tablets in the West Wing refer to textile production and aromatics. Similarities occur in the evidence of architecture and ritual at the other palace sites concerning the control of access to vitally important storage capacity.

Adjacent—south—of the Room of the Column Bases is the *Room of the Chariot Tablets* (nearest the Court, with stone benches). Here a further archive of Linear B tablets was found with the evidence for wooden boxes in which they had been stored, together with a number of seal impressions. In the large room behind (to the west) of this, immediately south of the paved corridor, Evans found a number of Minoan stone vases of ritual type which he concluded had fallen with debris from the Central Treasury above when the upper floor collapsed in the LMIII destruction. However it is now suggested that the vases may have been stored where they were found, as a valued collection of rarities of superb quality, antique already in Mycenaean times.

At the southern end of the Court (24) a replica of the well-known Priest-King figure from the Procession Fresco stands poised to lead the procession into the Central Court. (One academic article puts forward the iconoclastic suggestion that this figure should be interpreted as a boxer.) Fragments of the floor pattern noticed at the start of the Procession Corridor are preserved also here at the end of it.

You now cross the angle of the court to the *East Wing* to descend the ***Grand Staircase** (25) to the *Domestic Quarter*. (The gypsum block passed in the court is the base of an observation tower used during the excavation.)

The gypsum staircase is one of the masterpieces of Minoan architecture. Four gentle flights are preserved, with the landings, and there is evidence for a fifth flight above. This side of the palace is built into the slope of the hill, which had partially retained the staircase and buildings as they collapsed. The Shield Fresco on the first balcony depicts the ox hides stretched and sewn on a figure-of-eight frame which Evans thought hung in the Hall of the Double Axes below. The Upper East–West Corridor leads past the fresco out to the Upper Hall of the Double Axes, where only the ground plan is restored. A LMII fresco fragment was found here—part of a larger-than-life leg and foot of a bull (now in the Herákleion Museum). Linear B tablets found in the Corridor were referred to by Evans as the 'percentage tablets' because the figures on them tended to add up to 100. They are now seen to deal with very large flocks of sheep, and administration connected with the wool industry. It is noted that a fight of steps from the east could have provided convenient access for dealings with the outside world.

The Grand Staircase descends again, to a suite of rooms at the bottom of the light-well which from their scale and elegance seem designed for the ruler or rulers of the palace. From the staircase you pass (right) into the Hall of the Colonnades (26). Continuing ahead along the Lower East-West Corridor (27) a second right turn takes you into the *King's Megaron* also known as the *Hall of the Double Axes* (28) because of the distinctive masons' marks on the ashlar blocks of the adjacent light-well. (One can be distinguished on the opposite wall of the well, at eye level right of centre.) The Hall is a large double room opening off the light-well, and at the far end is a broad L-shaped portico, sheltered from Crete's prevailing winds. The double doors give great flexibility to this room space, and the balance of pillars and columns is architecturally effective. Scorched remnants are preserved of what may be a plaster-backed throne.

From the south-west corner of this Hall you pass by a dogleg passage to the *Queen's Megaron* (29) with its Dolphin and LMII rosette fresco (original in Herákleion Museum, Gallery XIV). A strong body of opinion now holds that this was floor decoration. Stone benches line the portico walls and a verandah gives on to a light-well. Below the floor, near the LMI jar, part of the irregular paving of the Old Palace floor can be seen. Alongside the Queen's Megaron is a *bathroom*, with clay tub. Beside the bathroom a narrow corridor leads to a *toilet* (30) with a drainage system to allow flushing. Light is provided from the adjacent Court of the Distaffs (31), again named for the masons' marks on its wall.

Return to the Queen's Room (29) and leave the 'Domestic Quarter' by the Queen's Verandah. There is an alternative staircase up from the Hall of the Colonnades; at very busy periods you may have to follow a circular one-way route.

To visit the south-east area of the palace climb the steps on the right outside the Queen's Verandah to find (roofed and gated for protection) the tiny postpalatial *Shrine of the Double Axes* (32), of LMIIIB (13C) date. Miniature horns of consecration and terracotta figurines with drum-shaped bases were found on the ledge at the back, and clay vases lay scattered on the pebble floor in front of them. The small corridor immediately west of the shrine was named the *Corridor of the Sword Tablets* after an important find of tablets of this class with Linear B inscriptions. Before leaving this part of the palace you may visit the *House of the Chancel Screen* (33), the *South-East House* (34) (see below), both MMIII–LMI buildings, the MMIA Monolithic Pillar basement (35) and a Minoan (LMI–II) kiln (36).

The **South-East House** is reached down a double flight of stairs. On the north side of the house is a *pillar room* with two double-axe stands and a wall niche, also a cist let into the floor. The main rooms on the south side opened off a *peristyle court* or miniature cloister, its covered walk paved with gypsum, the open centre with more weather-resistant stone. Note an interior wall of gypsum slabs laid on end.

For a shorter visit keep left (round to the north) from the Queen's Verandah, past the broad porticoed *terrace* of the King's Megaron. The terrace was noted before from the interior of the King's Megaron (Hall of the Double Axes). You walk through to the *East Portico* (37), and find the corridor behind and parallel to it (west) which passes a small storeroom (38) with blocks of Spartan basalt (lapis Lacedaemonius), raw material for stone vases and seals imported from the sole source near Sparta in the Peloponnese. The corridor opens into Evans's 'School Room' (with a bench along the wall) which was probably a craftsman's workshop (39), and you cross this to the *Court of the Stone Spout* (40). Ahead are the *Magazines of the Giant Pithoi* (41), with mighty vases dating from the Old Palace (MMII c 1800 BC) and beyond them to the north were the Royal Pottery Stores, also MMII.

A staircase descends to the *East Bastion* (42) above the East Entrance. A stone water channel descends beside the steps, in a series of parabolic curves and small settling basins to break the flow of storm water and debris down the steep slope.

Ascending the stairway past the Giant Pithoi and an area which may have been stalls for animals, you reach the *Corridor of the Draught-Board* (43) where the magnificent inlaid gaming board was found (Herákleion Museum, Gallery IV). Below the corridor the clay pipes of the palace's elaborate drainage system are visible: notice how they taper (in this case to produce a greater head of water). From the corridor you pass a stone drain (which runs into the Court of the Stone Spout) to enter the Magazine of the Medallion Pithoi (44). A similar pithos in stone was found in the Tomb of Klytemnestra at Mycenae. From here you could return to the Grand Staircase along the *Corridor of the Bays* (45), the thick walls of which must have supported spacious rooms above, but a staircase (before the corridor, right) leads back up to the Central Court.

Cross the Court diagonally to leave it by the North Entrance Passage (46). To the left was a complex of rooms (47) in which the Saffron Gatherer Fresco and Miniature Frescoes were found. Below these rooms were MMI stone-lined pits, perhaps granaries, or dungeons as Evans thought; on account of its massive construction he called this area the North Keep. The *North Entrance* is dominated by the intimidating stucco relief of a charging bull (48) (remains of original in Herákleion Museum, Gallery XIV). For the New Palace this entrance was narrowed, and the North Pillar Hall (49), with double row of gypsum pillars, was added outside it. Turn left, past the North Portico to the *North Lustral Basin* (50), where careful restoration has provided a clear example of these typically Minoan features. Signs of burning on the gypsum facing, and the oil jars found in the MMIII destruction material suggest a ritual of cleansing and annointing before entry to the palace. Near the Lustral Basin was found the alabaster lid with a cartouche of the Egyptian Hyksos King Khyan—an important clue to dating the construction of the New Palace.

The stepped *Theatral Area* (51) is superimposed on the *Royal Road* and looks west along it; it has been suggested that the area had a role in the welcoming of visitors. The road, with central flags bordered by drains, continues west into the Minoan town of Knossós and a branch turns north to the Little Palace. A further stretch was picked up 200m west of the modern (Herákleion) road.

The Royal Road was lined with houses, perhaps similar to those portrayed on the faience plaques of the 'Town Mosaic' (see Herákleion Museum, Gallery II) found in Middle Minoan levels in the palace. On the left was the (MMIII) *House of the Frescoes* where Evans discovered the stack of fragile slabs of painted plaster now pieced together in the Herákleion Museum, including the striking 'Blue Bird' scene. The right (north) side of the road was the site of the Arsenal or Armoury.

Beside the Armoury further excavations in 1957–61 produced pottery deposits from EMII to LMIII, as well as a fine series of ivories of LMIB date. Excavations (1971–73) along the left side of the road have revealed building remains stretching from EMII (mid-third millenium BC) to the 4C AD, and at the far end traces of another similar road leading off south. Built at the same time as the Old Palace, around 1900 BC, these Knossós examples are among the earliest urban roads in Europe.

You can return to the West Court past the gypsum horns of consecration (broken) and the scant remains of the North-West Treasure House (52) where a rich hoard of bronze vessels was found.

The South House (53) merits a visit, as do the House of the Sacrificed Oxen (54) and the House of the Fallen Blocks (55), named after the massive blocks of masonry hurled into it from the palace's south façade during the violent earthquake which destroyed the Old Palace.

The *South House* is now reached by steps from the Corridor of the Procession Fresco, but in Minoan times it lay beside the road leaving the palace towards the southern part of the island and the harbours on the Libyan Sea. The building, partially restored on three levels, is set in a deep cutting (down into Neolithic and Early Minoan levels) which preserved up to eight courses of its back wall. The reconstruction includes several typical features of Minoan domestic architecture: a hall with central paving bordered by gypsum flagstones and related to a lustral basin and adjacent light-well; a pillar-room with stands for a double axe and for other cult furniture or offerings; basements constructed as pillar crypts. The original entrance was at the south-east corner.

South across the valley Evans's Caravanserai marks the line of the imposing southern entrance to the palace by way of the Minoan viaduct and the Stepped Portico. Sadly this area is now closed to the public, as are all the other great dependent buildings listed below (see area plan p 94). In some cases a little can be seen from outside the fences.

A modern path from beyond the bridge on the main road leads down to the *Caravanserai*. Springs feed a shallow trough or footbath and the adjacent hall was decorated with the much-illustrated partridge and hoopoe fresco (original in the Herákleion Museum). Just outside (to the west) is the small *Spring Chamber*, with basin and a niche in the back wall, perhaps for a lamp, and ledges for offerings. This was the setting for a vegetation cult in Postpalatial and Subminoan times (see also p 99). The Caravanserai is interpreted as a resting-place for those approaching Knossós from the south before they followed the road across the great viaduct (remains of foundations dating back to MMI) and up the ramp and Stepped Portico to the palace.

Along the main road to the south is the *House of the High Priest* (below the road on the left) with a stone altar set behind a columnar balustrade between stands for double axes. Further, c 1km from the bridge at the end of the village, on the right-hand side, is the partly reconstructed *Temple Tomb*, built in MMIII but remaining in use until the final destruction of the palace. An open paved court led to the Inner Hall and Pillar Crypt, beyond which was the Sepulchral Chamber. From the Inner Hall there was a small stairway to the upper floor which consisted of a two-columned room. The masonry of the lower rooms is excellently preserved. (No public access.)

North-east of the palace is the *Royal Villa*, built in MMIII. The track circumnavigating the palace affords a grandstand view over the excavation. The main hall, fronted by a portico with two columns, has a gypsum balustrade at its inner end and a throne set in the wall behind it. A fine purple stone lamp stood in the opening. To the north of this hall is a *Pillar Crypt* in which the slots in the masonry for the roof beams are visible. From here a stairway leads to the upper floor. To the south of the hall is another ascending staircase; on its landing was found a magnificent LMII Palace style jar (Herákleion Museum) with papyrus in relief.

The *Little Palace* lies on the right of the main road from Herákleion just before the village of Knossós is reached. This building (unfortunately always closed to the public), the largest explored at Knossós after the main palace, consists of a series of stately halls on the east side, including a *peristyle hall* or court (comparable to that at Phaistós). The east façade seems to have had a columned portico. To the west is a complex of smaller rooms and a staircase with two flights preserved. North of this a Lustral Area was used as a shrine—the *Fetish Shrine*—in the later (LMIII) period, with rough-hewn stones as images In this reoccupation phase the columned balustrade was walled up, thus preserving the impression of the convex fluting of the earlier columns. At the north end of the building is a paved lavatory served by a drain behind it running east–west. The south end of the palace consists of a series of *Pillar Crypts*. The one in the south-west corner has a tiny walled recess on its north side in which were found the famous *Bull's Head Rhyton* (Herákleion Museum, Gallery IV), a double-axe stand, and other ritual objects. The Little Palace was built in MMIII and finally destroyed at the time of the great LMIII fire in the main palace; as in the main palace, Linear B tablets were found in the debris.

Immediately to the west, and linked to the Little Palace by a masonry bridge, Evans uncovered the façade of another great building which he named the *'Unexplored Mansion'*. From 1967 to 1973 this site was comprehensively excavated by the British School (M. Popham and H. Sackett) revealing a well-planned complex of rooms, pillar basement, staircases and storerooms. The Unexplored Mansion turned out to have been constructed after the Little Palace but some unified purpose is suggested by attempts to harmonise the orientation and appearance of the two buildings. After a LMII destruction by fire (which did not affect the Little Palace) the poorly preserved northern half of the mansion had been reoccupied in LMIII, but the southern half had never been cleared, and was filled with fine-quality painted pottery, stone vases, stone and clay tools and implements. (There is a good exhibit, including a goddess figurine, in Herákleion Museum, Gallery V.) Much scrap bronze, with a number of clay crucibles, suggested a bronze foundry located in or near the building, and a shrine on the upper floor may have been connected with this activity. This excavation contributed valuable evidence for the arrival of the Mycenaeans at Knossós at the beginning of LMII, some 50 years before the palace was destroyed in LMIIIA, but it is emphasised that much, particularly in the realm of religious practice, remains essentially Minoan.

West of the palace, further excavations (P. Warren, 1978–82) revealed a continuation of the Minoan *town* of Knossós, dating from the first period of urban expansion (MMIA) before the founding of the Old Palace, and with uninterrupted occupation through the Middle and Late Minoan periods. Most important is the discovery of a LMI house (destroyed at the end of that period) which, to judge from its contents of fine ritual pottery, was used as a cult centre. In a basement room of this house were found the bones of at least three children; ten per cent of these (unburnt) bones show knife-cut marks which indicate that the flesh had been deliberately cut away.

The excavator suggests that in this context the most likely explanation is connected with some form of offering to the gods, possibly even preparations for a ritual meal.

As was the case with the remains of the Little Palace and 'Unexplored Mansion', Minoan levels at this town site were in places much disturbed by overlying Dark Age, Hellenistic and Roman building belonging to the later phases in the history of Knossós.

3 Excursions from Herákleion

A. To Týlissos, Anóyia and the Idaian Cave

A quiet country road, 13.5km to the Minoan villas at Týlissos, and on to 33km (20.5 miles) Anóyia on the north flank of Mount Ida.

You can continue via Axós to join the Réthymnon–Herákleion road (Rte 11B) for a round trip from Herákleion of c 100km (63 miles).

From Anóyia up to the Nída plain and the Idaian cave (at 1500m) it is 20km on a mountain road—conditions variable according to season.

Two short excursions from Herákleion to Krousónas and Rogdiá are also described.

Buses: five daily to Anóyia, from the bus station outside the Khaniá gate. Reduced Sunday service.

Leave Herákleion to the west by the Khaniá Gate on the Old Road to Réthymnon (Rte 11B), keeping straight on past the major junction with the north coast highway.

1km further, a right fork keeps parallel to the sea, with access through an area of piecemeal holiday developments to a long beach. This area may be reached on some of the No. 6 town buses, which serve a clutch of large hotels at the far end of the beach. (See Herákleion bus information.)

The Old Road continues through *Gázi*, site of the LMIII (postpalatial) shrine from which came impressive clay figures now displayed in Herákleion Museum (Gallery X). One goddess, 75cm tall, in the typical position with arms raised, has three poppy-heads in her crown.

Just after Gázi you pass under a bridge carrying the highway and, with urban sprawl left behind, can look forward to spectacular views of Mount Ida; in the high crevasses the snow often lies until June.

For a recommended short excursion to the mountains above *Krousónas* (c 50km round trip from Herákleion) leave the Old Road at the junction just beyond the bridge. The narrow but surfaced road winds up the valley between vineyards before turning towards the peaks. The village, hidden till the final approach, is dramatically situated across the head of a valley and the main street sweeps round in front of the church. Continue to the end of the village and then keep right, signed 3km to *Ayía Eiríne*. The nunnery buildings (destroyed by the Turks in the 1821 rebellion) were only reconstructed during the last 50 years, but they stand in tranquil isolation at 700m on the last cultivated slopes before the bare rock of the pass over to Zominthós and the Nída plain (Rte 3A).

Continuing from the highway bridge on the Old Road to Réthymnonon, at c 8km from Herákleion a by-road to the right (signed) loops back to the highway and then climbs (6km) to Rogdiá and to the Savathianá nunnery—another recommended short excursion from Herákleion (c 45km round trip, direct by the New Road and leaving it to hug the shore at the cement works and jetty just before the Pandanássa bridge, Rte 11A).

Rogdiá clings to the hillside 300m above the sea with magnificent coastal views, and taverna terraces from which to enjoy them. The village was part of a Venetian feudal estate, and the ruined façade of a grand house can still be seen near the church. You can continue (signed, sharp uphill left at the beginning of the village, and after 1km curve right to follow round the flank of the hill) 5km north-west into cultivated uplands to the Savathianá monastery founded during the Venetian period. A community of more than 20 nuns now flourishes here and proudly welcomes visitors to one of the most delightful gardens on Crete, in the shade of trees alive with songbirds. The road ends at the gates of the nunnery (open: 08.00–13.00 and 16.00–19.00) with a red-roofed church in view against the cliffs across the valley.

The nunnery's main church, dating from 1635, is dedicated to the Panayía (the birth of the Virgin, festival 8 September), but c 200m along a path through the garden, the red-roofed Ayios Antónios protects the grotto which was the original nucleus of the monastery. The path crosses an old bridge (inscription 1535) where springs feed a stream.

The road continues through Rogdiá village (rough in places) to the north coast highway (Rte 11A), for Ayía Pelagía by the sea, or on to Akhláda and Phódele.

At 10.5km from Herákleion on the Old Road to Réthymnon, branch off left towards Týlissos. This is the Malevísi district, famous at least from Venetian times for the strong sweet wine known as Malmsey which found its way to western Europe. These same fertile slopes must also have contributed to the prosperity of prehistoric Týlissos, which lay on the route from Knossós to the west of Crete by the northern foothills of Mount Ida.

13.5km. The pleasant village of **Týlissos** preserves its prehellenic name, which occurs on Linear B tablets as tu-ri-so. The Minoan villas are on the edge of the modern village, signposted from the main street left and left again. They were excavated (1902–13) by J. Khatzidákis after the chance find of the great bronze cauldrons now on display in Herákleion Museum, Gallery VII. More recently N. Pláton reinvestigated the site. (Open: daily 08.30–15.00, closed only on public holidays. Small entrance charge.)

Týlissos was inhabited in the Early Bronze Age, and there are traces of MMI occupation (c 2000 BC), but of the excavated remains interest centres on three large MMIII–LMI houses contemporary with the New Palace at Knossós. Probably these should be thought of not as an isolated group of country houses but as part of the wealthy area of a prosperous town (comparable to Palaíkastro in eastern Crete) flourishing at the height of the Minoan civilisation. The LMI finds were numerous and of the same high quality as material from the palaces; many are on show in Herákleion Museum (Gallery VII) including a bronze statuette of an older man in the typical votary position, hand to forehead. A number of large clay storage jars had survived.

After the destruction of the Minoan villas at the end of LMI there was considerable reoccupation of the site in the LMIII period, including the building of a big circular cistern at the north-east corner. There was also later Greek Classical period occupation and Týlissos at this time was an independent city-state with its own coins. Thus the excavated remains of the three original Minoan buildings (dense black on the plan) are complicated by vestiges of earlier and later construction.

House A is the most easily intelligible of the three. Its plan (max. dimensions 35m by 18m) consists of two blocks or wings, linked by a partially covered court.

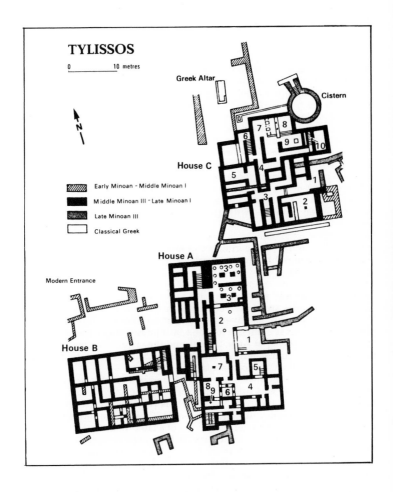

You can walk right, round the south edge of the site, to appreciate the finely dressed ashlar masonry and to reach House A's *entrance*, an angled passage leading into a small paved court (1 on plan). The passage, now restored, had been cut into by LMIII reoccupation walls. On two sides of the court (west and north) was an L-shaped *peristyle* (2); note the central column base, pithos stand, and a window lighting the staircase on the west side. North of the peristyle are two large *storerooms* (3). The pillars would have supported the upper floor, from which fallen fragments of painted plaster indicated important rooms; by analogy with the Palace at Mállia it has been suggested that here was the Banqueting Hall. Food could have been prepared in the small ground floor rooms west of the storerooms, where there is a convenient second staircase. Some of the *storage jars* still in situ (3) have holes near their bases and are set on stone slabs for tapping the liquid contents, presumably oil.

A *passage* south from the peristyle court leads to the heart of the south wing. Here the main room (4) has a *lustral basin* (5) beside it. The hall (4) has an irregularly paved floor, and the typical pattern of double doors opening on to a colonnaded *light-well* (6) which also has a window in its west wall. The drain at the south-west corner of the light-well can be followed on the other side of the wall. The portico to the north of the light-well leads to a *pillar crypt* (7), where the excavator found a pyramidal stand for a double axe, similar to those in the 'Corridor of the Magazines' in the Palace of Knossós. Reached from the pillar crypt are two small rooms (8 and 9) which may have been treasuries. From hereabouts came the three huge bronze cauldrons, the chance find which led to the discovery of the site. The storerooms also held Linear A tablets and a bronze ingot similar to those found at Ayía Triáda.

The lay-out of the small rooms in the south-west corner, with a short passage from the central room and the proximity of a private staircase, has suggested parallels with the presumed women's quarters in the palaces.

House B, set on traces of earlier walls, is a notably rectangular building with few recognisable architectural features except a staircase in the north-east corner.

House C is basically square but with a characteristic irregular outline. The Minoan walls are preserved almost to the second storey in places. The villa was cut into and overlaid by later buildings; still in situ above the Minoan levels is evidence for the LMIII house (which resembled the LMIII period building at Ayía Triáda), and the cistern complex which is contemporary with it. There are also bases for columns or statues, and an altar stone from the Classical levels.

The *entrance* (which was, like that of House A, partly destroyed by later walls) is on the east side (1), and a clear system of *corridors* connects the various parts of the house. On the left as you enter is a supposed *cult area* including a room with central pillar (2). Then, at the staircase (3) the corridor turns right (4), under the paving of a later floor. On the west side of the house is a block of storerooms (5); the raised *column base* here is from the LMIII reoccupation level. Off the corridor is a *staircase* (6); the lower flight dates from the original MMIII/LMI house, and the upper from the later Classical period building. Across the corridor from the staircase, at the north end of the house, is the *residential quarter*, where a main room with paved floor (7) opens east through a pier-and-door arrangement on to a large porticoed *light-well* (8). The big window, now restored, lit the adjacent room (9). A corridor ran east-west outside this room to reach a staircase (10) to an upper floor, and a toilet equipped with a drain through the outer wall. To the north-east of the house, and built over its corner, is a circular **cistern** of LMIII date entered by a staircase from the north. The water reached the cistern by a *stone channel* on the west side, having first been decanted in a basin or trap at the west end of this channel. North of the channel are remains of a large early structure

(EM–MMI), and also an altar stone from the Classical period. A paved *Minoan road* runs along the west façade of House C.

After the village of Týlissos the road climbs steadily away from the coast, and the landscape becomes wilder. Beyond a war memorial you pass through a rocky defile, above a stream bed, and into a long valley with the village of Goniés spread out across the head of it. Soon (19.5km) the road cuts across the façade of the large Minoan villa of **Sklavókambos**, the excavated remains of which suffered further damage during the last war.

This substantial country house did not exhibit the architectural refinements noticed at Týlissos. It is more crudely built, of partly worked boulders, and the floors were apparently unpaved. But the quality of the pottery and the number of seal impressions found here show that the life of the occupants was far from crude. The main façade was along the line of the modern road with a *pillared verandah* at the Goniés end looking north across the valley. Behind this was a small open *court* with three pillars to support the peristyle roof. The *main entrance* to the house was from the east, behind the façade, and in the entrance passage were found several clay sealings with bull-leaping scenes. The same seal impression has been recognised at Zákros, Gourniá and Ayía Triáda, which suggests a system of travelling merchants, or middlemen, in an extensive trading system.

At 26km *Goniés* stands on a hill of chloritic and serpentine rock. The road, dominated by the Psilorítis mountain range ahead, reaches a crest at the nome boundary.

32km. **Anóyia** (ΑΝΩΓΕΙΑ) occupies a commanding position (730m) on the northern foothills of Mount Ida, with two distinct village centres, one along a saddle on the road in from Herákleion, and the other at the little plateía on the slope below. There are tavernas and modest hotels as well as rooms for rent. Anóyia is noted for its traditional brightly coloured weaving. Many of the houses have their own looms, and attractive local products are everywhere for sale.

The village has a long history as a centre of resistance and revolt, and bitter experience of the inevitable consequences. In August 1944 it was totally destroyed by the Germans, partly as a reprisal for sheltering, earlier that year, the captors of General Kreipe (see Rte 3B). The German indictment also described Anóyia as 'a centre of English espionage and asylum for resistance bands'.

At 2456m Mount Ida (or Psilorítis) is the highest mountain on Crete— the Greek name means the High One. At the Herákleion end of Anóyia a road (partly surfaced but still rough in places after bad weather) sets off south into the mountains for (20km) the upland plain of *Nída*, and, a little above it, the **Idaian cave** (Ιδαίον Αντρον). A major long-term excavation at the cave's shrine of Zeus means that the site is likely to be closed. The waymarked climb to the summit of Mount Ida from the Nída plain is a project only suitable for experienced long-distance walkers. Consult the Greek Alpine Club in Herákleion.

However, the mountain road up to the plain is highly recommended, especially to wild-flower enthusiasts as the snow recedes in late spring and early summer. There is intensive use of the high summer pastures for great flocks of sheep and goats, and you will notice the 'mitáta', round stone-built huts where the shepherds make their cheeses. The traditional method of roofing these huts in stone with a true corbelled vault has been cited in connection with the unsolved problem of roofing the circular Bronze Age tombs of the Mesará, none of which was found intact.

After 15km a rough road is signposted left, west through the hills to Krousónas. In 1983 an unusually well-preserved *Minoan villa* was discovered here; the site is now known as **Zóminthos** after the nearby spring which, interestingly, has retained this prehellenic place-name. In Minoan times the complex would have stood (at 1187m) at the meeting of major routes on this northern approach to Ida.

Excavation has uncovered a large (54 x 37m) LMIA building dating back to c 1600 BC. Walls stand up to 2.20m in places, including one door lintel, and with some wall plaster in situ. On a shelf in a small niche in one room were a terracotta bull rhyton and three vases. Fallen debris included burnt timbers and broken pots (the result of destruction by earthquake) and confirmed the existance of an upper storey. A potter's workshop contained a wheel, appropriate bronze tools, a built pit for the preparation of the clay, and a large quantity of vases which seemed to have been stacked according to type.

At last amid magnificent scenery the *Nída plain* (c 1400m) is in view ahead. On the far side of the plain the road divides. Above the track to the right, as the snow recedes in late spring, are predictable sheets of mountain flowers including crocus and chionodoxa.

The left fork leads to a tourist pavilion (less predictable as to its opening arrangements) with convenient parking for the walk (15 minutes) up a track to the **Idaian cave**.

According to the myth (see also the cave of Psykhró on Mount Díkte, Rte 6) the infant Zeus was hidden from his jealous father, Kronos, in a remote cave in the mountains. He was nursed by the goat-nymph Amaltheia, and guarded by the nine Kourétes, the sons of 'Earth', who danced and clashed their weapons to cover the sound of the baby's cries. The most widely accepted tradition links this upbringing with the Idaian cave. The Cretan Zeus died and was reborn, and this recognisably Minoan concept was central to a cult of Zeus here on Mount Ida which was held in repute throughout the Classical world. The sacred cave was thus a place of pilgrimage in historical times; Pythagoras visited the sanctuary, with the Cretan religious teacher Epimenídes.

The cave was first investigated in 1885 by the Italian Mission, and was immediately recognised as a highly important Iron Age sanctuary. A pedestal in front of the cave mouth would have held a larger-than-lifesize statue of Zeus. Votive offerings dated back at least to the 9C BC, and continued down to the Roman period. In the 1950s the Greek archaeologist, S. Marinátos, demonstrated that the cave was much frequented in Minoan times, and probably for cult purposes. There was a wide range of terracotta and bronze figurines, wine jugs and basins, as well as numerous objects in gold and ivory (Herákleion Museum, Gallery XII). Tripod cauldrons, characteristic offerings in the great Geometric sanctuaries of Greece, were found in numbers only exceeded at Olympia and Delphi.

Outstanding among the finds were the ceremonial bronze *shields from the Orientalising period c 750–650 BC (Gallery XIX) and a bronze drum portraying Zeus between two Kourétes figures. It is thought that a guild of metalworkers from the Near East, established on Crete, was responsible for these pieces.

The current excavation (begun in 1982) under the direction of I. Sakellarákis is one of the most ambitious archaeological projects on the island at the present time. The programme has involved re-examination and then the clearing (with the aid of trucks running on rails) of the areas and levels disturbed by earlier work, in order to prepare, both inside and immediately outside the cave, for systematic exploration of the cave's undisturbed deposits.

The progress reports so far indicate a greatly increased understanding of the detailed topography of the cave; the identification of structures: walls, hearths etc.; the confirmation of Final Neolithic use of the cave in the fourth millenium and further evidence of cult activity developing in Middle Minoan times. Many unusual cult objects continue to appear among the votive offerings. There is sometimes valuable information when newly discovered fragments join with material from earlier excavations.

Among the many finds of exceptional quality were pieces of 8C–7C BC ivory artefacts from the Near East, with some important north Syrian material. Cretan ivories include a superb pin, its head carved in a Janus-arrangement of two women's heads, and part of a plaque with the figure of a woman in the Daidalic style, perhaps a Mistress of Beasts. From the Geometric period (c 750 BC) there were ivory block seals carved with a design of man and horse. There were also fragments of large statues in both bronze and terracotta; one painted terracotta head had an inlaid faience eye. Jewellery includes a gold pendant in the shape of a woman's head, and many rings including Roman examples with engraved bezels. Roman lamps are a poignant reminder of the last generations of pilgrims.

Limited tests in the undisturbed deposits led to the discovery of a complete bronze shield (similar to those described above) decorated with sphinxes and griffins; this is particularly important because for the first time the exact find place of one of these shields has been recorded.

From Anóyia the road descends, but **Axós** is another beautifully situated village clinging to a high ridge. At 41.5km, on the last bend before the houses, a ruined *chapel* is dated to the Second Byzantine period by 10C–12C pottery let in above the door. The building incorporates older material including fragments of columns; only tantalising traces of wall paintings remain.

As you enter the village three roads meet by the tiny cruciform church of Ayía Eiríne (14C/15C). Beyond the church a track (signposted) leads uphill to the left for 400m to the site of *ancient Axós*, a city-state which flourished in the Archaic and Hellenistic periods. The magnificent bronze *helmet, with cheek-pieces in the form of winged horses, now in Herákleion Museum (Gallery XVIII), came from this site. Little of the city survives above ground, but the extensive view makes the 5-minute walk worthwhile. The Greek Archaeological Service has recently returned to the site for further exploration.

A north-south saddle connects two hills with the steep southern *acropolis*—to the right as you approach; occupation extended down the north-east slope. On the saddle the cemetery church of Ayios Ioánnis is built into the central nave and apse of an earlier basilica. (The church has remains of late 14C–early 15C frescoes; the key is kept in the village.)

On the extreme top of the acropolis, a *temple* of the Archaic period, possibly dedicated to Apollo or Athena, was excavated by the Italians at the end of the last century. The massive *temple platform* can be distinguished most easily at the extreme south of the summit of the hill, now overlooking the many circular threshing floors and the modern village in the valley below.

In the middle of Axós village, by a fountain (and kapheneíon), are the ruins of the double-naved Byzantine church of Ayios Mikhaíl Arkhángelos.

The minor road through Zoniáná (left in Axós) winds across the foothills of the Ida range towards Pérama and Réthymnon. But on the circular itinerary keep straight on, descending through Garazó to join (53km) the Réthymnon–Herákleion road (Old Road, Rte 11B) 8km east of Pérama. Turn right for the return (a further 45km) to Herákleion.

B.   To Arkhánes and Vathýpetro

15km (c 10 miles) from Herákleion to Arkhánes. A further 5km to the
Minoan villa of Vathýpetro, with the opportunity to drive or walk, only
4km off the valley road, to the summit of Mount Júktas. Unsurfaced roads
in the beautiful country south of Arkhánes are being widened and
upgraded.

Buses to Arkhánes approximately hourly (except Sundays) from the main
bus station by the Herákleion harbour, with a convenient stop in Plateía
Venizélou. Pýrgos or Khárakas buses can be used for the return from
Khoudétsi.

Take the Knossós road (Rte 2) out of Herákleion. 2km beyond the palace a
fine *aqueduct* supported by two tiers of arches spans a ravine; it was built
during the brief interregnum of Egyptian rule (1832–40) to improve the
Herákleion water supply. This aqueduct had a Roman predecessor. The
road climbs through *Spiliá*, and passes the turning (left) for Skaláni (see
Rte 3C). After 9.5km keep right where the main road bends left signed
Arkalokhóri and Viánnos.

At 10.5km there is an acute right turn at a T-junction where in April 1944 Patrick
Leigh Fermor and W. Stanley Moss, with their band of Cretan resistance fighters,
kidnapped the German General Kreipe while he was being driven from his headquarters in Arkhánes to his residence in the Villa Ariadne at Knossós; after 18 days
in hiding as they crossed the Ida mountain range, the party was picked up by a
Royal Navy submarine from a cove at Rodákino on the south coast. (The story was
told by Moss in his book *Ill Met by Moonlight* which was later filmed—see also
Crete: the Battle and the Resistance by A. Beevor, published in 1991 to coincide
with the 50th anniversary of the German invasion of the island.)

The road runs through the hamlet of Káto (lower) Arkhánes before you
reach the small town (pop. 3700) of Epáno (upper) Arkhánes, usually
referred to simply as Arkhánes. (Good tavernas on the road into town,
and in the plateía at the far end of it where the bus turns.)

Sir Arthur Evans was the first to uncover Minoan remains in **Arkhánes**.
While excavating the massive ashlar masonry of a monumental *well-
head* or reservoir he noted that Minoan walls had been incorporated in
some of the neighbouring houses. Since the early 1960s the Greek
Archaeological Society has conducted a major programme of excavations
in the locality under the direction of I. and E. Sakellarákis. Three major
sites have been investigated: Turkogeitoniá, a Palatial-style complex
partially overlaid by the buildings of the modern town; Phourní, a cemetery which produced an exceptional series of rich burials with offerings
which included jewellery and ivory work, now among the most outstanding exhibits in the Herákleion Museum; and Anemóspilia, a Minoan
sanctuary site with dramatic suggestions of human sacrifice. None of
these three excavations is at present open to the public, but directions
are given for those interested in assessing them through the fences.

A phýlakas, official custodian of all the archaeological sites described below, is
based in Arkhánes. It may be possible to arrange for him to unlock closed sites or to
open the wine-press storeroom at Vathýpetro. Enquire at one of the kapheneíons in
the plateía at the top of the village where the bus turns.

The approach to the Turkogeitoniá site takes less than 5 minutes on foot from the clock-tower near the war memorial and the three-aisled church (Panayía Vatiótissa) on the right of the road into town, and just before the one-way street system begins. Start up the left fork, against the traffic flow, but immediately take the narrow street left. At the end turn left, and follow the bend to the right; 50m further turn right again where the site gate is in view.

Minoan Palatial-style buildings were first located in 1965, and an intensive programme of excavations since then has gradually uncovered a site of exceptional interest. Both the architecture and the contents of the buildings so far investigated have confirmed the original hypothesis that the site is comparable with the known Minoan palaces.

Wall decoration included miniature frescoes and painted shallow reliefs, and among many examples of the minor arts of the Minoans were fragments of ivory statuettes from a group similar to the bull-leaper from Knossós. Other finds included faience, sections of tusk and a lump of imported red jasper for which the most likely source is Iran. A large rectangular altar, of a type familiar from numerous artistic representations, is the first to be found complete in an excavation.

There was evidence for two distinct destruction levels, in LMIA and LMIB. (Mycenaean artefacts were also noted.) An intense fire destroyed the LMIA building and its upper floor collapsed, but from a study of fragments of frescoes in the debris it was clear that walls on both floors had been decorated. The masonry was a combination of poros ashlar blocks and courses of bricks. One particular area is cited as an example of the architectural sophistication of the building: a propylon gave access, along a corridor, to an L-shaped peristyle from which a monumental staircase led to an upper floor where the peristyle colonnade was repeated on a smaller scale. Paving consisted of irregular slabs, in varying colours and pointed with red and yellow plaster. With such a clear understanding of the original building the excavators believe that in due course an attempt at reconstruction will be jusified.

Excavations in 1966–67 brought to light a *Minoan cemetery* on the hill of *Phourní* just to the north-west of the town. To find the site return to the three-aisled church. On its Herákleion side is a large neo-classic school building (ΣΧΟΛΕΙΟΝ); beside this (signed) a by-road has been improved to take cars 600m round the flank of the hill, keeping left at a fork, to an olive grove where a roughly paved path (an overgrown kalderími) leads uphill between two walls, 5 minutes to the site fence. Keep left along the fence, and after 150 paces strike right on a trodden path for vantage points on the uphill side of the excavation. (In April the hillside is a wild garden.) The old kalderími leads on temptingly to a crest with a fine view over the Bay of Herákleion.

The principal discoveries during the early excavations at Phourní were an *ossuary* of c 2500 BC and three well-preserved *tholos tombs* of LMII date, one containing the first unplundered royal burial found in Crete. The sealed *larnax* held 140 pieces of gold jewellery, now displayed in Herákleion Museum, Gallery VI. A group of white marble idols of Cycladic type are among more recent finds. In 1971, at a short distance north of Tholos A, a Mycenaean-type *grave circle* was uncovered. It comprised seven shaft graves, each with a pit for cult purposes, and each containing an empty larnax. Bronze vases and stelai were found but no bones, suggesting that the bodies had been deliberately exhumed at a later date in antiquity.

Excavations resumed in 1986 concentrated on early (Prepalatial) burial areas and on various architectural features. In one southern sector of the cemetery a new series of mortuary structures came to light, some in use c 2000 BC, containing a great number of burials: in larnakes, in pithoi and on the floor between. In one place there was a stack of 18 successive burials. An important missing link (MMIA) was established, confirming for the first time an unbroken series of burials throughout the Minoan period. Among the wealth of grave-gifts now expected from this site (vases, seals, jewellery) was an unusual terracotta sistrum.

The sanctuary of *Anemóspilia* (discovered in 1979) is across the deep valley to the west of Phourní, 3km north-west of Arkhánes on the flank of Mount Júktas looking out to the coast.

From the same three-aisled church (see above) continue into the town. Notice, almost straightaway, the start of the one-way traffic system, and 100m along it take the first turning right. The narrow but surfaced road follows the stream, bears left after 300m, gains height steadily and then climbs steeply as it nears the site. The excavation (fenced) is up a bank, left of the road, 3km from the turning out of the town. (*View to the coast, with the Knossós valley away to the right.)

The *Minoan shrine*, within an enclosure wall, had three rooms preserved along the uphill side of a central corridor; two of them contained a great quantity of fine pottery including a chalice, ritual vases and a large stone basin, as well as pithoi for storage. In the central room life-size clay feet probably belonged to a wooden idol, and in the room to the west there was a free-standing altar. The shrine was destroyed by the great earthquake which destroyed the Old Palaces at the end of MMII (c 1700 BC). In the debris, evidence for ritual at first pointed to animal sacrifice, but the bones found on the altar with a long bronze knife were those of a young man. Two other human skeletons were found nearby; a gold ring and an agate seal were associated with one of them. Taking account of forensic evidence, the excavators concluded that the youth on the altar had been sacrificed minutes before the building was destroyed by the earthquake disaster which the ritual was perhaps designed to avert.

South from Arkhánes the road runs directly below Mount Júktas and then passes (5km) the excavated Minoan villa at Vathýpetro. Just off this road is the frescoed *church of Ayios Mikhaíl Arkhángelos*, Asómatos. The key used to be held in Arkhánes at the Taverna Miriophitó (in the plateía by the bus terminus) but this arrangement may have been discontinued; ask in the plateía and if necessary contact the phýlakas (see above).

Just over 1km from the plateía on the Vathýpetro road there is a turning left to Ayios Mikhaíl Arkhángelos. Soon curving right, the track runs between vineyards for 1.5km. At a sharp bend across a stream-bed, the trees down to the left hide the little church, all that remains of the Venetian settlement of Asómatos. The frescoes (1315–16) include a remarkable Crucifixion, and a Fall of Jericho. On the west wall (bottom left) the donor Mikhaíl Patsidiótis, with his wife, reverently offers a model of his church to his patron saint the Archangel.

Below the church a water source was until modern times the main supply for Herákleion.

From the Vathýpetro road the church of Aphéndis Khristós (Christ the Lord—great festival on 6 August) is conspicuous on the summit (811m) of **Mount Júktas**. Just below the summit, on the northern shoulder, is the site of a Minoan peak sanctuary.

3km out of Arkhánes a road to the right, rough but passable, climbs the hill (keep right at the fork just off the valley road), or you can walk from the turning, 4km to the summit; *view. There is a direct path from Arkhánes which is shorter but very steep.

On the last bend before the church a footpath leads right along the flank of the hill (10 minutes) to the telecommunications relay station (OTE). This is built over part of the *peak sanctuary* first investigated by Evans, who found substantial structures with a massive temenos wall of a cyclopean character unusual on Crete. In 1977

A. Karétsou of the Greek Archaeological Service returned to this large enclosure near the summit of Γιούχτας (transliterated Iúktas in excavation reports). While systematically exploring the open area of the shrine and the associated buildings within the enclosure, she has established that the peak sanctuary was in use as a place of cult at least from the late EMII period through to LMIIIB. As an important centre for pilgrimage it would have been visible from a great distance, and certainly from the Minoan settlements at Knossós and Arkhánes.

The main shrine area blocks the path just before you reach the OTE station. The site is fenced but the sure-footed can scramble up to vantage points on the hillside above it. Here, at the upper (south) end of the temenos, is the distinctive feature at the heart of this peak sanctuary, a natural cave-like rock-cleft or chasm. The cleft was defined on its east and south sides by a retaining wall, two terraces and a rectangular enclosure clearly designed for cult practices. Across the cleft (on its west side and facing east) a stepped altar was constructed in two phases dated successively to the Old and New Palace periods. Associated with the cleft were rich finds of offerings, pyre material, vessels for libations and remains of sacrifices. The large quantity of votives cleared from the cleft itself ranged in date from EMII–III material such as 'sheep bells' and Pýrgos ware through to the (headless) model of a sphinx which proved the continuity of the sanctuary into Mycenaean times.

The offerings included hundreds of terracotta figurines, both human and animal, but also many artefacts (vessels, figures, seals, jewellery) in more precious materials such as stone, bronze, faience, gold leaf and rock crystal. Fragments of numerous stone offering tables, many with Linear A inscriptions, all came from LMI levels. It used to be thought that peak sanctuaries were a Protopalatial phenomenon, but these finds pointed to the importance of cult practices here in Neopalatial times.

Finds from the excavation are on show in Herákleion Museum, Gallery II.

Beyond the OTE equipment the north end of the temenos extends apron-like over a lower slope to a northern entrance in the wall, and buildings that have been investigated there are recognised as installations of the sanctuary. A two-storey building, with a short life during the early years of the Neopalatial period, produced evidence of workshops and a potter's kiln.

Before leaving the hill it is worth scrambling up the (precipitous) rocks beyond the four-naved church of Aphéndis Khristós for a bird's-eye view stretching from the Lévka Ori in the west to Lasíthi in the east, and south across the island to the Asteroúsia mountains. According to legend the ridge along the summit of Júktas is the burial place of the Cretan Zeus.

The valley road continues to the LMI villa of **Vathýpetro** (5km from Arkhánes), signposted 200m right of the road at a fountain. The site is fenced, but not always locked (officially open mornings only). The villa, contemporary with the New Palaces, destroyed at the end of LMI, was excavated by S. Marinátos (1949–52), but his findings have not been fully published. Interesting evidence was discovered for the self-sufficiency of this large country house; as well as weaving equipment, there were both wine and olive-oil presses and probably also a potter's workshop.

To the west the site commands a superb view across the north–south route from the coast through to the Mesará plain; in the middle distance to the north west you can distinguish the twin-peaked hill of Prophítis Ilías (Castle of Témenos, Rte 3D).

The *main entrance* to the house, on the south east, is along a corridor (1 on the plan). On the left are storerooms (2) (roofed and locked for protection, but see phýlakas above), where elaborate *wine-making equipment* is in a good state of preservation. At the end of the corridor the staircase (3) led to an upper floor over the storerooms. The main room (4) has four central pillars and a paved floor. Along the west façade is a miniature paved *West Court* (5) with drains running out of the villa wall. The *oil press* with basin was found here. This façade has a deep recess (6)

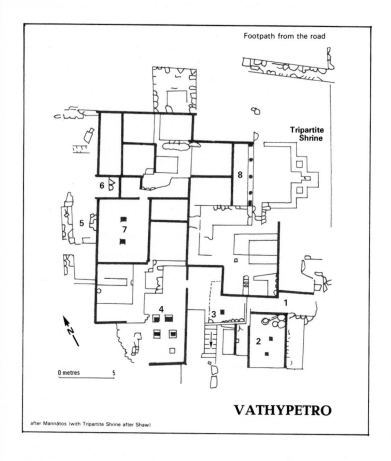

Footpath from the road

Tripartite
Shrine

6

8

5

7

4

3

1

2

N

0 metres   5

VATHYPETRO

after Mannátos (with Tripartite Shrine after Shaw)

which may have held a small shrine. The roofed area (7) is another pillar basement where 16 giant *pithoi* are still in situ. To the north is a set of rooms (poorly preserved and complicated by two periods of building) which are thought to have been the private living quarters. The entrance to this part of the house was through a *three-columned portico* (8); to the east of it, across a small court the excavator identified a **Tripartite Shrine** with a central recess flanked by two square niches, recalling both the shrine in the Miniature Frescoes found at Knossós and the sanctuary carved on the Mountain Shrine Rhyton from Zákros. A grander version, but on the same principle, is the tripartite shrine beside the Central Court of the Knossós Palace (for fresco reconstruction see p 105).

The road continues from Vathýpetro, 3km to Khoudétsi, at 440 m, on the main Herákleion–Pýrgos road (see Rtes 3C, 4 and 8). A circular tour could include Moní Epanosíphi (p 159).

C. The Pediáda District

This itinerary is a circular drive from Herákleion of c 80km (50 miles) through a fertile upland landscape, with opportunities to visit (22km) the Kazantzákis Museum, (23km) the Angárathos monastery, (25km) the potting village of Thrapsanó, (c 40km) the site of ancient Lýttos, as well as a number of frescoed churches of the Pediáda district.

Also described (diverging after 19km) is the main road south east from Herákleion to (63km, c 40 miles) Viánnos; this can be used for a day's expedition to the beaches of the south coast between Tsoútsouros and Mýrtos, or as the first stage of the journey to eastern Crete by the route south of Lasíthi.

Buses from Herákleion to Kastélli Pediádas, also one service daily to Ierápetra (via Viánnos), from the Oasis Bus Station outside the New Gate. A long-distance walk via Lýttos uses the Lasíthi bus for the return trip.

Leave Herákleion as for Rte 2 by the Knossós road, and continue towards Arkhánes (Rte 3B). After 8km you pass the Skaláni turning where the direct route (left, 8km) is clearly signed all the way across-country to the Kazantzákis Museum.

At 9.5km the main road turns left, for Arkalokhóri and Viánnos. 17km *Pezá* is the centre of a prosperous wine-growing area, where wine co-operatives, often by introducing advanced methods of viticulture, are engaged in a determined effort to improve quality and expand trade, including the export of Cretan wine. (A consistently reliable wine from this region is marketed as Logádo.) The grape harvest begins soon after the great holiday for the Feast of the Assumption (15 August). Pezá also has one of the largest processing plants for Cretan olive oil.

At the fork just beyond the village, one main road south is signposted, right, for Pýrgos and Khárakas, the large villages at the eastern end of the Mesará plain. (See Rtes 3B, 4 and 8; see also the Epanosíphis monastery 13km from this junction.) However, the recommended itinerary keeps straight on to (19km) *Ayiés Paraskiés* and then left into this village when another main road to the south curves sharply right, signed for Arkalok-hóri (13km) and Viánnos (45km) (see Rte introduction above and p 128).

For Thrapsanó and Kastélli Pediádas you proceed east from Ayiés Paraskiés through the fertile and intensively-cultivated Pediáda countryside.

22km from Herákleion, a left turn is signposted to the KAZANTZAKH Museum in the village of *Mirtiá* (formerly Varvári, the home village of Níkos Kazantzákis's father).

Recommended detour (2.5km) to the museum, opened in 1983 to honour the distinguished Cretan writer Níkos Kazantzákis (1883–1957). On the Mirtiá road, pass the fork right to Astráki, and at the beginning of the village bend left, following the main street until, at the church, it turns right into the plateía in front of the museum. (Ahead is the road back to Herákleion via Skaláni.) Mirtiá is an attractive and particularly well-tended village which welcomes visitors.

The museum is open (March–October): Monday, Wednesday, Saturday and Sunday, 09.00–13.00 and 16.00–20.00; Tuesday and Friday, mornings only; Thursday closed. Entrance charge.

The **museum** is very well arranged to illustrate Kazantzákis's personal, literary and political life in Greece and abroad, with extensive background notes in both Greek and English by the door of each room. The author of the novel *Zorba the Greek* was born on Crete in 1883; he took a degree in law at the University of Athens, and afterwards continued his literary and philosophical studies in France, Germany and Italy. Between the two world wars he worked from his home on the island of Aíyina. Briefly in 1945 he was Minister of Education in the Greek Government.

Among Kazantzákis's most admired books are *Freedom and Death, Christ Recrucified* and *The Odyssey: A Modern Sequel;* some have been made into films and plays, but he also wrote specifically for the theatre. On display are contemporary photographs and documents, personal articles, and copies of all his books, including a great number in translation. There are also theatrical memorabilia, and one room is entirely devoted to his best-known character, Zorba. Kazantzákis died in Germany in 1957; in line with his somewhat unconventional views was his request for burial on the Martinengo Bastion of the Herákleion city walls (see p 61).

At 25km on the main Pediáda route (3km beyond the museum detour) there is a by-road, left, which leads in 4km to the tranquil **Angárathos monastery**, formerly one of the most important religious houses on the island. After a glimpse of the monastery ahead in trees below the skyline, you descend 1.5km to a stream-bed, and from just beyond the bridge the buildings are again in view. Here walkers may be tempted by the short-cut along field tracks.

The exact date of the monastery's foundation is not known, but it is mentioned in 16C manuscripts in the British Museum and St. Mark's Library, Venice, and the records of its abbots go back to 1520. After the fall of Constantinople, Angárathos rivalled the Sinai college in Herákleion as a seat of learning, and a number of abbots went on to distinguish themselves elsewhere in the Christian world as churchmen and academics. The monastery flourished during the first half of the 17C, but at the time of the Turkish invasion of 1645 its precious objects and documents were taken for safety to the island of Kýthera, where the abbot's family had property. These valuables included a treasured icon of the Panayía (Virgin Mary); the name Angárathos enshrines the belief that the original church was built on the spot where this icon had been found, under a bush of the tall herb αγκαραθιά (Jerusalem sage).

The present church, dedicated to the Assumption of the Virgin (Feast Day 15 August), dates only from 1894, but it is surrounded by a triangular courtyard of picturesque buildings which preserve many early features. Several of these are dated by inscription: the gateways at both north and south entrances (1583 and 1565 respectively), a sarcophagus built into the north side of the court (1554), and a lofty barrel-vaulted storeroom opposite the west end of the church (1628). The old north gate is to the left of the modern approach.

Back on the Kastélli road, a turning is almost immediately (300m) signposted right to *Thrapsanó.* This village is known for its pottery, in particular the plain earthenware which includes the traditional large jars or 'pithária', little changed from the storage jars of Minoan times. A Cretan monk, Agápios Lándos, whose work was published in Venice in 1642, commented even then that all the men of Thrapsanó were potters. You can continue straight ahead to Kastélli, but the recommended route takes the right turn.

31km **Thrapsanó** is a long village set on a hillside. Pots are for sale on the main street, but most of the workshops, especially those for the very large jars, are down the hill to the left. From the little triangular plateía, you can walk downhill, but with a car it is easier to go on through the village, turning left towards Kastélli in front of the big church at the end. Out of Thrapsanó, the first track to the left leads past a prominent modern church, and along a stream-bed until it bends right and crosses it. There are *pottery kilns* and workshops not far from the bridge; you can ask for the potters specialising in the large pithária.

Potting is a seasonal occupation. As soon as weather permits in early summer the potters work a seven-day week. A primitive production line obtains, through potting, drying and firing; each pot may take up to a week from start to finish. Most of the potteries welcome visitors, and their products are for sale.

The road to Kastélli continues past (34.5km) *Evangelísmos* and (37km) *Arkhángelos*.

In the middle of the first of these villages, the cruciform church of Ayios Evangelísmos has unusual (14C) frescoes. Uncovered in 1981 in the west arm of the cross, they include Old Testament scenes, rare on Crete, of the Creation of Adam and Eve, the Garden of Eden, and the Expulsion from Paradise.

Ask for the church key at the blue-painted kapheneíon across the street (Kyría Katerína).

At 37.5km, in *Sklaverokhóri*, is the church of Eisódia Theotókon (The Presentation of the Virgin), with particularly well-preserved *frescoes (graffito date 1481). For a single example, during this excursion, of the widely-admired Byzantine wall-painting of Crete, these frescoes would be a good choice. Turn right in the village before a left bend, and the church is at the end of the short street. Ask for the key (for the Panayía) at one of the houses on the right, just before it.

In the customary position in the apse is portrayed the Panayía Platytéra, the Virgin Mary symbolising the Incarnation in Orthodox iconography, framed by angels, hierarchs and deacons; and on the arch above, the Ancient of Days. In the nave: the birth of Mary and the presentation in the temple (vault), as well as scenes from the life of Christ, including a baptism with male and female river gods; on the south wall, St. George slaying the dragon, and rescuing a princess (the daughter of the King of Alassia), with her parents watching from the city walls and God's hand outstretched from above. The figures opposite include St. Francis, one of only three examples on Crete of the portrayal of this subject derived from the Latin hagiography.

If you continue past the church, you almost immediately rejoin (turning right) the direct Ayiés Paraskiés–Kastélli road.

39km **Kastélli** (pop. 1300), the traditional centre of the Pediáda district, is named after its Venetian castle which survived until the early years of this century. On the main street the circular route keeps left following signs for Khersónisos and Herákleion.

A detour right, on the Arkalokhóri road, takes you in 2km to Ayios Ioánnis, Lilianó, a picturesque church of considerable architectural interest (no frescoes). Half-way up the hill out of town keep right opposite a conspicuous tree. After 2km there is a sign for Lilianó (right), and 100m before this second turn to the village, a metalled road opposite a guardhouse runs straight to a military airfield. Between these two parallel side-roads the church is in view among olive trees.

The architectural history of Ayios Ioánnis is unclear because of a puzzling mixture of Venetian influence and features usually associated with much earlier churches. The three-aisled ground-plan ending in three apses and divided by two pairs of columns (Ionic and plain abacus capitals) indicates a basilica, though the short, square nave is not typical; in an older phase it was perhaps covered by a dome. The church now has a saddle roof of wooden construction, and across the west end a barrel-vaulted narthex supporting a bellcote. The narthex is reminiscent of the vaulted storerooms at Angárathos.

Material reused from older buildings is particularly noticeable outside the church in the lower courses of both north and south walls; the block serving as a bench outside the west wall has an inscription in ancient Greek, and a fragment of an Early Christian altar is let into the threshold at the church door.

The basilica plan (with floor lower than that of the narthex and c 1m below the present level of the cemetery) combined with the antiquity of the building material suggest an early date. (The city-state of Lýttos, not far away, was still flourishing in the First Byzantine period.) However the roof construction, other architectural details such as corbels, and the narthex all show unquestionable Venetian influence. On the south wall, near a low window, five stone steps and part of a column are probably the remains of a pulpit which suggests the practice of the Latin rite, and would put the final adaptation of this church at least no earlier than the 13C.

From the centre of Kastélli, take the Herákleion road, and when it turns left (still in the town) keep straight on for (3.5km) Xidás and the site of the historically important city-state of Lýttos.

Approaching (43km) *Xidás*, the modern church is visible for some distance. Across the valley to the left is the tiny (frescoed) chapel of *Ayios Yeóryios*, set among cypresses and orange trees.

To visit Ayios Yeóryios stop by the war memorial below the modern church. From the terrace of the kapheneíon opposite, the chapel is in sight in the valley, and steps lead down to a path which passes within 50m of it. Indistinct remains of frescoes (dated by inscription 1321) are preserved in the apse and on the south wall.

Beyond Xidás the road (signed Aski) climbs for 2km to **Lýttos**. There is little above ground of the Greco-Roman city, but the ascent is recommended for the site's majestic position against the wall of the Lasíthi massif, overlooking the Pediáda plain. Homer speaks of 'broad Lýttos' and the exploits of the Lýttian force under Idomeneus, leader of the Cretan contingent (in 'eighty black ships') at Troy. Before the crest, two white chapels on the skyline (right) mark the site, and the path (5 minutes to the top) starts directly below the northern or left-hand of these two, which is dedicated to Tímios Stavrós (the Holy Cross). If you miss the path, the road bends right and, 300m further, a field-track offers an easier route with the little churches almost in line ahead along the ridge.

Lýttos, one of the most powerful and warlike of the city-states, was a deadly rival of Knossós, at least from the 4C BC. Its territory extended from the north to the south coast, with control of the Lasíthi plateau; its port was at Khersónisos. In the war of 221–219 BC Lýttos resisted the alliance between Knossós and Górtyn which aimed to control the whole island. The Lýttian army embarked on an expedition against Ierápytna (modern Ierápetra on the south coast), unwisely leaving the city unguarded, and Knossós seized the opportunity to destroy Lýttos utterly. The rebuilt city was to put up strong resistance against Quintus Metellus, in 67 BC, and Lýttos survived to flourish under Roman rule and into the First Byzantine period. Statue inscriptions dedicated to Trajan and Hadrian are particularly numerous.

Systematic investigation at this huge site has only recently been begun (by the Greek Archaeological Service); previous understanding depended largely on inscriptions and chance finds. Interest attaches to the excavation of a Hellenistic house, where four column bases and a built altar were preserved in a main hall, as well as storage and workshop areas. It appears that the house was destroyed by fire in 221-220 BC, presumably as a result of the war with Knossós described above.

The church of Tímios Stavrós (see above) is built over the foundations of a large 5C basilica; the area around it was apparently the agorá or centre of the ancient city. The second church, Ayios Yeóryios on the southern peak, lies on a 2C AD building in which painted wall plaster was found. Built into the east wall of the church are architectural fragments from ornate piers, with crosses set in delicately carved acanthus foliage. Nearby part of the city's Bouleuterion or council chamber has been excavated, revealing a large area with built platforms or benches; this was destroyed by earthquake c 200 AD.

The relatively small hilltop area between the two churches was enclosed by a formidable *wall* which can still be traced in places, most easily along its outer face. It is of rubble faced with squared stones in the Roman style, and has been compared to the fortifications of the acropolis at Górtyn. Its probable dating is 7C AD. A theatre, the largest recorded on Crete, was planned in the 16C by the Italian antiquary, Onorio Belli (appointed physician to the Proveditor General of Candia in 1583) but its exact location is now uncertain.

Crossing the narrow valley to the south east are remains of the massive walls of an *aqueduct* which brought Lasíthi water to Lýttos.

The panoramic view may be enjoyed without exploring the site of Lýttos by continuing 500m up the road to the watershed. Away to the left the road from the north coast (see Rte 6) climbs past the Kerá convent into the mountains, and straight ahead, directly across the valley, a carefully constructed mule track or kalderími, one of the eight ancient ways up to the Lasíthi plateau, starts towards the Tsoúli Mníma pass. (On the Lasíthi side, bulldozers recently gouged out an unsightly track for vehicles.) In the opposite direction you can distinguish on a clear day the Levká Ori, or White Mountains, near the western extremity of the island.

Beyond the watershed the road surface is variable, and in a car it is better to return from Lýttos to Kastélli.

Walkers who have made the stiff 6km ascent, and are planning to continue 12km to the main Lasíthi road (and bus route) at Avdoú, can now look forward to a gradual descent in this beautiful landscape along the country roads and tracks which connect the villages in the valley below. Turn left after 2.5km in Aski; there are signs all the way for Avdoú.

Back in Kastélli on the circular itinerary, turn right for Herákleion. Less than 1km outside the town, a dirt road (signed right) leads in 2km to the interesting old church of **'Ayios Pandeleímon** dating to the Second Byzantine period, (frescoes transitional 13C–14C).

Passing (right) a stretch of well-preserved ancient paved road, the track keeps straight ahead at a fork, and bends left when joined by another track from the right. Soon the church almost blocks the way, shaded by two spreading oak trees, in an area kept green by a nearby spring. In the summer months there is a simple taverna (EΞOXIKON KENTPON) delightfully situated on the slope below the church, and the key is kept here; if the taverna is closed, ask in Piyí (see below).

The church stands on the foundations of an Early Christian basilica, and Hellenistic inscriptions as well as architectural fragments suggest a previous sanctuary. Ayios Pandeleímon is the patron saint of healing, and this, together with the health-giving waters of the spring, makes it likely that there is continuity on the site from an Asklepieion.

Almost a ruin when Gerola saw it at the beginning of this century, Ayios Pandeleímon was carefully restored in 1962. The three-aisled church is a structure without parallel, incorporating many reused architectural fragments and decorated blocks, as well as inscriptions of Hellenistic and Roman date. The partially restored blind-arcading in the south wall is thought to relate to a previous building phase, perhaps a larger cruciform domed church. One of the interior columns consists of four superimposed Corinthian capitals resting on a square abacus plate.

Frescoes are preserved in the apse and on the walls of the nave, dated stylistically to the late 13C–early 14C. As well as the full-length figures of the soldier saints on the north wall, there is an unusual scene of Ayía Anna nursing the infant Mary.

You can continue along the track (1km) to rejoin the road at the nearby village, formerly Bizarianó, now renamed *Piyí* (meaning a spring). This water source fed the Roman aqueduct which supplied ancient Khersónisos; ruins of the aqueduct's foundations can still be seen (right, c 500m) near the junction with Rte 6 below.

From Piyí it is 8km till you reach the Lasíthi road (Rte 6) to turn left for another 5.5km to the north coast highway, and the return (23km) to Herákleion.

To Viannos

The main road runs south from Ayiés Paraskiés (see p 123) through extensive vineyards, where the vines for the 'rosákia' table grapes are laboriously trained on tall wire trellises.

32.5km from Herákleion is *Arkalokhóri* (pop. 2500), a busy agricultural centre. The nearby sacred cave of *Prophítis Ilías*, first explored by J. Khatzidákis, was fully excavated in 1932 by the Greek archaeologists S. Marinátos and N. Pláton.

The cave had been a place of worship from the Early Minoan period to the time of the New Palaces. Among the rich series of votive offerings was a large number of bronze rapier blades (MMIII/LMI) recalling weapons in Grave Circles A and B at Mycenae, also many miniature double axes in bronze, silver and gold, some decorated with traced ornament; one has a vertical inscription in Linear A. (See Herákleion Museum, Gallery VII.)

The main road turns sharp left near the end of Arkalokhóri, and runs towards the Lasíthi range, where *Mount Díkte* is often snow-capped till May.

38km. At a meeting of five roads turn right for Viánnos.

45km. *Aphráti*. The hill to the right is the site of the Classical city-state of Arkádes. The city was destroyed during the war between Knossós and Lýttos (221 BC), and again at the time of the Roman invasion. Nothing remains above ground today.

The Italian Archaeological Mission under D. Levi, excavated an important Geometric and Orientalising *cemetery* here, and from the latter period some particularly fine cremation urns with rare figurative scenes are exhibited in Herákleion Museum, Gallery XII.

At 49km *Embaros*, just off the main road (left), is a recommended (500m) detour for the church of Ayios Yeóryios which has much-admired frescoes by Manuel Phokás (1436–37); compare Avdoú (Rte 6) and Epáno Sými (Rte 8). Tracks lead from the village into the Lasíthi mountains.

At 58km there is a right fork for a 3km detour to *Khóndros*. A Bronze Age site here is one of the few excavated settlements known to have been founded in LMIIIA–B, after the widespread destruction of Minoan sites across the island at the end of LMI.

The excavation comes into view on a low double-peaked hill immediately above the village. Round a sharp bend at the first group of houses, two tracks diverge right. Take the left of these, at an acute angle to the road ahead. After 800m this track forks, and here the site is 3 minutes away, uphill to the left. In early spring the orchids around the site may prove a distraction.

The settlement is divided into two complexes linked by double walls, and each complex consists of a number of house units rather than one large building. The architecture is said to exemplify that of LMIII: walls up to a metre thick, stone-flagged floors, low benches and fixed box-shaped hearths. The western complex (away from the modern village) had a weaving area, and a group of ritual objects, fallen from above, suggested a shrine on an upper floor.

From the village an improved road continues c 9km to the coast at Keratókambos (see below).

63km Ano (upper) **Viánnos**, on the site of the classical city-state of the same name, is a large and picturesque village (pop. 1400) with several interesting churches, notably *Ayía Pelayía* which has well-preserved frescoes dating from 1360. From the huge plane tree on the left of the main street at the far end of the village, you can make your way up the stepped side-streets. The key for Ayía Pelayía is kept at the priest's house on the third or fourth level, and the church itself is on a terrace near the top of this part of the village. On the way up is the 14/15C church of *Ayios Yeóryios* with fine doorways and bellcote.

A decent road now descends (via Khondrós) 12km to the sea at Keratókambos. Until recently this stretch of coast retained a delightful sense of isolation quite untouched by organised tourism, but it may soon be affected by development at neighbouring Tsoútsouros. The improved dirt road along the sea has a fine modern bridge across the Anapodáris river.

For this newly accessible coastline and for the main road east to Arvi, Mýrtos and Ierápetra (respectively c 20, 24 and 40km from Viánnos), see the last part of Rte 8.

D.   To Prophítis Ilías and the Castle of Témenos

This is a short drive, 19km (12miles), in beautiful country behind Herákleion, recommended after a morning's sightseeing, or for a leisurely half day between strenuous excursions. There is a choice of longer routes for the return.

Leave Herákleion by the Khaniá Gate. Immediately outside the walls, at the traffic lights, turn left uphill. The road crosses above the north coast highway, and (c 7km) passes a turning for *Phinikiá*, centre of a famed Venetian vineyard, and still a wine-producing area. At first you follow a fertile river valley which must always have contributed to Herákleion's prosperity, and was one of the main routes from the north coast through to the plain of the *Mesará*. Then the road climbs through (15km) *Tsagaráki*; you look across to the craggy south west slopes of *Mount Júktas* before the final stretch where the village of *Prophítis Ilías*, and the fortification wall round the hilltop above it, come into view ahead. Note the white chapel dedicated to the Panayía immediately above the village.

Prophítis Ilías was until recently known as Kanlí Kastélli ('bloody castle'), because of a battle here in 1647 when the Venetians inflicted a great defeat on the Turks. The modern name is taken from the dedication of the principal village church.

Above the village is a twin-peaked hill. After the Byzantine general Nikephóros Phokás had driven the Saracens from the island in 961, he decided to build a great castle on this hill and called it **Témenos**. His plan was to establish a new capital

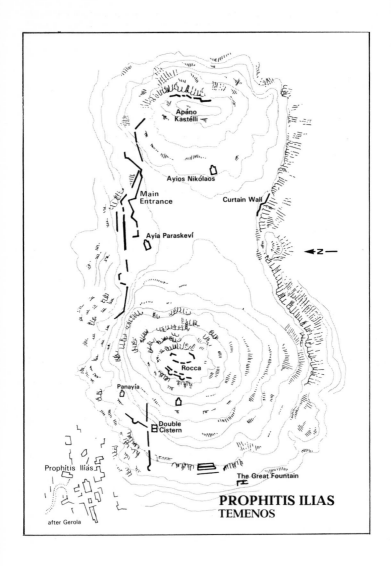

Apáno
Kastélli

Ayios Nikólaos

Main
Entrance

Curtain Wall

Ayia Paraskeví

← N —

Rocca

Panayía

Double
Cistern

Prophitis Iliás

The Great Fountain

PROPHITIS ILIAS
TEMENOS

after Gerola

inland, less exposed to the danger of pirate raids, and to transfer there the population of Khándakas, as Herákleion was then called. But the move lacked popular
support, and in 968 when Phokás was recalled to Constantinople as Emperor, only
the fortress had been completed.

In the first decade of the 13C Témenos was occupied briefly by the Genoese,
under Enrico Pescatore, but they were soon expelled by the Venetians in whose
documents the castle is referred to as 'oppidum fortissimum'. The first Venetian

Duke of Crete, Giacomo Tiepolo, took refuge here at a time of rebellion in Candia. The fortifications were restored after an earthquake in 1303, and again in the 16C when the Turks began to threaten the island.

Cars may be left at the top of the village near the church of Prophítis Ilías where the chapel of the Panayía, no longer in sight, is directly above you. From here an easy track runs left along the northern flank of the double hill (see below) but if you ask for the path to the Panayía, it will bring you (10 minutes uphill) to the main west summit—see Gerola's sketch-plan. On this hill, known as the *Rocca*, Nikephóros Phokás built his castle.

More than 1000 years earlier this was the site of the Greco-Roman city-state of Lýkastos and near the chapel of the Panayía is a well-preserved double *cistern*, probably Roman in date.

On the summit nothing is preserved except traces of rock cutting. The view is extensive, with an angle of Mount Júktas unfamiliar from the north coast, and the Minoan villa at Vathýpetro (Rte 3B) discernible below the quarry scar to the south east across the valley. From the Rocca summit you can make your way down to the saddle to reach the eastern height, *Apáno Kastélli*. To the south is a fine stretch of curtain walling. North of the church of Ayios Nikólaos (rebuilt on old foundations) are the remains of substantial buildings, probably Venetian. The protected saddle, designed as a haven in times of trouble in the surrounding countryside, slopes down to the main *north entrance* where formidable overlapping defence walls are excellently preserved. In places the walls reuse Hellenistic material, presumably from Lýkastos.

Ayía Paraskeví has only the tantalising remains of the frescoes which the Italian scholar Guiseppe Gerola admired at the beginning of this century. It is possible to walk here directly (avoiding the scramble to the summit) by the track which will now lead you back from the church round the flank of the hill to the village (10 minutes).

It is worth walking south into the village round the foot of the hill to the Venetian *fountain* known locally as Η Μεγάλη Πηγή (megáli piyí), the great fountain. There is a precipitous path or stairway up the steep rock face above it, and remains of guard houses with conspicuous brick courses in their walling.

You can continue on a quiet country road c 10km to Veneráto (see Rte 4 to Phaistós) with a possible detour on the way, left in Kipárissos 4km to Rukáni. On the edge of the village the (recently restored) domed cruciform church of Ayios Ioánnis dates to the Second Byzantine period (11/12 C). Alternatively return through Tsagaráki, and c 2km beyond this hamlet turn right on a quiet by-road for *Ayios Sýlas* and *Vasiliés*. Through Fortétsa, this emerges on the Knossós road (Rte 2) opposite the University buildings, and you turn left for Herákleion or the north coast highway.

4   Herákleion to the Mesará and the Palace of Phaistós

Direct route 64km (40 miles) to the major Minoan sites of Phaistós and
Ayía Triáda. 30km Ayía Varvára; 46km Górtyn, the capital of Roman
Crete. Continue to the south coast at (75km) Mátala or (84km) Ayía Galíni.

A number of alternative routes branch off this direct road: a 65km round
trip from Herákleion through Ayía Varvára taking in the Archaic site of
Priniás; a branch road from Ayía Varvára through the southern foothills of
Psilorítis (Mount Ida) to (57km) Kamáres, which passes two important
frescoed churches; an alternative return route to Herákleion from Ayii
Déka along the Mesará plain and then north through the Témenos
countryside; a road through the Asteroúsia mountains to the south coast
at Léndas, site of ancient Lebéna (78km from Herákleion). These
alternatives are noted at the appropriate junctions on the way to Phaistós,
but are described separately at the end of the direct route.

There are buses to all these destinations from the bus station ouside the
Khaniá Gate in Herákleion. Frequent services to Phaistós.

The road leaves Herákleion to the west by the Khaniá Gate, becomes a
dual-carriageway and (2.5km) turns left (signposted Míres and Phaistós).
This is also the junction for the north coast highway (New Road), but
keep straight ahead under the bridge. From other north coast bases you
can join the route here, in which case you should deduct c 3km from distances given below (and on the new kilometre posts along the road which
are measured from central Herákleion).

At c 2km after the highway junction a minor road (signed for Ayios Mýron and
Asítes) turns right and runs parallel to the main route which it rejoins (after c 30km)
at Ayía Varvára. This alternative route, slower but relatively free of traffic, is
described as part of a leisurely excursion to Ayios Mýron and the Archaic site of
Priniás (see p 154).

The main road climbs gently through a valley planted with vines and
olives, the cypress trees scattered with dramatic effect. Occasional
glimpses of hills are a foretaste of mountain views in store. Continue
through (19km) *Sivá*. At 20.5km, soon after entering *Veneráto*, a (signed)
detour left leads in 2km to the Palianí monastery.

400m after leaving the main road, turn right where the monastery sign is painted on
a wall, and almost immediately at a fork keep right downhill. (An alternative
approach to this fork is also signed from the main road.) Across the valley the road
then climbs to the monastery, with the reward at the top of a wide retrospective
view. The village on the summit of a hill away to the north is Ayios Mýron.

Moní Palianí is an ancient foundation, documented as an antiquity (palaiá meaning old) even in 668. Nowadays a nunnery, this is a flourishing self-supporting community. The nuns are hospitable and will point out interesting features of the old
buildings; their fine handwork is for sale.

The 13C church (the narthex a 15C–16C addition) retained the plan of the underlying three-aisled 6C basilica, but in the last century it was much restored after Turkish destruction and earthquake damage. Some Early Byzantine (6C) capitals and
impost blocks are preserved; two capitals are in situ, four support the altar, and
others lie outside in the courtyard.

In the 14C, authority over the wealthy monastery was disputed at great length
between the powers of the Orthodox and Latin Churches, in the shape of the Patriarch of Constantinople and the Latin Archbishop acting under instruction from
Pope Clement IV.

Veneráto now adjoins (at 21km) *Avyenikí*, after which the road begins to gain height through olive groves. 3km further, on a sharp bend, you pass left the turn for (5km) Ayios Thomás on a ridge (here the watershed) which geologists recognise as the spine of the island linking the mountain peaks of Ida and Díkte. The village, at 530m above sea level, is curiously situated around a conical rocky eminence.

The main road continues to climb to a less cultivated level, dominated to the right by a chapel on a craggy outcrop. Here, in the Archaic period, was the acropolis of the city-state of *Rizenía*; some important Daidalic-style sculptures from its temples can be seen in the Herákleion Museum. The site is immediately to the north of the modern village of Priniás, by which name it is now usually known.

The circular rock formations in the valley below are a strong erosion feature; locally they are called 'the old lady's cheeses'. The Phaistós bus will put you down at the start of the roughly paved 'Turkish' road or kalderími, for the cross- country walk (c 1 hour) to the ancient site; ask for Priniás 'me ta pódia' (on foot), and for the kalderími, which is the second of two tracks, 200m before the 27km post.

30km *Ayía Varvára*, where the little church of Prophítis Ilías perched high on a rock called Omphalos (navel) is said to mark the centre of Crete. In the middle of this long village the minor road from Priniás and Ayios Mýron joins the main road (5km from this junction to the start of the path to the archaeological site—see p 155).

At the end of Ayía Varvára is a turning (right) for the monastery of Valsamóneros and Kamáres; this route too is described among alternative excursions below (p 156).

Shortly after Ayía Varvára on the main road to Phaistós, the *Mesará plain* comes suddenly into view, spread out below to the left; beyond, to the south, are the Asteroúsia mountains and beyond them the Libyan Sea. The plain is an alluvial basin of the Quaternary period. From the foothills of the Díkte range to the Bay of Mesará, it lies parallel to the south coast, watered by two great rivers and their tributaries: the Anapodáris (at the east end of the plain) and the Ieropótamos (ancient Lethaíos, Lethe) flowing into the sea below the Minoan site of Ayía Triáda. The rich soil and benign climate in the shelter of the island's central spine of mountains have favoured settlement through the ages, and this is still an area of great agricultural prosperity.

First occupied at the end of the Neolithic period, the Mesará experienced rapid population growth during the Early Bronze Age, with many settlements along the slopes of the Asteroúsia range, and the first appearance of the monumental collective tombs, on a circular plan with entrance from the east, which have become known as the Mesará type. By the beginning of the second millenium, Phaistós had begun to emerge as the great palatial centre and economic focus of the region. At a later period the city of Górtyn on the northern edge of the plain became the capital of Roman Crete, and retained a position of power until the second half of the 7C.

The road winds down from the hills and in summer the temperature increases at every bend. The wild flowers of the Mesará are strikingly larger and taller than anywhere else on Crete.

43km. An acute left turn signposted for *Pýrgos* is an important junction for routes to south-eastern parts of the island. One possibility is an alternative return drive (c 63km) to Herákleion, east along the Mesará plain, and then north through Khoudétsi and Pezá, entering Herákleion by the Knossós road. Details are given on p 158. Alternatively, from Pýrgos you can continue east on the recently completed section of the south coast road towards Viánnos and the extreme south-east of Crete (Rte 8).

44km *Ayii Déka.* The name, the Holy Ten, commemorates ten Christian martyrs of the Persecution of Decius (AD 250). The *church* is signposted left of the through road, in the older part of the village.

This much-restored 13/14C building incorporates re-used material from the neighbouring city of Górtyn. In the nave an icon portrays the martyrdom, and below in a glass case is a stone on which the ten are supposed to have knelt to be executed. Many of the old houses around the pleasant tree-shaded square in front of the church also incorporate ancient fragments from Górtyn.

A path leads (5 minutes) to the south-west outskirts of the village, and to a crypt beside the portico of a modern chapel where six tile graves are venerated as the tombs of the martyrs.

46km GORTYN (the English rendering of Γόρτυς) was the most powerful Greco-Roman city on the island, and capital of the Roman province of Crete and Cyrenaica. The main road cuts through the middle of the still largely unexcavated city which lies in the olive groves where the foothills of Mount Ida and the Mitropolianós, tributary of the Ieropótamos, ancient Lethe, meet the Mesará plain. The ruins of the basilica of Ayios Títos mark a convenient stopping-place on the right of the road (see area plan) whether you spend a whole day at Górtyn or make a brief stop to see the *basilica* and the 5C BC *law code*, both within the area, now enclosed, of the Greek-period agorá.

This area is open 08.30–15.00 every day except Monday (closed). Entrance charge. The small museum in a loggia beside it (no charge) houses a dozen large pieces of Górtyn's sculpture. There are also contemporary photographs (labelled in Greek and Italian) of the earliest excavations at the turn of the century; one of the Odeion and the associated reconstructions shows the Venetian water-mill on the stream beside the acropolis.

The rest of the huge site may be explored at will, though excavations usually have to be viewed from vantage points outside a protective fence. Major finds from the site (except as above, and from the basilica—see below) are displayed as appropriate chronologically in the Archaeological Museum in Herákleion.

The site was first explored in the 1880s by the Italian archaeologist, Federico Halbherr; with his primary interest in epigraphy, he was drawn here by earlier travellers' tales of fragments of inscribed blocks. Almost immediately he was able to locate the major part of the Law Code inscription, still one of the most important known in the Greek world. The Italian Institute returned to the site during the early part of this century, and again from 1954–61 when the acropolis was investigated, and work has continued in recent years. The whole area of the city is littered with ploughed-out architectural fragments and pottery, and only a number of major buildings at the centre, and some cemeteries, have been systematically excavated. A recent topographical survey resulted in a plan incorporating the most up-to-date understanding of ancient Górtyn; a large-scale version is now displayed at strategic positions around the site.

History. There was a settlement on the *acropolis hill* from the end of the Bronze Age (Subminoan, c 1000 BC) until the 7C BC, during which time it became a place of religious and military significance. The acropolis was fortified in the Geometric period and parts of the *bastioned wall* still stand. The city spread on to the plain below and was flourishing by the first half of the 5C BC, the date of the Law Code. By the time of the defeat of Phaistós (2C BC), Górtyn extended south to modern Mitrópolis and east beyond the temple of Apollo Pythios and, with the additional strength of two harbours (Mátala and Lebéna), was intermittently at war with either Knossós or Lýttos. The Carthaginian general Hannibal visited Górtyn (189 BC) after the Battle of Magnesia.

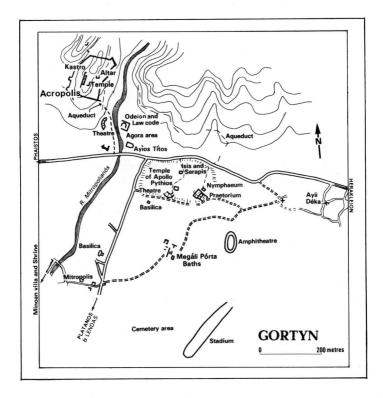

At the time of the Roman invasion (65 BC) the city put up no resistance to Quintus Metellus, and while Knossós was destroyed, Górtyn went on to flourish as the capital of the new Roman province. Many of the great public buildings date from the Imperial period, particularly from the 2C AD. St. Titus, commissioned by St. Paul to convert the island, was installed here as the first Bishop of Crete. The Byzantine city spread over the plain to the south during a period of great expansion; six basilicas and smaller churches are known to have existed contemporaneously in one small area (100m long) between Mitrópolis and the River Lethaíos. The region suffered a number of severe earthquakes, and at last, towards the end of the 7C, Górtyn was destroyed by Arab raiders. The basilica of Ayios Títos was rededicated in the 10C and there was a Venetian monastery on the Praetorium site, but the great city was never rebuilt.

The **Basilica of Ayios Títos**, traditionally the burial place of the saint, is by far the best-preserved Early Christian church on Crete. Its foundation is tentatively attributed to the Justinianic period (early 6C), but it underwent many reconstructions. Originally it was an imposing church, built of unusually large limestone blocks; the three-aisled basilica with narthex (see ground plan) was elaborated by the addition of a cross-dome, reflecting the influence of Eastern architecture. The ruins of the *bema* are still impressive.

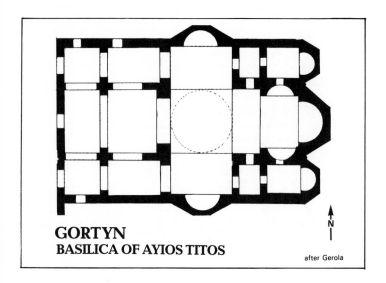

GORTYN
BASILICA OF AYIOS TITOS

after Gerola

After a study by the Italian Guiseppe Gerola in 1900, the church was excavated by Greek archaeologists in 1902 and again in 1920. The ground plan remains intelligible: narthex, nave with side-aisles, central cross with side-arms which end in apses. Around the central dome, the nave and the arms of the cross were barrel-vaulted. In the triconch chancel each side-chapel had an anteroom. Architectural fragments dating from the 2C suggest a previous building, probably a temple, on the site or nearby.

The Historical Museum in Herákleion preserves stone carvings and liturgical furnishings from Ayios Títos.

The basilica stands beside the unexcavated *Agorá* or *Forum* (see area plan). A path leads north west to the *Odeion*, a theatre used for musical performances or contests; the excavated remains are those of a 1C BC structure restored under Trajan after earthquake damage in the early 2C AD. In the foundations of an earlier circular building (of Hellenistic date) on this site were re-used stone blocks inscribed with the famous **Law Code of Górtyn**. The code, now displayed beyond the Roman Odeion, is written in a form of the Dorian dialect dating to the first half of the 5C BC, and is therefore the earliest law code yet known from the Greek world.

The *inscription* is divided into 12 columns, 600 lines in all, 17,000 letters. It is written 'boustrophedon': this word describes the pattern of oxen ploughing a field, so alternately one line reads from left to right, the next from right to left. The inscription codifies in great detail the laws relating to property in respect of marriage and divorce, the sale and mortgage of property, the rights of heirs and the division of property among children, including adopted children. It deals with the procedure for adoption. It covers cases of seduction, rape and adultery, as well as general assault; also the position of slaves, and much else besides.

Across the Mitropolianós stream from the Odeion the outline can be detected of the *Larger Theatre* cut into the lower slope of the acropolis hill; in Roman times the stream ran through a culvert. The plan of the theatre is known from the drawings by the Italian antiquary Onorio Belli, who was appointed physician to the Venetian Proveditor General of Candia in 1583, and during a tour of the island with him (designed to 'rectify disorder') recorded for posterity invaluable information about Roman monuments still surviving at that time.

The **acropolis** (outside the main fenced site) is reached by a track from the road along the west bank of the stream. Beyond the theatre, a gate marks the start of the path, and the easiest route gains height across the south slope, to reach the flat summit at its south-west corner (10 minutes from the gate, a recommended climb if only for the view).

On the southern brow of the hill are the excavated foundations (fenced) of the 7C BC *temple of Athena* (a rectangular building with cella and central bothros or circular pit), which continued in use, restored on several occasions but not basically altered, into early Roman times. Below the temple, terraced into the east slope, was an associated *altar of sacrifice* (8C–3C BC), which stood on a wide platform supported by a massive ashlar wall. The cult statue from the temple, remains of decoration including the naked feminine triad in relief, and Geometric and Archaic finds from the rich votive deposit at the altar site, are in Herákleion Museum, Galleries XVIII and XIX; they include notable exhibits in the Daidalic style.

In the 6C the temple was succeeded on the same site by a Christian basilica.

These fenced remains are over-shadowed by an unexcavated but well-preserved Roman building known as the *Kástro*, which consists of a spacious hall sunk up to 6m into the rock. Its function, probably as some offical building, is uncertain.

The acropolis was fortified as early as the Geometric period; the Hellenistic circuit was restored in Byzantine times, and parts of this *bastioned wall* of concrete with good stone facing can still be traced.

On either side of the stream archaeologists have found branches of the great *aqueduct* that brought water to the city from Zarós on the slopes of Mount Ida.

The rest of the site of interest to visitors lies across the main road, east of the turning to Plátanos and Léndas. Paths are signposted (see area plan).

The *Temple of Isis and Serapis* is a simple rectangular cella with on its south side a crypt complex, probably for initiation ceremonies. The cella has a tripartite podium in the east wall for the statues of the Egyptian divinities; the third was possibly Hermes Anubis. A stylobate of six Ionic columns fronted the west façade. This temple is dated 1–2C AD from the dedication of Flavia Philyra and her two sons.

To the south is the **Temple of Apollo Pythios**, the main sanctuary of pre-Roman Górtyn. The original 7C temple was a simple cella with rectangular bothros just inside the doorway (right). In the Hellenistic period a pronaos was added with six half-engaged columns of the Doric order. Between the columns, four inscribed stelai displayed Górtyn's 2C BC treaties with other Cretan cities and with Eumenes II of Pergamon. The stepped *monumental altar* in front of the temple and the small *heroön* just to the north east were built at this period. During the Empire (2C AD) the temple was converted, with the addition of an apse and arcaded Corinthian columns, into a three-aisled *Christian basilica*, which continued as the religious centre of the city until c 600 and the construction of Ayios Títos.

Near by (to the south west) are the remains of the *'Smaller Theatre'*, the best-preserved Roman theatre on Crete. It is built in brick-faced concrete with a double-tiered 'cavea' or seating arrangement.

To the east along the track (or it can also be reached on a signed path off the main road) is the **Praetorium**, the grand palace complex of the Roman governor of the Province; this can be viewed from outside the fence along the north side, which follows a fine stretch of Roman (and medieval) road. Excavations have revealed several phases of building. The early 2C AD construction, contemporary with the rebuilt Odeion of the Trajanic period, probably replaced an Augustan palace, and then was itself enlarged and rebuilt in the 4C after earthquake damage. The architectural fragments on the site include marble columns, and capitals of both the Ionic and Corinthian orders. The 4C reconstruction created the large *basilica audience hall* (27m by 12m) in the north-west corner of the site; it was built of concrete, faced in this case with stone, and the floor was paved. Along the outer wall the dedicatory bases intended for statues of prominent citizens of the Roman world are preserved. East of this was the bath suite. The 2C *Nymphaeum* to the north was supplied by a branch of the city's main aqueduct (see above). The Praetorium building survived in part as a monastery during the Second Byzantine period, and the Nymphaeum became a public fountain.

South east of the Praetorium (c 150m) are the remains of the almost unexcavated *Amphitheatre* (late 2C AD). Further south the *Stadium* or Circus is scarcely discernible under cultivation.

To the west of the Amphitheatre are the remains of the Roman building which was given the name 'Megáli Pórta' or Great Gate. This has not been excavated but is recognised as a 2C AD *public baths* complex, with the arch being part of a large hall.

Almost opposite Ayios Títos is the turning for the road south to Plátanos and Léndas. This route is described below (see p 159); included is the detour to the Minoan villa or farm near Kanniá, less than 2km from Mitrópolis.

52km from Herákleion on the main road is *Míres* (pop. 3500), not superficially an attractive town but the thriving centre of this agricultural region, with a busy Saturday morning market in the wide main street. A minor road to the left is the direct way (18km) to Mátala (see below), but for Phaistós keep straight on through the town.

About 3km beyond Míres, the site of the Palace of Phaistós comes into view ahead slightly to the left of the road, at the end of a low ridge jutting into the Mesará plain.

The rich Kalývia cemetery lay on the slopes to the right of the road. Postpalatial tombs were excavated early this century (finds in Herákleion Museum, Gallery VI) and more recently Protogeometric burials have also been discovered.

At 57km Moní Kalvyaní is one of the most flourishing ecclesiastical establishments on the island; the nuns run an orphanage and school. An avenue of clipped bougainvillea leads to the big modern church with Italianate campanile; behind it is the 14C frescoed chapel of the Panayía Kalivianís.

The newly established **Museum of Cretan Ethnology**—for the study of the development of the Cretan culture after 1000 AD—lies just off this main road and is a recommended detour at some time in the day's itinerary. The museum is open daily: 10.00–21.00; small entrance charge. Follow signs past the Phaistós junction and then almost immediately turn right 1km to the attractive village of *Vóri* on a minor road up to Kamáres and Mount Ida (see below). An old courtyard building near the church has been well converted to house the remarkably comprehensive collection relating to the arts, crafts and social history of the island. The exhibits are clearly labelled and explained in English as well as Greek, and there is also an illustrated catalogue.

2.5km beyond the Kalyvianí convent turn left to cross the Ieropótamos and climb to (61km) **"PHAISTOS**. From the bus stop and car park, a paved path leads up to the palace site, and a Tourist Pavilion (café).

The Minoan palace occupied a superb position overlooking the Mesará plain. To the north is Mount Ida, snow-capped for half the year, and to the south the Asteroúsia range running parallel to the coast. The nearby

Minoan site known as **Ayía Triáda*, at the western end of the same ridge, had sea views to the west over the Mesará Bay. The relationship between the two sites is still uncertain, and is an area of great interest for archaeologists working in this field.

Note that opening hours for the two sites are not identical; Ayía Triáda closes before Phaistós.

Phaistós: 08.00–18.00, Sunday 09.00–15.00. (Ayía Triáda open, including Sundays 08.30–15.00.) Entrance charges.

Hours may be extended in high summer, and are reduced in winter. If in doubt check with a Tourist Information Office, or telephone the NTOG in Herákleion (81) 228 225.

The Palace of Phaistós and the surrounding area were excavated by the Italian Archaeological Mission on Crete. Work began in 1900 and continued for nearly a decade, with L. Pernier as director; the results were published in the 1930s. From 1950–66 Doro Levi (for the Italian School of Archaeology at Athens, which had absorbed the Mission) conducted further extensive excavations in the southern and western sectors of the site, revealing a considerable area of the Old Palace (First Palace in the Italian terminology) and of the surrounding Minoan town. Exploration and study still continue.

The site was inhabited in Neolithic and Early Minoan times; pottery deposits of these periods are found beneath the earliest palace floors, and Prepalatial structures have been uncovered west of the area of the later West Court. The Middle Minoan palace was built in MMIB (c 1900 BC; see chronological outline p 18). Levi's excavations revealed three distinct phases for this building before it was destroyed, like Knossós, at the end of MMII. The ruins of the Old Palace were levelled and consolidated to provide foundations for the New Palace (excavators' Second Palace) which is mainly what visitors see today. The New Palace was destroyed, like many other major sites on the island at the end of LMIB. There was some reoccupation in LMIII, towards the end of the Bronze Age, and in the Geometric period (8C BC). Of the Classical-Hellenistic era are remains of a temple and some substantial houses. The city, mentioned in Linear B tablets and by Homer ('Iliad', II, 648, where it is described as 'well inhabited'), was important in the later periods and minted its own coins, until it was destroyed by Górtyn in the 2C BC.

As at Knossós, Mállia and Zákros, the palace was built around a large Central Court and has a Grand Entrance, with an elegant staircase from a West Court (see plan). The main reception rooms are immediately to the north of the Central Court, and beyond them, on the northern edge of the palace with an uninterrupted view of the mountains, are the main living quarters, comparable to the Domestic Quarter at Knossós. Also as at Knossós, the wing on the west side of the Central Court has a religious area next to storerooms, and palace workshops tucked away to the north east. Features distinctive to Phaistós are the Grand Staircase, the Peristyle Hall and the formal north façade of the Central Court.

From the modern entrance to the site, you cross the *Upper Court* diagonally to a flight of stairs. (On your right are the remains of Hellenistic buildings.) You descend a staircase to the *Theatral Area* (1 on the plan) and the **West Court**. To the right of the staircase, along the north side of the West Court, is a retaining wall for the Upper Court, and below it tiered rows provided seats for the events and ceremonies that took place here.

From the West Court two successive palace façades are still visible. When the New Palace was built (in MMIII) its façade was set back about 8m behind that of its predecessor, and the level of the new West Court was raised accordingly. Its new paving was laid above more than a metre

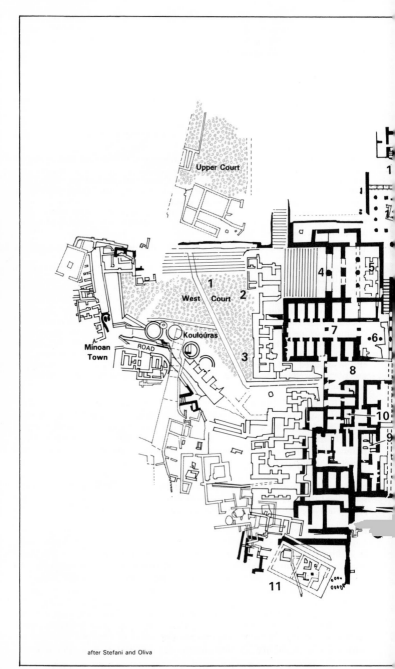

after Stefani and Oliva

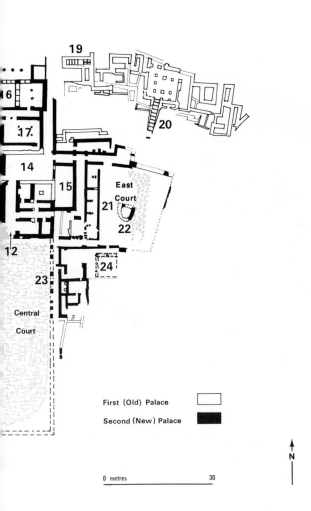

19

6

17.

14

15

East
Court

21

22

20

12

24

23

Central
Court

First (Old) Palace

Second (New) Palace

0 metres 30

N

PALACE OF PHAISTOS

of cement-like fill, in the process covering the lower tiers of the Theatral Area. During excavation this paving and fill were removed, leaving the Old Palace West Court that you now see, with its *raised paths* a distinctive Minoan feature, and (outside the fence) *kouloúras* similar to those at Knossós and Mállia.

To the south and west of the Theatral Area, beyond a fine Minoan *paved road* (also outside fence), lies part of the *Minoan town*. The Italians have been excavating here since 1966, uncovering important houses that were destroyed at the same time as the Old Palace. From this complex has come an astonishing number of polychrome vases in the *Kamáres ware*, named after the sacred cave where it was first identified, but thought to have been made only at the palace workshops of Knossós and Phaistós.

The distinctive decoration is in white, red, orange and yellow on a black ground, the curvilinear motifs flowing over the whole surface of the pot. Kamáres ware provides some of the finest examples of the Minoan potter's art, rarely equalled in prehistoric times; a superb collection of these vases from both palace and town at Phaistós is displayed in Gallery III in the Herákleion Museum.

At the north-east corner of the West Court, a group of small rooms (2 on plan) is a *shrine complex* of the Old Palace; two adjoining areas have benches round the walls. These rooms contained a large clay 'table for offerings', stone vases, a triton shell and other cult objects now forming the central exhibit of Gallery III (see above). In a sacrificial pit to the north of the main room, charred animal bones suggested burnt offerings.

To the south of the shrine is the *west façade* (3) of the Old Palace, recessed, as was the later version, for the windows of the storey above. Behind this the excavated Old Palace rooms, MMIIA (Levi's phase 1B), have been covered over to form a level surface in front of the *New Palace façade*. They ended to the south at a corridor which provided a monumental West Entrance for the Old Palace. Down the hill south of the corridor (fenced off and in places roofed for protection) work continues on the wing where the New Palace did not extend over the ruins of its MMI–II predecessor. This has allowed archaeologists a unique opportunity to investigate Old Palace remains.

From the Theatral Area of the West Court, the monumental **"Grand Staircase** into the palace, walled in fine ashlar masonry, leads up to the *Propylon* (4). This was a porch with a massive central column, in front of a pair of double doors leading to a narrow anteroom and a large colonnaded *light-well* (5). This imposing entrance changes character at this point, for from the light-well only small unimposing exits led left by a roundabout route to the Reception Rooms, or right to the Central Court. Take the staircase which descends to the right to the level of the Court.

On the right, at the foot of the stairs and under the Propylon light-well, are *storerooms* of the Old Palace where large pithoi with painted decoration have been left in position on their stands.

The square *hall* (6) was built with two internal columns, and there is an oval column base (very unusual in Minoan architecture) on the same line and between two pillars in the colonnade on the court; massive doors closed from both sides on to the column that rested on this oval base. The hall seems to have controlled access to the double row of storerooms behind it, as well as being associated in an administrative capacity with them; beneath the floor of the building and dating to the earlier palace, were discovered in 1955 tablets in the Linear A script, and an extensive archive of *clay sealings*. From over 6500 seal-impressions on small lumps of clay, nearly 300 different motifs have been identified; a display in Herákleion Museum, Gallery III, illustrates the wide variety of subjects. Study of the material, including the impressions on the backs of the clay lumps, suggests that many of the objects sealed were not as had been thought vessels or containers but wooden door-handles, a discovery with interesting implications about the administration of storage.

Behind the columned hall, the *storeroom block* (7) is a tangible reminder of the importance of storage and redistribution to the Minoan palace economy; the solid construction and the central pillars would have supported an upper floor, and the gypsum slabs, dadoes and column bases found in the storerooms had fallen from it. At the end of the row (right) *giant pithoi* of the New Palace period are visible behind a grille.

To the south of the storeroom complex was a *corridor* (8), walled with massive stone blocks; it formed an impressive entrance on this west side of the court, and could be closed at both ends by double doors. The area south of this is poorly preserved, and is now partly fenced off. Several of the rooms here seem to have had religious purposes: there is a *pillar crypt* (9) with a bench round it as at Knossós, and behind this a *lustral basin* (10).

Down the slope at the south-west corner of the site, at an oblique angle to the Minoan remains, are the lower courses of the walls of a *temple* (11) of the Classical period (on 8C foundations), perhaps dedicated to the Great Mother, Rhea.

The palace buildings to the south and east have been lost owing to the erosion of the hillside; however, part of the *drainage system* survives in the south-west angle of the court and is exposed near the site fence.

Looking north at this point, up the great paved **Central Court** (51.50m by 22.50m), the view is dominated by the distant mass of Mount Ida. One of its southern bluffs has distinctive twin peaks with a shallow saddle between them, and a little below the right-hand peak a large dark spot, especially dramatic when there is snow on the mountain, marks the Minoan sanctuary, the *sacred cave* of Kamáres.

Both long sides of the Central Court had *porticoes* along their frontage, and some of the stone bases for wooden columns or pillars still survive; those on the west side, and at a lower level, belong to the portico of the earlier palace. The buildings on the east side of the court are preserved only at their northern end (described below).

The court's *north façade* of ashlar blocks has a *central doorway* designed with a formality known only at Phaistós. This is framed by half-engaged columns (originally wood) and by recesses which are considered to be *sentry boxes*. The plaster which lined them was decorated with a lozenge-pattern fresco, dark lozenges on light ground. Sockets can be seen in the threshold block for the double doors which opened into a passage (12). Just inside the passage is a further recess for a sentry (also showing traces of lozenge-pattern fresco). Next to this is a *staircase* (with a pithos under it) which would have given access to important reception rooms on the upper floor. Perhaps, as has been suggested in similar positions at Mállia and Zákros, these included a dining hall.

The staircase was one of the routes to the important Peristyle Hall which could also be reached from an anteroom of the Propylon, or by the staircase from the Central Court, as well as from the grand private quarters to the north (identified by their protective cover). If you take the stairs from the north west corner of the Central Court, you pass two LMIIIB (reoccupation period) pithoi, and a stone block with double-axe masons' mark, which may have been the base of an altar. At the top of the stairs an anteroom leads into the *Peristyle Hall* (13). Part of the foundations of an earlier (Prepalatial) building have been left uncovered in the centre, but the colonnade of the hall would have produced an effect similar to a cloister, with the north side open to the mountain view from an elaborately paved verandah.

Return down the staircase noted above which leads directly to the sentry boxes guarding the entrance to the palace's north wing (at 12). A drain running down the centre of the paved passage suggests that it was unroofed and took rainwater from the buildings on either side. It leads to the *North Court* (14) which separates the main block of reception rooms on the Central Court from the grand private quarters ahead towards the trees on the slope of the hill. Over to the east is a large open area (15), its well-preserved *ashlar masonry* similar to that of the North Court; it may have been a walled garden.

The (fenced and roofed) *Private Quarters* can be viewed from several vantage points. Here the most luxurious room of the block (16), nearest the edge of the hill, has an elaborate plan similar to that of the Hall of the Double Axes (King's Megaron) at Knossós. Pier-and-door arrangements on the north and east sides of the main inner area allowed this space to be securely enclosed or to be thrown open to the *verandah* with mountain views to the north, or to the portico giving on to a sheltered *light-well* to the east. This light-well has a drain for rainwater through the wall at its north-east corner. Across a passage to the south (with staircase up to the Peristyle Hall) the room with four columns, gypsum bench and dado (17) has been compared to the Queen's Megaron at Knossós.

From the south-west corner of the larger hall, a dogleg passage leads to (18) a *lustral basin* (best viewed from west side) which has been re-lined with gypsum slabs (from nearby quarries at Ayía Triáda); the original choice of this soluble material suggests that the basin was not intended to contain water. West of the lustral basin, the outer of two small rooms was a lavatory, with a hollowed stone connected to a drain.

Proceeding east round the flank of the hill you come to a series of chests (19) built of mudbrick and originally faced with plaster. In one of them was found (1903) the mysterious **Phaistós disk**.

The disk, of baked clay c 16cm in diameter, is inscribed on both sides in an unknown ideographic script. The signs (241 in all) are set in a spiral thought to run from circumference to centre. Despite many ingenious attempts to decipher the script, the disk (prominently displayed in Herákleion Museum, Gallery III) remains an enigma.

On the north-east edge of the hill lies a further complex of rooms reached by a long staircase (20). The underlying levels visible here date from the Old Palace, and the area with columns at the foot of the staircase may have been a *peristyle* anticipating the plan of the Peristyle Hall (13, above).

Returning, by the stairs, towards the centre of the site, you pass craftsmen's workshops (21) along one side of the East Court. In the middle of it (fenced), are the remains of a large *furnace* for metalworking (22); scraps of copper and bronze were found still adhering to its walls.

A ramp connected this East Court to the north-east corner of the Central Court, and the foundations of a set of rooms known as the *East Wing*

(23). This self-contained suite demonstrates all the most delightful embellishments of Minoan domestic architecture: a versatile main hall, a peristyle court, a bath, even a bench outside the door to the Central Court. The finds here included LMI vases, a table for offerings and several bronze double axes. The *colonnaded court* (24) was surely designed to benefit from the uninterrupted prospect of the Mesará plain, to the Asteroúsia mountains and the distant Lasíthi range, and three and a half thousand years ago this would have been, as it remains, a magnificent sight.

To *Ayía Triáda

Open (including Sundays) 08.30–15.00. Entrance charge.

Leave the Phaistós car park at the far end towards the picturesque ruined church, all that remains of the monastery of Ayios Yeóryios Phalándras. Opposite it the footpath (usually marked) strikes off to the right around the northern flank of the hill, with views of Mount Ida, and approaches the site through groves of orange trees (c 30 minutes). By car (3km) keep right at the fork near the church along the south-facing slope, where in April and May the hillside is densely covered with pink Cretan ebony.

Ayía Triáda is beautifully situated, overlooking the plain at the mouth of the Ieropótamos river where it runs into the Bay of Mesará; in the Bronze Age the sea may have come right up to the foot of the hill. The ancient name of the site is unknown—though tentatively identified with the 'da-wo' of a Knossós Linear B tablet—so archaeologists named it after the double-naved Venetian church (in view from the car park) which lies close to the river bank, 250m south west towards the sea.

The site was excavated by the Italian Mission (1902–14), under the personal supervision of its director, Federico Halbherr, but for various reasons the full results were not made available at that time; the definitive publication of the structures and material of the New Palace period (chiefly the work of L. Banti) happily coinciding with the 1984 celebrations for the centenary of Italian archaeology on Crete, has gone a long way to fill this gap. Excavations to re-examine the stratigraphy with the benefit of modern methods have been in progress since 1977.

There is evidence of continuous occupation dating from the Neolithic period to the 13C BC, but the chief interest of Ayía Triáda is focused on the LMI and LMIII (New Palace and Postpalatial) phases, and especially on the relationship between the Minoan buildings—the so-called Royal Villa—and the contemporary New (Second) Palace at Phaistós. The quantity and quality of the LMI finds marked this site as exceptional. They included alabaster facings, carved stone vases, fresco paintings and one of the most important archives of tablets inscribed in Linear A so far known on the island. There was extensive reoccupation in LMIII after the widespread LMIB destruction of the palaces and other Minoan sites on Crete; the megaron-type building here (reflecting Mycenaean influence) is the earliest known on the island, and the area of the lower town was reconstructed at this time.

In the Geometric period part of the villa site seems to have had cult associations, for clay and bronze figurines of this date were found here. Later there was a Hellenistic shrine dedicated to Zeus Velkhanós. The little Byzantine church above the excavation, Ayios Yeóryios Galatás, has remains of *frescoes* (1302) including (sadly worn) a rare scene in the apse with the Christ child representing the elements of the Eucharist. (Key with site guards.)

You can get a preliminary understanding of the site from the mound beside the apse of this church, where you are looking out across the excavation to the broad river valley and Mount Ida away to the north.

The irregular remains of paving immediately in front of you indicate the position of the *Upper Court* (see plan), and the Palatial-style Minoan buildings (contemporary with the New Palace at Phaistós) occupied an L-shape along the north and west sides of it; there was evidence for an upper storey. Beyond (to the north) is the *Lower Court* with its surrounding buildings, reached by a (later) staircase, and beyond that the excavated remains of the settlement or town.

At the eastern end of the L-shape (under the plastic roofing) is a set of rooms where the quality of the architecture suggests an important residential or reception area, with, adjoining to the west, its own storerooms. The grandest residential apartments, with the best view of the sea, named the 'signorile' quarter by the Italian excavators, lay in the northwest corner (the angle of the L). Between these two areas was the main storeroom block of the Minoan complex, with many large clay pithoi. Finally to the south of the 'signorile' quarter (level with the west end of the church) was a more modest block, perhaps for servants or attendants, which included storerooms and a kitchen.

The Minoan buildings of Ayía Triáda have traditionally been known as the *Royal Villa*, perhaps a summer palace of the rulers of Phaistós. Now the economic and administrative aspects are being emphasised, especially with regard to the important Linear A archive found here.

The excavation report points out that architecturally the structures divide themselves into separate sectors, linked together but distinct according to their function. A peculiarity of the Minoan levels is that each quarter, whether grand or modest, had its own storage area, not for merchandise or provisions which were held in the main north storeroom block, but for valued possessions such as articles of pottery, stone and bronze. Each quarter had an independent entrance, and its own staircase to an upper floor; moreover it seems that none of the existing entrances was a principal one for the whole villa complex.

Recently it has even been argued that in the distinct east and west wings we may be dealing with the remains of not one but two villas, comparable with those for example at Týlissos, and part of the recognised network of estates playing a crucial role in the system of collection and distribution that was the basis of the Minoan economy.

Over part of the Minoan wing on the north side of the Upper Court, there were erected, in the later (LMIII) phase, two large rectangular buildings (unshaded on plan) on different axes from the LMI construction; architecturally they resemble the megaron of mainland Mycenaean type. Abutting the first of these 'reoccupation' buildings and associated with it, a loggia with rectangular flagstones and a column base faced on to the Upper Court.

Near the eastern end of the Upper Court (below the guardian's hut) two short flights of a narrow *staircase* (1) lead down into the **East Wing** of the L-shape described above. In the Minoan period this wing, which was open to the east on to a forecourt, consisted of a set of rooms (2) with windows on to light-wells, gypsum stairs, dadoes, benches, and a drainage system; the remains hint at the refinement of the architecture. (The upper levels of the drainage system belong to the LMIII reoccupation period.)

Originally (in LMI times) the Lower Court was a private open space; the broad staircase now leading down to it was a later adaptation. The court was bounded on its east side by a five-columned portico, and on the north by a massively built structure (3) known as the *Bastion*, possibly a warehouse. The paved *Minoan road* to the sea, the 'Rampa al Mare', led out of this court, along the north façade of the villa buildings. (The stepped section of the road is a LMIII alteration.)

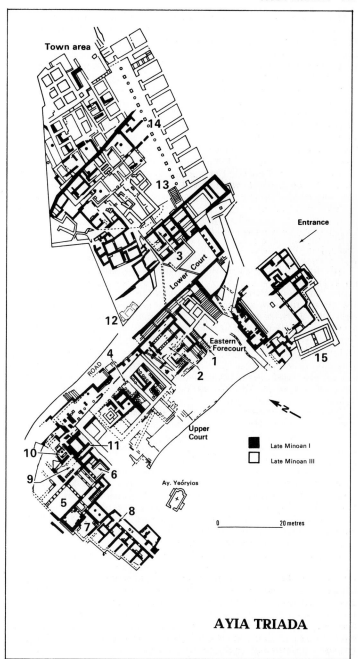

Town area

14

13

Entrance

3

Lower Court

12

Eastern
Forecourt

4

ROAD

1

2

Upper
Court

10

11

9

6

5

7

8

Ay. Yeóryios

■ Late Minoan I
□ Late Minoan III

0 _____ 20 metres

15

AYIA TRIADA

The main *storerooms* (4) still contain a number of pithoi, and one, up stone steps, has five gypsum pithos stands, all severely burnt, as is the threshold itself; here is a vivid reminder of the fire which destroyed this LMI (Minoan) phase of Ayía Triáda.

At the point where the 'Rampa al Mare' is no longer exposed, turn left up into the **West Wing** where the grandest residential apartments of the LMI period, in what was surely a matter of deliberate choice, enjoyed the sea view. Another paved road runs along the west façade below the retaining wall.

The largest room in the villa (c 6m by 9m) is the *hall* (5) with pier-and-door arrangement on two sides. The inner doors lead into two columned porticos (a scheme unusual in Minoan architecture), with breccia column bases, and black and white pebble floor with sunk rectangular basin; then across a narrow light-well to a small *inner chamber* (6) with benches round the walls. These were covered with a gypsum facing (now restored), with red stucco filling between the slabs; note the recesses for wooden beams. This room leads on the left to a smaller chamber which also, originally, had access to the light-well. The huge, slightly raised *gypsum slab* in the paved floor has been interpreted as a divan base, and it is now suggested that it could have held a wooden bed similar to one found in the excavation of the Minoan town at Akrotíri on Théra. Both rooms were lit by tall pedestalled stone lamps (originals in the Herákleion Museum).

It is considered that this suite provided the public rooms for entertaining guests, and alongside it (to the north—see below) were those for business affairs. There was an upper floor, over both sets of rooms, which could have been used for official receptions. It certainly contained valuable artefacts, for among the scattered pieces found fallen from above in the destruction debris were the Harvester Vase and the Boxer Rhyton (fragment also in Upper Court) carved in relief from serpentine, and among the most important examples of Minoan stone vases yet discovered, valued both for the skill of the carver, and for the scenes of Minoan life that they portray.

The conical beaker known as the Chieftain Cup came from an upper room in the block to the south of this; the scene carved on this cup is thought to show a Minoan official receiving tribute of animal hides. All three vases, believed to be products of a Knossós workshop, are prominently displayed in Herákleion Museum, Gallery VII.

The block to the south, adjacent to the reception rooms, is seen as servants' quarters and storerooms. The paved area (7) has been plausibly interpreted as a kitchen, with the built-in platforms with circular depressions serving as mortars for the preparation of food. Six pairs of rooms open on to a long north–south corridor (8) which leads in from the south entrance; one storeroom held pithoi and other coarse-ware vessels, clay sealings and loomweights.

North of the reception rooms, in the suite of private or business apartments, is the *archives room* (9). Here, in a gypsum chest, was found a deposit of over 200 clay sealings (bearing impressions of numerous sealstones) thought to have been used to secure bundles of documents. The walls of the inner part of this room were covered with exquisite frescoes (Herákleion Museum, Gallery XIV), including a lady seated in a garden and a cat stalking a pheasant. There are stairs to a little *porticoed light-well* (10) which had a central bowl for rain water; on the stucco plaster of the walls were scored graffiti in the Linear A script.

The Harvester Vase (Herákleion Museum, Gallery VII)

Behind this group of rooms, and not apparently connecting with it, is the *Treasury* (11), a small narrow space from which came the 19 bronze 'talents' or ox-hide ingots (raw material of a metalworking industry) now exhibited in the Herákleion Museum in the same gallery as the stone vases.

The 'Rampa al Mare' leads back to the Lower Court, passing on the left the remains (12) of MMIA structures (c 2000 BC). Beyond the Bastion a LMIII stairway (13) descends towards the excavated *town*. Much of this is of LMIII date (14C–13C BC), a number of houses being built over or adapted from (LMI) Minoan buildings. On the right at the foot of the staircase, opposite the town houses, was what seems to have been a row of *shops*, of a regular size, and all with large threshold blocks. Along the front was a columned portico (14) on the same principle as the design of later stoas. This *agorá* is a feature with, as yet, no exact parallel in Bronze Age excavations on Crete.

Finally, returning across the Lower Court and up the broad staircase out of it, you pass near the *Shrine* (15), subject of an important reassessment as a result of the 1978 stratigraphical examination of the foundations. The building used to be tentatively dated to MMIII–LMI, the New Palace period, though the shrine furnishings, belonging to LMIII, were thought to indicate reuse at that time. It is now clear that the structure (cella and vestibule) is purely LMIII (probably IIIA2, early 14C BC), including the frescoed floor with a seascape of octopus and dolphins, remains of which are now in Herákleion Museum, Gallery XIV. The New Palace period walls which caused the confusion are remains of a substantial Minoan house.

To reach the *cemetery area* turn left on to the path outside the site gate. You pass the (covered) excavation of a LMI potters' *kiln*—rectangular in plan with the fire-chamber at the front and a series of hot-air conduits.

The path leads (in less than 5 minutes along the hillside) to the scant remains of two Prepalatial circular stone-built *tombs* of Ayía Triáda. The better-preserved (eastern) one, Tomb A, was in use EMII–MMI, mid third to early second millenium, and had annexes outside it used as ossuaries as well as for offerings. The chamber and annexes held in all about 150 individuals; the grave goods included bronze daggers as well as many small clay and stone vases. Tomb B, approximately contemporary, was cleared out and re-used in the Postpalatial (LMIII) period. On the slope above this tomb was a rectangular chamber-tomb that contained the famous *painted sarcophagus* made of limestone (dated to LMIII) which is now the centre-piece of the main fresco room in Herákleion Museum (Gallery XIV). A tomb nearby with four compartments like rooms cut out of the rock produced an Egyptian seal of Queen Tyi (1411–1375 BC), wife of Amenhotep III, and also a Hittite sphinx.

A little way further along the path through the olive grove (north east of Tomb A) remains of Early Minoan buildings have been uncovered with pottery in the Ayios Onoúphrios style; they are likely to be part of the settlement for which the great round tombs were the cemetery.

From Ayía Triáda a rough road descends to join the main Míres–Timbáki road c 1km west of the Phaistós turn. As it involves fording the river, it is not recommended for vehicles, but the river banks may appeal to bird-watchers. Returning to Phaistós along the way you came there is a choice at the junction in front of the ruined monastery church. You can pass the palace and go back down to the main road to turn left for (c 20km) *Ayía Galíni* (Rte 12B) (and the detour to the Museum of Cretan Ethnography at Vóri—see above). Or you can turn right downhill on the minor road in a southerly direction, 11km to the coast at *Mátala*—also possible by bus.

1km from Phaistós the Mátala road bears right on the edge of the village of *Ayios Ioánnis* (rent rooms and tavernas). Just past this bend the little church of *Ayios Pávlos*, hidden behind cypresses in a cemetery surrounded by an old wall, reflects in its architecture a long period of Cretan history.

Ayios Pávlos (restored 1972) is the product of three building phases. The oldest part, which now serves as the bema, is thought to be pre-Christian in date; originally it consisted of no more than a cupola supported by four massive piers between open arches, on a square ground plan. This design recalls the Spring Chambers of Late Roman times, and it may be significant that there is still a well immediately behind the cemetery. In due course the nave was added, with dome resting on a drum, and the open arches under the cupola were blocked where necessary to form the bema as we see it today. (The narthex, with open pointed arches in the Venetian style is a later addition, 15/16C.)

A frieze round the dome above the nave carries a painted inscription; it is dated 1303–04 but it is not clear whether this refers to a time of construction or of subsequent redecoration. The inscription describes the church as: 'dedicated to the Apostle Paul in a village called Baptistiras [taken to mean the village of St. John, Ayios Ioánnis], restored and surrounded by a wall', and further states that 'the decoration of a venerable historic building was at the command of the Emperor Andronicos II Palaiologos (1283–1328), his Empress Irene (Yolanda Montferrat) and their son Michael'. The dedication to St. Paul may have been inspired by the legend of his brief stay at Kalí Liménes, on the coast less than 10km away, when he commissioned Titus for the conversion of Crete.

If a Spring Chamber of antiquity came to serve in due course as a Christian baptistery, that would make this 'venerable historic building' one of the earliest ecclesiastical buildings on the island still in existence.

There are remains of *frescoes* dated by the inscription (1303–04): best preserved are the Punishments of Hell on the west wall, and on the pendentives the Evangelists Matthew (south west) and Luke (north west).

Immediately opposite Ayios Pávlos, a dirt road offers a detour through the olive groves to (3.5km) the Minoan vaulted tomb of ***Kamilári**, one of the best preserved of this Mesará tomb type. The nearby village of the same name has several pension and simple rent-room establishments, and can be recommended as a base for exploring this part of the island.

After c 2km on the side-road from Ayios Pávlos, you reach a crossroads near houses, and continue on the track ahead. (Village left at cross-roads, but for direct road see below.) Pass a rutted cart-track (right) but take the first field track after it (right, c 200m from the crossroads), follow it c 1.5km to a T-junction and turn left. (If this track is boggy after wet weather, the next one parallel curves round to join it on the higher ground.) 100m from the T-junction the site is on top of the low hill left; the Archaeological Service fence is a useful landmark—vantage points up the slope of the hill.

Built at the beginning of the Palatial era, in MMIB (c 2000 BC), this large communal tomb was in use for several centuries. Its thick stone walls still stand 2m high, and the evidence from the excavation (under the direction of the Italian archaeologist, D. Levi) suggested a roof structure of wooden beams supporting masonry. A complex of five small rooms, beside a paved area outside the entrance to the circular tomb, was used for funerary cult purposes, and in the later periods also for burials.

The Kamilári tomb was robbed in antiquity, but three important clay models found by the excavators are now in Herákleion Museum, Gallery VI. Tentatively dated to the Late Minoan period, these illustrate different aspects of a precise funerary rite. Two are connected with banquets or ritual offerings for the dead; on one of them offerings are being placed on small altars in front of four figures seated in a shrine. The third model shows a group of dancers in a circle, reminiscent of Cretan dance today. The addition of horns of consecration and doves emphasises the ritual setting of the events.

From Ayios Ioánnis the asphalt road continues towards the coast. After 2km you reach the direct Míres–Mátala road and turn right on to it. After less than 2km there is a crossroads, right (signed) direct to Kamilári village, and left for Sívas; note that this is the junction described below at the start of the excursion to the Odiyítria monastery and the Ayiophárango.

7.5km from Phaistós you pass through *Pitsídia* (rent rooms and tavernas). Just over 1km beyond the village, at the crest of a hill, is a track (recently improved) to the right for the site of *Kommós*, believed to be one of the main harbours of Minoan Phaistós, and later, in the first millenium BC, an important sanctuary area.

A major programme of excavation and study has been in progress here each summer since 1976, directed by J. Shaw (University of Toronto) under the auspices of the American School of Classical Studies.

After 500m the track forks. In a car take the right fork and the site (with guardian's hut) is in view down by the shore. (There may be a small charge for parking.) On foot you might prefer to keep left at the fork and continue (1km) along the contour of the hill to a chapel where a steep path drops down to the beach for the

5-minute walk (north) through the tamarisk trees to the excavation. This is not (at the time of writing) open to the public but can be viewed quite well from outside the fence.

The west-facing bay has one of the finest beaches on Crete (though for archaeology the sand has presented many problems); swimmers may notice ancient remains under the sea.

In Minoan times Kommós was probably the major entryway by sea to south-central Crete. During the period MMIII–LMIII the town consisted of houses up the slope, to the top of the low hill at the the north end of the site, and below, down by the shore, buildings of a different scale and quality of construction suggesting an administrative complex presumably linked to aspects of harbour activity. The architectural evidence appears to support Evans's original assumption that this was an important Minoan harbour with a customs post.

At shore level (under the later sanctuary remains) the excavation uncovered a monumental courtyard building (LMI), using Palatial-style ashlar masonry and enormous orthostats, some of which are the largest cut blocks recorded in Minoan Crete. The part of the building next to the shore had been damaged by the sea, but adjoining it on the inland side was a portico or colonnaded hall also massively built, and also facing (south) on to the large paved court. Running up from the beach along the north side of these buildings is a broad slab-paved road which probably continued inland to link Kommós with the neighbouring Minoan centres of Phaistós and Ayía Tríada.

During the Greek period a series of temples (10C–1C BC) was built above this LM complex, of which only the latest sanctuary (4C–1C BC) is now visible. There is a temple, a hall thought to be a dining-hall, and ancillary buildings grouped around a courtyard containing four altars; abundant evidence was found for sacrifice and feasting. The 10C temple is one of the earliest known in Greece and fragments of Phoenician pottery associated with its foundation may suggest eastern religious influence.

At 11km from Phaistós (75km from Herákleion) is *Mátala*. The cove around which the village has grown up offers good swimming under cliffs spectacularly honeycombed with rock-cut Roman tombs. These date back to the 1C–2C AD but they have been exploited through the ages and a team from the Greek Archaeological Service and the University of Crete is now engaged in studying the history of their various uses.

There are a number of waterfront tavernas, and also accommodation (rent rooms and C/D-class hotels), but Mátala, partly because of its proximity to Phaistós, has been taken over by organised (and disorganised) tourism, and in high season the noisy result may be unappealing. Rooms in the villages back from the coast, mentioned above along the road from Phaistós, are suggested as more tranquil alternatives.

To the Odiyítria Monastery and the Ayiophárango

This detour from the Phaistós–Mátala road uses unsurfaced roads, perhaps rough in places: c 9km to the monastery (closed 13.30–16.30), 4km further towards the Bay of Kalí Liménes for the recommended walk (less than an hour to the sea) down the Ayiophárango, or 'holy gorge'. In high summer the number of campers in the gorge may spoil the sense of remoteness which, for the rest of the year, is one of the principal attractions of these western slopes of the Asteroúsia mountains.

The detour begins from the Kamilári–Sívas crossroads (noted above) 4.5km from Phaistós on the main road to Mátala. Take the road which leads after 1km into the village of *Sívas*, and keep straight on across the plateía with the church on your left. The dirt road winds through olive groves interspersed with cypresses, and climbs steadily into the foothills of the Asteroúsia mountains, the range which rises from the Mesará plain to drop steeply to the sea along the south coast. After about 3km the

White Mountains of western Crete (60–70km away) are in view on a clear day, with in the foreground the distinctive angular Mount Kédros, and the Paximádia islands in the Bay of Mesará. At 5km from the main road, in *Lístaros*, turn right downhill in front of the church. The recently constructed road climbs to a less fertile level, technically garigue (in Greek phrýgana), the scrubby upland typical of so much of the island's landscape; many groups of beehives are scattered about the hillside.

At 9km the *Odiyítria monastery*, probably founded in the 16C, comes into view. It is dedicated to the Panayía Odiyítrias (Our Lady Guide). The epithet is applied iconographically to the Virgin pointing to the Christ Child in her arms as the way to salvation. The archetype, believed to be the work of St. Luke, belonged to the Odigon monastery in Constantinople; it was invoked for the protection of the city and in times of danger was even carried in procession round the city walls.

The monastery, isolated in this nowadays remote corner of Crete, commands a ridge high above a tributary of the River Ayía Kyriakí which flows to the sea through the Ayiopharángo. The position set back from the sea afforded some protection from the pirate raids which plagued the coast in medieval times. The rambling buildings, whitewashed and only partly surrounded by a wall, are dominated by a massive rectangular stone-built tower.

Gerola came here at the turn of the century, and remarked on the familiar pattern: quadrangular enclosure, a large courtyard around a church, but the enclosing wall substantial only on the north and west sides where it bordered on the road. He noted the three gates, a gravestone with an inscription of 1564, the kitchen garden, and was much impressed by the tower of Xopatéras. This was the nickname, meaning ex-priest, of a disgraced monk who achieved fame as leader of a local band of warriors in the 1828 Revolution. The avenging Turks pursued him to the refuge of the tower where, after a heroic struggle against hopeless odds, he perished with all his family. Legend has it that the attackers had to contend with beehives hurled from the roof of the tower. The climb up the tower is worthwhile for the view from the roof. A giant key to unlock the door is held by a monk whose living quarters are at the top of the stairs in the far right-hand corner of the courtyard; he also opens the church.

In the church the remains of frescoes have been uncovered on the vault of the nave, with scenes from the life of the Virgin. The Odiyítria has a highly regarded collection of icons; the depiction of Christ with the twelve apostles in the branches of a vine is by the 15C painter Angelos, one of the few artists of this date who signed his work. A 15C icon of Ayios Phanoúrios has been removed to hang (No. 4) in the collection in Ayía Aikateríni in Herákleion (see Rte 1D).

For the Ayiophárango take the fork left just beyond the monastery, towards Kalí Liménes. The road descends for 2.5km, until (immediately after crossing the river-bed) you come to a farm on the right; a large flock of sheep winters here. 1km further, before a bend, a track turns back at an acute angle (right) and drops down to the river, leading (after 500m) to the start of the walk down the gorge. (If walking from the monastery you can get down to the river-bed sooner, at the farm.)

At first there is a clear path, but nearer the sea it is necessary to follow the stream-bed, so this expedition is not advisable in early spring or after heavy rain.

Gradually the valley narrows, and after about 30 minutes the vertical walls of the gorge loom ahead—up to 100m high for a length of 600m. At the far end, with the sea almost in sight, the substantial domed church of

Ayios Antónios is built into the rock wall (left), enclosing the grotto chapel asociated with Ayios Ioánnis Xénos, the 11C evangelist, who was born in Sívas in 970, but is principally associated with the Katholikó on the Akrotíri near Khaniá (see p 271).

Once back on the road, it is possible for the adventurous to continue (4km) to the coast, though the surface may be exceedingly rough in places. The beautiful bay of *Kalí Liménes* has one of the very few extensive beaches on the south coast of the island, and is still relatively unspoilt. The bay has been used since antiquity as a sheltered anchorage for ships of passage, 'secure for 10 galleys' according to a Venetian document, and was the Fair Havens of St. Paul (Acts 27,12). Paul knew that 'the harbour was unsuitable for wintering', but in the strong southerly winds that are a feature of the weather along this coast there is some shelter in the lee of the two off-shore islands, Megalónisi and Ayios Pávlos. St. Paul's ship left here to sail westward in the lee of the land to the safe winter harbour of Phoínix (modern Loutró), but with a change of wind it was driven by the unfavourable 'Euroclydon' (probably a strong northerly meltémi) south of the island of Gávdos and onward to shipwreck on Malta.

The idyllic view of the bay has been radically altered by the building of an oil bunkering station on one of the islands, but as there is very little associated shore activity, the installation is not necessarily a deterrent. (Limited accommodation, and tavernas, at scattered points on the long bay.) The double-naved chapel on the western headland is dedicated to Ayios Pávlos.

In the Greco-Roman period the anchorage was controlled by the city-state of Lasaía. The centre of the city was on the cliffs above an islet 100m off-shore at the eastern end of the beach. (There is also evidence for Minoan settlement on the acropolis as well as associated chamber tombs in the vicinity. It has been suggested that nearby copper-workings could have been exploited in antiquity.)

Nothing of the city has been excavated officially (though considerable damage has been caused by illicit activity) but a survey of the headland has identified the site of a temple and a probable basilica church, as well as house walls, cisterns and an aqueduct. An unusual feature is the breakwater, built of loosely piled stone blocks, running out from the shore to the islet; a narrow channel was left at the southern end, allowing boats to be moved to sheltered water according to changes of wind. It is known that this coast was relatively deserted from medieval times, so the breakwater is likely to be an ancient structure.

A dirt track continues along the coast 10km to Léndas. A broad but unsurfaced road strikes inland to (c 25km) Míres, via Pigaidákia (asphalt after that) and Pómbia; improvements are promised but some sections may still be rough.

To Ayios Mýron and Priniás

A round trip from Herákleion of c 60km.

Leave Herákleion as for Phaistós (see start of Rte 4), but at 4.5km (2km beyond the north coast highway) turn right for Ayios Mýron; distances are from this junction. The road crosses the stream (keep right at the fork after 1.5km), and winds through a valley densely planted with vines, gaining height gradually. After 7.5km you pass through *Voútes*, and at c 10km there is a fine view back to the sea, and over the main valley running inland from Herákleion, the central line of communication across the island from coast to coast. At 11.5km pass a turn for Kitharída to climb up to (13.5km) *Ayios Mýron*. This attractive village, built on the site of ancient Rávkos, is named after the 3C martyr saint who was born here, and became bishop of Knossós; keep right, on the lower road, to pass his grotto. Steps from it lead up to the big 13C–14C church, cross-domed in plan with the later addition of a domed narthex; the drum supporting the main dome is designed with eight linked arches framing slender windows. (The village priest has the church key. Enquire at the kapheneíon opposite.)

At 15.5km *Pirgoú* has a view west across to the lower slopes of Mount Ida and the villages strung along its eastern flank at the limit of the cultivable land. 19km *Káto Asítes*.

Here a recommended detour leads in 2km to the Gorgolaíni convent. At the beginning of the village fork right and after 150m turn right at the end of the little plateía. The road climbs steeply to the nunnery which enjoys from its terrace a *view unsurpassed on this route. Except for the church of Ayios Yeóryios, the buildings of *Moní Gorgolaíni* are of no great age, but the well-tended grounds are shaded and airy even in the heat of summer.

200m below the main gate on the way back to the village, on a sharp bend, a rough track diverges left for walkers, crosses a valley through olive groves, and climbs west into the high pastures of the Ida foothills.

Very soon after Káto Asítes is (19.5km) *Ano Asítes* (lower and upper), and just beyond the village a glimpse of an angular hill ahead. At c 22km, the distinctive flat-topped rock formation dominates the view, with the white chapel of Ayios Pandeleímon perched on the eastern brow, overlooking the north–south valley route. This, the Patéla hill of **Priniás**, was the acropolis of the ancient city of *Rizenía*. The path to the hilltop starts at the crest at 23.5km; it is 10 minutes to the summit (686m, *view).

500m before this you pass the site of the cemetery of Siderospiliá, on a slope facing south east across to the acropolis. Its 680 excavated tombs yielded a continuous sequence of material and of burial rites (late 13C–mid 6C BC), its development being contemporary with that of the settlement on the Patéla. The cemetery consisted of pit-graves, inhumation in tholos tombs, and cremation burials.

A number of crouch-burials, without grave gifts, were probably associated with the nearby Prepalatial settlement. Roman tombs were also found.

The Italians excavated on the *Patéla* (1906–08) and returned here in 1969. They identified a refuge site dating from the end of the Bronze Age (LMIII), comparable to Karphí or Vrókastro. From the sanctuary near the eastern edge of the plateau came a goddess figurine with cylindrical skirt and raised hands similar to those from Gázi and Karphí on display in Herákleion Museum, also numerous votive terracottas including snakes and the curious tubes with columns of loop handles associated with the snake cult. The sanctuary continued in use till the Archaic period.

At the western end of the hill are the ruins of a square Hellenistic fortress with corner bastions, but the most important remains on the acropolis are the excavated foundations of two 7C *temples* (fenced in the middle of the plateau).

The earlier, and better preserved, *Temple A*, is said to show Minoan influence on the Archaic Greek 'templum in antis' plan. Instead of the expected two columns at the front of the porch (pronaos) between the 'antae', or side-posts, Temple A had one central pillar, and in line with this inside the temple, on the long axis of the cella, there were (as at Dréros, Rte 7) two wooden columns on low stone bases with a hearth between them. Some of the sculptures which decorated the entrance to the temple were retrieved, and are well displayed in Herákleion Museum, Gallery XIX. They include two seated female figurines in the Daidalic style, from above the doorway into the cella, and fragments in low relief from friezes depicting lions and a procession of mounted spearmen.

The road continues through the village of *Priniás*, and, 5km from the site, rejoins the main Phaistós route in Ayía Varvára.

From Ayía Varvára to Valsamónero and Kamáres

At the end of the long village of Ayía Varvára (p 133) a road branches off right, signposted Yérgeri and Kamáres, to run along the southern foothills of the *Ida* massif. This recommended route (c 26km from Ayía Varvára) is scenically most rewarding driven from east to west. At the first bend out of the village there is a glimpse of the Libyan Sea ahead. Beyond (10km) Yérgeri is a fine view of the *Paximádia islands* in the Bay of Mesará.

At 15km, at the beginning of *Zarós* a major road left, signed Míres, runs down from the mountains to join in 10km the Herákleion–Phaistós road across the Mesará plain. Zarós is a large village (pop. 2000) with abundant water; the springs here used to feed the aqueduct that supplied the numerous fountains of the great city of Górtyn. Just above the village there is a Class C hotel in a tranquil situation beside a stream.

To the north west of Zarós is the Monastery of Ayios Nikólaos where a curious little church has frescoes of two periods (14C and 15C).

You can reach the monastery by car: 500m beyond the end of the village take a track right that climbs 2km up a valley. On foot there is a shorter path: 200m before the end of the village a narrow street, surfaced in concrete (the first right after the turning signed for the hotel) leads up, past a chapel set back from the road, to the old route (c 20 minutes) between village and monastery.

This is a flourishing monastic community. The north aisle of Ayios Nikólaos was the original church, and has the earlier (14C) paintings, including a tender scene, on the north side of the bema, of the birth of the Virgin. The monastery lies at the bottom of a gorge. You can ask for directions to the cave church, also painted, of Ayios Evtímios (c 45 minutes up the hillside), or follow the path up the gorge, a walk of a little under 2 hours to the chapel of Ayios Ioánnis at the top.

At 21km from Ayía Varvára, the ***Monastery of Vrondísi** is signposted (right uphill, 2km). The main gateway was destroyed in 1913, but an inscription from it dated 1630–36 has been set above one of the cell doors. Outside the monastery, shaded by two great plane trees, is a 15C Venetian *fountain* with figures (damaged) of Adam and Eve. The terrace enjoys an extensive view across foothills to the Mesará plain.

In the monastery courtyard is the two-aisled church with bell-tower. The older south aisle, dedicated to Ayios Antónios, preserves the remains of some admired frescoes dating from the first half of the 14C; these are early examples of the widely-diffused style known as *The Cretan School*, a specific trend in Palaiologan painting. In the vaulting of the apse is painted the Last Supper, a scene that occurs in this position at no other church on Crete; below it is the Apostle Communion. Also unique on Crete (in wall-painting) is the figure, on the right of the Hierarchs, of Simeon holding the Christ child.

By the end of the Venetian period Vrondísi was one of the most influential monastic communities on the island, renowned as a centre for scholars and artists. The six icons by Damaskinós, now in the Ayía Aikateríni collection in Herákleion, hung in this monastery church until 1800.

Back on the road it is 3km to the village of *Vorízia*. On the way you can see across the valley the red roof and triangular gable of the bellcote of the •church of Ayios Phanoúrios, which contains one of the finest displays of fresco painting on the island.

Towards the end of the village a side street drops awkwardly downhill left, signed for **Valsamónero**. It immediately bends left and after 150m the house of the 'phýlakas' or guardian is on the left, opposite a small general store. The arrangement is that he has the church open 08.00–13.00, but if necessary you can return here and make enquiries; avoid the siesta hours in summer.

Keep right from the house in the village, across the bridge over a stream shaded by plane trees, then left at the fork level on a track (way-marked with red paint) or gradually descending along the contour as the valley opens out ahead, until after 2.5km a slightly uphill stretch brings the church into view ahead.

The church of *Ayios Phanoúrios* (a Rhodian saint) is all that remains of the once influential Valsamóneros monastery. Its exterior is one of the best examples on the island of Venetian influence on Byzantine church architecture; on the south façade the main doorway has carved rosette decoration and over the door into the narthex is a Venetian coat-of-arms with a wreath and interwoven leaf motif. As a result of several building phases Ayios Phanoúrios has acquired a highly unusual ground plan: there are two parallel *naves* or *aisles* on the usual east–west axis, and a third at right-angles across their western end forming a *transept*. Alongside this, there is also a *narthex*.

The original nave along the north wall, erected in 1328, is dedicated to the Panayía (Virgin Mary). She was depicted in the bema above the Apostle Communion, and on the barrel vaulting of the nave there is the most complete set of scenes from her life (the *Hymns to the Mother of God*) known in Cretan fresco painting.

The south aisle (just inside the main door) is dedicated to Ayios Ioánnis Prodrómos (the forerunner, St. John the Baptist). The new addition was completed by 1406–07 but was not decorated until 1428. The frescoes include a scene of Ayios Ioánnis in the desert, where the elongated figures have been compared to the work of El Greco.

The transept honours Ayios Phanoúrios. The frescoes were painted by Konstantínos Ríkos in 1431 (inscription next to the doorway through to the narthex). In the east wall at the south end of the transept there is a miniature apse, with the Pantokrátor in the vaulting, and below this the Communion of the Angels, with Christ as high-priest offering communion to the richly-clad angels in heaven. This rarely-found scene here replaces its counterpart in the theme of the Divine Liturgy, the Communion of the Apostles. Scenes of the miracles of Ayios Phanoúrios are preserved on the east wall, and on the pillar he is depicted as a soldier-saint.

From Vorízia it is 3.5km on along the road to *Kamáres*. Just out of Vorízia the track into the mountains has been widened by bulldozers, mainly for the benefit of shepherds, at the start of the old route round the flank of Mount Ida to the Nída plain above Anóyia (Rte 3A). From the village of *Kamáres* a very steep path climbs (4–5 hours) to the **Kamáres cave** which gave its name to some of the finest polychrome pottery of the prehistoric world (Herákleion Museum, Gallery III, and see p 143).

The cave, at 1524m, was discovered by a shepherd only in 1890. It was investigated in 1904 by the Italians (under L. Mariani) who found the first examples of 'Kamáres ware' dating from the period of the Old Palaces (c 1900–1700 BC). In 1913 the site was fully excavated by the British. There was evidence for occupation during the Neolithic period, after which the cave became a sanctuary.

The climb to the cave is definitely an expedition only for experienced walkers; the route is marked rather erratically with orange paint, but these splashes are not always easy to see on the descent. Guides are sometimes available; enquire at the kapheneíon by the church (just left of the through road). There is simple overnight accommodation in the village.

At the Herákleion end of Kamáres, the walk to the cave starts up a side-street almost opposite the cemetery; after 200m, leave the track (before it is blocked by a new building) and up the bank (right) look for the first of the paint splashes. The path climbs steeply up the watercourse following a pipeline. The first landmark (after about 1 hour), is a group of water troughs. Then you strike east to the edge of the trees, looking for marked rocks which lead up to a second water point: troughs and a spring. From here it is a further hour's climb to the *cave* which is soon in view. For many years the cave-mouth has been the home of a noisy colony of Alpine choughs.

There are time-honoured paths north west to the summit of Psilorítis, and north around the shoulder to the other great sanctuary on the mountain, the Idaian cave (see Rte 3A), but for these expeditions a guide is definately advisable. Consult the Greek Alpine Club in Herákleion, tel. (81) 227 609.

From the village of Kamáres a minor road runs down to Vóri (past the recommended new Museum of Cretan Ethnology p 138) and (20km) Phaistós. Looking back there are dramatic views of the rock wall of Mount Ida. (The fast road between the mountains and the plain runs from Zarós—see above.) Alternatively you can continue (c 12km) to Apodoúlou at the southern end of the Amári valley (Rte 12A).

Ayii Déka to Pýrgos 25km across the Mesará plain, for an alternative return route to Herákleion of 65km (40 miles) or to continue (c 40km) by the south coast route to Viánnos for south-eastern Crete (see Rte 8).

This road branches off the main Herákleion– Phaistós route 1km on the Herákleion side of Ayii Déka (p 133), and runs east along the intensively-cultivated Mesará plain. You pass (4km) *Gagáles*, and at *Stóli* and (10km) Loúres keep right (ignoring left turns for Ayios Thomás that cut back to the main Herákleion road). Continue through (12km) *Asími*, a larger rural centre. The road through olive groves turns towards the Asteroúsia mountain range. At 19.5km, skirting *Protória* you arrive at a T-junction on the main Pýrgos–Herákleion road: turn right for Pýrgos (5km) and Viánnos. (For Herákleion turn left—see below.) All this fertile region is watered by the upper reaches of the Anapodáris and its tributaries.

Taking the Pýrgos road you turn left almost immediately, at a crossroads, on the last approach to the foothills of the Asteroúsia mountains. During the Venetian period *Pýrgos* was a fief of the Latin clergy in Candia. At the upper end of the village is a frescoed church of that period dedicated to Ayios Yeóryios and Ayios Konstantínos. In depicting episodes from the life of the Emperor Constantine the Great (so commonplace in the iconography of western Christendom) these frescoes are unique in the Byzantine world.

Keep straight on up the hill on the way in, and at the top turn left, signed for Tsoútsouros. The church is on the right at the end of this narrow main street, 50km before a sharp left bend. The key is held at a house down an alleyway opposite the church (ask for Kyría Anastasía).

This was a triple-naved church but the aisle dedicated to Ayía Eléni (the Emperor's mother) had to be sacrificed during widening of the village street. At least three phases of wall-painting can be detected within a relatively short period in the surviving decoration—the earliest in the *north aisle* of Ayios Yeóryios. The Constantine cycle is in the *south aisle* with a donor inscription in the apse giving a date of

1314/15. Extant (lower registers of the eastern half of the vault) are: the birth of Constantine; his parents with the young Constantine on horseback with his father; the crowning of Constantine's son; the battle of the Milvian bridge when Constantine's vision of the Cross is traditionally said to have determined the future religion of the Roman Empire. The style of these frescoes is as yet uninfluenced by the technique of the new Palaiologan movement in Constantinople, which is however well illustrated in the (slightly later 14C) wall-paintings in the west bay of this aisle.

From Pýrgos a fairly recently completed road runs east towards (c 40km) Viánnos, with the possibility of a diversion to a newly accessible stretch of the south coast at (25km) Tsoútsouros or (35km) Keratókambos, and to link up with the main road from Herákleion to south-eastern Crete (Rtes 3C and 8).

The road north to Herákleion from the T-junction near **Protória** (see above) leaves by an avenue of gum trees across the fertile valley of the Anapodáris river and climbs to *Ligórtinos* and *Tephéli* (c 7km from the junction). It winds through the vineyards and olive groves of the upland valleys of central Crete often with wide views east to the Lasíthi mountains, and ahead to the sharp-nosed profile of Júktas, the isolated peak behind Herákleion, legendary burial place of the Cretan Zeus and site of one of the most important Minoan peak sanctuaries on the island (Rte 3B). 8km beyond Tephéli, at a crest, there is a turning left signed for a detour to (c 3km) *Moní Epanosíphi*; the view ahead (half left) now includes Prophítis Ilías and the walls of Témenos (Rte 3D).

The Epanosíphis monastery is thought to have been founded towards the end of the period of Venetian rule, c 1600; the original church, dedicated to Ayios Yeóryios, was destroyed in an earthquake in 1856. This was a particularly wealthy monastery with valuable land and property, and the community still flourishes, now under the jurisdiction of the cathedral in Herákleion. During the Turkish period it was a centre of learning, and, like so many other monasteries on the island, gave constant support to the cause of Cretan nationalism, for which it suffered severely.

There are great celebrations here on the feast of Ayios Yeóryios (23 April unless this falls in Holy Week). At other times it is a tranquil, well-tended place with a beautiful view from the terrace below the church over fertile but sparsely-populated countryside. The 19C traveller Robert Pashley remembered the cypresses and palm trees of this 'retreat from the busy hum of men'.

The route across the island continues over less cultivated upland 5km to *Khoudétsi*—at 440m the highest village on this route—and then descends past Ayios Vasílios to join the main Herákleion–Viánnos road (Rte 3C) just outside Pezá. On this road you enjoy one of the less familiar views of the Palace of Knossós, and shortly afterwards (see Rte 2) reach the outskirts of Herákleion.

From Górtyn to Léndas (Lebéna), c 30km (18 miles).

On the main Herákleion–Phaistós road, just before the church of Ayios Títos at Górtyn (see p 134), is the left turn for Léndas on the south coast. (Distances from this junction.) After 500m, in *Mitrópolis*, you pass (right) the excavated remains of another of Górtyn's basilicas, with an unusual tri-conch plan; this 5C building was perhaps a martyrion. The mosaic floor found in the south apse (but sadly no longer on view) ranked among the finest mosaics on the island, with a border of bands and guilloche framing a free design of birds among flowers, all in polychrome using some 15 colours.

From Mitrópolis there is a recommended detour to (1.5km) the remains of a *Minoan villa* or farm near Kanniá. 750m from the main road, the Léndas road widens slightly at a small plateía. Take an unsigned narrow street to the right. By the big red-domed church at the end bear right and left, cross a stream (Mitropolianós, see Górtyn), and turn left along it. After 600m you pass (left) a white chapel (Ayios Phanoúrios) and 500m beyond it take the first track to the right. Stop after 150m where the track bears right and the (roofed) excavation is in view ahead. The site is fenced but there is a good vantage point on the far side.

This was a LMI farmhouse with a large number of storerooms containing pithoi (many still in situ). It was destroyed (like so many other Cretan sites) at the end of LMIB but was reinhabited in LMIII. A household *shrine* from that period (contents in Herákleion Museum, Gallery X) had clay goddesses in the typical posture with raised arms.

The road south now crosses the Mesará plain, watered by the Ieropótamos (ancient Lethaíos or Lethe), to (5km) *Plátanos*.

On the edge of the village are the excavated remains of two Early–Middle Minoan *tombs*, circular stone-built communal burial chambers dating back to the third millenium BC and in use over a long period. They are signposted to the right in the village, and after 300m you turn right again. There are many of these tombs throughout the Mesará, and a few elsewhere on Crete, but Tombs A and B at Plátanos are the largest known; the internal diameter of Tomb A is 13m, and its wall is nearly 3m thick. These tombs are always free-standing, with a single low entrance on the east side. For the smaller ones the vault may have been completed in stone, but these Plátanos tombs were probably roofed in a lighter material: mudbrick or small stones on a framework of wooden beams, brushwood and thatch have all been suggested.

A walled trench outside Tomb A (the first you come to on the site) contained a very large number of small stone vases, presumably for ritual use. In Tomb B was found the Babylonian haematite cylinder seal of the period of Hammurabi, 1792–1750 BC (Herákleion Museum, Gallery I).

The Léndas road continues 2km to *Plóra*, and on the far side of the village keeps left at a fork towards Apesokári. The right fork leads in 10km to the isolated **Moní Apezanón**, founded in the Venetian period. At the turn of the century G. Gerola, in his survey of Crete's Venetian monuments, described the impressive pentagonal wall enclosing the monastic buildings, with towers, a defended gateway, turreted and loop-holed battlements, and enough still remains (despite modern additions and restoration) to convey some of the original effect. There is an active community, with eight monks in residence.

From Plóra (part asphalt surface and improvements nearly complete) you climb to a less cultivated level with rewarding views across the foothills of the Asteroúsia range. Continue 6km, through *Ayios Kýrillos*, and just above the village fork right (sign). 2km further on, fork right again beside a red-roofed chapel; from a long way off a line of cypresses marks the Apezanés monastery buildings. The original *north entrance* is a little beyond the modern gate into the courtyard.

The Léndas road (from Plóra) arrives at an oblique T-junction just short of *Apesokári*, and you turn sharp right for the steep climb south into the *Asteroúsia* mountains. On the left of this next stretch of road, on the hill just south west of the village of Apesokári, is one of the best-preserved tombs of the Mesará type, with circular chamber standing to over 1m high, and ancillary ossuary chambers.

At 12km, on a spur, the road has cut through an unexcavated MMIII site. The cliffs to the left of the road are often of interest to bird-watchers. Looking back you can distinguish the Palace of Phaistós on its ridge jutting out into the Mesará plain; in Minoan times it must have been an impressive sight on this approach to the plain from the coves of the south coast.

18.5km *Miamoú*, where a cave site (now under the houses of the village) was excavated by the Italian A. Taramelli in 1895; the finds dating back to the Neolithic period included hearths and food debris, including shellfish remains. The evidence pointed to human occupation from the Final Neolithic to early in the EMII period (c 2500 BC) when the cave became a burial place.

The road descends, with fine coastal views. The prominent conical hill to the east is *Kóphinas*; on the precipitous summit the Minoans established a peak sanctuary.

At 29km you reach **Léndas**, site of ancient Lebéna. Therapeutic springs made this a renowned sanctuary for healing, with a *temple of Asklepios* dating from the 4C BC and still important in Roman times; it was restored in the 2C AD, the great building period at Górtyn, of which this settlement was a harbour. The Hellenistic sanctuary was superimposed on a preceding cult of water deities. At the beginning of the century the Italian Mission excavated here.

The sanctuary site (fenced but not always locked) lies on the left of the road at the beginning of the modern village. The temple, on an artificial terrace, consisted of a simple *cella* (12m by 13m) with a *podium* for the statue of the god against the inner (west) wall. Two *granite columns* still stand in front of the podium area. In the Hellenistic period the walls were of stone, but in the Roman restoration they were given a lining of brick. Near the statue base dedicated by Xenion (inscription on loose fragment) is a scrap of Roman mosaic. At the north-east corner of the temple was the *treasury*, which has a Hellenistic (3C BC) pebble mosaic floor executed in black, white and red, depicting a sea-horse framed in a scroll of waves, with two delicate palmettes. The floor was damaged in antiquity by the sinking of a shaft to hold offerings (see dedicatory inscriptions). Leading north from the treasury was a colonnaded *stoa*, a free-standing portico, and along the whole length of the east side of it a broad flight of marble steps (traces preserved) gave access to the raised level of stoa and temple. 15m to the east of the steps is a *tiled arch* which the excavators recognised as part of the building above the Asklepieíon's therapeutic spring. (On the hillside a little below the temple were two great basins, perhaps for the total immersion of the sick.)

The sanctuary complex included a hostel to lodge the pilgrims; this building had texts inscribed on its walls. The ritual apparently included the reading of votive tablets in a local Doric dialect. The therapeutic powers of the god are vividly described: one sufferer from sciatica was cured whilst he slept.

Bounding the Lebéna Bay on the west is Cape Léndas (lion) and on this promontory with a profile which suggests a crouching lion there was a Minoan settlement. In the vicinity of Léndas the eminent Greek archaeologist S. Alexíou excavated five large Early–Middle Minoan *tombs* of the circular Mesará type (see Plátanos, above). One lies east at Zervoús, two just west of Léndas at Papoúra, and two others c 2km to the west at Xerókambos. One of these last two produced a great deposit of vases of EMI date, and out of the whole group of tombs came three Egyptian scarabs (11th Dynasty).

In the village there is a local phýlakas, a guardian for the archaeological sites, who will help with directions; ask at the kapheneíon set back from the beach. Léndas has expanded from the original cluster of tavernas on a cove, but in a simple style, with plenty of rooms to rent associated with two long beaches, one a 15-minute walk over the promontory to the west.

A fair dirt track leads west along the coast 10km to *Kalí Liménes* (see p 154).

II EASTERN CRETE

5 Herákleion to Mállia and Ayios Nikólaos

Direct route to Ayios Nikólaos by the north coast highway (New Road)
70km (43 miles). 7km Amnisós—26km Khersónisos—37km Palace of
Mállia.

The first stretch of the Old Road serves the archaeological sites of
Amnisós and Nírou Kháni, as well as the airport, beaches and tourist
hotels, and therefore is described below as an alternative exit from
Herákleion. The detour to the Skoteinó cave could make an easy half-day
excursion (round trip c 50km).

Frequent bus service to Mállia and Ayios Nikólaos from the main East
Crete bus station near the harbour, operating on both the New Road and
Old Road routes. For the Palace of Mállia, which is beyond the town, take a
bus going on to Ayios Nikólaos and get off at the palace turning.
   In summer, a blue 'town' bus (No. 1) runs every 20 minutes from the
centre of Herákleion, Plateía Eleftherías, to the Amnisós beaches (see bus
information under Herákleion, Rte 1). Out of season, long-distance buses
on the Old Road will stop.

Join the north coast highway from the Knossós road (Rte 2). Distances
along the **New Road** route are from this highway junction. (The roadside
kilometre posts are calculated from Khaniá.) Soon the airport is in view
below left, and beyond it the off-shore island of Día.
   It is 7km to the exit for *Amnisós*, see below, and the alternative Old
Road close to the shore, and c 16km to the junction near Goúves where
the two roads merge again.

The **Old Road** leaves the centre of Herákleion from Plateía Eleftherías
below the Archaeological Museum, and runs through the unattractive
modern suburb of *Póros*, in Minoan times one of the harbour areas of
Knossós.

Here the Greek archaeologist S. Alexíou excavated a Late Neolithic settlement, and also an important Postpalatial cemetery. At Póros, in 1971, in a LMIIIB floor deposit, was found a scarab of Ankhesenamun, wife of Tutankhamun, significant in determining the absolute chronology of Late Minoan Crete.

After 2km the road crosses the bed of the Kaíratos, the stream which runs down the Knossós valley. This suburb, now the edge of town, is Néa Alikarnássos. 300m beyond the bridge, an insignificant right turn is signed for the New Road. The Old Road continues past this turning and at 3km takes the right fork signposted Ayios Nikólaos. (The spur straight ahead ends at the airport.) You bend left round a military establishment and run parallel to the highway before descending, beyond the airport, to the Bay of Amnisós.

At 6km a small cave church (right) is dedicated to Ayios Ioánnis Pro-drómos (the Baptist; feast day 29 August).

At 7km the *municipal beach*, Karterós, is signposted. There is a token charge for simple facilities: cabins, chairs, umbrellas. A bar serves light refreshments. There are also some beach hotels along this bay, otherwise the bathing is unrestricted, and very popular in high summer with both local people and tourists. There are several access points between a track opposite the cave church (see above) and the extreme eastern end of the bay, surprisingly named *Tobrouk* (good fish tavernas). Far out in this bay the currents can sometimes be treacherous and even strong swimmers should take care.

8km **Amnisós**. Mentioned in Linear B tablets, this was another of the harbours of Minoan Knossós; from here Idomeneus set sail for the Trojan War. A turning right for Episkopí is also the junction with the north coast highway.

To visit the Amnisós antiquities turn left towards the sea, just beyond the highway junction, on a signed track. The low hill which rises from the sea-shore has Minoan remains around its base. The ruins on the summit are of a 16C Venetian village.

Under the east side of the hill is the excavated site of a *Minoan villa* contemporary with the New Palace at Knossós. This is known as the *House of the Lilies*, from the graceful floral frescoes that decorated its walls (see Herákleion Museum, Gallery XIV).

The site is fenced, but there is a vantage point on the seaward side where the villa's flagged *terrace* is immediately in front of you. This had a fine view out to sea, and behind it a spacious room which, with six sets of folding doors, could be a cool retreat open to the terrace, or an enclosed hall protected from winter storms. The *frescoes* were found in the south-west area of the house, the main room with bases for two columns. The *west façade* was built of massive ashlar blocks, some of which have been toppled out of place, presumably by earthquake action. Burnt patches on the stones are a reminder of the fierce fire that destroyed the villa at the end of the LMI period.

The site was excavated in the 1930s by the Greek archaeologist S. Marinátos and re-examined in 1983 by a team from Heidelberg University. This was one of the sites where Marinátos found a quantity of the laval by-product pumice, which led him to relate the LMIB destruction level here and at many other sites on Crete to an eruption on the volcanic island of Théra (Santorini) only c 100km to the north. The relationship was never universally accepted, partly because pottery styles suggested that the destruction on Crete was at least 50 years later than the eruption which engulfed the Bronze Age sites on Santorini. However three learned sessions of the 'Thera Congress' (1971, 1978 and most particularly 1989) attended by archaeologists and a wide range of interested scientists have first established an agreed correlation between the two islands, and then begun to examine new (and much earlier) scientific dating for the volcanic eruption, which appears to challenge the traditional chronology of second millenium Minoan Crete. (See also LMIB destruction in Historical Background p 19.)

You can walk along the Amnisós beach under the hill. On its west side (fenced) is the Archaic (6C BC) *Sanctuary of Zeus Thénatas* also excavated by Marinátos. Associated with a large round open-air altar were two life-size eagles in stone (Herákleion Museum, Gallery XIX). The massive foundation wall re-uses blocks from a Late Bronze Age building. A little further west where the rocks run down into the sea are the remains of substantial constructions below the shore line. These are thought to be LMI harbour works from the ancient port of Knossós.

On the hill-side above Amnisós is a *cave* sacred to Eileíthyia, goddess of fertility and childbirth. This was an important place of worship from Late Neolithic (see Herákleion Museum, Gallery I, case 1) to Roman times, and was known to Homer (Od. XIX 188). The cave entrance is closed. Most people will probably be content to identify the sanctuary site, but for those who wish to explore the cave, the Archaeological Service guardian has the key at the nearby Minoan site of Nírou Kháni (see below).

At the Amnisós junction with the New Road follow signs, leading under the highway, for Episkopí. The road climbs, at first westward across the hill, but after a sharp bend the drop to seaward is on the left, and (1.5km from the highway) the cave is signed (left), just before a gully which the road crosses on a culvert. The cave entrance is 30 paces below the road under a fig tree. Walkers can approach straight up the gully, from which the tree is also visible.

The cave, first investigated early this century by J. Khatzidákis, was fully excavated by S. Marinátos (1920s). It has stalagmites, round one of which was a low wall suggesting that it played a part in the cult rituals of Eileíthyia; the small terrace in front of the cave mouth also showed signs of ritual activity.

From Amnisós the Old Road follows the coast to the next sandy bay. At the far end of it, below a large hotel, stands the chapel of Ayii Theódori. A Minoan harbour and dockyard were investigated here in the 1920s; swimmers may notice remains of the installations under water.

This stretch of coast and the immediate hinterland are popular with birdwatchers, especially at the time of the spring migration.

At 13km a bridge crosses a gully just before (right) the excavated villa of **Nírou Kháni** (sign on left). Open Tuesday–Sunday 09.00–14.30; Monday closed. Small entrance charge.

This was a large Minoan building of at least two storeys (LMIA, contemporary with the New Palaces), and the remains are among the best preserved of their kind on the island. The interior of the house is railed off, but all points of interest can be viewed from outside it.

See Plan: 1. paved courtyard with *raised paths* across it;

2. stepped platform where part of *horns of consecration* was found;

3. *main entrance* between two columns, and then through a typically Minoan pillar-and-door scheme to 4., a *hall* with gypsum dado and decorative floor paving;

5. *corridor*, originally frescoed, leading west to the central block of the house;

6. a room where four large, thin and therefore presumably ceremonial double axes were found, along with a heap of ashes, possible evidence for a *shrine* with a hearth for burnt offerings.

The main rooms are best seen from the far end by area 9. On the way round the south side you pass (7) the foundations of the *staircase* and its return. At the centre of the house is the *Room of the Benches* (8) with its integral light-well (9). There was a room above, also with benches, and also opening on to the light-well, thus creating a sheltered environment here at all seasons. Behind the Room of the Benches, and accessible only from it, is room 10, where four stone lamps were found. Rooms 11 and 12 contained about 40 tripod *tables for offerings*, stacked in piles. In 13 there is a built seat, and 14 contained a further three tables for offerings. In the light of these curious finds suggestions have been made about possible missionary activity, or the export of ritual paraphernalia from the harbour of Ayii Theódori (see above). The religious element is recognised in the name given to the site, the 'House of the High Priest'.

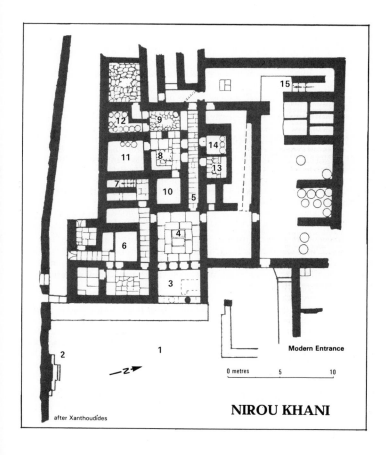

NIROU KHANI

after Xanthoudídes

On the way out you will notice five storage bins (15) built of mud-brick, with steps up to them, and to the south a deposit of large storage jars.

Finds from the villa are in Herákleion Museum, Gallery VII, where the double axes are strikingly displayed on (reconstructed) poles and bases.

The route continues past an American Air Force Base. Soon afterwards the Old Road joins the north coast highway below a prominent hill crowned by a radar station (16.5km from Herákleion by the highway).

In less than 1km a turning to the right is signposted for *Goúves*, for (8.5km) the **Cave of Skoteinó**. The detour across upland (230m) behind the village to this Minoan sanctuary is also feasible on foot; buses stop at the turning on the highway.

The road climbs gently to (1.5km) *Goúves*. There are seats provided along the way and the village has several kapheneíons in the plateía. At 3.5km is a sign-posted turn right to (4.5km) the village of *Skoteinó*. Keep left through the village and at 6km, on a corner, a track branches off to the right, signposted for the last 2.5km to the cave. At the final rise the sea is in view (right) and Mount Díkte to the south-east is behind you. Ahead, on bare upland, a white church (Ayía Paraskeví, dating from the period of the Venetian occupation) marks the mouth of the cave. From the crest beyond the church there is a fine view across the centre of the island.

The huge cave of Skoteinó (the name means dark) is one of the most important sanctuary sites on Crete. 160m deep, with four levels and steeply sloping galleries, it was first investigated by Sir Arthur Evans and has been thoroughly studied by the French speleologist P. Faure. In 1962 the Greek archaeologist C. Daváras excavated here; the finds ranged from MMI (c 2000 BC) to the Roman period, and included three important bronze statuettes, LMI male votaries. Dating from the last great flowering of the Minoan culture, these figures wear only the loin-cloth and stand in the typical position, right hand raised to forehead (Herákleion Museum, Gallery III).

At 23km on the highway is the turn for the Plateau of Lasíthi (Rte 6).

26km. The holiday resort of **Khersónisos** is strictly Limín Khersonísou (Khersónisos harbour), because the original village now lies a short distance inland. (On the way into the town there is a signed turning for a minor road that climbs inland 2km to *Piskopianó* and a small folk museum.) The main road runs straight through Khersónisos, and is lined with souvenir shops, motor bikes for hire and the garish trappings of tourism. A turning left signed to the *port* leads down to the noisy waterfront lined with bars and tavernas.

Khersónisos was an important Greco-Roman harbour town, with a famous temple dedicated to Britomartis (mentioned by the 1C BC Greek historian, Strabo) and secure anchorage sheltered and defended by the rocky headland to the north called Kastrí. This was the port of Lýttos c 15km inland, but must have been autonomous at least by the 4C when it issued its own coinage. The city continued to flourish in the Roman period, when a great aqueduct brought water from the Kastélli Pediádas region (Rte 3C).

Halfway along the waterfront (see plan) the road narrows, and bends around a much restored Roman *fountain*, in the form of a pyramid with a stepped channelling system and remains of mosaics (2C–3C AD) of a fishing scene.

Off the little point here are vestiges of ancient harbour works, which can be seen in the water because the sea level has risen by about a metre since the Roman period. At right-angles to the shore is the southerly *mole*, its surface awash. With a second, L-shaped, quay on the line of the modern one jutting out from the Kastrí, this formed the Roman *harbour*, the safest anchorage on the north coast between Herákleion and Oloús (Eloúnda). Breakwaters of large boulders outside the moles gave increased protection. To the left, north of the same point by the fountain, are

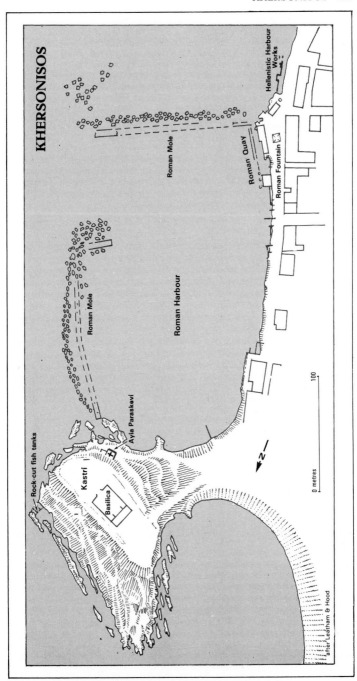

KHERSONISOS

Hellenistic Harbour Works

Roman Mole

Roman Quay

Roman Fountain

Roman Mole

Roman Harbour

Rock-cut fish tanks

Kastri

Ayia Paraskevi

Basilica

0 metres 100

after Leatham & Hood

remains of the Roman concrete *quay* along the shore. This is preserved for 30m or so above the water and the northern section has a line of rectangular bollards 8–9m apart on its seaward edge; it has been estimated that the Roman harbour provided 330m of wharfage. On the shore, just to the right (south) of the point, large dressed stone blocks are the remnants of earlier Hellenistic harbour works.

The rocky headland of *Kastrí* marked by the white chapel of Ayía Paraskeví was fortified in the Late Roman period. On its top (reached from the steps to the left of the large modern café) are the excavated remains (A. Orlandos, 1959) of an early 6C triple-aisled basilica *church*, one of the largest basilicas known on Crete and probably once the seat of the local bishop. Its spectacular position must have made it an impressive landmark for shipping. The mosaic floors are not well preserved, but note a 2C AD Attic sarcophagus lid re-used as an altar base, and the apse is unusual in being included in a rectangle.

On the seaward side of the basilica, the headland meets the sea in a flat rock-shelf, and at the east end of the shelf, just submerged, are three rock-cut rectangular compartments (the largest 4m by 3m) thought to be Roman *fish-tanks*. These were enclosed by a wall and had a system of cut channels for a constant supply of fresh sea-water.

30km *Stalís* is a nebulous area of inexpensive holiday accommodation. A side-road climbs steeply by zigzags, 9km to *Mokhós*, a village set around a large shady plateía (now on a main route up to Lasíthi).

At 34km you reach modern *Mállia*; there is a fine long sandy beach (sign in the centre of the town) but the atmosphere of the resort is typified by the road down to the sea: a kilometre of bars, pubs and discotheques.

The archaeological site is 3km to the east beyond the modern town, signed left (500m). The walk along the beach, longer but more pleasant than the busy main road, now passes a large seaside hotel at the edge of the archaeological area.

The Minoan palace and town of **Mállia** (ancient name unknown) lie on the narrow coastal plain just inland from the sea, on the natural lowland route between central and eastern Crete, and immediately to the north of the mountains girdling the Lasíthi plateau. The little church of Prophítis Ilías sits on a spur level with the site, and rising steeply behind is the dominating bulk of *Mount Seléna* (1559m).

Open 08.30–15.00, Sundays and holidays included, but closed Mondays. Entrance charge. (Bookstall but no refreshments.)

The site was first explored in 1915 by Greek archaeologists under J. Khatzidákis, but since 1922 both the palace and a series of large houses, part of a *Minoan town* of considerable size, have been systematically excavated by the French School at Athens which publishes the excellent 'Guide des fouilles françaises en Crète'. The original site plans here distinguished 'Quartiers' (sectors or areas) by the Greek alphabet. The early excavators left on view remains that are largely of the Neopalatial buildings, but in recent years work has tended to concentrate on Protopalatial features both within the palace and in the surrounding town, in particular Quartier M (pronounced Mu) where a system of modern walkways has been constructed to allow visitors access to the excavation covering c 2700 square metres. Panels with commentary are to be provided at points of particular interest.

In 1987 work began on an ambitious project to erect new covers over areas particularly vulnerable to weathering. Several phases are already completed, and the soaring translucent roofs, specifically designed to avoid any echo of the original Minoan architecture, are a striking innovation. The digging of postholes for the supporting frameworks offered a valuable opportunity to re-examine the stratigraphy recorded by earlier archaeologists.

There was Prepalatial settlement on what became the town site—EMIII/MMI buildings have been excavated (see chronological sequence on p 18). The Old Palace at Mállia was certainly in existence by the MMII period, contemporary with

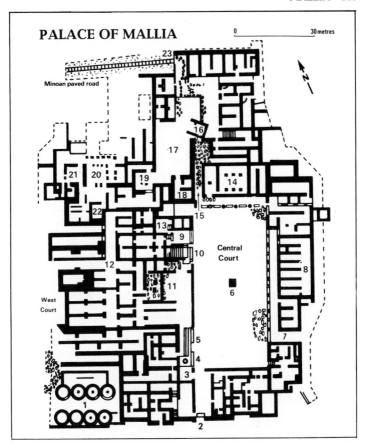

PALACE OF MALLIA

0   30 metres

Minoan paved road

21   20   19

18

17

16

14

15

13   9

22

12

10

Central Court

11

6

8

West Court

5

4

3

7

1

2

those at Knossós and Phaistós, and it suffered, as they did, damage by a major earthquake at the end of MMII. After rebuilding, the New Palace flourished until LMIB when both it and the main dependent buildings were destroyed. A few parts of the site, notably House E, were reoccupied in LMIII.

The palace excavation is approached from the paved *West Court*; note the flagstone paths forming raised walks, a typical Minoan device. One of these paths serves the North Entrance (see below), and another runs along, though not exactly parallel to, the West Front. At the south end of this façade, and dating from the Old Palace, is a double row of circular structures (1 on plan), eight in all, each 5m in diameter. These pits were probably used as silos or granaries, and from the evidence for central pillars it is deduced that they were roofed.

Follow the *south façade* of the (New) Palace, just inside the wire fence on your right, past the narrow opening to a shrine, to the *main entrance* (2). The flagged passage of the entrance was probably cut off from the Central Court by an extension of the wall at its north end, so that entry was effected indirectly, by turning left through a door into an antechamber (3), which gave on to a paved terrace (4) from which two steps led to the Court. Set in the terrace floor is a circular limestone table known as the Mállia *kernos*, with a large hollow at its centre and 34 smaller ones round the circumference. This has been interpreted as an offering table for rituals associated with harvested first fruits, or the fertility of seed, but many other explanations have also been advanced. Just to the north are the lower steps of a monumental *staircase* (5).

The **Central Court**, which has been shown to date to the Old Palace period, is more than twice as long as it is wide (48m by 22m) and lies on the same north-north-east/south-south-west axis as those at Knossós and Phaistós. It is not certain whether the surface was paved all over, or only in certain areas. In the exact centre is a shallow *pit* (6) lined with mud-brick, and with four mud-brick stands in it. This may have been an altar, perhaps associated with the cult of the pillar crypt in the west wing, as it is aligned between the pillars of that room (see below). It has also been suggested that its exact central position was of technical significance in the original laying out of the court and its surrounding buildings. Along the east side of the Central Court was a gallery or portico supported by alternate columns and pillars, a stylistic arrangement much favoured by the Minoans, presumably for decorative reasons. Pairs of round post-holes between each pillar and column base may indicate a balustrade.

Behind the portico, at its south end, is the *east entrance corridor* (7) and north of it the *east storeroom block* (8) previously hidden from view but now displayed under an elegant new roof protecting the mud-brick construction. These storerooms would have held oil and wine. The equipment can be seen to include raised platforms for storage vessels with spouts for drainage near their bases, also separating tubs for oil and channels for collecting spilt liquid.

On the west side of the court a more imposing complex consisted of a raised platform (9) known as the *Loggia*, perhaps for ceremonial purposes, and beside this the *Grand Staircase* (10), which would have led up to a set of large rooms above. The central part of the ground floor of this *West Wing* is occupied by the *hall* (11) and its interconnecting rooms. It opens to the west into a flagged *pillar crypt* (paved area on the plan). This would have been a dark enclosed room remarkably like those near the Temple Repositories at Knossós. There are double axes carved on the pillars. Behind this cult area are storerooms, indicating a juxtaposition of functions found also at Knossós and Phaistós. By the long *west corridor* (12) you can return past a huge pithos to the area behind the loggia. Here (13), on a floor dating from the Old Palace, were found the ceremonial stone axe in the shape of a leopard, and a great bronze sword with rock crystal hilt; both these outstanding examples of Minoan craftsmanship are on display in Herákleion Museum, Gallery IV.

The *North Wing* lay behind a colonnaded portico, of which the column bases are preserved. The large *hall* (14) has six rectangular pillars in it, presumably to support a grand room on the floor above. Cooking pots were found in the small room to the west and, by analogy with pots and food debris found in a comparable position at Zákros, it has been suggested that the upper storey was a dining hall. To the east part of a staircase to this upper storey remains, and there is another further north.

The paved *corridor* (15) which sets off towards the North Entrance is partly obstructed by a later building (16) on an oblique alignment. This is thought to be a shrine, but its dating is uncertain. The corridor passes (left) the *North Court* (17).

At the south end of the North Court, up three steps, is the solidly built structure known as the *Keep* (18). West of this is a small court (19) with a portico to the south from which a dogleg passage leads west to the so-called *Royal Apartments*, the private quarters of the palace. The *main hall* (20) has a broad colonnaded verandah to the north which may have looked out over a garden; the excavated walls now visible here belong to the Old Palace. On its east and south sides the hall gave on to light-wells which could be shut off when necessary by means of a pier-and-door arrangement. To the west is a smaller paved hall (21) (usually compared to the 'Queen's Room' at Knossós), and off this (south) is a lustral basin or bath. West of these rooms was found the famous 'Acrobat's sword' (also in Herákleion Museum, Gallery IV), with the figure of an acrobat arched across a gold disk on the pommel. The *Archive Room* (22) yielded tablets in hieroglyphic script as well as in Linear A.

From the light-well east of the main hall (20) a passage leads back to the North Court (17) and from here you can leave the palace by its *North Entrance* (23), near which stand two giant *pithoi*; the one inside the entrance shows dramatic evidence of burning. A fine Minoan paved way which serves this entrance will lead you west into the *town*.

Immediately to the north lies the area known as the *agorá*, excavated in the 1960s. This turned out to be a walled space—in use by the Old Palace period—measuring c 29m by 40m and with a plaster floor. It is uncertain whether it functioned as a market place but if so it would have been the earliest such feature known on Crete.

On the west side of the agorá is the so-called *Hypostyle Crypt* (sometimes more elegantly the Columned Crypt); its plastered walls are now protected by the conspicuous new roof. The building is below ground level, approached by a flight of steps, and consists of a series of storerooms and two interconnected halls with benches round three sides. The puzzling lack of finds from these halls has led to the suggestion that they served as some kind of council chamber.

Behind (west of) the dig-house is Quartier Δ (closed to the public). This series of houses with a paved road between them includes House Δα, cited as a particularly well-preserved example of Minoan domestic architecture of Neopalalatial date; it has a main hall opening on to a light-well with single column, a lustral basin with white plaster walls and red dado, and a toilet, as well as the usual storerooms.

A track (dotted on area plan, now upgraded for vehicles) starts from near the car-park, opposite the south-west corner of the palace fence, and runs out to the sea (10 minutes on foot). This passes the Quartier M excavation (see below) recently opened for public viewing under its new roof. (An alternative, quieter, path hugs the fenced area—keeping right—and strikes off from the north corner towards the sea.)

Quartier Mu consists of administrative buildings and workshops developed at the time of the Old Palace. The economic functions are defined as production, storage, record-keeping and the redistribution of goods, but the excavator concluded that the principal purpose of this sector of the town in the Protopalatial period was connected with religious administration. Important finds of sealings and tablets, including a hieroglyphic archive deposit discovered in 1968, were considered alongside discoveries in the workshops of a stonemason's unfinished kernos, and a potter's clay moulds from shells and agrimi horns; both shell and horns, in association with figurines, are recognised furnishings of Minoan shrines.

The refined architecture is also notable. The oldest part of the buildings, near the (first) main entrance, has the earliest sunken *lustral basin* yet known. This is associated with a complex consisting of *main room and anteroom* with the addition of an *inner room* with a hearth or table for offerings, also a nearby row of storage magazines. One line of thought compares this complex with the original (MMII) phase of the Throne Room area at Knossós, and suggests for both areas a similar cultic function.

Some of the remarkable finds from Quartier Mu are displayed in the Ayios Nikólaos Museum.

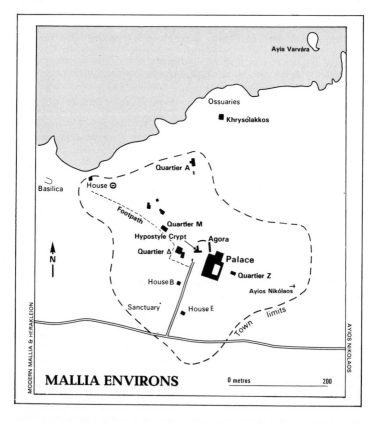

As the car track nears the shore (see above) a resort hotel is now conspicuous to the west. In that direction the ruins of an Early Christian basilica (6C–7C) cover the site of a tomb which contained an imported Attic sarcophagus of the Antonine period (2C AD but here probably re-used); this is now in Herákleion Museum, Gallery XX.

If you turn right on to the coastal path and follow it east for a further 10 minutes (to a rise where the islet of Ayía Varvára comes into sight) just on the right (fenced) is **Khrysólakkos**, a large rectangular enclosure dating to the MMI period (early in the life of the Old Palace) from which came the well-known gold pendant of two conjoined bees (Herákleion Museum, Gallery VII), one of the masterpieces of the Minoan goldsmiths' art. The Greek name translates as 'pit of gold'—as the area was known locally long before archaeologists began their investigations. (It has been suggested that the 'Aegina treasure' now in the British Museum was actually plundered from here during the latter part of the 19C.)

The enclosure is elaborately built of well-dressed stones; it is divided into many compartments, with a paved area and along its east side an extended portico, an architectural feature unknown elsewhere on Crete at this early date.

The function of Khrysólakkos is uncertain. It has traditionally been thought of as an ossuary or cemetery, even, because of the quality of the finds, a royal burial-place. However the buildings resemble no other funerary structure known on Crete. The presence of clay idols indicates that some of the rooms on the east side were certainly used for cult purposes, and the enclosure may have served as a sanctuary.

On the rocky bluff immediately to the north of the excavated site are caves which were used as ossuaries during MMI, while to the east around the Ayía Varvára Bay are further remains, including workshops, also of early date, from the period of the Old Palace.

Walking east to the sea from Khrysólakkos the path follows the line of a defensive wall built at the beginning of the Old Palace period. Such walls have only recently begun to be recognised in the Minoan record.

To the east of the palace, outside the fence and level with the East Entrance (7 on palace plan), is Area Z. Here three houses have been excavated; the one to the left of the paved road shows the best construction. Note its paved hall with column base and door jambs.

Two further excavated areas may be visited on the way back to the main road. On the eastern side of the palace approach road is the large *House* E, of MMIII–LMI date, but reoccupied during LMIII, after the LMIB destruction of the palace. Off the opposite side of the approach road remains of another building have been found. The horns of consecration incorporated in its construction suggested that it was a shrine.

1.5km after you rejoin the main road to Ayios Nikólaos there is a left turn for a detour to the coast at (5km) Sísi or (10km) Mílatos.

A section of the Old Road to Ayios Nikólaos (by Vrakhási) briefly runs parallel to the highway. After 3km turn left. (Very soon you pass the by-road signposted, right, for Mílatos.) *Sísi* grew up around a picturesque rocky inlet with agreeable tavernas and an empty beach beyond the eastern headland, but the village has rapidly changed its style as it develops the tourist potential of mushrooming holiday apartments on harbour, headland and beach.

At *Mílatos* (see road turning above) c 6km east along the coast, a cave in the hills behind is a place of modern Cretan pilgrimage on account of a Turkish atrocity against the Christian populace committed there in 1823.

There was a Bronze Age settlement at Mílatos and important LMIII tholos tombs have been excavated (finds in the Ayios Nikólaos Museum). The city-state of the Classical period, a contemporary of neighbouring Dréros, was destroyed by Lýttos in the 3C BC. According to legend the great Ionian city of Miletus in Asia Minor was founded from here, and in fact Minoan influence has now been identified in the archaeological record of that city.

In Mílatos village (inland of the beach settlement) you can turn right to follow the asphalt road signed to the cave, and then continue by good dirt roads across unspoilt uplands, through (a further 2km) *Kounáli*, and then south, following a deep valley, to rejoin the Neápolis road at Latsída. A recommended 3km detour (with extensive views between mountains and sea) takes a turning left at the T-junction in Kounáli, then 1km byond Tsámbi right at a stone-built farmhouse where the road drops away into a valley before a rise to the tranquil long-abandoned monastery of Ayios Antónios.

After the Sísi turning the New Road strikes inland through the gorge of Selenári where the holy icon of Ayios Yeóryios is said to exert a benign influence on travellers. The foothills of the Lasíthi mountains (right) provide a grand scenic background.

At 49km the highway bypasses *Neápolis*, a pleasant market town (pop. 3500) which is the administrative centre of the eparchy (district) of Mirabéllo and seat of the district law court. (See Rte 7 for the site of Dréros and a recommended cross-country drive to Eloúnda.)

Near present-day Neápolis was the birthplace of Pétros Phílargos, the Cretan who became Pope Alexander V. Born 1340 and, as an orphan, brought up by the Catholic friars of nearby Ayios Antónios, he went on to study at the renowned friary of St. Francis in Candia (on the hill where the Herákleion Archaeological Museum now stands) and took orders in 1357. A career as an academic and theologian led him to many European universities including Oxford. He travelled as an evangelist to Lithuania, and was appointed ambassador to the court of the Duke of Milan, Giovanni Visconti. On 26 June, 1409, in the city of Pisa, he was proclaimed Pope but the following year, before reaching Rome, he died and was buried in Bologna. There were rumours of poison.

Derelict windmills enhance the landscape before a tunnel brings the road out above the Bay of Mirabéllo.

At 70km on the outskirts of *Ayios Nikólaos*, a wide crossroads offers (left) the Eloúnda road (avoiding the centre of town), and (right) the bypass leading on into eastern Crete. Ahead, in Ayios Nikólaos, a one-way system now operates so it helps to be familiar with the town plan. (You will be diverted right leaving the hospital on your left, and then bear left and right to Odós Plastíra high above the town's lake.) On a short visit you may prefer to park where you are diverted right, and walk downhill against the traffic flow, past the Archaeological Museum, five minutes to the harbour front.

For details of Ayios Nikólaos turn to Rte 7.

6   The Lasíthi Plain and the Cave of Zeus

57km (34 miles) to Tzermiádo, principal village of the upland plateau of Lasíthi, continuing to (70km) Psykhró for the Diktaian cave.

The road climbs to the pass which cuts through the girdle of mountains round the fertile plateau of Lasíthi, irrigated in the dry season by white-sailed wind pumps. The Diktaian cave, a traditional birthplace of Zeus, has become one of the principal tourist attractions of the island. (Suitable shoes and a sweater advised.) There is simple accommodation on the plain in the villages of Tzermiádo, Ayios Yeóryios and Psykhró.

Bus service, twice daily from Herákleion to Psykhró. Also once a day from Ayios Nikólaos.

Take the north coast highway from Herákleion in the direction of Ayios Nikólaos (see Rte 5) until at 23km you turn inland for the Lasíthi plateau.

At 29km a road branches off right to Kastélli Pediádas (Rte 3C). Shortly after this, in the ravine below the road (right) are the ruined piers of a Roman *aqueduct* built to supply ancient Khersónisos (Rte 5) from springs around Piyí near Kastélli—see Ayios Pandeleímon (Rte 3C).

At 32km, before the village of Potamiés, a large sign indicates the track left up to the frescoed Byzantine *church of the Panayía, all that remains of the Gouverniótissa monastery. Passing almost immediately the chapel of Sotíros Khristós (Our Saviour Christ), also frescoed, you climb 1.5km to the monastery church which looks out from the hillside over the Langáda valley.

If the church is closed, with no notice of opening hours, enquire for the guardian (phýlakas) at the kapheneíon right of the main street in Potamiés.

The cruciform church of the Panayía (dedicated to the Assumption of the Virgin; festival 15 August) has a ground-plan in which three arms of the cross are of equal length, with central dome resting on an octagonal drum lit by blind-arcaded windows. The *frescoes* date from the second half of the 14C. The paintings are best preserved in the west arm, with a double tier of gospel scenes above the worshipping saints. The church is dominated by the Pantokrátor in the dome, above the four evangelists on the pendentives.

The carved wooden iconostasis, sanctuary doors and a group of 16C icons from this church are now displayed in Herákleion's Historical Museum (p 89).

Beyond Potamiés the road levels out as it approaches the dramatic wall of the Lasíthi mountains. The knob shape conspicuous on the skyline is Karphí, meaning the Nail. Clinging to its precipitous slopes (see below) are the remains of a refuge settlement built at the very end of the Bronze Age by a community still adhering to Minoan religious traditions 300 years after the collapse of Minoan power.

39km *Avdoú* is an unspoilt village with several interesting churches.

Ayios Konstantínos, 1.5km outside the village, has frescoes painted by the brothers Mánuel and Ioánnis Phokás, dated by the donor's inscription to 1445 (compare frescoes by Mánuel dated 1436–37 at Embaros, Rte 3C, and Epáno Sými, Rte 8).

The owner of the first kapheneíon on the right of the main street will direct you to the nearby house of the keyholder. The track to the church was right of the road as you entered Avdoú (50m back from the kapheneíon). On the track bear right and continue (along a stretch of old paved road) to a bridge; 500m beyond it is a fork, where the church precinct is in view among the trees right.

The church of *Ayios Antónios* is in the middle of the village (signed, opposite the above kapheneíon, left and immediately left again). Its 14C frescoes of gospel scenes are interesting for their powerful draughtsmanship executed largely in tones of brown paint.

The cruciform church of *Ayios Yeóryios* stands in a cemetery on the north edge of the village. Little remains of its frescoes, but a visit to the church is an excuse to explore Avdoú on foot. Turn off the main thoroughfare as for Ayios Antónios but follow this street (without turning left again) as it winds through the village. The main plateía is to the right.

From *Goniés* the climb begins in earnest. At 41.5km a road diverges downhill to *Mokhós*, scene of an animated festival on 15 August. (This would also be the route up to Lasíthi from the coastal region around Mállia.) At 44.5km a loop (left) off the main road takes you through the delightful village of *Krási*. On one side of the plateía water from springs is harnessed through vaulted draw basins opposite an enormous ancient plane tree which 12 people with outstretched arms cannnot girdle (well-sited cafés).

Near by, one of the earliest known examples of a circular stone-built tholos tomb (EMI, c 3000 BC), originally noticed by Evans, was excavated in 1929 by S. Marinátos.

48.5km. Just below the road (right), at *Kerá*, is the convent of the Panayía Kardiótissa. The epithet, a particularly popular one on Crete, suggests the quality of tenderness. (Festival for the Birth of the Virgin, 8 September.)

The convent is open 08.00–13.00 and 15.00–19.00. *View from the terrace, and a well-tended garden that benefits from the mountain climate.

The highly unusual ground plan of the church is the result of four successive building phases, though it is interesting that care was taken with windows, stonework and decorative tiling in order to achieve a homogeneous exterior. The original three-apsed chapel serves as the bema of the present convent church. To enlarge this chapel an extended narthex was added, forming a short three-aisled nave or triple transept, with steps to adjust to the slope of the hillside on which the convent is built. Parallel to this is a conventional narthex which is now the entrance to the church. A further addition is a small chapel to the north of the original one. The frescoes in the bema are dated to the early 14C; those elsewhere in the church were painted later in the same century, and show the influence of the Macedonian school.

Beyond the hamlet of Kerá, the road climbs to (52.5km) the *Selí Ambélou pass* (900m) marked by a row of stone-built windmills which continued to grind corn until early this century. (The windmills have recently been joined by less romantic modern buildings—usually with a café among them.) The *view from the pass extends back to the coast and forward to Mount Díkte, at 2148m the highest peak in the range.

The excavated Subminoan refuge of *Karphí* is on a summit to the left (east) of the pass. To reach it, it is possible to follow the crest of the ridge from the windmills, or take a very steep path from Kerá, but the recommended route is a walk of less than an hour up from the plain (see Tzermiádo, below).

Below, at 817–850m lies the **Lasíthi plateau** (Oropédio Lasithíou). There are several of these fertile upland plains on Crete but Lasíthi is the only area above 800m that is inhabited all the year round. There is a strong sense of community among the 20 or so villages around the edge of the plain. In winter the passes may be blocked by snow, so preparations in autumn are still a serious business.

The plateau's fertility depends on the rich alluvial soil brought down from the mountains by the melting snows which drain into a swallow hole at the western end near Káto Metokhí. The Romans tackled the problem of drainage to cope with spring flooding but the grid of ditches (known as 'linies') which now gives much of the plain the appearance of a chessboard was installed by engineers from Padua. Recent research has made it possible to date the construction of this system very precisely to 1631–33, at a time when the success of the wheat crop was of particular importance to the rulers of the Venetian empire. The irrigation system employed countless picturesque windpumps, each with four to eight triangular sails of white cloth revolving anti-clockwise to draw water to the surface, and during the dry season, many of these (despite the mechanised competition) still operate.

Lasíthi lies above the olive-tree line, but its apples and potatoes are now valued in the markets of Athens as well as throughout Crete. Some cereals are still grown, also other fruit crops and an abundance of almonds. The plain is a splendid sight at blossom time.

There is evidence for Neolithic occupation with an important sanctuary at the

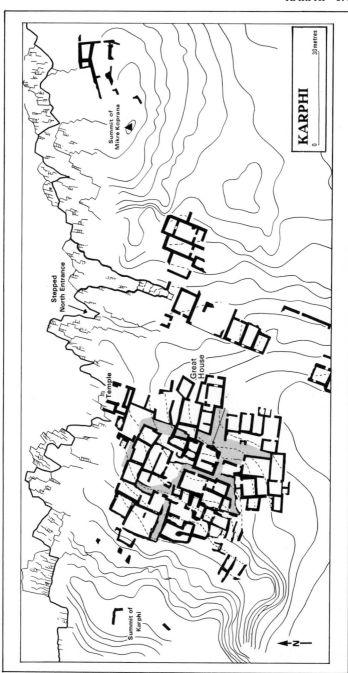

KARPHI

0 _____ 30 metres

Summit of
Mikre Koprana

Stepped
North Entrance

Temple

Great
House

Summit of
Karphi

←N→

Trapéza cave. The great cave at Psykhró was a place of pilgrimage from Middle Minoan times to the 7C BC, a period of a thousand years. In Hellenistic times the area was under the control of Lýttos (Rte 3C), a powerful city-state to the west just outside the girdle of mountains, and there is plenty of evidence for Roman settlement presumably exploiting the rich soil.

The Lasíthi plain, with only eight natural passes through the encircling mountains, has always been an easily defended refuge, and hence at many periods (up to recent times) the chief base in eastern Crete for rebellion and revolt. During the early part of Venetian rule the situation was so critical that in 1263 the authorities forcibly cleared the population from the plain, and forbade tillage or pasturage for nearly two centuries—a desparate decision considering that Crete made a considerable contribution to the granaries of Venice.

Descending 1.5km from the Selí Ambélou pass, you come to the road which makes a circuit of the plain. To the right it is 8km to the Diktaian cave at Psykhró; you pass after 3km the ruins of the Vidianí monastery. The following route circles the plain in the opposite (clockwise) direction. Turn left and continue through *Lagoú* to *Tzermiádo* (4km from the pass, 56.5km from Herákleion), the principal village (pop. 1200) of the eparchy or district of Lasíthi. (Pension and rent-room accommodation available.) On the edge of the village there is a track into the mountains, the beginning of the easiest of several routes up to the excavated Subminoan site of **Karphí**.

Just before you enter the village you pass, left, large modern buildings, the KENTPO ΥΓΕΙΑΣ or district health centre. On the village side of this complex a track (recently improved to take vehicles) leads north into the mountains. You climb gently for about 20 minutes (or drive) to the *Níssimos plateau*, a small fertile area probably also cultivated in ancient times. In April and May the wet gullies in the surrounding hills still shelter the creamy white peony indigenous to Crete, *P. clusii*.

The track would take you straight across the Níssimos plain to a paved kalderími through the hills towards the north coast, but your destination, a saddle between two peaks at the top of a conspicuous long narrowing gully, is now visible to your left and can be reached only on foot. Leave the track and keep left along the edge of the plateau, to pick up a path which gains height up the left incline of this gully. You pass the Astividerós spring. The path ascends in a fairly straight line until it crosses the gully near the top, before leading you between outcrops of rock up the slope from which the excavated remains are in view. The concrete survey post should mark the peak to your right. There are two groups of small tholos tombs along this path, with a circular vault usually covering a roughly rectangular chamber.

There was a Middle Minoan peak sanctuary on the knob at Karphí but the settlement, excavated (1937–39) by the British School under J. Pendlebury, dates from the very end of the Bronze Age (11C BC) and continues into the Protogeometric period. This desolate site, presumably chosen for defensive purposes, was occupied for perhaps 150 years and then peacefully evacuated, limiting the excavator to a partial view of the Minoans who built this remote refuge. They certainly worshipped Cretan gods some 3–400 years after the destruction of the political power of the Minoan palace civilisation, and the many ritual features revealed by the excavation may mean the site was of particular religious significance.

The settlement clings to the south-east slopes of 'the Nail' and spreads across the saddle between the two peaks (see plan). The houses were roughly built of stone without plaster, and only thresholds and doorjambs were of carefully cut blocks. Pendlebury's *Great House* can be identified by its superior construction; a series of bronze finds confirmed the relative importance of this building. The paved streets (shaded on plan) give shape to the town, though individual house plans, where clusters of rooms are huddled together in agglomerative fashion, are not so easy to make out. There was a stepped entrance from the top of the steep northern ascent. The *Temple* or civic shrine was also at the edge of this precipice and part of it has been eroded away. The largest room with remains of an altar was entered from the east and had two small adjoining rooms opposite this doorway. Among the furnishings left behind in the shrine when the settlement was abandoned were clay goddesses with the traditional cylindrical skirt and hands raised in a gesture of blessing. One, nearly a metre high, has birds perching in her crown. A unique rhyton is in the form of a chariot drawn by three oxen represented only by their heads (all in Herákleion Museum, Gallery XI).

There is an alternative return route to the Lasíthi plain. Follow the ridge west, passing a second water supply, Vitsilóvrisis, the Fountain of the Eagles. (The modern inscription commemorates the British archaeological team which excavated Karphí.) You can see a white chapel on the outer slope of the hills. A little beyond this you meet a path crossing the ridge, and turning left on to it you very soon start the descent to Lasíthi on a stepped stone-built kalderími, another of the eight ancient ways through the girdle of hills. You reach the Tzermiádo road 500m west of the Lasíthi Health Centre and the track at the start of the ascent.

In the middle of Tzermiádo an acute left turn is signed for the *Trapéza cave*, but by car it is better to continue through the village in the direction of Psykhró, for soon a new road leads off to the left, and 300m along it the path (10 minutes) is signposted—to Krónio. *View from terrace in front of cave mouth. The site was frequented from the Neolithic period (5th millenium BC). It is disputed whether the earliest levels show evidence for occupation, but the cave was certainly used for Neolithic burials, and later as a sanctuary. In the Middle Minoan period it seems to have been abandoned in favour of the Diktaian cave at Psykhró. The nearby hill of Kástellos (just to the east) was the site of a Middle Minoan settlement.

The road turns south, passing (61.5km) *Moní Kroustalenías* at the junction with the road down to Ayios Nikólaos (see below). You follow the eastern edge of the plain through *Ayios Konstantínos* to (65.5km) the village of *Ayios Yeóryios* (good tavernas and simple accommodation). The well-arranged *Folklore Museum is open daily, 10.00–16.00; small entrance charge.

At 70km you reach *Psykhró* (pension and rent rooms). At the end of the village, a turning (left, signposted 'Spileon') leads up to a Tourist Pavilion and car park, from which there is a superb *view over the plain. A stepped path ascends (15 minutes) to the **Cave of Psykhró**.

Open 08.00–17.00; tickets at cave entrance. Guides are available but not essential. Donkeys may be hired for the ascent from the Tourist Pavilion.

There are many rival stories but according to one tradition, this is the Diktaian cave where the Hymn of the Kourétes says Zeus was born. Many thousands of visitors are drawn to the cave each year on this account, though some scholars dispute the location.

An oracle had decreed that Kronos, the youngest of the Titans, would be dethroned by his son, so his wife Rhea contrived to give birth in a cave deep in the mountains of Crete (hence the title Zeus Kretagenes, Cretan-born). In Hesiod's version, Kronos had swallowed his five previous offspring, but in this case he was duped with a stone wrapped in swaddling clothes; meanwhile the infant Zeus was spirited away, traditionally to the cave on Mount Ida, to be raised by the goat-nymph, Amaltheia. (See also Idaían Cave, Rte 6.) All six children proved to be immortal, and in due course Kronos was succeeded by Zeus.

The cave (1025m above sea level and 150m above the village of Psykhró) attracted the interest of a number of archaeologists (including Evans) at the end of the last century, and enough material was brought to light to suggest that the site was rich in votive deposits and a cult centre of antiquity. The cave was excavated (1899–1900) by D.G. Hogarth for the British School, and yielded remains from Middle Minoan to Late Geometric times. Notable are libation tables, most in serpentine or limestone, one (purchased by Evans, now in the Ashmolean Museum, Oxford) inscribed with

Linear A signs, and a series of small bronzes: human and animal figurines, and models including a chariot, as well as double axes, rings, pins and blades (all these in Herákleion Museum).

The descent into the cave is steep and slippery, and the lower depths are chilly. The upper part of the cave (the north-west area to the right of the entrance) contained pottery and animal bones consistent with sacrificial offerings, and there was an *altar*, roughly built and about 1m high, round which most of the fragments of libation tables were discovered. The innermost recess, against the cave wall, was a *temenos*, or sacred precinct, defined by a wall and roughly paved. To the south (ahead) is the entrance to the main cavern which descends 65m; at the bottom water now lies for most of the year. Bronze votives were found in great numbers in the pool, in the vertical crevices formed by the fine stalactites, and sometimes embedded in the stalactites themselves. Almost all the finds from this lowest level were of LMI date. This was the main period of use, but there was a lesser revival of ritual activity in the 8C–7C when openwork bronze plaques were the characteristic votive offerings.

The road now completes in a further 8km the circuit of the plain, to the deserted *Vidianí monastery* (19C foundation), and the junction below the windmills on the road back to Herákleion.

About 4km from Psykhró, just beyond *Káto Metokhí*, you pass the swallow hole that drains the plateau; this is frequently a rewarding area for bird-watchers. Here, by the fine new bridge, is the start of the old kalderími over the girdle of mountains by the Tsoúli Mníma pass towards Lýttos. The path may be obstructed in places as a result of work on a shepherds' vehicle track up to the high pastures. Allow about an hour to the pass; then the kalderími snakes down by a circuitous route to Tíkhos, where the ancient aqueduct carried Lasíthi water to Lýttos. From the pass there is a magnificent view over the Pediáda countryside (Rte 3C).

From the Plateau of Lasíthi to Ayios Nikólaos, 40km (25 miles).

From the junction by the Kroustalénia monastery take the road (heading in an easterly direction) signposted for Ayios Nikólaos. Through *Mésa Lasíthi*, you climb steeply out of the plain (*view) to a high pass, *Patéra ta Seliá* (1100m), and then descend to (10km) *Mésa Potamí*. The road continues along the river valley among holm-oaks and fruit trees below Mount Seléna to (13.5km) *Exo Potamí*. A second col with the derelict stone-built windmills of Katakaloú marks the boundary between the provinces of Lasíthi and Mirabéllo. The road runs between Makhairá (1486m) to the north and Katharó (1664m) on the southern side.

Beyond (17km) *Zénia* there is a sharp descent. At c 26km you pass a turning left for (6km) Neápolis and the north coast highway. For the direct route to Ayios Nikólaos on minor roads, keep right here, and then keep right again through *Exo Lakónia* and *Phlamourianá* to cross the Ayios Nikólaos bypass at the junction with the road to Kritsá (Rte 7).

7   Ayios Nikólaos and Excursions in the Locality

AYIOS NIKOLAOS, a little harbour town beautifully situated on the west side of the *Bay of Mirabéllo*, has developed into the most popular tourist resort of Crete without losing its charm. The modern town has grown up only since the second half of the last century, and is now the administrative centre of the province of Lasíthi, which comprises the whole of eastern Crete. (See town plan at the end of this Guide.)

The short tree-lined avenue, ΛΕΩΦ. ΚΟΥΝΔΟΥΡΟΥ (Leophóros Koundoúrou), more often referred to by foreigners as the 'main street', descends from ΠΛΑΤ. ΗΡΩΩΝ (Plateía Iróon) to the crowded *harbour*, the social centre of the town. To the left a channel dug in 1867–71, and crossed by a bridge, links the harbour with the small picturesque *Lake Voulisméni*; there was a tradition that this was bottomless, but it is now known to be funnel-shaped to a depth of 64m. The backdrop is a steep cliff; to enjoy the *view from the top, take ΟΔΟΣ Ν. ΠΛΑΣΤΙΡΑ (N. Pla-stíra) west from the main street (see above). The combination of lake and harbour is the basis of Ayios Nikólaos's particular attraction.

The town prides itself as one of the best shopping centres on Crete, and among the ubiquitous souvenir shops can be found some better-quality establishments for clothes, rugs, leather goods and jewellery. The broad esplanade running north from the harbour offers a stroll by the sea past a sheltered anchorage to the promontory with a retrospective view of the town; this is also the road to Eloúnda.

From Herákleion airport to Ayios Nikólaos, one hour by road. (Taxi fare in the region of £30; consult notices in the airport and confirm fare in advance.) Frequent buses from the Herákleion main bus station near the harbour (New Road route for express buses).

Tourist Information: the Municipal Information Office is on the waterfront, in the ground floor of the Port Authority building at the north end of the bridge between the lake and the harbour. Open daily: 08.30–21.30; tel. 22 357, English spoken. *Area code* 841.

Olympic Airways office: 20 Nik. Plastíra (tel. 22 033), on the cliff above the lake.

Bus Station: by the sea, down the hill south of the central Plateía Iróon (see town plan). Services to Mállia and Herákleion approximately hourly until early evening; to Eloúnda and to Kritsá frequently; to Siteía and to Ierápetra five or six times daily. Detailed information is clearly displayed in the office—or consult Municipal Information.

Boat connections: for many years there has been at least one weekly service through Ayios Nikólaos on the Athens–Rhodes route, with intermediate calls at various Cycladic islands to the north, and Siteía, Kásos, Kárpathos and Kos to the east. Recently there has been an experimental overnight service direct to Piraeus, but note that domestic boat schedules are liable to alter every year. All NTOG offices have current timetables. Shipping agent in Ayios Nikólaos: Massarós Travel, 29 R. Koundoúrou, on the right half-way up the main street, tel. 22 267.

Hotels: the NTOG lists some 70 hotels and pensions between de Luxe and Class C, the majority geared to package holidays arranged from abroad; in high season the best in any price bracket are liable to be fully booked with tours from all parts of the world. Ayios Nikólaos, above all places in Crete, is to be preferred outside the high season. The luxury hotels (with bungalows) are all beautifully situated on the bay and can be recommended. If you need medium-priced accommodation for a few nights during a touring holiday, look along the sea front in the direction of Eloúnda, ΑΚΤΗ Σ. ΚΟΥΝΔΟΥΡΟΥ (Aktí S. Koundoúrou), around the lake, or out on the bay between the ferry quay and Kitroplateía. In case of difficulty or for cheaper accommodation consult Municipal Information (see above). For longer periods consider also Eloúnda and Pláka (recommended below p 194) or Istro, formerly Kaló Khorió (Rte 9).

Youth Hostel: 3 Stratigoú Koraká.

Restaurants: prices may be higher than comparable establishments elsewhere on Crete, and more geared to international notions of eating; sample menus are displayed outside most premises. Recommended: the Kitroplateía area.

Tourist Police now occupy an office in the regular Police Station, ΟΔΟΣ Κ. ΠΑΛΑΙΟΛΟΓΟΥ (Odós K. Palaiológou), on the left before the archaeological museum (see town plan).

Tourist agencies abound, running coach tours to all the main tourist attractions on the island; if necessary ask Municipal Information for recommendations. There are *motor boat excursions* around the Mirabéllo Bay and weekly day-trips to Théra (Santorini).

Swimming. Ayios Nikólaos did not become famous because of its bathing beaches. From the south-west corner of the harbour ΟΔΟΣ ΣΦΑΚΙΑΝΗ (Odós Sphakianí) leads over the promontory to the small pebbly beach, called Kitroplateía because of its traditional association with the shipping of citrus fruits. There is also a long beach stretching south from the bus station, and another, attractively reed-fringed, is 10 minutes further on foot, just outside the town at the start of the road to Siteía (Rte 9).

In the early Hellenistic period the settlement here on the bay was the harbour of Lató (Λατώ η Ετέρα), the city-state in the hills near modern Kritsá. The harbour town was known as Lató 'pros Kamára' ('towards the arch') and it has been suggested that the arch in question is the cliff which overhangs the lake at Ayios Nikólaos. This coastal settlement flourished in Roman times, on the low hill jutting into the bay between the modern port and the Kitroplateía.

Under the Venetians, a cove a short way along the bay north west towards Eloúnda became the harbour, named the Porto di San Nicolo after the little Byzantine church overlooking it. Almost completely sheltered from the prevailing winds, the cove still provides a safe winter anchorage for small boats. (The recently restored church preserves evidence of some of the earliest frescoes on Crete—see below.)

To protect this Porto di San Nicolo, there was the medieval castle of Mirabéllo, built by the Genoese during their brief stay on the island after 1204. The castle occupied the height on the neck of land south of the lake, and between present-day Plateía Iróon and the sea. The castle was sacked by a Turkish raiding party in 1537, more than a century before the Turks finally captured Crete, and nothing remains today. When the Turkish threat became even more serious, the Venetians assigned the defence of the Mirabéllo Bay to the almost impregnable fortress of Spinalónga (see below).

The Byzantine church of *Ayios Nikólaos is in sight from the Eloúnda road on a headland next to the Minos Palace hotel. (The key is available from the hotel reception desk in exchange for a passport as security.)

This is a single-nave church with three bays, the central one supporting a dome. The building is difficult to date architecturally, but restoration work in 1968 uncovered frescoes which go back at least to the early years of the Second Byzantine period (late 10C–early 11C), not long after the island had been reclaimed for Christendom from the Arabs. Two layers of paintings were found: there are remains of 14C work, including fragments of the Pantokrátor in the conch of the apse, but unique on Crete (and rare in Greece) is the evidence for the earlier frescoes. These can be seen to have consisted of formal designs of geometric motifs such as crosses, lozenges, interlocking circles, quatrefoils and blossoms, consistent with the principles advanced in the 8C–9C by the Iconoclasts, who banned the representation of the divine or saintly form in religious art.

The Goddess of Mýrtos, an Early Minoan rhyton (Ayios Nikólaos Museum)

On the road uphill from the bridge by the lake (Odós Palaiológou) is the ***Archaeological Museum.** Open: 08.30–15.00, Sundays and holidays included. Closed Tuesdays. Entrance charge.

Built in the early 1970s with eight rooms around a central court, the museum houses finds from sites all over eastern Crete. The clearly-labelled cases are arranged in roughly chronological order, and the first three rooms contain Bronze Age material of exceptional quality. (The museum likes to accommodate finds of outstanding interest from current excavations, so a minor rearrangement of the display is sometimes necessary.)

For visitors with a particular interest the official publication, by the eminent Greek archaeologist, C. Daváras, describes the major exhibits and sets them in context; it is also beautifully illustrated. (On sale by the same author is 'Guide to Cretan Antiquities', recommended in the Bibliography.)

Room I. Neolithic and Early Minoan. The first case you come to contains a stone idol from Pelekitá, a remote cave with Neolithic material on the seaward side of Mount Traóstalos, north of Káto Zákros.

Five cases are devoted to finds from the huge Early Minoan cemetery (first half of the third millenium BC) at Ayía Photiá on the coast just east of Siteía; characteristic is the pottery's burnished surface (perhaps imitating wood) and incised decoration, often with white clay filling. Typical shapes include the biconical goblet or 'chalice' and the 'frying pan', and multiple vases are well represented. Note a lidded *double vase on a tall foot. A *bird-shaped vase with incised decoration (used here to suggest plumage) is one of the earliest in a long tradition of this shape in Cretan pottery. There are also fine displays of obsidian blades and bone tools. Among the bronze weapons is one deliberately bent to render it harmless.

Room II, Early and Middle Minoan (c 2600–1700 BC). The highly unusual *'Goddess of Mýrtos', an EMII libation vase, deservedly has pride of place. The Mýrtos site (Phournoú Koriphí) west of Ierápetra is a settlement of the EMII period (c 2600–2150); in the centre case are disks from its potter's workshop, a primitive form of slow wheel.

The distinctively mottled pottery with a slightly lustrous surface, here and in the next room, is Vasilikí ware, named after the type-site on the isthmus of Ierápetra. The effect is thought to have been achieved by uneven firing and perhaps by the use of different coloured slips on the same vessel. The 'teapot' with exaggerated spout is a common shape.

On the left wall are finds from EMII burials at Mókhlos, a tiny off-shore island halfway between Ayios Nikólaos and Siteía. Note especially the delicate gold jewellery, also the stone vases with the veining of the material superbly exploited. *Diadem decorated with three heads of Cretan ibex in dot-repoussé technique; 'teapot' vase in brecchia.

In the next case are stone libation tables with Linear A inscriptions, from Petsophás, the peak sanctuary above Palaíkastro. The cases between giant pithoi from the Palace of Zákros contain grave groups from the Myrsíni tholos (the first tomb of Mesará type to be excavated in eastern Crete), and from the MM burial enclosures at Zákros. Bronze tools and weapons are in the central case.

Room III, Late Minoan. First, either side of the door, are votive offerings from various peak sanctuaries; those on the right are chiefly from Petsophás which, as one of the most important of these places of pilgrimage, was still frequented in Neopalatial times. The terracotta figurines throw interesting light on the physical appearance of the worshippers, and on their needs and desires. Note the quadruple horns of consecration, with religious connotations.

In a wall case, right, is one of the museum's outstanding exhibits. The steatite *triton, a rare and extraordinary piece of Minoan workmanship, was found (1981) in an excavation near the north-east corner of the Palace of Mállia. The relief carving is a scene of two facing genii, one pouring a libation from a double-spouted vase into the outstretched hands of his companion. In the same case are a tiny ivory crocodile and a sphinx from the LMIII cemetery at Mílatos, about 5km east of Mállia.

The 1970s' excavation of the LMI villa at Makryialós, on the Libyan sea east of Ierápetra, produced finds which vividly illustrate the quality of life in the large Minoan country houses and estates contemporary with the New Palaces (c 1550–1450 BC). The Marine style pottery (wall case, at far end of room) is thought to come from the Knossós workshop, and the marble *chalice (centre) from Zákros.

This room displays a fine collection of Minoan clay sarcophagi. These were of two types: chests (larnakes) with low feet and gabled lids, and the oval 'bath-tub' shape, often with drainage holes suggesting that they had functioned as bath tubs. The decoration includes birds, fish and the stylised octopus. With them are pithoi also used for burials.

The central cases contain seals, ivory work and jewellery. Note the superbly decorated gold pin with an inscription of 18 Linear A signs; this was presented to the museum by the Belgian archaeologist J-P. Olivier, who had purchased it in Brussels.

At the far end of the room there is material from the LMIII cemetery at Myrsíni near Siteía. Outstanding is the female figurine on drum base with hands joined suggesting an attitude of worship. The pottery includes incense burners and conical clay rhytons pierced at the tip for use as libation vases.

Room IV, Late Minoan III (Postpalatial) and Early Iron Age. An infant burial (centre) is displayed exactly as found in the transitional LMIII–Protogeometric cemetery at Kryá, south of Siteía. The exhibit of material from the Myrsíni cemetery is completed in this room, with wall cases (left) containing pottery from sites in eastern Crete dating from the last phases of the Bronze Age (14C–13C BC) including the cemeteries in the Siteía region and at Kritsá. The new straight-sided cremation urns are characteristic, but the typically Minoan horns of consecration motif still occurs in the painted decoration—as on the vase from Apáno Zákros. The potter's wheel from Kritsá complements the display of primitive clay disks (the early slow wheel) from Mýrtos seen in Room II.

The Early Iron Age covers the Subminoan, Geometric and Orientalising periods. During this time the pottery from this part of the island is relatively uninspired and rustic, and by contrast accentuates the quality of contemporary pieces from central Crete (cf. especially Herákleion Museum, Galleries XI and XII).

Room V. Terracotta Collection. Geometric and Orientalising pottery from Siteía overflows into this room which is otherwise given over to finds of the Archaic and Classical periods (7C–5C BC), mainly from the city-state of Oloús near Eloúnda, and from a rich deposit (presumably associated with a shrine) discovered near the centre of modern Siteía. Many of the female figurines, heads and plaques are fine examples of the Daidalic style; some retain traces of the paint which originally adorned them. *Archaic head from Siteía, separately displayed. Note the collection of clay animals from Oloús near Eloúnda.

The anteroom (VI) completes the display of terracottas from this site, with some contemporary vases.

Room VII. Greco-Roman material, much of it, including the glass, from an important Roman cemetery on the edge of Ayios Nikólaos, the Lató pros Kamára of the Roman period. There are various types of lamp, and from a tomb at Eloúnda red-figure vases.

At the far end of the room is an outstanding exhibit, a skull still adorned with a gold wreath; the bronze aryballos in a nearby central case came from the same burial which is dated by the associated silver coin of Polyrrhénia to the early 1C AD.

To Spinalónga

There are boat excursions every afternoon in summer (sea conditions permitting) from Ayios Nikólaos harbour to the ruined Venetian fortress (and one-time leper colony) of **Spinalónga**, built on a rock at the northwest corner of the Mirabéllo Bay.

Duration of trip approximately 4 hours, usually including a stop for swimming. (The fortress can also be reached by small boat from Eloúnda or Pláka.)

The boats from Ayios Nikólaos pass close to Ayii Pántes (All Saints), the island reserve for the 'agrími' or Cretan ibex. The protected herd has grown to some 200 animals, and the adult male is a fine sight. The route follows the coast north to the peninsula of Spinalónga; the neck of land now joining it to the mainland was the site of the ancient city of Oloús (see p 194).

The Spinalónga *fortress* controlled the entrance to the anchorage of Eloúnda as well as defending all the Mirabéllo Bay. Built in 1579, it remained in Venetian hands till 1715. The Turks then held it until 1903. From 1903–55 the fortress was used as a leper colony.

The guided visit includes a tour of the Venetian fortifications both from the sea and from the battlements of the island, usually with a sympathetic account of the recent history. Most of the buildings within the enceinte, including the lepers' village, are in an advanced state of decay, and for reasons of safety independent exploration is discouraged.

Across from the islet on the north-eastern shore of the peninsula is the quarry from which came blocks for the Venetian ramparts.

To Kritsá and Lató

A round trip of less than 30km (c 16 miles); 9km to the frescoed church of the Panayía Kerá outside the attractive village of Kritsá, which is dedicated to a tradition of weaving, and on to Lató, an excavated example of a city-state of the Greek period beautifully situated in the hills.

Above Kritsá, 16km west into the Lasíthi mountains, is the upland plain of Katharó.

Frequent bus service to Kritsá. From Kritsá to Lató on foot, one hour. Also morning bus to Kroústas, east of Kritsá.

From the central Plateía Iróon follow the one-way street signs for Siteía as far as the bypass, but then continue straight across the main road clearly signed to (9km) Kritsá. After 100m a road to the right sets off for the plateau of Lasíthi (see Rte 6). The Kritsá road climbs through the outskirts of Ayios Nikólaos and landscape scarred by quarrying, and then levels out among olive groves, with the village of Kritsá clinging to the wall of the Lasíthi mountains ahead. 7km from the bypass, clearly signed on the right of the road is the **church of the Panayía Kerá** (Our Lady of Kerá).

Open: 09.15–15.00 (Sunday –14.00). Winter hours may be reduced. (Check first with Tourist Information if possible.) Entrance charge.

On sale at the church: 'Panaghia Kera: Byzantine wall-paintings at Kritsa' by M. Borboudákis is a knowledgeable and well-illustrated commentary; the author is Ephor (director or inspector) of Byzantine Antiquities on Crete.

The church dates from the early years of the Venetian occupation and its frescoes are among the finest and most complete on the island. Recent restoration work afforded an opportunity for a chronological reassessment.

The domed three-aisled church is dedicated to the Assumption of the Virgin, as is its CENTRAL AISLE or nave which is now considered the original structure (mid 13C). Two phases of painting have been identified in this aisle, both dated stylistically within the 13C. Remnants of the earlier decoration are preserved only in the apse and on the flat surfaces of the arches supporting the dome. On the *south arch* is the figure of a female saint, but better preserved, in the *apse*, is the Ascension above four Hierarchs holding open scrolls and dressed in chasubles decorated with crosses; on the jambs the two deacons, Stéphanos and Romanós.

The *dome* and the *nave* are decorated in the later style. Instead of the conventional Christ Pantokrátor in the dome, there are four gospel scenes (an arrangement perhaps dictated by the quadrating effect of the reinforcing ribs), but some expected elements are preserved: four angels in the apex triangles, the twelve prophets round the cylinder of the vault, and the four evangelists on the pendentives. The four gospel scenes in chronological order and anti-clockwise from the west are: the Presentation, the Baptism, the Raising of Lazarus and the Entry into Jerusalem. Further scenes from the gospel cycle also occupy their usual place on the *vault* of the nave. In the handling of these scenes there is a noticeable observation of detail charmingly rendered in contemporary medieval terms, for example the Venetian glass and pottery on the tables laid for the Last Supper and Herod's Feast. On the side walls are the worshipping saints, among them (on the north-west pillar) a rare St. Francis, or Frantzískos, showing the strength of the influence of the Western Church.

On the *west wall* are the remains of a portrayal of the Crucifixion; the Centurion's soldiers wear 13C armour. Below are gruesome scenes of the Punishment of the Damned.

The SOUTH AISLE (early 14C) is dedicated to the Virgin's mother, Ayía Anna, who looks down from the quadrant of the *apse*. The *vault* of the aisle is decorated with a robust series of scenes narrating, with much human tenderness, the life of the Virgin; they are largely inspired by the Apocrypha. The scenes are arranged in pairs on either side of the vault, beginning at the east end with the House of Joachim (the husband of St. Anne), and the angel's answer to Joachim's prayers for his barren wife. After the rejoicing the story continues through Mary's birth, her presentation to Zacharias in the temple, Joseph's Sorrow (his early misunderstanding of his wife's pregnancy) and 'the Water of Trial', a test of the Virgin's chastity. Finally there is the Journey to Bethlehem, and Mary triumphant with the Infant Christ encircled above a closed gate that, as in the vision of Ezekiel (with arms raised in prayer), would not exclude the Lord God of Israel.

On the west wall is an inscription naming the donor, Antónios Lámeras, and the village of 'Kritzea'. The date here is now worn away but is recorded as 'the century beginning 1292'.

The NORTH AISLE is dedicated to Ayios Antónios (patron saint of the donor), and the frescoes (dated to the mid 14C) proclaim Christ's Second

The Embrace of Joachim and Anna, from the frescoes in the Panayía Kerá, Kritsá

Coming, in the most ambitious treatment of this theme known from Crete. Below the ascended Pantokrátor in the bema are the Hierarchs holding the text of the Second Coming. Towards the east end of the vault the enthroned apostles and the massed ranks of angels, with below them the saints, wait in prayerful readiness for the salvation of the world. On the reinforcing arch the angel holds a scroll of stars (book of Revelation). Next in the vault (south side) is the depiction of Paradise, a walled garden with fruit trees and birds—the four rivers of Paradise (Tigris, Euphrates, Geon and Phison) named only by their initial letters; beside the enthroned Virgin, the Patriarchs, Abraham, Isaac and Jacob, protect the souls of the just. The gate of Paradise is guarded by St. Peter who admits the righteous thief. Opposite: the dance of the female martyrs and saints entering Paradise. Two panels of the wise and foolish virgins, symbolised by candles lit and extinguished, are unusual in this context.

In the scenes at the west end of the vault the Earth (with snake) and Sea (with boat) are delivering up their dead on the Day of Judgement. And high up on the west wall, above the recording angel supervising the judgement scales, the Archangel Michael sounds the last trumpet call which proclaims the Second Coming.

Of exceptional interest on the wall in the north-west corner is the period treatment of the *portrait of the donor*, Yeóryios Mazizánis, with his wife and child. This aspect of church wall-painting is documented in an exhibit in the new wing of the Herákleion Historical Museum.

There are a number of other frescoed churches in this region of interest to specialists: the cemetery church of Ayios Ioánnis (dated 1370 by an inscription which also records a financial contribution by the Skordílis family); Ayios Yeóryios Kavousiótis on the Kroústas road out of Kritsá, which has remains of frescoes by two painters (late 13C and mid 14C); and Ayios Konstantínos (1354–55). These churches are locked and not always accessible. You can consult the head guard at the Panayía Kerá about the current arrangements, but persistant enquiries in Kritsá will probably lead to the Papás. (See also Ayios Ioánnis Theológos, on the road to Kroustás.)

At the entrance to the village you pass the turn (right) for Lató (also see below).

The village streets of **Kritsá** (pop. c 2000) are terraced across the hillside, with extensive views down to the coast, and cafés and tavernas from which to enjoy them. (Some rooms to rent.) The old streets are narrow, so for a visit it is best to leave a vehicle in the signed car-park and walk.

Kritsá is renowned for its weaving, long considered among the finest on Crete. The most characteristic pieces are either in natural wool colours of cream, grey and brown, or sometimes in a strong red. Nowadays you may have to persist to find the traditional designs based on geometric patterns or natural variations in the wool among the windmills and dolphins thought more suitable for the tourist trade.

In the village a good road forks left (past Ayios Yeóryios—see above) to *Kroústas*. 1.5km along it, *Ayios Ioánnis Theológos* (Evangelist) is superbly situated at the head of a valley. The triple-aisled church dating back to the Second Byzantine period became an annexe of the monastery of Toploú at the eastern tip of the island (key held by the Papás in Kritsá).

There are convenient buses up to Kroústas from Ayios Nikólaos, and the walk (5.5km) back to Kritsá, past this church, is recommended. Alternatively, serious walkers will enjoy the old routes, with a choice of unfrequented dirt tracks across pine-clad upland or a (way-marked) kalderími, north from Kroústas c 2 hours to Pýrgos and Kaló Khorió. (Good north coast bus service for the return to Ayios Nikólaos.)

From the far end of Kritsá village street a well-maintained dirt road sets off for (16km) the **Katharó plain**, 1100m up in the Díkte range of mountains, under Mount Lázaros. The steep climb leads to empty hills, and the drive is recommended for wide views, for the wooded area along the way, and (in spring and autumn) for alpine flowers. In April the yellow *Arum creticum* is a striking sight. The track crosses the plain, which is inhabited only during the summer months. The right branch ends near the start of the old kalderími over the mountains to the Kroustalénia monastery, one of the eight traditional passes into the plateau of Lasíthi (Rte 6).

To Lató

At the beginning of Kritsá, 10km from Ayios Nikólaos, a one-way traffic system begins. 300m after this, beside a chapel, is the dirt road, right, for (3.5km) Lató. After 400m bend right, and then at the next two forks in the road keep right again. The track ends at the site, known locally as *Goulás*, which covers two acropolis peaks and the saddle between them where the centre of the ancient city lay.

Open 09.00–14.30, entrance free. The site is currently closed Mondays, but for confirmation of opening consult Ayios Nikólaos Municipal Information Office (see above).

The city-state of Lató (Λατώ η Ετέρα) was founded in the Archaic period (7C BC) and flourished down to Early Hellenistic times but, with hardly any evidence of Roman occupation, it is clear that there was a decline in importance by that time in favour of the harbour 'Lató pros Kamára' (see Ayios Nikólaos), and the city here in the hills is known to have been destroyed c 200 BC.

Though securely identified by an inscription during the French School's exploration of 1899–1900, Lató was largely ignored in favour of Minoan remains until excavations were begun again in 1967; it is now the most thoroughly excavated site of its period on the island. The principal interest lies in the detailed evidence of the town plan, and the light it throws on the character and organisation of the city. Lató can also be enjoyed for the dramatic beauty of its position, which offers from the north acropolis a panoramic view of eastern Crete.

The visit begins (at the down hill end of the site) at the *city gate* in the fortification wall (see plan). The gateway, designed for easy defence, leads through two inner doorways into a small square court from which a long stepped *street* leaves at right angles. The street is bordered on the right by shops and workshops, which open from the steps and back on to the defensive wall itself. On the left a stout wall ascends the steep slope; it is interrupted by several narrow doorways leading into the northern sector of the town. This wall is given added strength by two *towers*, which were found to serve in a dual capacity as houses. The street bends right and then left to reach the *agorá*, a pentagonal area with in the centre a deep square cistern and a shrine. From the shrine (probably an open-air structure) came many figurines dated to the 6C BC.

The agorá in its present form dates to the beginning of the Hellenistic era, 4C–3C. The west side is bounded by a *stoa* that has stone benches round three walls behind a Doric colonnade. (The southern end is cut by a modern threshing floor.) On the south side of the shrine, set at an angle, is an *exédra*, a rectangular shelter open to the court.

To the north, flanked by two towers, an elaborate staircase consists of a triple flight of broad steps separated by narrow ones for easier ascent. The towers buttressed the building above, and also contributed to the monumental effect of the design which suggests both the Minoan 'theatral area' that is so characteristic a feature at Knossós and Phaistós, and the seating arrangement of a Greek theatre. The staircase gives access to an upper terrace on which stood the Hellenistic *prytaneíon* essential to the administration of the city-state. These civic buildings are often compared to a town hall, but they had an additional function because a fire

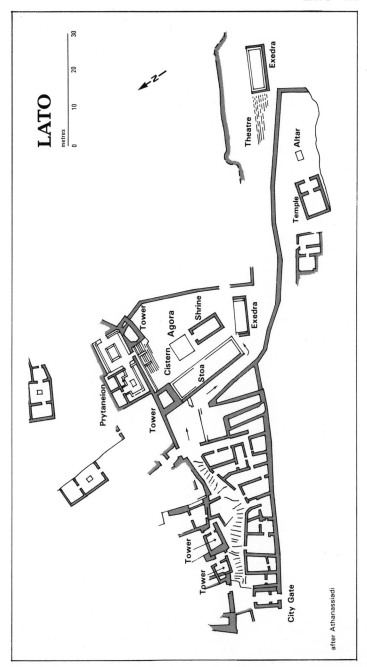

LATO

metres

0   10   20   30

N

Theatre

Exedra

Temple

☐ Altar

Tower

Cistern Agora

Shrine

Stoa

Exedra

Prytaneion

Tower

Tower

Tower

Tower

City Gate

after Athanassiadi

was kept burning continuously on an altar of Hestia as a sign of the city's continuity with its past. On the east side of the building is a peristyle court which leads west into the main hall which has benches and a central hearth. The small rooms behind, to the north, are thought to have held the city's archives. An inscription found here, recording a treaty between Górtyn and Lató, was important for the identification of the prytaneíon.

Across the agorá, above its south-east corner, is a terrace supported by a well-preserved retaining wall of rustic polygonal masonry; on the terrace there remain four courses of a *temple*, dated late 4C–early 3C, approximately contemporary with the major civic buildings. The temple was rectangular, with pronaos and cella, and without columns; outside the entrance (east) stood a stepped altar. Further east, below the temple terrace, there are traces of a semi-circular area facing north, understood as a small theatre, and beside it is another exédra similar to that on the edge of the agorá.

The summit of the northern acropolis is reached by a rough path and the view repays the effort required to climb up to it.

To Dréros and Eloúnda

A round trip of c 50km (30m) to (16km) Dréros, a city-state of the classical period where (20 minutes on foot from road) an important early temple has been excavated, returning by Eloúnda and the site of ancient Oloús. Eloúnda is only 11km along the coast from Ayios Nikólaos, but the recommended drive down from the hills provides a spectacular *panorama of the Bay of Mirabéllo.

Seven buses a day between Ayios Nikólaos and Eloúnda. Frequent service to Neápolis (Herákleion schedule) for a walk to Dréros.

Leave Ayios Nikólaos along the road past the museum, to join the north coast highway running west towards Herákleion. At 13km the exit for *Neápolis* is signposted right. For the town, the slip-road describes a circle to cross above the highway, but just before the bridge there is a turning uphill (left) for the site of Dréros, signposted also to Kouroúnes. After 2km keep right at a fork and 1km further the road ends at the start of the path to the site.

On foot, from the centre of Neápolis leave the big plateía at its north end, to pick up signs for the New Road. At the T-junction at the end of the square these lead left and immediately right. Cross the bridge over the highway and turn uphill right. (Then see above; from the plateía to start of path up to site, 3km. At the end of the asphalt look out for any marked path.)

A stony path first climbs the southern flank of the hill (with splendid views across the valley to the Lasíthi range) and then levels out along the contour to reach (15 minutes) the saddle between two peaks where the centre of the city lay. Cross the saddle keeping to the left (west) slope. The temple excavation, now protected by a stone-built shed, lies just over the crest.

The city's ancient name is known from an inscription of c 220 BC vividly detailing an oath of loyalty taken by the young men of Dréros. Other inscriptions found include an early code of constitutional law and an important text in Greek script but in the older Eteocretan language (see Praisós, Rte 10B). The city was flourishing by the Geometric period.

The city plan is to some extent comparable with that of Lató: an agorá with retaining wall and bordered by a flight of steps, cistern, temple and nearby public building (perhaps a prytaneíon) to the south of the agorá, but here all is much less well preserved. There are house remains down the far (northern) slope of the hill.

The majority of finds from the site date to the Geometric and Archaic periods, but the huge *cistern* below the temple was constructed in the Hellenistic period (3C BC). Two of its walls were rock-cut and two were built; all were faced with plaster. The city declined in importance before the end of the 2C. It flourished again during the Second Byzantine period, and there are traces of Byzantine and Venetian occupation on the east acropolis hill which takes its name from the chapel of Ayios Antónios on the summit.

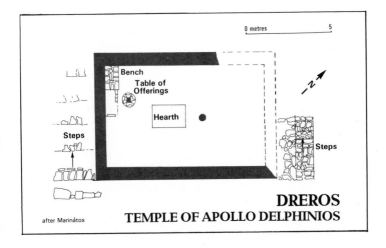

0 metres 5

Bench

Table of Offerings

Hearth

Steps

Steps

DREROS
TEMPLE OF APOLLO DELPHINIOS

after Marinátos

The **Temple of Apollo Delphinios**, dated to the second quarter of the 8C, is one of the earliest temples known in all Greece. It was approached from the south-west corner of the *agorá* by a flight of steps. The temple, orientated north east–south west, consists of a simple cella (see plan) with entrance probably in the north wall. (The north corner was destroyed by the construction of a kiln.) On the long axis is a central rectangular sunken *hearth* lined with stone slabs, and a base for a wooden column; it is believed that there were originally two columns. On a ledge in the south-west corner were an early 6C gorgoneion, vases and terracotta figurines, and in front of this on the floor a stone 'table for offerings'. Three important bronze statuettes (c 650 BC) found in the temple would probably have stood on the ledge. They are made by the sphyrelaton technique—hammering bronze plates over a wooden core—and are thought to represent Apollo, Artemis and Leto (Herákleion Museum, Gallery XIX). Beside the ledge was a later addition, a low altar in the form of a stone box filled with the horns of young goats, recalling the horn altar at Delos around which Theseus and the Delian maidens performed the crane dance after his triumphant return there from Crete.

On a walking expedition it is possible to make your way down the northern slope of the hill, but the going is rough in places. One path joins the dirt road below at a large water trough, and a right turn will bring you out on the Eloúnda–Neápolis at Kastélli road, 5km from Neápolis; or you can make a short cut round the base of the east acropolis on to the same road.

By car you return as you came, to cross the bridge over the highway towards the centre of Neápolis, but instead of turning into the main square keep straight ahead (signposted for Ayios Nikólaos by the Old Road). After 1.5km, in *Nikithianós*, watch for the left turn for Eloúnda. After leaving the Old Road there is a steep climb with the site of Dréros above left, where the little church of Ayios Antónios can be seen as a landmark on the hill top. 4km from Nikithianós you pass through the village of Kastélli and on along an avenue of gum trees to Fourní.

Just beyond Phourní, 9 km from Neápolis, an acute left turn is signed for Doriés and Karídi. This offers a short detour (7km) to the recently restored *Moní Arétiou* (founded 16C), once the wealthy seat of the local bishopric but now peaceful and isolated among cypresses and cedar trees, at a height of 400m above sea level. On the way up to the monastery, Ayios Konstantínos in Doriés has an icon of historical interest, now the earliest remaining on Crete. This icon of the Panayía Odiyítria (somewhat restored and altered) is dated to the end of the 14C; the painting became part of a double-sided icon, the reverse being a slightly later Crucifixion. (Key with the Papás who lives near by.)

Continuing from Phourní towards the coast, suddenly the **Bay of Mirabéllo** fills the view, with the island of *Pseíra* and the hills of eastern Crete in the distance. You descend steeply, several times crossing the old stone-paved route, and, at 18km from Neápolis, reach the coast on the outskirts of *Eloúnda* and turn right into the village. There are good tavernas on the waterfront around a harbour busy with fishing boats. Eloúnda is unashamedly a (small) holiday resort but it has a comfortable air of permanence as compared to many seaside hamlets which have expanded artificially during the last decade. It has the advantage of an idyllic setting equalled but rarely excelled elsewhere in the Mediterranean. The centre is likely to be noisy at night but the coast road out to the north, towards Pláka (also recommended), offers quiet rooms on the shore.

500m towards Ayios Nikólaos a left fork is signposted to Oloús. The track leads along the shore, past salt-pans dating from the Venetian period, to the isthmus of Póros which joins the Spinalónga peninsula to the mainland. This is the site of the Greco-Roman city-state of **Oloús**. During the occupation of Crete by the Great Powers at the turn of the century, French sailors were detailed to cut a narrow channel through the isthmus, thus opening up the southern end of the natural harbour of Eloúnda to the open sea.

The track crosses the channel by a bridge near a restored windmill. The sea level has risen and structures can be seen in the water on either side of the isthmus, and along the shore right (to the east) level with a white chapel. Just north west of this chapel, and reached by a path beside a taverna, is an excavated Early Christian *basilica*. Its exact date is uncertain, but it may be a two-phase building, as the 4C black and white *mosaic floor* appears to belong to a smaller church. The unusual asymmetric design of geometric and natural motifs includes panels of lively dolphins and two inscriptions naming the donors. The mosaic was dated from the style of the writing.

This is all that has been excavated and all that remains visible above ground of a city that is known to have had great temples to Zeus Talaios and Britomartis. In the Hellenistic period Oloús maintained close relations with Rhodes, and an inscription of 200 BC gives details of an agreement by which Rhodes could use anchorages here for her drive against piracy.

Outside the summer season this isthmus is a tranquil place, and a walk out along the peninsula of Spinalónga (recommended to bird-watchers) offers fine coastal views.

On the east coast of the peninsula opposite the little island of Kolokýthia was a small Hellenistic and Roman settlement, and there are remains of another basilica at what is now the water's edge. An ancient road, of Roman or possibly Hellenistic date, can be picked up crossing the rise between the two sites.

The road from Eloúnda runs south following the coast. The glorious views of the Bay of Mirabéllo are enjoyed by several of the most select and luxurious hotels on the island.

At *Elliniká* in 1937 the French School excavated a 2C BC temple dedicated to Aphrodite and Ares; this became a 'border temple' in settlement of a dispute between Lató and Oloús. (Nothing remains to visit.)

You keep left along the coast into (11km) Ayios Nikólaos.

8 Ayios Nikólaos to Ierápetra and the South Coast

This itinerary follows the north coast towards Siteía (as for Rte 9) as far as (21km) Pakhyámmos, and then crosses the island at its narrowest point to 35km (21 miles) Ierápetra. There is an alternative route (c 36km) through the hills via Kalamávka. From Ierápetra you can turn east to Makryialós (Rte 10B) or west to (17km) Mýrtos, (42km) Viánnos and (by Rte 3C) on to Herákleion. The upgraded stretch of road parallel to the south coast—from Viánnos to Pýrgos on the Mesará plain (37km)—makes it possible to cut across to Phaistós and south-western Crete, and to explore on the way the newly accessible coast between Arvi and Tsoútsouros.

Good bus service from Ayios Nikólaos to Ierápetra. Twice daily (except Sundays) Ierápetra to Viánnos.

Leaving Ayios Nikólaos you join the bypass and turn towards Siteía. For road directions and places of interest along this stretch of coast as far as Pakhyámmos, including (at 18.5km, p 204) the important archaeological site of Gourniá, see the beginning of Route 9.

After 9.5km a minor road (right), signed Kaló Khorió and Kalamávka, offers a recommended alternative route (c 25km) through the pine woods of the hills around Priná (especially recommended to walkers) to the south coast at Ierápetra. *Kalamávka* is dramatically sited in a cleft on the spine of the island; from a watershed (on the north side of the village) there is a fine view encompassing both coastlines. In spring a great variety of orchids flourishes in this hilly terrain.

At 21.5km, just beyond the village of Pakhyámmos, you turn away from the coast to cross the island to Ierápetra. This is the narrowest part of the

island, 14km coast to coast, and the valley road is dominated to the east
by the massive Thryptí range cut by a dramatic cleft, the gorge of Monastiráki.

Opposite the cleft, at 24km, is a right turn for (300m) **Vasilikí**, an important EMII settlement (c 2900–2200 BC). The guardian's hut is a landmark
from the approach road and there is a sign at the start of the path to the
left (3 minutes up the rise). Vasilikí is renowned for its profusion of wild
flowers in spring.

The site was investigated in 1904 by the American archaeologist E. Hall and further
explored in 1906 by her compatriot R. Seager. During the last decade A. Zois has
been re-examining Vasilikí for the Archaeological Society of Athens.

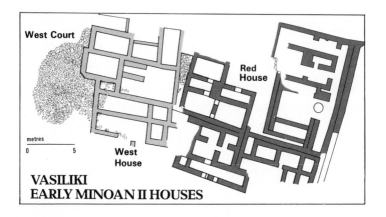

The path along the flank of the hill (leaving the hut on your right) brings you first to
the level ground of recent work. Up the slope behind this is an area easily identified
from the depth of the excavated (basement) rooms; the house walls still stand in
places to near a man's height. This complex, named by Seager 'The House on the
Hill', and dated to EMII, was generally regarded as the most luxurious building of
this early date that had so far been excavated, and as an important step towards the
splendid architecture of later Minoan times.

Erosion of the northern slope of the hillside confused the picture, and it was
thought that only the south-west and south-east wings of the House on the Hill, with
a paved West Court, were preserved. These two wings have now been shown
by Zois to be two separate buildings, named the Red House and the (slightly later)
West House—see plan—both of which have been dated within EMIIB. The West
Court paving was used for both buildings.

The deep basement rooms belong to the Red House. The rough construction of
the walls was concealed by a hard red lime plaster, which at other sites in later
periods was to provide an ideal ground for Minoan fresco painting. Small patches of
this red stucco are still preserved, as are channels for structural timbers.

The original excavations brought to light many distinctive clay vases with mottled
decoration; the site gives its name to this EMII Vasilikí ware. The specialised firing
technique achieved a semi-lustrous surface, with mottled patches from red through
orange and brown to black. The unusual shapes of these hand-made pots, often with
beak spouts or elongated horizontal ones (the so-called 'teapot' shape) are well
illustrated in the first two rooms of the Ayios Nikólaos Museum.

28km In the middle of the village of *Episkopí*, below the road (left) is an interesting medieval church with a double dedication to Ayios Yeóryios and Ayios Kharálambos (key with village priest but access is often difficult).

This was not the bishop's church of medieval Episkopí. A bishopric (of Ierápetra) is recorded as early at 343, but the episcopal church, only finally destroyed in 1897, stood in the same position as the conspicuous modern one, just above the through road. (Decorative marble fragments of the episcopal basilica are preserved in Ayios Yeóryios and Ayios Kharálambos.)

The 19 blind arches round the drum below the dome are outlined with an elaborate decoration of tiles set upright in mortar and fringed with a band of rosettes, a scheme rarely found on the Byzantine churches of Greece. (Similar decoration on mainland churches, including two at Mistra in the Peloponnese, uses a glazed fabric.) The closest parallels occur in Bulgaria dating from the end of the 12C, and in conjunction with the complete absence of Venetian influence here at Episkopí, they help to date this church to the 12C–13C, the years just preceding or at the beginning of Venetian rule.

The unusual ground plan of the little church consists of a south nave (Ayios Kharálambos) which was added to an earlier domed church (Ayios Yeóryios) with conch-shaped east and west cross-arms and a small (strictly rectangular) north aisle or inner room, now reached only from the main body of the church. There are two altars in the east conch or apse, but originally there was no west portal opposite. (The existing doorway in the west conch was opened up during the Venetian period.) The conch plan suggests that the church may have been designed as a martyrion. Recent examination (1981) by the Service for Byzantine Antiquities under M. Borboudákis led to the further intriguing suggestion that a martyrion may have been associated with a system of Early Christian catacombs perhaps reached through the north inner room.

During road building in 1946, LMIII chamber tombs with larnax burials (c 1300 BC) were found under the village street. One particular clay larnax with remarkable painted decoration has long been accessible only to specialists but is now on display in Ierápetra (see below).

At the end of Episkopí a left turn leads to *Káto Khorió* just off the main road, and the start of a 12km dirt road into the mountains to the hamlet of *Thriptí*.

35km. Ierápetra, the only sizeable town (pop. 10,750) on the south coast of Crete, benefits as a holiday resort from its long beaches and warm dry climate. It is also the busy centre of a district which owes its prosperity largely to horticulture. The modern sea-front promenade is geared to holidaymakers who enjoy a wide variety of eating-places, noisy bars and discotheques, but there is plenty of accommodation away from this area, with a dozen or so B–C class hotels, and, especially in the older part of town immediately to the west of the harbour, pensions and rooms to rent which may provide a satisfactory base for exploring this corner of the island.

The centre of the modern town (signposted *kéntro* on a rigorous one-way street system) is a small plateía on the sea-front between the town hall and the police station. The *Municipal Information* Office is here, on the corner of the main road west to Mýrtos and Viánnos (Odós K. Adrianoú). The office is open 09.00–21.00, weekends –15.00; useful for a town plan, advice on accommodation, buses and excursions including the boat trip (leaving daily at 10.00) to the uninhabited island of Khrysí (formerly

Gaidouronísi). The town's *covered market* is 200m along the Mýrtos road on the left-hand side. Next door to the information office is a small *archaeological museum*.

The gallery was opened in these new quarters in 1991. The star exhibit of the collection is the LMIII (Postpalatial) larnax from Episkopí (see above): the clay coffin in the shape of a rectangular chest is decorated with scenes of hunting, a chariot procession and a stylised octopus in 12 painted panels, with the gable of the lid ending in a bull's head and tail. The museum also houses antiquities from the Greco-Roman city of Ierápytna, with pride of place rightly given to a recently discovered statue of Demeter (2C AD).

Ierápytna destroyed neighbouring Praisós c 155 BC to become the main rival to Itanos at this extreme east end of the island, and then put up strong resistance to the Romans in 67 BC, but flourished later in the Roman period as a seaport on the route to the eastern Empire and well placed for trade with Africa. The ancient city covered a larger area than the modern one, but little has yet been excavated and nothing remains above ground of the amphitheatre, two theatres, temples, baths and aqueducts mentioned by earlier travellers.

There has been a *fortress* guarding the harbour at least since the early years of Venetian rule. It was twice rebuilt: in 1626 (after earthquake damage) by Francesco Morosini to counter the Turkish threat, and again during the Turkish occupation, and recently its walls have been repaired.

The attractive (less raucous) part of the town, the old Turkish quarter, is just inland from the harbour. If you walk westwards from the castle along the quay, past the bell-tower and the fishing-boats, and continue 200m on the road close to the shore, you come to a plateía with a Turkish fountain in front of a derelict mosque.

From Ierápetra to Mýrtos and Viánnos. The road runs west along the coast; distances are calculated from Ierápetra.

At the edge of the built-up area a minor road (signed) leads off into the hills at the start of a recommended alternative route across the island to (12km) Kalamávka (see p 195), Kaló Khorió and (c 25km) Istro on the north coast.

The main road, built about 20 years ago as part of a projected south coast highway, stays close to the shore. The scenery is not improved by the universal use of plastic sheeting to protect the crops of the intensively cultivated plain. After 4.5km, in *Gra Lygiá*, there is a turning inland (signed Anatolí) for a side-road to (c 22km) *Málles*.

This village clings to the well-watered slopes of Mount Díkte at a height of 580m, and is a popular starting-point for a walk into the mountains. To return to the coast you can continue to the far end of the village and then turn sharp left on to a dirt road (signed Mýthi). The road is rough in places and needs to be taken slowly, but it descends to one of the most beautiful valleys on Crete, and to the Mýrtos river. 10km from Málles you come to *Mýthi* and 2km further, in *Mourniés*, there is a crossroads where you can turn left for Mýrtos on the coast and the return to Ierápetra, or keep straight on to rejoin very shortly the main road (4.5km north west of Mýrtos) and proceed west towards Viánnos.

Staying on the coast road at Grá Lygiá you pass (12km from Ierápetra) a good beach at *Ammoudáres* and then (2km further) come to *Néa Mýrtos* with a domed cruciform chapel a landmark on a knoll behind the beach. Opposite, on the hill beyond the bridge, is the first of two interesting excavations in the neighbourhood of the modern village of Mýrtos (which is 3km further west); this Early Bronze Age settlement is known as *Phournoú Koriphí* after the summit on which it stands.

The site was intensively excavated by the British School (P. Warren) in 1967–68, when c 90 rooms were uncovered. These represent two periods of urban occupation of EMII date, c 2500 and c 2170 BC. Much evidence was found for the manufacture of pottery and textiles, and a room at the south-west corner of the site proved to be the oldest known Minoan domestic shrine. The remarkable clay goddess figurine, and some of the 700 clay vases and other objects of daily life, are displayed in the Ayios Nikólaos Museum.

The path to the site is easiest from the west side of the hill (15 minutes).

MYRTOS PYRGOS
Minoan Villa

0 metres   5

after Cadogan

16.5km. Overlooking the Mýrtos river is a second Minoan site; it surrounds the summit of a hill called Pýrgos (a tower in Greek) from the watchtower which stood here during the Turkish occupation, and the Minoan site is therefore known as **Mýrtos Pýrgos**. The path (10 minutes) starts just on the east side of the bridge, striking off uphill from the track beside the river bed.

This site too was excavated by the British School (G. Cadogan, 1970–75). It proved to be a Minoan settlement of long duration. There was EMII occupation contemporary with Phournoú Koriphí, and also a destruction by fire at the same time (c 2200 BC) but, unlike Phournoú Koriphí, Pýrgos was reoccupied and a Minoan town continued to develop on the slopes of the hill.

Visible today from the early phase is a stretch of fine paved road on the north-west side of the hill (not on plan) which led to a built communal tomb; at its southern end was a pit used as an ossuary in which was found a large jar of bones surrounded by neatly stacked skulls.

By the time of the New Palaces (MMIII–LMI, c 1600 BC) the settlement was dominated by a grand building on the summit of the hill and facing across a court to the sea. This house, which produced a quantity of finds consistent with the elegance of its architecture, was built on two or possibly three floors, and the lower floor—cut into the rock of the hilltop—is what you see today.

A *stepped street* (1 on plan) from the town leads up the eastern slope of the hill to the paved *courtyard* (2). The plaster-lined *cistern* (3) dates from the Old Palace period, and when the house was built it was filled with 22 tonnes of river pebbles, perhaps as an ornamental soak-away for storm water. A *raised walk* (4) of flagstones bordered in purple limestone ran along the front of a gypsum-floored *verandah* (5) which had two wooden columns on purple limestone bases either side of a pillar. The building (6), of uncertain use, completed an L-shaped façade for the courtyard. The *main entrance* (7) at the west end of the verandah opened into a passage which led to a staircase (8) with a *light-well* (9) beyond, and opposite that a bench (10). Both staircase and bench are of gypsum and have had to be covered over for protection from the weather. The *staircase*, which showed no signs of wear, had a stepped parapet with traces of wooden columns, recalling in a modest form the Grand Staircase at Knossós. The floor of the light-well, of purple limestone set in white plaster, sloped to a central basin. The bench had gypsum back panels, and triglyph decoration, perhaps imitating legs, below the seat. Beside it a rock-cut *pantry* (11) held a large tub and a quantity of plain cups.

In the east wing a passage (12) led to storerooms (13 and 14) which contained large pithoi; clay and stone vessels, found in the street among the debris resulting from the fire, suggested the existence of a grander room above. The fire which destroyed the house at the end of LMIB was so fierce that it splintered the ashlar masonry, vitrified pottery and fired mud bricks (as well as a Linear A tablet), and yet it did not touch the houses of the surrounding town.

If you walk round the hill starting down the stepped street (1), and then left along the contour of the east slope, you pass a deep *cistern* dating from the Old Palace period, the largest of its kind known from Minoan Crete. When it burst over the edge of the hill it was not repaired, so that from then on all water had to be carried up from the valley below. Above the path are terrace walls and the lower courses of what may have been a defensive tower. The path leads to the EMIII–MMIA paved street and tomb noticed above, and then on down the hillside back to the road.

A track beside the river leads north to a Venetian bridge on the old road to Ierápetra.

At 17km the coastal village of *Mýrtos* has good tavernas, two small hotels and rooms to rent.

The dirt road along the shore runs west past banana groves and the inevitable plastic-covered greenhouses through the hamlet of *Tértsa* to *Arvi* (see below). For vehicles the track is still rough in places and its condition varies from year to year— ask in Mýrtos. For walkers it is always recommended, as is the hill country up the Mýrtos river valley.

The main road climbs inland passing outcrops of serpentine rock. (After 6km there is a turning right into Mourniés where the key is kept for the frescoed church at Epáno Sými—see below. Ask for Pápa Nikólao.) You continue among olive and almond trees towards the Díkte foothills; as the road climbs the scent of pines begins to fill the air. At 31.5km there is a right turn to (2km) *Káto Sými* signed to a war memorial and antiquities. High above the village (1200m up on Mount Madára) an important *sanctuary of Hermes and Aphrodite* has been excavated in recent years by K. Lembéssis for the Greek Archaeological Service. The side-road follows the stream up the valley, beside plane, walnut and fig trees.

The war memorial (on the right before the village) commemorates a battle between German troops and a Cretan Resistance band. In September 1943 the fall of Mussolini led to confusion about the role of the Italian military command which controlled the eastern end of the island. In the highly-charged atmosphere of the time, retaliation for the incident here was particularly severe. Six villages were destroyed and 500 civilians shot by the Germans.

The improved hard-packed dirt road into the mountains (5km from Káto Sými) is very steep in places, with tight hairpin bends. (Stiff but rewarding walk.) Keep left at the fork beyond the village where there is a modern house in the angle above right.

The right fork leads (2km) to the church of Ayios Yeóryios, Epáno Sými, with frescoes, dated by inscription to 1453, by Manuel Phokás (cf. Embaros and Avdoú). The church key is held by the Papás in Mourniés—see above.

Keeping to the left fork you climb for c 3km till a track (from Epáno Sými) comes in from the right across a ford below a waterfall. 1km further the site is above the road right—securely fenced (landmark) and locked, but a path circumnavigates. On the uphill side of the sanctuary water springs from the rock. It falls through channels to a valley now filled with deciduous trees alive with song-birds. The mountain wall above shelters eagles and vultures.

The sanctuary occupies a series of platforms on the mountainside. This isolated spot was a place of worship from the Middle Minoan period to the 3C AD, and provides a rare example of continuity of religious practice from Minoan to Postminoan times; Hermes and Aphrodite are seen as a transformation of the Minoan goddess and her young consort. Great quantities of votive offerings were brought to the sanctuary over the centuries, and some of the more remarkable finds are a recent addition to Herákleion Museum, Gallery XII.

At 34.5km on the main road, 3km beyond the mountain detour, a left turn leads through Amirás to Arvi (see below) and a coastal detour to Tsoútsouros.

Continuing along the main road you soon pass a second turn and another explicit monument recalling the wartime episode related above.

42km Viánnos (Rte 3C, p 129). For the recently improved road west across the Mesará plain to Pyrgós, see below after the detour to the south coast.

A good road tackles the steep descent from *Amirás* (see above); it keeps left at the fork at the end of the village for the coast (11km), and then turns left to (in 2km) **Arvi**. The village already caters for visitors and is expanding; there is a small hotel as well as rent rooms and tavernas behind a narrow beach. You can walk to the monastery of Ayios Antónios, 15 minutes inland, at the entrance to the narrow gorge which is in view from the village. The monastery's buildings are of no great age (late 19C) but its position is ample compensation. A monk from here is credited with the introduction of banana cultivation to Crete from Egypt soon after the end of the First World War.

The recent upgrading of the former coastal track between Arvi and Tsoútsouros (c 25km) is a significant improvement for anyone travelling by car in this region, for it has given easy access for the first time to a beautiful stretch of coast previously empty except for horticultural activity and long-distance hikers. It is surely not destined to be empty for long.

Leaving Arvi keep west along the coast past the turn up to Amirás (signed ahead 10km to Keratókambos). Soon the hard-packed dirt road turns inland. There are encouraging signs painted on walls as you climb high above the sea into olive groves. 7km from Arvi turn left at a T-junction, downhill to the coast and along to *Keratókambos*, an as yet unspoiled village on a long (c 2km) beach of pebbles with a scattering of rocks. (Direct road here from Viánnos is asphalted.)

The improved dirt road continues out of the village and along the coast (past the familiar plastic hot-houses) and crosses the mouth of the Anapodáris, one of the four major rivers of Crete, on a modern bridge of unusual design. There is an attractive beach on the west side of the broad (mostly dry) river bed, but the wading birds that frequent this area still seem to be regular visitors. The road climbs over headlands and down to the tamarisk-lined beach and strikingly clear sea at *Tsoútsouros*. Close inshore the water is unusually deep, which made it a favoured landing place for undercover agents joining the Second World War resistance movement.

The cave of Inatos (at the back of the beach 200m before the haven where fishing boats tie up) was an important sanctuary of Eileíthyia, goddess of childbirth. The cave was excavated in 1970 but then sealed up. The remarkable votive offerings, including figurines invoking the blessings of children, as well as some Egyptian material, were mostly from the Geometric and Archaic periods (see Herákleion Museum, Gallery IX).

Along the coast is the best approach to Tsoútsouros for the bulldozers have moved in to transform the seaside hamlet into a resort. Extensive terracing of the hillside above the beach has been completed; it is too early to be sure what the final result will be but the first buildings did not look promising.

The hard-packed dirt road (destined for asphalt) climbs steeply inland high above a narrow valley where in summer the river-bed glows with oleander. At the ridge you pass a traditional double-naved church, completed in 1991, before (11km from the sea) Káto Kastellianá on the route described below.

From Viánnos to Pýrgos. This 37km 'missing link' stretch of the projected south coast road is now completed, and is convenient for a circuit of the island, linking as it does the traditional routes without the need for a return to Herákleion. (No east–west bus service at time of writing; enquire at Tourist Information Office in Herákleion or Ierápetra.)

From Viánnos follow the main Arkalokhóri road (Rte 3C) for 10.5km, and then take the second of the roads signposted (left) to Mártha. The route leads south west down a river valley towards the Asteroúsia mountains. It is 7.5km on the broad new road to *Skiniás*, and after this a further 6km, across the Anapodáris at *Demáti*, to *Káto Kastellianá* and the junction for (11km) Tsoútsouros on the coast (see above). You continue along the southern edge of the Mesará plain, through *Mesokhorió*, and reach *Pýrgos* 37km from Viánnos.

From Pýrgos (see p 158) the main road runs north 50km to Herákleion. 5km along it there is a left turn for (20km) Ayii Déka, to link up with the main Herákleion–Phaistós road (Rte 4).

9   Ayios Nikólaos to Siteía

70km (43 miles) on the north coast highway. 18.5km, the excavated
Minoan town of Gourniá; 25km, Early Iron Age excavations at hill-top
sites above Kavoúsi; at 39.5km a detour to Mókhlos on the sea. The
roadside kilometre posts on this section of the highway are calculated
from the centre of Ayios Nikólaos.

Buses five times a day to Siteía; Gourniá is also served by the Ierápetra
bus.

Leave Ayios Nikólaos following Siteía signs on the one-way system from
Plateía Iróon, and at the bypass turn left. At the 2km post you pass a popular reed-fringed beach. The road winds close above the shore around the
scenic Mirabéllo Bay.

After 9.5km you come down to the waterfront at *Istro* (formerly part of
Kaló Khorió). At the new bridge there are two roads inland: the first for
Pýrgos, the second for (2km) Kaló Khorió and (13km) Kalamávka on the
spine of the island (see Rte 8)—both recommended for wooded hills and
good walking country.

Above Istro is *Vrókastro*, a refuge site of the Early Iron Age on a steep
limestone spur 300m above the sea. The site was excavated (1910–12) by
Edith Hall of the University of Pennsylvania. The plan of the settlement
is hard to make out, but the remains of houses clinging to the hilltop are
evocative, and the view from the summit is superb.

As you approach the bridge on the way into the village, the site is on the left or
seaward summit of the hills ahead, with a terraced gully pointing up to it. There is a
choice of routes to reach the site. At the far end of the straggling village (at c 12km)
a track to the gully (offering a stiff 20-minute climb to the top) starts just before the
road bends right around the next bay. Once the climb begins you are aiming, with
the help only of goat tracks, for the saddle which connects the highest peak on your
left with the hills behind. (For the alternative approach, longer but by an easier
gradient, see below, 500m further along the road.)

After the stiff climb to the saddle an easy path leads left to the peak, around which
is a tangle of house walls, the irregular plan reflecting the nature of the terrain. The
rooms are huddled together, and separate houses are difficult to distinguish. All the
floors were of trodden earth, but column bases were found in three presumably
grander areas. The excavator speculated that the choice of such an uncomfortable
refuge suggested danger from seaward, and the site has obvious advantages as a
look-out post. There is Bronze Age occupation over a long period in the neighbourhood, especially on the slopes either side of the Istron valley, also Early Minoan (3rd
millenium) cave burials in the hills behind and a settlement site on the shore below.
There are traces of Middle Minoan on the hill-top itself. The pottery from Vrókastro
shows continuity from the end of the Bronze Age (LMIII) through Protogeometric to
the Geometric settlement, 11C–8C BC.

At the far end of the village of Istro, opposite two large tavernas, is a
sandy bay with good swimming.

Just before the 13km post is the start of the alternative route up to
Vrókastro. At a big concrete culvert over a gully, with a wide parking
space on the seaward side, you can see the path following the gully into
the hills to approach from eastward the saddle behind the site.

At 16.5km a track is signposted right for *Moní Phaneroméni*. (Immediately opposite the turning to the convent from the main road is the
approach to a long-established camping site. Good swimming from
rocks.)

A steep climb (about 6km of careful driving) brings the reward of the austere convent buildings on a rock ledge with extensive coastal views. In the foreground is the Vrókastro site. The convent church, dedicated to the Panayía (Assumption of the Virgin, Feast Day, 15 August) is built around a hermit's grotto. There was a religious foundation here in the Second Byzantine period, before the island fell under Venetian rule.

To enjoy further the sense of isolation, walk on past the main door and the modern church hostel; a dirt road brings you out on to the uplands behind the convent.

In March the roadside for the next few kilometres is covered with the brilliant yellow *Ranunculus asiaticus*; the yellow form is notably localised in its distribution. Orchids also abound in the uncultivated areas.

At 18.5km the archaeological site of **Gourniá** is spread across a low hill (right) overlooking a sheltered cove of the Bay of Mirabéllo. The total size of the settlement is known to have been up to four times greater than the excavation on the acropolis, and houses were located down by the shore. The geographical position was a major advantage for trade and communication with the south coast of the island; the alternative in ancient times to a hazardous sea voyage around the eastern capes was a mere 12km journey across the gently undulating terrain of what is now the isthmus of Ierápetra.

The site is open 08.30–15.00 including Sundays and holidays; closed Mondays. Admission free. The entrance is signposted (150m off the road). You are required by the guardian to stay on the paths to avoid damaging the walls.

The Minoan town, ancient name unknown, was intensively excavated (1901–04) by Harriet Boyd Hawes, a member of a team of American archaeologists in the area at that time. There is evidence for occupation from the Early Bronze Age (3rd millenium), and there were houses on the hill in the Middle Minoan period—with the street pattern already in place—but most of the remains now visible are of the Neopalatial period. Like so many other Minoan sites Gourniá was destroyed by fire in LMIB. There was limited reoccupation in LMIII, the period of Mycenaean rule at Knossós.

The street plan of the Minoan town, and the ground floors or basements of houses are unusually well preserved. The narrow streets, which are wide enough for pack animals but not for wheeled transport, are cobbled and stepped, and equipped with an efficient drainage system. In places the houses still stand to a man's height and there were certainly second storeys, because five stone staircases were found as well as evidence for wooden steps. Stone was used in the building, but also mudbrick, often faced with plaster. The doorways were carefully constructed, with limestone thresholds level with the street. If the visitor is already impressed by the grand scale of the palaces, it is here at Gourniá that the everyday domestic life of the Minoan civilisation comes alive.

A street around the outside of the excavated town leads up from both directions to the top of the hill, where the *Palatial quarters* are located (heavy bold outline on plan). Archaeologists differ as to whether this complex should properly be identified as a palace: it is smaller in area (not quite half that of the Palace at Zákros) but may be sufficiently similar in design and function to be ranked with the other known Minoan palaces. Architecture and provision for cult practices compare well; there is a court, though it is not laid out as a central focus of the palatial buildings; there are storeroom blocks though not, perhaps crucially, the Linear A archive which would indicate a literate bureaucracy and corresponding political influence in the surrounding region.

If you keep left inside the entrance gate you arrive at the large open space which the excavator called the *Town Court* (1); it has been compared to an agorá or market place.

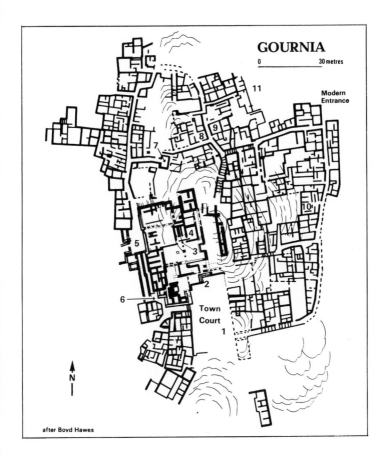

GOURNIA

0   30 metres

Modern
Entrance

Town
Court

N

after Bovd Hawes

At its north end, in clear contrast to the domestic architecture of the town, the remains of two porticoes in the north-west angle of the court flank the entrance to the palatial quarters. An L-shaped *staircase* (2) recalls, on a miniature scale, the Theatral Area at Knossós. (North of the staircase there was access to an upper floor.) The west flight of the staircase leads up to the *North Portico*, which is paved with limestone slabs, one unusually large and pierced at its south-east corner. It has been suggested that this slab was the setting for the bull sacrifice connected with bull-leaping sports in the court, with the hole as a drain for blood. Fragments of horns of consecration which had fallen into the court from the pillars of the portico identified this as a cult area, and the room immediately to the west has a fixed stone *kernos* indented with a ring of 32 hollows, a further sign of ritual activity.

The *West Portico*, on the court and directly south of the kernos, has been compared in design and function to the Tripartite Shrine at Knossós. Behind it is the *South Wing* of the palatial quarters (or palace).

It is not certain whether the central area (3) with alternate pillar and column bases along its west side was an open court or a large room similar to the Hall of the Double Axes (King's Megaron) at Knossós. To the north were associated *storerooms* (4), and there are others behind the west façade (see 5) at what was then basement level. There would have been grand ground-floor rooms above this important west storeroom block.

There is a narrow cobbled *West Court* in front of the west façade (5) which is of imposing ashlar sandstone construction and is recessed for windows on a floor above. Ashlar is generally regarded as a sign of rank and wealth in Late Minoan society. A corridor, paved—and originally roofed—leads south from the West Court ending (at the level of the south wing noted above, behind the West Portico) in a small square open space (6). Here an irregular stone slab (conglomerate) c 1m long by 0.75m high stands on an east–west orientation in a little court apparently designed to accommodate it. This is thought likely to be a sacred stone for in association with it, just to the east, are a stone kernos, a double-axe mason's mark and part of a terracotta channel.

To the south-west of the Town Court are houses of the LMIII reoccupation period. These show an architectural scheme influenced by the Mycenaean megaron of mainland Greece. Contemporary with these houses (i.e. Postpalatial) is a small *shrine* (7), reached by the cobbled street running north from the West Court. Off this, right, a sloping path is carefully paved with a central pattern of evenly matched cobbles. The shrine, up three steps, is a simple room (3m by 4m) with a ledge for cult objects. The finds (now in Herákleion Museum, Gallery X) included a low tripod altar in clay, goddesses with raised arms and bell-shaped skirt, clay tubes with snakes modelled in relief, a sherd with a double axe in relief, terracotta bird figurines and serpents' heads.

The finds from the LMI town increased understanding of economic and industrial aspects of Minoan life: of particular interest was the evidence for stone vase-making, also the set of carpenter's tools (found at 8), the workshop of a potter (9) and of a bronze-smith (10). Near the modern entrance a press was found with other equipment for the production of olive oil or wine.

At this north-east corner of the site the excavators found traces of a MMI house (11), the earliest building recorded on the hill.

In 1910 the American archaeologist, R. Seager, excavated a cemetery on *Sphoungarás*, the hill-slope right above the sea at the eastern end of the cove below the site. He found 150 pithos burials, the majority of Neopalatial (LMI) date (contemporary with the last phase of the Minoan town); the grave gifts included an important series of seals.

The road climbs away eastwards from Gourniá with a fine general view over the site. (On foot a rocky mule path offers a short cut.) At 20km you descend sharply through several bends to *Pakhyámmos* on the coast. The name means 'deep sand'. To the right on the hillside is the single-storey stone house built by Seager.

In 1914 he excavated, at the back of the wide beach, a large Minoan cemetery exposed by a severe storm. Apart from six chests, or larnakes, he found upwards of 200 *pithos burials* mostly dating from the MMIII–LMI period, with a few from EMIII (c 2100 BC). The body was folded head down into the pithos, which was then buried with the base uppermost. Seager found many such jars below the present water level, and because of the labour which would have been required to sink them into wet sand, he took this as confirmation of a rise in sea level on this coast since the Bronze Age.

Pakhyámmos has basic accommodation and waterside tavernas.

Beyond the village (21.5km) is the parting of the ways to Ierápetra on the south coast (Rte 8) and Siteía.

For Siteía keep straight on. At about 23km an angular knob is conspicuous jutting out from the wall of the Thriptí mountains running parallel to the road. This marks the Kástro refuge site above the village of (25km) *Kavoúsi.*

Several sites inland of the village were briefly excavated at the beginning of the century by the young American archaeologist Harriet Boyd Hawes; her discoveries included the two principal sites (Vrónda and the Kástro) and she excavated the completely preserved (but looted) tholos tomb of Skouriasménos. In 1901 she began to explore the Minoan town of Gourniá, and Kavoúsi returned to relative obscurity.

Since 1978 the area has been subjected to a systematic re-examination by a team from the American School of Classical Studies in Athens (W. Coulson, L. Day and G. Gesell). There was some Middle Minoan activity in the area, but no settlement of that period has yet been found, and attention centred on the Early Iron Age sites along and overlooking the old road up to the Thriptí plain. Excavation began in 1987 and has concentrated on two sites: on the lower ridge named Vrónda (meaning thunder) and high above it, around the pinnacle of the Kástro which was noticed from the main road. (For footpath directions, see below.)

At *Vrónda* there is a sizeable settlement (c 60m by 40m) of LMIIIC date (12C BC) with associated cemeteries including, on the north slope, a number of stone-built tholos tombs with chambers approached by a short trench or abbreviated dromos. Boyd excavated eight and others have since been cleared. There has been some erosion of the ridge, but the picture is further confused by re-use of the area as a cemetery in the Late Geometric period.

On the summit of Vrónda the large building with a paved court on its south side (Boyd's 'House on the Summit' and now known as Building A) was part of the LMIIIC settlement. Its function is unclear but it appears to have been (peacefully) abandoned during the succeeding Subminoan period. In the north part of the court a flat kernos-stone has 24 small circular depressions set in an oval ring. Similar objects at other sites (Gourniá, Mállia) have usually been interpreted as cult-related offering tables, but a gaming use has also been suggested. A cobbled street ran west from the court, and structures on its south-east side are interpreted as basement storerooms, with one area for the preparation of meals. The massive wall here is confirmed as a terrace wall rather than a defensive one. A kiln also belongs to this period.

In 1987 scattered fragments of LMIIIC goddess figurines were found, suggesting a *shrine*, and the following year the shrine building was uncovered, on the south-west slope of the ridge, with some of the furnishings still in situ. There was a bench along the east wall and beside it six nearly complete snake tubes and seven kalathoi (one decorated with horns of consecration on a flaring rim and a miniature kalathos set into it, one with snakes modelled inside it). There were also a terracotta plaque (pierced with holes for hanging and with horns of consecration on its rim) and fragments of the torso of a goddess with upraised hands. By 1989 the excavators had evidence (from a total of more than 2000 fragments) for at least 17 goddess figurines.

The recent excavation has also added new information about funeral ceremonies and burial practices in the Late Geometric period (8C BC). In some cases earlier tholos tombs were re-used but there are also cist graves, in two of which a cremation burial was followed by an inhumation. Remains of pyres showed that cremations sometimes took place in abandoned LMIIIC houses, with the bones and grave gifts afterwards roughly covered; there were also secondary burials with the already cremated bones brought there to be covered by stones or a pithos. The variety of practices may indicate significant changes in burial customs, or may perhaps differentiate between the status, sex, age etc. of the deceased. In contrast to the sparse offerings in the earlier tholos tombs these 8C burials were accompanied by a surprisingly rich array of iron tools and weapons. The intriguing question remains as to whether these people lived in some as yet undiscovered settlement on the ridge. It is thought on the whole unlikely that they came down from the Kástro to bury their dead.

The refuge site on the *Kástro* towering above Vrónda clings to a jutting pinnacle which commands one of the passes into the hills behind, giving rise to curiosity about the (no doubt compelling) reasons that led to the choice of such a precipitous position. Successive generations built and re-built here despite the structural problems compounded by earthquake damage. There is evidence for settlement in the LMIIIC period (Postpalatial, 12C), and notable expansion during the Late Geometric period, especially on the saddle on the seaward side of the main peak; part of the site was still occupied in Early Orientalising times (early 7C BC).

The original (1900) excavation on the main peak revealed houses occupying narrow terraces around the pinnacle, of much more regular construction than at Vrókastro (see above). Each complex is carefully rectangular, and large blocks are employed in foundations and doorways; there were stone benches outside the houses either in the streets or in small private courts.

The recent American excavations have greatly enlarged the scope of the investigation, and have shown that the Kástro settlement was far larger than was originally thought. It extended across the saddle to the false peak to the north-west, and on terraces down the slopes overlooking the coast. Late Geometric buildings were found 100m inland (south) of the settlement on the summit.

On the west slope the earliest (LMIIIC) levels show that the occupants exploited the wide natural fissures there, using the inner rock wall for the back of their dwellings. On the terraces of the eastern slope interest attaches to a room where two centrally aligned column bases were found with a hearth between them, an arrangement recalling the excavation at Dréros (Rte 7). A little to the north of this, on the most precipitous part of the east slope, movement between the various levels of the long narrow terraces may have been restricted to wooden ladders.

The many interesting finds included some unusual figurines of a crude unpainted type. Study of the pottery is expected to throw more light on the sequence of activity at this remarkable settlement.

The view from the Kástro pinnacle is stunning, and the strenuous walk (90 minutes–2 hours from the village) is highly recommended, regardless of archaeological interest.

A new dirt road leaves the main road just before the bridge at the end of Kavoúsi, and climbs as far as Vrónda, but unless there have been recent improvements it is not recommended for normal hire cars. You can walk by this track, but more agreeable is a roughly paved path, the old Turkish road or kalderími, marked by occasional splashes of red paint, which passes between the two archaeological sites on its way over to the upland valley of Thriptí. It is cut in places by the new dirt road.

At the crossroads in the middle of Kavoúsi (beyond the big modern church) turn right off the main road; there is a kapheneíon on the corner. After 250m, by a kiosk, turn left and continue uphill, then right into the picturesque ΟΔΟΣ ΔΕΡΜΙΤΖΑΚΗΣ (Odós Dermitzákis). At the end of the houses, passing (left) the old village school and a cemetery church, the kalderími sets off into the hills. At the second road crossing there is the choice of following the kalderími (which strikes left) or taking the easier footpath ahead beside the water channel. (In this case, at the road again, turn left and in 200m take another footpath right which will rejoin the old paved way.) The Panayía Kardiótissa church (on the dirt road) is now in view above left, with the

Kástro pinnacle towering behind it. Watch for a split in the path; the red-splashed kalderími continues ahead, but for Vrónda take the right fork uphill. In 5 minutes the church of Ayía Paraskeví, with a ruined building adjoining it, comes into view, and the old cottages of the summer-pasturage village of *Vrónda* appear on the sky-line (right). A path between them leads over the hill (5 minutes) to the excavation of the settlement and cemetery (see above).

From Vrónda the path to the Kástro passes in front of Ayía Paraskeví and rejoins the old paved way, climbing steadily. When this reaches the head of a cultivated valley it turns right, away from the site, and on to Thriptí. Leave the (red-splashed) kalderími, cross the head of the valley, left, on a terraced path making for the saddle behind the pinnacle. From here the easiest approach to the summit is round the further flank.

From Kavoúsi the highway climbs high above the coast. At Plátanos (31km; 4km beyond Kavoúsi) a well-sited café (left) commands a fine view across to the island of *Pseíra*. R. Seager (see Sphoungarás and Pakhyámmos) excavated on the island in 1906–07, uncovering a prosperous Minoan settlement founded in EMI and continuously occupied until its final destruction in LMIB (finds in Herákleion and Siteía Museums). It is possible (but expensive) to arrange to visit the island from Mókhlos or Ayios Nikólaos.

In 1985 archaeologists returned to the island, in a Greek–American collaboration headed by P. Betancourt and C. Daváras, to clean and re-examine Seager's settlement, and the associated Minoan cemetery (Final Neolithic – Middle Bronze Age). The settlement's streets and lanes, not plotted by Seager, were traced and plotted, contributing interesting information on settlement organisation and access. Work during the 1989–91 seasons concentrated on defining the town square (the plateía) and the major buildings around it.

39.5km *Spháka* offers the easiest of several signposted roads for the detour (6.5km) to the seaside village of Mókhlos (also the most convenient bus stop).

On the descent keep right at a fork after 1km, and the coastal plain soon comes into view with a large hotel on the shore. The modern hamlet at the far end of the bay is still relatively unspoilt and is recommended for very simple accommodation and waterfront tavernas. (Two modest hotels, also rooms for rent.)

Mókhlos was an important settlement in Minoan times. The small island, now 150m offshore, was attached to the mainland by a narrow isthmus, which made for a versatile harbour and shelter from the prevailing north-west winds. At various periods settlement covered what is now the island (which was also a cemetery area) and extended along the shore of the bay. After the Bronze Age there appears to be a long gap in the archaeological record until Late Roman (Early Byzantine period) fortifications are noted above the island's northern cliff, with traces of a tower behind an east–west curtain wall. They may have been a defence against 7C–8C AD Arab raiders. There was an extensive town in the area of modern Mókhlos up to the Second Byzantine period.

R. Seager (see Pakhyámmos) worked here in 1908, excavating the settlement remains on the island (on the south slopes facing the modern village) which proved to date from the Middle Minoan and Late Minoan I periods, with traces of Early Minoan occupation. But his most exciting Mókhlos finds came from tombs nearby. At the western end of the island he identified Early Minoan rectangular chamber tombs built against the cliff and resembling house structures. The tombs would have had flat roofs of reeds and clay. Some have doorways which could be closed with large stone slabs; one group opened on to a roughly paved court. The rich burial gifts included spectacular *jewellery* and *sealstones* as well as one of the finest collections of *stone vases* known from Minoan Crete. The materials include rock-crystal, marble, steatite and brecchia (Ayios Nikólaos Museum, Room II, and Mókhlos case in Siteía Museum).

In recent years the cemetery was reinvestigated by the Greek archaeologist C. Daváras and this study led on to a major programme of new excavation begun in 1989 (a joint Greek and American project with J. Soles). The scope of this work covers: further tombs in the cemetery with particular attention paid to the associated funerary cult; Prepalatial settlement (including a paved street) beneath Seager's Neopalatial houses on the island; the street system of this Neopalatial settlement and at least three new houses, including a large terraced ashlar building which have been found with their contents still intact. The same area has seen the discovery of a house (and street) of the later (LMIIIA/B) period of Mycenaean influence. Then comes the chronological gap. On the island Early Byzantine buildings in some places overlie the Neopalatial settlement with 7C AD walls resting directly on those of the 16C BC.

All the new evidence at this site (from the pottery sequence and the findings of volcanic ash in the stratigraphy) confirms that the Minoan civilisation continued to flourish on Crete during the LMIB period which followed the eruption on the island of Théra (Santorini). The discovery in 1990 of a LMIB settlement on the mainland, behind the modern village, with a bench shrine and evidence for workshops (in bronze and stone) indicates the arrival of new settlers at this time.

There is often rough water and a current in the strait, but in calm weather a local boatman will ferry you across. The chamber-tombs are easily reached from the landing place by a path along the west slope of the island.

Beyond Spháka the highway, attractively planted with cypress and oleander, continues past a number of villages along the foothills of Mount Ornón.

At 43.5km the road skirts *Myrsíni*, but it is worth stopping to walk up into the village. The terrace of the restored church enjoys a good view of this stretch of the coast. To the left, the village of *Tourlotí* is prominent; there was a LMIII cemetery on the hillside below. On the Aspropiliá hill near the sea, north of Myrsíni, 12 rock-cut chamber tombs of the same Postpalatial period, excavated by N. Pláton in 1960, yielded a rich variety of vases, weapons and utensils, now on show in the Ayios Nikólaos Museum.

Also on the slopes below Myrsíni a much earlier circular tomb, the first of the Mesará type to be found in eastern Crete, contained over 60 burials dated by associated finds to the EMIII and MMI periods.

The road crosses a high spur to (50km) *Mésa Moulianá*. Nearby in the place known as Selládis, two tholos tombs were excavated in 1903 by S. Xanthoudídes. These were LMIII tombs re-used during the Protogeometric period; it is interesting that at this time of transition from interment to cremation, there was evidence for both burial rites within the same tomb. The rich LMIII grave offerings included a gold mask, bronze vessels and a sword reflecting the Mycenaean influence. Particularly remarkable is a Protogeometric bell-krater (10C BC), with on one side a hunting scene with two wild goats (probably the 'agrími' or Cretan ibex), on the other a man on horseback, the first such representation known from Crete (Herákleion Museum, Gallery XI).

The wine from the Moulianá region is highly regarded.

At 56km ruined stone windmills are a landmark on the last crest before the Bay of Siteía. Here a track leaves the road (right), signposted for

Khamaízi, a Minoan site which rewards a detour (1.5km). On the track take the second turning right, the one just beyond the windmills (possible by car, or a 15-minute walk).

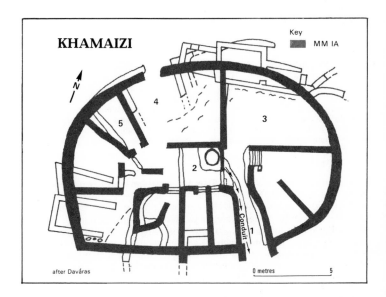

Key
▮ MM IA

KHAMAIZI

N

4
5
3
2
Conduit
1

after Daváras

0 metres   5

Khamaízi, visible for some distance on top of a conical hill, is the only Minoan building so far discovered that is roughly oval in plan. The site was first excavated in 1903 by S. Xanthoudídes. After controversy in the archaeological world about the function of the building it was reinvestigated in 1971 by C. Daváras.

There is a paved entrance from the south-east (1 on plan). The rooms are set around a small courtyard also paved (2), an arrangement which no doubt offered some protection from the fierce winds which sweep across this eastern tip of the island. Raised in the north-east corner of the court is a deep circular cistern, or well, lined with masonry. The conduit system can still be traced.

A find of figurines now in Herákleion Museum, Gallery II, had led to the suggestion that the building was a peak sanctuary rather than a dwelling, with the cistern interpreted as a votive pit, but the discovery of the conduit made this hypothesis less convincing and it is now agreed that the three figurines probably furnished a small household shrine; the area (3) to the north east of the court contained a movable hearth and fragments of a clay altar. In 1979 a second entrance was found, and this lessened speculation about the fortress-like aspect of the building. The walls of the room (4) into which the entrance leads were faced with schist and limestone, and adjacent (5) was a staircase to an upper floor.

There had been discussion whether the choice of a curved exterior wall was a deliberate architectural decision or was determined by the shape of the hill-top. The 1971 excavation found earlier (EM) rectangular buildings, discernible now on the site (unshaded on plan), which suggest that the curved walls of the MMI construction were a new and presumably deliberate design.

In the village of *Khamaízi*, the Folk Museum preserves some of Crete's rapidly vanishing past, including a rare type of loom. (Opening hours are erratic: in theory 09.00–13.00 and in high season 17.00–19.00. Stop on chance or enquire in Siteía. Small entrance charge.) It is best to park on the main road and follow the signs into the village on foot.

At 60km *Skopí* is below the road right. 4km further there is the chance of a detour—suggested as an excursion from Siteía—to a former monastery near the coast. Moní Phaneroméni (Φανερωμένη) is now disfigured by a huddle of modern buildings but its dramatically sited (Venetian period) chapel is unscathed.

The detour (signed, 3km from Siteía, 6km on a track to the chapel) is also recommended to walkers—good bus service along the main road. At the coast the track runs west (c 2km) below white cliffs, but towards the end of the bay (usually signed) the monastery lies a short distance inland. The frescoed church (graffito date 1465) is dedicated to the Panayía Phaneroméni (the Virgin made manifest); it is built over a grotto associated with the miraculous appearance of an icon of Mary, but some experts believe that this arises from confusion with the monastery of the same name in the hills behind Gourniá (see above). Perched on the edge of a ravine looking down to the sea, the tiny north–south oriented church became the nucleus of an important monastery. The grotto is still revered.

The main road runs down into **Siteía**, a small harbour town (pop. c 8000) much less hectic than Ayios Nikólaos but well-equipped to welcome visitors and an agreeable base for exploring this extreme eastern region of Crete. The effective town centre (with convenient car park) is the Plateía Iróon Polytekhníou in the angle formed by the sheltered harbour at the north end of the long beach. The tree-shaded waterfront is lined with cafés and tavernas, and the attractively colour-washed modern houses rise steeply, tier on tier, behind. A conspicuous red-domed church is the seat of the local bishop. Cretan raisins are exported through Siteía and a lively 'Sultana Festival' takes place in August.

The Siteía Archaeological Museum opened in 1984 to concentrate on the cultural development of this eastern tip of the island. The story is brought up to date in the newly-housed and expanded Folklore Museum.

There was Final Neolithic occupation (with similarities to the Neolithic of the Dodecanese archipelago) at various points on the bay, followed by settlement in Minoan times at Petrás on the ridge 1km east of the centre of the present town.

Excavations since 1985 under the direction of the Greek archaeologist, M. Tsipopoúlou, have been uncovering a major settlement on a series of artificially terraced slopes, and a substantial retaining wall supporting a Palatial-style building on the top of the hill, with a shrine on the upper floor. An impressive list of artefacts includes hundreds of vases, with numbers of large pithoi, also metal objects, terracotta figurines and a wine press. Examples are on display in the Siteía museum. Potters' marks were detected on vases and other clay objects. The 1990 find of a well-preserved Linear A tablet pointed to the existence of an administrative archive. At the foot of the hill, on the seaward side, a fortification wall of monumental construction with large square towers is preserved to a height of 3.5m. The site was abandoned following destruction by earthquake in LMIA; it was partly reoccupied in LMIIIA.

Greco-Roman Eteía is mentioned by Stephanos of Byzantium as the birthplace of Myson, one of the Seven Sages of Classical Greece. There has been a town on the present site of Siteía since the First Byzantine period, before the 9C Arab conquest. During their brief stay on the island (early 13C) the Genoese strengthened existing fortifications, and under Venetian rule Siteía flourished as a fully walled city; above the harbour, one of the forts of the wall has been restored and is used as a theatre in summer. The Venetian city was twice damaged by earthquake, and frequently by Turkish raids until, in 1539, it was sacked by the renowned Turkish pirate, Barbarossa. When the Turks blockaded the city in 1648, the Venetians forcibly evacuated the reluctant population to safety inland. The Kástro held out for three years, but the town was utterly destroyed and lay in ruins for two centuries. Not until 1870 did the Turkish authorities decide to build a new administrative centre here. The new town was laid out, but unfortunately little more than the regular street plan survives.

Siteía is proud of its association with the Hellenised Venetian family of Kornáros, distinguished in the spheres of art and learning. Its most famous member is Vinzétzos Kornáros, author of the 16C epic poem, 'Erotókritos'.

Hotels: Siteía has a number of pleasant, well-equipped Class C establishments, some right on the harbour front, and many houses offering rooms to rent. For relative quiet at night, explore out to the north east by the ferry quay.

Youth Hostel: 4 Odós Therissoú near the outskirts of town on the road from Ayios Nikólaos.

Tourist Information Office (high season only) run by the municipality in a caravan on Plateía Iróon Polytekhníou in front of the Hotel Itanos. Tel. (843) 24 955.

National Bank: also on Plateía Iróon Polytekhníou.

OTE: Odós Kondiláki. Area code 0843.

Post Office: at the town end of Odós Therissoú (main road in from Ayios Nikólaos).

Bus station on Odós Praisoú, part of the dual-carriageway running down to the harbour.

Ferry services regularly connect Siteía with Kásos, Kárpathos and Rhodes, and with various islands in the Cyclades en route to Piraeus. The schedule alters each spring. Tourist information offices should have details, or check direct with the Tzortzákis travel agency (tel. 28 900), whose office is on the quay by the inner pier.

Olympic Airways: 56 Odós El. Venizélou, almost opposite the National Bank, tel 22 270. Siteía has a small airport 10 minutes from the town centre with scheduled flights at present only to Kásos, Kárpathos and Rhodes.

From just west of the inner pier, broad steps lead up to the episcopal church of Ayía Aikateríni in Odós Gabr. Arkadíou. This street runs out to the restored *Fort*, known locally as the 'Kazárma' (Casa di Arma) which provides, especially in the evening light, a superb view of the bay and the eastern hills of the island.

A lively evening 'volta' (the traditional hour of strolling and chatting) takes place to and fro along the harbour quays. On the seafront beyond the Port Authority building, rock-cut *Roman fish-tanks* have been recognised just below the present water-level. They are comparable to those at Khersónisos (Rte 5), but less easy to make out. The water-front walk diverts a few paces inland to avoid old buildings, and the fish-tanks are just beyond them, level with the Star hotel.

The *Folklore Museum* has recently reopened in Odós Therissoú on the outskirts of town (right side of the road leaving for Ayios Nikólaos).

Open (Apr–Oct) 09.30–15.30, closed Sundays. Entrance charge.

The collection concentrates on domestic crafts (especially weaving), including both the products and the equipment. The antique hand-spun and handwoven silk bedhangings are particularly fine.

The **Archaeological Museum** stands back from the seafront, inland of the bus station, at the main junction with the road south across the island signposted for Lithínes.

Open daily: 09.00–15.00 (Sundays 09.30–14.30). Entrance charge except Sundays free.

The building, opened in 1984, is attractively designed around a courtyard. The display of finds from this eastern end of the island is arranged chronologically with each section introduced by explanatory notes and a relief map.

Prominently displayed just inside the main room is the chryselephantine statuette from Palaíkastro. Pieced together from fragments excavated successively over recent years this figure, in characteristic pose with left leg slightly forward, is now known as the *Palaíkastro Kouros. At least eight pieces of ivory (derived from the hippopotamus) were carved separately for the figure and fitted together with dowels. (A ninth piece forms an ivory pommel from a missing dagger.) A rectangular ivory peg behind the face fits a cavity in the serpentine head. Eyes of rock crystal are worked at the back, apparently to take an iris, perhaps a small stone. The gold seems to have belonged to foot coverings, bracelets and the typical Minoan belt.

Behind the Kouros a free-standing case contains material from the important Neolithic site of Pelekitá, a cave on the seaward slope of Mount Traóstalos, north of Zákros; there is also an impressive exhibit of Neolithic stone axes.

Left of the entrance are two cases of finds from the cemetery of Ayía Photiá, 5km east along the coast, where more than 250 tombs (EMI/II, c 3000–2500 BC) were excavated. The material is interesting because of the strong Cycladic character of some of the finds emerging from a clear Early Minoan context; the 'frying pans' (also well represented in the Ayios Nikólaos Museum) are a local variation of a type characteristic of the Early Bronze Age in the Cyclades and on the Greek mainland. There is a good exhibit here of obsidian pressure blades.

Next come Minoan votive terracottas from various peak sanctuaries, the majority from Petsophás above Palaíkastro. (A large proportion of the known sites of this type are located in eastern Crete.)

The adjacent central case contains material from EM/MM tombs on the off-shore islet of Mókhlos. Note the garlanded bull figurine, also a lamp on the lower shelf. Next in the centre are finds from the Minoan settlement on the island of Pseíra, including a fine stirrup-jar in the Marine style, probably a product of a Knossós workshop.

Along the wall are cases of Early and Middle Minoan material from various sites in the Siteía region, and near by (towards the centre) an exhibit of bronze objects. Finds from the Minoan town of Palaíkastro have a wall-case to themselves. Note the horns of consecration in stone, and the same motif used to decorate a pottery rhyton for ritual use; also two multiple vases or kernoi, one in clay (four cups) and one in stone (two). Then comes a case of Late Minoan (Neopalatial) pottery from other sites in the region.

The *Palace of Zákros* is the subject of the next section, but first, in the corner, there is a well-preserved *wine-press from the Minoan villa (LMI, contemporary with the palace) just outside the modern village of Ano Zákros; it was found with a pithos inscribed in Linear A (now in the Zákros display in Herákleion Museum). The bronze saw was found in the palace. The next wall case holds large pots with signs of burning from the great fire which destroyed the palace at the end of LMIB. The nearby exhibit of Linear A script is a forceful reminder of the Minoan palace's administrative function. The free-standing giant pithoi emphasise the importance of storage and redistribution in the palace economy, and, between the two largest pithoi, a selection of Minoan cooking pots and basins illustrates one of the domestic aspects of Minoan life. These exhibits are followed by cases with a selection of finer wares from the palace, including a good display of spouted jars. In the corner are stone offering tables and lamps. Finally a centre case holds objects associated with

Minoan cult practices: horns of consecration, double-axe stands, kernoi, also an interesting trivet and a scorched alabastron, a further reminder of the final conflagration.

In the *Geometric and Archaic section*, note especially the display of Daidalic heads and figurines; this important deposit of terracottas was found in the centre of Siteía during road-works near the present post office. Roússa Eklissía also had an Archaic sanctuary with Daidalic material.

The last section is devoted to the *Hellenistic and Roman* periods. There is fishing equipment and other intriguing finds from the small island of Kouphonísi off the south-eastern corner of Crete, where a flourishing settlement owed its existance to the preparation of purple (or deep crimson) dye from a gland extracted from the shell *Murex trunculus*.

Finally, a large stone block with Greek inscription comes from a Roman-period building at Itanos.

Obtainable locally there is a detailed gazetteer for the region: 'Sitia' by the Greek archaeologist N. Papadákis (translated by J.M. Kaphetzáki).

10 Excursions from Siteía

A. To the East Coast

Direct road to the Minoan Palace of Zákros 50km. The recommended longer route (c 70km to the palace) includes: (16km) the Monastery of Toploú; (25km) the palm-fringed beach at Vái; (27km) ancient Itanos; (c 40km) the archaeological site of Palaíkastro with the opportunity of a walk up to the peak sanctuary of Petsophás.

One bus a day to Vái, two or three a day to Zákros via Palaíkastro.

The Zákros road runs east out of Siteía along the edge of the bay. At 5km is the village of *Ayía Photiá*, where an important EMI–II cemetery (on the low hill near the sea, just west of the Mare Sol bungalows) was excavated in 1971 by the Greek archaeologist, C. Daváras. There were more than 250 tombs, with multiple burials and a rich variety of grave offerings, many showing a degree of Cycladic influence. The outstanding finds of pottery, with bronze and stone artefacts, tools and weapons are exhibited both in the Siteía museum and in that of Ayios Nikólaos (Room I). Some graves were simple shallow pits but there was also a primitive form of chamber-tomb. The rock-cut tombs were closed with an upright blocking slab, and outside there was a small paved antechamber for the cult of the dead where many of the big pedestalled cups were found. On the next hill to the west, excavations have uncovered the settlement associated with the cemetery.

At 12.5km the direct road to Palaíkastro and Zákros runs straight on, but the recommended route takes the left turn to (3.5km) the fortified *Toploú monastery*, a striking sight standing out from the barren upland. The Turkish name (alluding to a cannon installed by the monks in Venetian times as a defence against pirates) has replaced the earlier

Panayía Akrotiriáni, the Virgin of the Cape. A 14C church (torch useful for icons) is the original nucleus of later (much restored) Venetian buildings; the monastery was fortified at the end of the 16C.

Only two or three monks remain in residence; one should be on duty at reasonable hours to open the church.

Toploú enjoys a reputation as one of the most influential and respected monasteries on Crete. During its chequered history it acquired great power and wealth, with dependent churches and monastic foundations scattered across the island (including a nunnery on the site of the present church of Ayía Triáda in Herákleion) and even today is a major landowner in eastern Crete. The monastery endured many acts of destruction and plunder by among others the Knights of St. John of Malta in 1530 and by the Turks in 1646, as well as severe earthquake damage in 1612. The monks maintained a tradition of support for the Cretan national cause, and suffered accordingly. During the 1940–45 war the monastery operated an underground radio transmitter, and for this the Abbot Silignákis was executed in the notorious Ayiá jail near Khaniá.

The main entrance is through the *Loggia Gate* into a reception and workshop area, and then by an easily defended double doorway into the monastery proper. The small *court* with patterned cobbles is surrounded by three levels of cells, as well as the abbot's quarters and a big refectory; above are the battlemented walls and tall Italianate *bell-tower*.

On the façade of the church, to the left of the doorway, four stone slabs are let into the wall. One is a relief of the Virgin with Child, Our Lady of the Cape. The two central inscriptions record the pious labours of the Abbot Gabriel Pandógalos, who restored the monastery after the 1612 earthquake with financial help from the Venetian Senate.

The *inscribed slab* at door level is part of the 'Arbitration of Magnesia', 132 BC. Two copies of this inscription have been found. One, from the Temple of Artemis at Magnesia itself, preserves lines 27–140. This fragment at Toploú overlaps with lines 1–86. Magnesia, a city of the Roman Empire in Asia Minor, was called to arbitrate in a complicated series of territorial disputes, first between Praisós and Itanos, and then after the destruction of Praisós, between Itanos and Ierápytna (modern Ierápetra). A central issue in the dispute was the control of the Temple of Zeus Diktaios at Palaíkastro. This fragment was brought to Toploú from Itanos to serve first as a tombstone and then as an altar table in the little cemetery chapel of Tímios Stavrós (the Holy Cross) outside the monastery. In 1834 it was noticed by the English scholar and traveller, R. Pashley, who suggested its present setting.

The two-aisled church has, as is usual, a double dedication: the northern and older aisle, of the Panayía Akrotiriáni, to the Nativity of the Virgin, and the southern to Ayios Ioánnis Theológos, the Evangelist (Feast Days respectively 8 and 26 September). *Frescoes* of scenes from the gospels recently uncovered in the north aisle are dated stylistically to the 14C. An *icon stand* painted with designs from bird and plant life bears the signature Stamation and the date 1770; such antique pieces are now very rare on Crete. Alongside this north aisle is a small room used in the past by women at the services.

There are several fine *icons* in the church. The outstanding one, displayed between the two aisles, is entitled 'Lord, Thou art Great.' Two inscriptions at the foot of the icon establish: the artist, Ioánnis Kornáros; the date, 1770; and the donor, Demétrios, with his wife and children. The work portrays 61 densely painted scenes each inspired by a phrase from the prayer of the Orthodox liturgy used on the Feast of the Epiphany. This icon is one of the great masterpieces of Cretan art.

The road continues for 6km across moorland to (22km) a T-junction. Turn left and (after 1.5km) right, for the beach at *Vái* set in a remarkable grove of tall palm trees. The grove was known already in Classical times.

Phoenix theophrasti greuter, a distinct species closely related to the date palm though its fruit is smaller, dry and inedible, is restricted solely to eastern Crete. The trunk may grow to a height of 10m.

There is especially fine swimming here from a sandy beach with theatrically placed off-shore rocks, but because of its exotic reputation Vái in summer can be very busy indeed.

If the crowds and noise are intolerable you can continue north a further 3km—back to the coast road and turn right—to the ruins of ancient Itanos, where there is a choice of small bays, the one to the south of the archaeological site being particularly recommended.

The road comes to an end at the site. Beyond is *Cape Síderos*, the extreme north-eastern point of Crete, but entry is restricted on the approach to a Greek naval establishment. (The small island of Elása, off Itanos, has ancient remains and is still used as a sheltered anchorage.)

The area is known locally as Erimoúpolis, 'the deserted place'. There was sufficient exploration here at the turn of the century to identify the ruins with **Itanos**, one of the most influential ruling cities of the eastern end of the island, with territory stretching to the south coast including the island of Kouphonísi. The French excavated in the 1950s but the results have not yet been published.

A LMI villa south of the Greco-Roman site is evidence of Bronze Age occupation in the area. It is not known when the city was founded, but according to a story in Herodotus (IV.151) it was flourishing by the 7C BC. There is a fine 5C silver coinage, and this prosperity continued through to the Early Byzantine period. Around 260 BC Itanos asked for Ptolemaic support against neighbouring Praisós, and an Egyptian garrison was established here, apparently without prejudice to the city's independence. Until the end of that century, and briefly again 50 years later, Egypt seems to have welcomed the opportunity to influence Aegean affairs, and East Crete was a convenient base for the vital recruitment of mercenaries. With the defeat of Praisós by Ierápytna (modern Ierápetra) c 155 BC, that city became the chief rival of Itanos, especially over the control of the important Temple of Zeus Diktaios at Palaíkastro. It took 20 years to settle this frontier dispute. The *Arbitration of Magnesia* (132 BC; see Toploú) is proof that by this time the Roman Empire was interested in the fate of Crete.

At least four temples are recorded here from Classical times, but the remains intelligible today are mostly from the First Byzantine period. Itanos was a double acropolis site on two low hills and the land between. The eastern hill rises sheer out of the sea; the western one has incongruous dwellings alongside the ancient watchtower and fine Hellenistic terrace walling. Traces of the city spread on to the rise beyond the bay to the south. The cemetery area is up the coast in the opposite direction.

On the inland slope of the main eastern acropolis are the excavated remains of a 5C–6C *basilica* which stood on the site of, and perhaps was converted from, an earlier temple to Athena Polias. The plan shows side aisles extended to the limit of the main raised apse, and the central aisle has unusual small apse-like niches in its long walls. The church was built partly of re-used material, and the floors were paved with stone slabs. Several incomplete marble columns survive. One large block has carved decoration of circles filled with rosettes (one with a Greek cross).

There are traces of two other basilicas on the slope behind the bay to the south.

Back at the T-junction beyond the Vái turn (with Toploú and Siteía right) keep straight on for Palaíkastro. After 2.5km there is a striking view ahead of a prominent flat-topped hill at the edge of the sea; this is known as Kastrí, and an important Minoan town lay on the coastal plain to the south (far side) of it. On this side of the hill a long stretch of beach with several access tracks (signed Koureménos) offers some of the best swimming in the area.

The modern village of Palaíkastro has several small hotels and simple rooms to rent. When you reach the plateía, turn left towards Zákros.

After 150m, on a right-hand bend, a by-road to the left (signed Marina Village Hotel) leads in 2km to the beach and the Minoan site. On the by-road keep straight ahead to the bridge over the stream-bed, and across it turn left skirting the hamlet of *Angathiá*. First follow signs to the hotel and then continue ahead, 1km to the sea. (For this route ignore any signs right to the archaeological site of Roussolákkos.) You should emerge from the olive trees on the shore at the base (south side) of the flat-topped hill, Kastrí. (Popular summer tavernas.)

The Bay of Palaíkastro (from Spratt, Travels and Researches in Crete, *1865)*

Palaíkastro was first investigated by R.C. Bosanquet and R.M. Dawkins (1902–06). In the 1960s a team from the British School at Athens returned to the site two years running under the direction of L.H. Sackett and M.R. Popham. There was evidence for occupation in the area from the Neolithic to the end of the Late Minoan period, with a continuing cult of Zeus Diktaios from Geometric down to Hellenistic and Roman times. Most of that excavation has been back-filled, but part of the *main street* can still be seen, and along it are the ground-floor plans of several LMI buildings. It was clear that Palaíkastro was a town on a grander scale and architecturally more elegant than Gourniá, but if, as seems likely, there were palatial quarters at Palaíkastro comparable with those at Gourniá they have yet to be discovered.

In 1983, at the invitation of the Greek government, the British School (L.H. Sackett and J.A. MacGillivray) returned once more to the site to carry out a topographical survey of the whole area with a view to defining more exactly the nature and limits of this harbour town. The survey established that (on the evidence so far available) this was, at 30 hectares, the second largest Minoan settlement on the island—after Knossós 70 hectares, Mállia 22 and Zákros about half that. The current programme of excavations and study was begun in 1986 (see below).

The scramble up *Kastrí* is worthwhile for the view (path behind the waterside taverna). Off-shore are the Grándes Islands. On a clear day you may make out Kásos and Kárpathos, 'stepping stone' islands to the east towards Rhodes. This was the notorious Kásos channel, a gateway to the Aegean Sea, through which the British Mediterranean Fleet so often had to risk its warships during the 1941 Battle of Crete; Stuka dive-bombers were based at the German-held airfield on Kárpathos. There was particularly severe loss of life after a courageous mission, during the evacuation of the island, to rescue the remaining garrison from Herákleion.

Excavations on Kastri in 1963 revealed walls (still visible) dating to EMIII and LMIIIC, that is early in the Bronze Age and at the very end of it, periods when the defensive potential of this hill was presumably of paramount importance.

The bay immediately to the south of Kastrí was the Minoan *harbour*. The excavated town occupies a stretch of land known locally as Roussolákkos (the red pit) a little back from the bay and from the salt-flats of the present shore line. The sea level is higher than in antiquity, but at the same time the silting process has raised the level of the valley floor.

The coastal track skirts the salt-flats and a broad path leads in 100m to the site. (Signed right, and guardian's hut in view from the track.)

Approaching from the sea, you come first to the fenced area of the newest excavations. The foundations of the Neopalatial buildings so far uncovered are aligned on a paved and walled road which runs up from the direction of the harbour (therefore named the *Harbour Road*) and widens at one point to a space resembling a miniature *plateía*—see plan. Lacking the characteristics of Minoan domestic architecture the complex is understood as a group of public buildings, though their function is still open to debate. Building 1 was a large LMI structure, with massive foundation slabs, still in situ, designed to carry the cut sandstone blocks probably to a height of two storeys. (This grand edifice was succeeded by a less imposing building of LMIII date, possibly a bench sanctuary of the type seen at Knossós in the Shrine of the Double Axes.) Diagonally across the plateía, under protective shelter, Building 5 (Neopalatial and only a small part reoccupied later) has remarkably well-preserved mudbrick walls which were faced with mud plaster; they subdivided an existing interior space with a colonnade or 'polytheron'. There is evidence for a system of storage, and the building had its own well. Beyond an alley on its southern side—and a formidable wall—an area was left open and entirely unoccupied at the height of the Minoan period; it may have been a garden.

A MMIII–LMI destruction deposit below Building 7 produced a Linear A inscription on a pithos rim, and fragments of a plaster tripod offering table decorated with narcissus in the fresco technique.

The most spectacular find from the recent excavations has been a chryselephantine statuette of a young male, roughly one-quarter life size, which was discovered during three seasons of digging, in innumerable fragments in the gravel surface of the open 'plateía' area and in Building 5 which is now regarded as its context. The figure, known as the *Palaíkastro Kouros*, is presumed to have cult associations, and taking account of the much later temple on the site (see below) it is tempting to suggest links with the worship of the Cretan-born Diktaian Zeus.

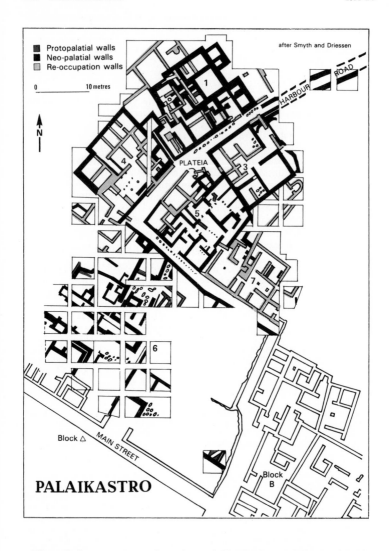

The cult figure seems to have been deliberately vandalised when the town was destroyed at the end of the final LMIB period. The fragments of ivory and gold leaf discovered in 1987 built up the torso and arms; the next year systematic sieving recovered scraps of neck, eyebrow, ear and then came a finely carved grey serpentine head that fitted neatly into a rectangular dowel at the back of the ivory face—which was completed by the finding of rock crystal eyes. In 1990 ivory legs joined ivory feet. The restored Kouros, the left leg set forward in characteristic pose, is on display in the Siteía Museum.

Inland of the new Roussolákkos excavations (at the west or Kastrí end of the exposed section of main street—see plan) is a separate excavation (1962 vintage) of the LMIB *house* N. The street entrance is on the north side. (The off-shore Grándes Islands lie roughly north-east.) The broad entrance passage leads to an inner *hall* with staircase to an upper storey. Two pyramidal double-axe stands (like those in the 'Corridor of the Magazines' at Knossós) and miniature horns of consecration had fallen from above, suggesting a *shrine* on the upper floor. The large *main room* at the back may have been a dining-room, for a pantry in one corner produced nearly 400 cups, many stacked inside each other as they had fallen from shelves, as well as large jars and a tripod cooking pot.

The *main street* is paved with irregular blocks of limestone and schist, and bordered by drains. On the right (south) side, opposite the newer excavations *house* Δ has a grand ashlar façade 40m long, with a wide doorway midway along it. A main hall is marked by four column bases round a large slab. East of the crossroads *house* B (MMIII–LMI) lies on the seaward side of the street; the entrance, across a large threshold block, is at the east end of the façade with evidence for a staircase to an upper storey just inside the doorway. The porticoed court ahead may have been a walled garden. It leads left into a *peristyle hall* with central impluvium, and adjacent lustral basin. The finds from this house were in keeping with the standard of the architecture, emphasising the prosperity of its owner. (See Herakléion Museum, Gallery IX, including superb Marine style vases believed to be products of a Knossós workshop—also a good display in the first section of the Siteía Museum.) Across the street is *house* Γ with another wide entrance (under an olive tree); this building lay in the angle of two town streets. From that point on, the earlier excavations have been covered over.

In this area, just beyond where the main street now disappears under the fill, R.C. Bosanquet's excavation identified the site of the *Temple of Zeus Diktaios*; it was already known that control of this sanctuary was disputed between the city-states of eastern Crete in the 3C BC and was one of the main subjects of the Arbitration of Magnesia in 132 BC (see Toploú and Itanos). The temple building had been completely destroyed, but architectural fragments dated from the 6C BC, including sections of a clay 'sima' or waterspout with a chariot scene in relief. The most important find was the scattered fragments of a limestone slab with an inscription, dated to the 3C AD, recording part of the Hymn to Zeus Diktaios, an invocation used in re-enacting the dance of the Kourétes around the infant Zeus (cf. the legend associated with the Idaian cave, Rte 3A). Both 'sima' and inscribed slab are in Herákleion Museum, Gallery XIX. Together they are taken as evidence of the longevity of a cult of Zeus Diktaios here, at least in historical times.

On top of the steep hill of *Petsophás* (215m), conspicuous to the south of Roussolákkos, the Minoans established an open-air peak sanctuary. First explored by the British in 1903, this was fully excavated in the 1970s by the Greek archaeologist C. Daváras. Tucked against the rocks on the summit, the walled precinct contained a small *shrine* with plaster benches. A great quantity of votive offerings was found, mainly human and animal fragments in clay, but there were also horns of consecration, and Linear A inscriptions on stone libation tables; examples are shown in both Ayios Nikólaos and Siteía Museums.

For the climb to Petsophás, a track (marked intermittently with paint splashes) starts from the little promontory on the shore south of the salt-flats, striking diagonally across the narrow coastal plain to a conspicuous ridge running inland. On the red earth up the hillside a tin roof (covering a well) offers a landmark beside the time-honoured route, a kalderími along the contour of the hill from the direction of Angathiá. To the left of this, where the ridge merges with the hillside, you turn left on to a well-worn path. Steadily gaining height the built path skirts the summit of Petsophás by the southern flank. At the highest point on the shoulder strike out to the right, less than 5 minutes to the peak. The sanctuary site overlooks the sea.

From Palaíkastro village the Zákros road leaves the coast and winds (for 20km) across windswept hills and through several villages. At 57km, just before *Adravásti*, a minor road (right) offers an alternative return route to Siteía (see below).

At 60km *Ano* (upper) *Zákros*. Originally settlement must have prospered because of the plentiful spring water, but now the village caters for visitors to the Minoan palace which is a further 9km on a good road down to the coast. (Simple hotel, also rooms for rent, and several tavernas.) In summer buses continue to the palace at Káto (lower) Zákros.

The traditional route to the site on foot (c 1 hour) is down a spectacular gorge carved by the river which flows into the bay at Káto (lower) Zákros. Caves in the gorge were used for burials during the Early and Middle Minoan periods, hence the local name, the Ravine of the Dead (Pháranga ton Nekrón). The gorge is subject to flash floods early in the year and after storms. Ask at one of the kapheneíons to be shown the start of the (way-marked) path, and if in doubt check for safety.

The car road to the palace from Ano Zákros is signposted (past the hotel) to the right from the central plateía. Just out of the village it cuts through a LMI villa where in 1965 a wine press and a pithos inscribed in Linear A were found; the wine-making equipment is well displayed in the new Siteía Museum, but the pithos is in Herákleion (Gallery VIII).

Within the last decade the road has been radically realigned so that it now makes the final approach to the palace along the coast from the south.

On the coastal stretch, looking back to further south, two islets mark Xerókambos, and way beyond is the island of Kouphonísi, port-of-call in the days of the Roman Empire for the 'purple trade' (see below).

Ahead the Bay of Zákros and the bottom of the Ravine of the Dead come into view, with the palace excavation a little back from the far end of the beach. The small bay, more enclosed then that of Palaíkastro, provides the best protected harbour on this coast. It was ideally placed for trade with Egypt and the Levant, as a landfall here avoided the voyage round Cape Síderos in the teeth of a contrary wind, the persistent 'meltémi' of the summer months. Valuable imports found in the palace debris indicate that the Minoan civilisation recognised and exploited this advantage.

The mountain to the north, beyond the bay, is Traóstalos, site of a Minoan peak sanctuary. Recent surveys have shown that in Minoan times all approaches to this bay except the main gorge were blocked by walls, and guarded by a series of watchtowers linked by a road laid out to serve this defensive system rather than for normal access to the palace. This new research, which is echoed in findings in several other parts of the island, is bound to encourage a reappraisal of the traditional assumptions about a 'Pax Minoica' and a land uniquely free from strife.

Káto Zákros, inhabited (because of flood danger) only from April to October, is no more than a cluster of low buildings with tavernas and a number of simple rooms for rent. Swimming is from a shingle beach usually well sheltered from summer winds.

The town site at Zákros was investigated by the British under D.G. Hogarth at the beginning of the century. But the spectacular nature of the continuing finds, including gold objects, unearthed locally, gave grounds for suspecting an undiscovered palace, and in 1962 the eminent Greek archaeologist N. Pláton began an exploratory excavation for the Greek Archaeological Society which immediately met with success. Work on the site has continued each year since then but only preliminary reports have been published. It appears that Zákros, like so many other Minoan sites, suffered a sudden and terrible catastrophe at the end of the LMI period which caused the buildings to collapse and burn. The inhabitants had time to escape, but though there was some rebuilding in the town area, the palace was left largely undisturbed. It was neither restored nor looted (possibly placed under a 'taboo') and therefore yielded to the excavators interesting evidence about the functions of the different areas of a Minoan palace and also a range of artefacts of exceptional quality. Gallery VIII in Herákleion Museum and a whole section in the new Siteía Museum are devoted to the Zákros material.

The site is open daily in summer 08.00–15.00. Out of season enquire about the current arrangement from Tourist Information in Ayios Nikólaos or Siteía.

The Palace of **˙˙ZAKROS** occupies flat land on the floor of the little river valley. The sea level has risen here since Minoan times and the palace site is often partly under water. The *harbour town* was terraced over the lower slopes of three surrounding hills, with narrow streets cobbled and stepped where necessary as at Gourniá. The most fully explored sector is on the slope to the north-east of the palace (see plan). The excavators have recognised larger villas or palace dependencies in the town.

The palace remains now visible are mostly of the LMI period, similar in plan to the other Minoan palaces, though much smaller, but traces of an older palace have been encountered, including evidence for a central court and features by the main entrance gate and beneath the west wing.

You approach the site at the north-east corner along a paved Minoan *road* (1 on plan) which came up from the harbour. The paving had a contrasting pattern of blue and white stones. On the left, the investigation of traces of Protopalatial features brought to light evidence for a *bronze foundry*, contemporary with the first phase of the New Palace, in the form of a horseshoe-shaped smelting chamber with four air ducts; remnants of the ore were still in situ.

The paved harbour road continues ahead into the town, but the principal entrance (2) to the palace is obliquely left through what was a *covered gateway*, now marked by a large limestone threshold block. You descend to the north-east court by a *stepped ramp* where the excavator compares the regular central slabs to a strip of ceremonial carpet. Some original fragments remain. The roofed area is a lustral basin or *bath* (3) with a bench, and column bases for a portico on its north and west sides. (Its proximity to the entrance suggests comparisons with the lustral basin near the North Entrance at Knossós, where visitors to the palace may have taken part in cleansing and purification rituals.)

In front of the roofed area you pass between two pillars (4) into the *Central Court*, on a north-east–south-west alignment differing very slightly from that found at the other three palace sites. At 30.30m by 12.15m this court is only about a third the size of that of Knossós. The façades of the surrounding buildings were in ashlar masonry incorporating vertical and horizontal timber beams as in the other palaces; the squared blocks came from a quarry at Pelekitá, 5km north up the coast. In the north-west quadrant of the court the square stone has been interpreted as the base of an altar.

The entrance (5) to the WEST WING from the court is across the massive threshold block in line with this altar base. Through an anteroom which had a slender central column was a square room characterised as a recep-

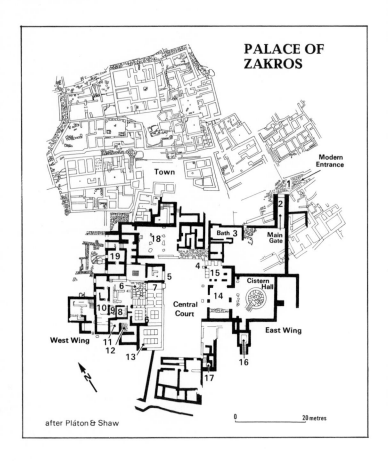

PALACE OF ZAKROS

after Pláton & Shaw

0   20 metres

tion lobby, and distinguished by a floor area with a central square of red tiles. A staircase behind led to a second storey. South of the lobby was a paved and colonnaded light-well (6); the floor here, of crazy paving with interstices of red plaster, was drained from its north-east corner.

In the light-well were found in pieces a chlorite bull's head rhyton and the *mountain shrine rhyton*. The latter is not only a finely worked stone vase originally covered in gold leaf, but also pictorial evidence of the greatest importance for an understanding of the Minoan peak sanctuaries. (See Herákleion Museum.)

The light-well also lit the north end of the *main hall* (7). The hall was designed with central columns and the space was made versatile by the pier-and-door arrangements characteristic of Minoan architecture. There were traces of wall paintings, and decorative panelling in the floor was framed by narrow strips of stucco originally painted red. These frames survived but, intriguingly, the material they outlined did not, with no trace of stone, nor archaeological evidence for wood.

This main hall communicated with the banqueting hall (13) to the south (see below), but also (in conjunction with the entance lobby (5)) controlled access to the inner areas of the west wing where the religious, administrative and economic functions can be deduced from the architecture and artefacts uncovered there.

Immediately to the south west of the light-well is a *lustral basin* (8) with eight steps down into it. Next to it (west) at the heart of the complex was the *central shrine* (9), with a ledge built into a niche across from a low bench. Nothing was found on the ledge, but on the floor were fine clay rhytons and pedestalled cups. Behind the Shrine was an *archives room* (10) where record tablets had been kept in bronze-hinged wooden chests stored on wooden shelves. Most of the tablets had been crushed but 13 were recovered, some inscribed in Linear A. This provision for ritual and for records of administration was integrally associated with a labyrinthine arrangement of workshops and pot stores.

Immediately south of the shrine was the *treasury* (11), equipped with eight clay chests, now restored. This room was found undisturbed, the chests tightly packed with fine vases, larger pots on the floor and probably on the chest lids as well; more pots had fallen from an upper floor. Here were some of the finest Minoan stone vases yet known. They included chalice shapes and jugs, and the exquisite *rock crystal rhyton* with bead handle and collar, which had been crushed into more than 300 fragments. A vase of porphoritic rock from Egypt had been adapted for pouring by the addition of a Minoan bridge-spout. (All exhibited in Herákleion Museum.) With them were bronze double axes, fine stone maceheads, artefacts in ivory and faience.

In this same sector of the palace, but in a room over the storerooms and workshops, were kept valuable raw materials. Among the debris of the collapsed upper storey the excavators found six bronze ingots and three large elephant tusks (also exhibited in the Herákleion Museum) which had fallen from above.

Next to the treasury was a *workshop* (12), the grouped flat stones perhaps a support for a craftsman's bench, and in the storeroom immediately to the south 15 storage pithoi were found.

Returning to the central court you pass the room (13) named the *banqueting hall* on account of the large number of drinking vessels found in the debris; the walls were decorated with a frieze of painted stucco and the room connected through a triple doorway with the main hall to its north.

Across the court the EAST WING, unfortunately damaged through the years by cultivation and by flooding, is designated by the excavator as the *royal living quarters*, to correspond with the two-storeyed private apartments found in the other palaces. Behind a pillared and colonnaded verandah are two main rooms (14 and 15), connecting by multiple doors. The northern room opened on to a light-well on the east side, but uniquely interesting behind the bigger room to the south is the **cistern hall**, a large area with a central basin or pool, built to retain spring water at a standard level. The substantial wall of the cistern was lined with plaster, and eight steps led down to it. The floor of the hall slopes inward for drainage, and column bases suggested that the area may have been at least partially roofed. The water came from the *spring chamber* (16) immediately to the south with its adjacent built *well of the fountain*, which constituted the main supply for the palace. Clearly the control of water was always a problem at Zákros. For much of the year these structures are now themselves submerged.

At the south-east angle of the central court is another stone-lined *well* (17). From this in 1964 came a conical cup containing olives perfectly preserved in the water for more than 3000 years. On exposure to air they shrivelled in a very few minutes.

At the other end of the central court the kitchen area (18) of the palace is to the north of the west wing. The six rugged column bases are taken to indicate structural support for a dining room above. The staircase is on the eastern side, and to the west the *storeroom block* (19) would also have had grander rooms above.

It is worth walking up the stepped streets of this sector of the town to the upper levels for the splendid bird's-eye view of the palace excavation.

500m inland along a track from the site gate is the bottom of the Zákros gorge.

On the return drive along the coast from the palace, the low-lying and now deserted island of *Kouphonísi* is in view (4km off-shore) on the southern horizon.

On this island (2km by 4km) there is evidence for settlement dating from the Early Bronze Age, and remains of a prosperous Roman town include a small stone-built theatre. Kouphonísi is known to have been a port-of-call on the trade routes from Rome to Egypt and Asia Minor. The Greek Archaeological Service has been excavating here since 1976 under the direction of N. Papadákis. During the Roman period the island played an important part in the Mediterranean textile industry known as the 'purple trade', which was based on the murex shell (*Murex trunculus*). A gland in this spiny sea-snail yielded a red dye prized by Phoenicians, Greeks and Romans. (The colour purple associated with Roman Emperors was more exactly a deep crimson.) The excavation uncovered vast numbers of murex shells and interesting evidence for dying installations. The murex was first exploited during the Minoan period—by the relatively simple process of crushing the shells. The Romans developed more sophisticated methods of harvesting the shells and processing the precious fluid from the glands (from each of which only a few drops of dye were obtained) in order to produce strikingly bright colours. (See exhibit in Siteía Museum. For possibility of visiting the island enquire in Makryialós, Rte 10B, or at Tourist Information in Ierápetra, Rte 8.)

From Ano Zákros a dirt road (sometimes rough in places) runs down to the coast in 9km to *Xerókambos*. It is well signed thanks to local initiative. There is a long beach (with developments already under way) and another striking gorge, with micro-environment that is, still, less disturbed by visitors than that of Zákros.

From Ano Zákros an alternative return route to Siteía (30km by minor roads) runs through deserted country that is a rich hunting ground for wild-flower enthusiasts. Part of the route is not asphalted but has a good hard-packed dirt surface.

Retrace the Siteía road for 3km to *Adravásti* (noted on the outward journey). Through the village a minor road left (signposted Karýdi and Sítanos) climbs to a plateau where in March you may find the distinctive *Tulipa cretica*. At 11km *Karýdi* is the centre of a network of upland roads (including those to Khandrás and Zíros, or across to the Siteía–Ierápetra main road, Rte 10B).

Turn right in the village for (14.5km) *Mitáto*, (16km) *Krionéri*, (22.5km) *Roússa Eklissía* and a descent, especially beautiful in the evening light, to the coast 3km east of Siteía.

B. To Praisós and the South Coast

Direct to Ierápetra 64km (40 miles). Suggested itinerary c 70km via (20km) the hilltop site of the ancient city-state of Praisós.

Using minor roads from (4km) Piskoképhalo there are alternative round-trip excursions from Siteía, to the Akhládia valley (c 18km) or through Zoú and Karýdi (c 40km).

Buses: eight a day to Ierápetra, one service to Néa Praisós.

The route to the south coast, signposted Lithínes, leaves Siteía from the junction in front of the Archaeological Museum. After 2km at *Manáres* the road cuts through the site of a Minoan villa (sign). Nowadays the site may look rather neglected but the remains are of a large LMI country house, contemporary with the New Palaces, that was terraced into the hillside and looked out eastwards over a fertile river valley. A well-preserved staircase at the northern end of the site gave access to the upper level. The lower level, which included storerooms, was protected by massive stone blocks, possibly as an embankment against a wider river below.

At 4km the cross-roads in *Piskoképhalo* (at a sign to the right for Khrysopiyí and Stavrokhóri) offers a choice of detours, one on each side of the road, both circling back to Siteía.

A left turn leads (1.5km) to the 11C church at Káto Episkopí, seat of the local bishopric soon after the island was regained from Arab domination for the Byzantine empire. The road continues (less than 5km) to another excavated LMI villa, at Zoú, and on to Karýdi.

From the turning in Piskoképhalo the narrow village street soon widens where the road is realigned to accommodate new banana cultivation. At the edge of the village *Káto Episkopí* is in view straight ahead—signed. (The road to Zoú here sets off right.) The objective, at the south-east edge of the village (best on foot, turning right into the narrow streets) is Ayii Apóstoli, a tiny cruciform domed church with octagonal drum and angled apse. This is now a cemetery church.

The well-engineered Karídi road first follows the river-bed, then crosses it and climbs into a side valley. The Zoú villa site is up the right bank of the road cutting (250m before the village below the road left). As at Manáres the house looked out over the fertile and cultivated land on which its economy would have depended. Beside the well-preserved entrance at the far (south) end of the façade is a small room with a stone bench. Two deep pits, right of entrance, suggest storage of grain. This Minoan farmhouse had its own pottery kiln.

The village of Zoú is noted for its plentiful spring water which now supplies Siteía. Just beyond the site the road sweeps left to cross the head of the valley and the recommended minor road continues across still unfrequented uplands through *Stavroménos* and *Sítanos* to (18km from Zoú) *Karýdi*, for a leisurely return drive (see end of Rte 10A) to the coast near Roússa Eklissía.

From the Piskoképhalo crossroads on the main route from Siteía, the minor road branching right begins a detour to the *Akhládia valley* for the site of an excavated Minoan villa, and also a well-preserved example of a LMIII tholos tomb.

After 3km on the minor road take a track to the left, perhaps signed, otherwise distinguished only by a nearby culvert. In 150m the track forks, and up the slope right are the Akhládia villa's massive foundations.

The site was excavated in 1959 by N. Pláton who identified two phases of a Neopalatial (MMIII) building destroyed in LMI. The approximately rectangular house had 12 rooms and a main entrance in the centre of the south-east façade. The main hall was through double doors on the left of the entrance passage. Three column bases remain along one line in the axis of the hall which opened on to an area with a stone bench at one corner. At the back, against the north-west façade, a cupboard and utensils in a small room suggested a kitchen. On the other side of the entrance passage was a group of storerooms.

The tholos tomb is 1km nearer Akhládia. On a right-angle bend not far before the village a track diverges to the left uphill, and climbs, round an awkward hairpin bend left, to (1km from the road) a T-junction. Turn left between concrete pillars carrying a modern aqueduct system, and 50m beyond them take a footpath (right) through an olive grove to a gap in a wall. Turn left and follow the terrace contour till it peters out on an upward slope. Just ahead in a vineyard is the tomb, hard to see until you are right upon it, but marked by a notice ΘΟΛΩΤΟΣ ΤΑΦΟΣ ΑΧΛΑΔΙΩΝ (Tholotós táphos, tholos tomb).

The tomb, excavated in 1940 (dromos 1952), dates from c 1300 BC during the period of Mycenaean control of the island. At the end of the 'dromos', or sloping approach, the two uprights of the low rectangular doorway support a massive lintel. The circular chamber is built of large stones, with the horizontal courses corbelled inwards to a keystone at the centre of the roof. Opposite the entrance is a small doorway against the natural rock; when found it was blocked by two walls and has been compared to the false door in Egyptian tombs through which the owner's spirit came and went. The tomb had been robbed—the hole in the roof is the robbers' entry—but three larnakes remained, one decorated with the double axe, horns of consecration and a griffin. The lid of another was shaped like the back of a bull, including head and tail at the gables. The finds, including pots and a stone lamp, were destroyed during the last war.

Back on the road, and 150m on towards the village of Akhládia, a good dirt road turns right along the valley to join (after 3km) the main north coast road 6km from Siteía. On the banks of a stream shaded by plane trees you pass *Kimouriótis*, a cluster of traditional stone-built houses with cobbled yards close to a church and a spring. The hamlet was practically deserted, but an attempt is being made to bring it to life again.

From Piskoképhalo the main Ierápetra road continues south to (11.5km) *Epáno Episkopí*. (At the beginning of the village a left fork, signed for Zíros, is the turn for the site of the city-state of Praisós.)

The village's name reflects the fact that it was the seat of the Catholic bishop of Siteía at least by the early 16C, when Turkish raiders, often under the command of independent corsairs such as Khaireddin Barbarossa, were a constant threat to the coast. A short loop right, off the main road, climbs to pass almost immediately the tall, slender basilica church (Panayía), its construction overcoming the awkward slope of the hill. On the west façade is a plaque carved for the Catholic bishop, Gaspar Vivianus. The Italianate bell-cote, pointed arches and details of the stonework and the doorway all emphasise the contrast with the typical domed cruciform plan for the Byzantine church of the Orthodox bishop at Káto Episkopí (noted above).

The Zíros road descends into the fertile valley of the Pantélis (Didymos) running below the hill-top on which the ancient city lay, and then climbs through *Ayios Spirídon* high above the valley to (18.5km) the village of *Néa Praisós*.

From the plateía a dirt road is signposted downhill left to the archaeological site of **Praisós**. After 1km, at a hairpin bend, keep on downhill to the right. After a further 800m you pass a low rocky hill just left of the track (the city's Third Acropolis; see below), and half left ahead is the First Acropolis, distinguished by a network of terrace walling. Continue (200m) to ruined buildings (remains of a Venetian village); they are just before a gate and signed footpath (left) to the centre of the site.

Praisós was the capital of the Eteocretans who were probably survivors of Minoan stock; their inscriptions using the Greek alphabet but for a non-Greek language form one of the most intriguing finds from the site. Despite their apparent ethnic origins, there is little evidence that their culture was anything other than purely Greek.

The area was first investigated in 1884 by the Italian F. Halbherr, who found the first inscriptions, and the main excavations by the British School under R.C. Bosanquet began in 1901. The city spreads across three hills designated as the First, Second and Third Acropolis; the third is also referred to as the Altar Hill.

The excavated cemeteries produced material dating from LMIII to the Hellenistic period. They included a number of chamber-tombs of which two produced indications of Bronze Age habitation in the neighbourhood. Bosanquet looked for continuity from a Bronze Age settlement, but found that the city of the Eteocretans was built mostly on the natural rock and had no earlier remains below it.

It is known that the Praisians had many contacts (both peaceful and warlike) with the neighbouring Greek cities of Ierápytna (modern Ierápetra) and Itanos. A major cause of dispute with Itanos was control of the important temple of Zeus Diktaios at Palaíkastro (see Rte 10A). At one stage in the Hellenistic period, the Praisians even shared citizenship with Ierápytna, but about 155 BC (Strabo X, 479,12) their city was destroyed by Ierápytna, and was never reoccupied.

An easy path leads round the western flank of the *First Acropolis* to the saddle between two peaks where the ancient city lay. On the summit of this acropolis scant foundations of a temple can be made out, and on the south side of the *Second Acropolis* (at the further end of the saddle) rectangular cuttings in the rock show where houses were cut back into the slope. These two hills were enclosed by a defensive wall which can still be traced in places. Looking across a broad gully the *Third Acropolis* (outside the wall) is identified as a flat-topped wedge formation, approachable with ease only from this direction. On the summit of this hill a primitive altar marked a sanctuary frequented, as the offerings prove, from the 8C–5C BC. In the late 5C–early 4C the temenos wall probably enclosed a small temple. Some of the more important finds, including figurines, are displayed in Herákleion Museum, Gallery XVIII.

Where the path meets the saddle, just uphill right on the slopes of the First Acropolis and looking across to the Second, are the excavated remains of a *Hellenistic house* (see plan) dating from the 3C BC. The outer walls are of ashlar masonry with carefully exact joints finished with lime mortar. The house is built on a terrace on the steep hillside, the upper wall making use of the native rock and the lower being carried down as a strong retaining wall. Water spouts act as drains through this lower wall. Traces of cobble paving remain but the usual flooring was native rock or hard clay. The roof was tiled.

The house, designed to fit into an existing street plan, is entered from a shallow-stepped street. A forecourt leads to a vestibule (1) before the main front door into the living quarters (2–4); wide doorways and substantial stone jambs are a feature of the architecture. The doors turned on pivots as did the windows which were fitted with wooden shutters.

The principal living-room seems to have been at the north-east corner, enjoying the coolest aspect of the house. (The unshaded walls on the plan are part of alterations to the original design.)

From the forecourt there is also an entance to three rooms of a different nature at the back of the house. A triangular vestibule (5) led to a large room (6) with an olive press in one corner, and in the centre a stone vat presumably for the storage of oil; it is fitted to take a wooden lid, and could have been lined with lead. There are the remains of a stone platform that ran round the walls of this room. Next door was a storeroom (7) which contained numerous pithoi, one with a projecting spout flush with the base for the drainage of liquids. The stone stairs are part of the lower flight of a staircase to the upper floor; the upper flight was of wood.

PRAISOS
HELLENISTIC HOUSE

after Bosanquet

From the forecourt, eleven steps lead down to a basement room (8) with a small rock-cut cellar in the rear wall. There may have been a room above with a door from the forecourt.

This building has always been known as the Almond-Tree House, for the tree which hung over it at the time of the excavation. There are still many almond trees on this hillside, though few visitors are there to enjoy the January blossom. Praisós is a site strongly recommended all through the spring to wild-flower enthusiasts.

From Néa Praisós the road continues towards the Zíros plateau. After 5km, just before Khandrás, the romantic ruins of the medieval village of *Voilá* are spread along the hillside to the left of the road. A by-road (left and right before you are abreast of the village) leads to a Turkish fountain at the start of what was the main street through the village. The ruins are dominated by the 15C double-aisled church of Ayios Yeóryios, and a tower of the Turkish period; the decorative carving on its doorway includes an inscription dated 1742. The track leads on into *Khandrás*.

Here one road keeps left to *Zíros* where the church of Ayía Paraskeví (left of the road in the middle of the village) preserves in the arch above the door the latest dated fresco painting on the island (1565).

A right turn in Khandrás leads through *Arméni* back to the main Siteía–Ierápetra route. You pass at *Etiá* the remains of a 15C •villa, highly praised at the turn of this century by G. Gerola in his study of the island's Venetian monuments; he attributes the building of the villa to a member of the Venetian De Mezzo family. Very few examples survive on Crete of the country houses of the Venetian period.

Writing an account of his travels on the island in 1856 Captain Spratt describes a castellated Venetian villa combining strength, luxury and taste. 'It has a vaulted basement, like a fortified tower, with well-constructed second and third stories above, and displays some architectural effect throughout. In the upper part were five windows in front, and in the lower, one on either side of a handsome entrance, approached by a flight of steps ascending from a paved courtyard, around which were the servants' dwellings and outhouses.' The house, by then Turkish property, was severely damaged during the 1828 Revolt, and fell into ruin before it was rescued and restored by the Greek Archaeological Service. Spratt's 'vaulted basement like a fortified tower' is what remains today.

In 2km you arrive at *Pappayianádes*, 20km from Siteía on the main road. This now climbs gradually south-west to the watershed and then descends, passing (after 4km) below the large village of *Lithínes* which is worth a short diversion to explore on foot.

Take the second turn and follow the one-way system up to the plateía in front of the main village church. Past the east end of this church, 50m downhill, is Ayios Athanásios (15C–16C); note the (contemporary) ceramic plates embedded in its south façade. A parallel street from the plateía (passing instead the church's west front—see above) leads to the church of the Panayía where a number of fine icons are preserved. The key is held by the Papás.

Soon the Libyan Sea is in view, with the mountains to the west rising to the heights of Thriptí.

Less than 10km to the east, perched above the shore, is the *Kapsás Monastery*. There are two signposts to it on the main road. The first is 4.5km from Lithínes, but the easier route is by the dirt road along the coast; this second sign (after fine sea views) is 4km beyond the first, at *Análipsi*.

The monastery is built into the cliffs above the sea just beyond the mouth of the Perivolákia gorge. According to tradition it was founded in Venetian times, but the present buildings (apart from modern intrusions) mostly date from the mid-19C when the much earlier grotto church—the present north aisle dedicated to Ayios Ioánnis Prodrómos (the Baptist)—was enlarged by the addition of a second aisle of Ayía Triáda (the Holy Trinity). The wooden iconostasis was installed at the same period. All this was achieved by an eccentric (some say saintly) character, a monk named Gerondoyiánnis, whose remains are still revered in the church.

Swimming is from a rocky pebble beach. The coastal track continues 4km to Goúdouras.

From Análipsi the main road turns west. The cliffs of the extreme south-eastern corner of Crete as well as the island of Kouphonísi are still in view, but ahead, on a clear day, the peaks of Díkte and Lázaros above the Lasíthi plateau stand out in the far distance. 2km beyond the Kapsás turn, a long strip behind the beach at *Makryialós* has suffered badly at the hands of developers. Level with the new harbour quay a Minoan villa was excavated by C. Daváras in the 1970s and produced a series of high-quality finds, some of which are on display in Room III of the Ayios Nikólaos Museum. However the site has all but disappeared under new buildings.

The villa lay 200m inland of the road. The ground plan resembled in miniature those of the Minoan palaces, with a monumental west façade, and a central court and a west court connected by a passage. The main entrance was probably on the villa's north side, but the central court also had an entrance from the east, and there may have been a walled east court. In the central court the excavator identified an altar with an associated bench.

From Makryialós the road follows the coast for 24km. Easy access to this stretch of shore has only come about within the last 20 years, but it has recently been followed by a boom in piecemeal development aimed at the cheaper end of the tourist market, and the result cannot be greatly recommended. At first the road passes a number of rocky coves where in spring the mountain streams flow down to the sea. Then the coastal plain opens out behind a long beach as you approach the town of *Ierápetra* (see Rte 8).

III   KHANIA AND WESTERN CRETE

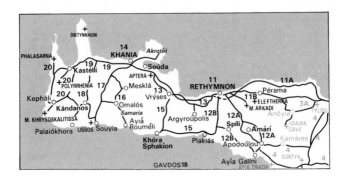

11   Herákleion to Réthymnon

A. Direct route 78km (48.5 miles) by the north coast highway or 'New Road': 15km Ayía Pelayía; 22km Phódele; 54.5km Pánormos. For the Monastery of Arkádi a short diversion is necessary on to the last stretch of the Old Road.

B. The Old Road, 79km (49 miles), is recommended for excursions or as part of a leisurely round trip: 20km Márathos, for the walk to Phódele; 55km Pérama for detour to ancient Eléftherna; 75km Plataniás, for (17km) Arkádi.

There is a good minor road (7km) up the river valley between Pánormos and Pérama.

Frequent (express) bus service by the New Road, two or three times a day serving the villages on the Old Road, both from the bus station east of the Venetian harbour, towards the Athens ferry quays (see town plan at end of book).

A.   The New Road

The north coast highway, which bypasses Herákleion, may be reached either from the Knossós road or 3km out along the Old Road which leaves town to the west through the Khaniá Gate—watch for signs for the New Road (Néa Odós). (Distances given below are from the west junction; the new kilometre posts operate in the reverse direction, calculated from Khaniá.)

The highway runs west passing oil-storage tanks and cement works. At 8.5km, there is an Orthodox seminary beside the Pandanássa Bridge, and soon after, at Palaiókastro, remains of a Venetian fort (1573) stand to sea-ward of Rogdiá, a village clinging to the hillside high up left (see Rte 3A.) Goats roam this territory, as they did long before the new road was built, and herds or stragglers are an attraction, but also a potential hazard to the fast-moving traffic. You climb out of the Bay of Herákleion, and (at 13km) almost immediately over the crest, a surfaced road leads off, right, 2km to *Ligariá*, where tavernas (with good swimming) offer a practical alternative to the town beaches after a morning's sightseeing in Herákleion.

This is the first of several independent by-roads leading to the sea around *Ayía Pelayía*. In the mid 1970s a large hotel was built on a headland here—on the site of the ancient city-state of Apollónia. More recently, development of a rather charmless kind has followed the hotel. At 14.5km a road, signed for Ayía Pelayía, leads left and then under the highway down to the main development, with a branch right by the chapel on the headland to the Bay of Ligariá recommended above. Ideally avoid Sundays at the height of the summer, for the crowds may be excessive.

Excavations have revealed extensive remains of the Classical–Hellenistic city of Apollónia, including what is probably the ancient prytaneíon. The city was destroyed in 171 BC by the people of Kydonía (Khaniá), in what came to be regarded as the most treacherous attack on record on a friendly city-state. The Apollonians went down to the harbour to welcome their allies who came streaming out of the boats to slaughter them. After this destruction the site was fought over by Górtyn and Knossós, and these squabbles led to one of the earliest diplomatic interventions by the Romans in a Cretan border dispute.

Excavated remains of the city are still preserved, scattered among the terraces and gardens of the hotel complex. (In the neighbourhood archaeologists also uncovered a LMI villa, one of the increasing number of country houses and estates of the Minoan period that have been examined in recent years.)

22km from Herákleion on the main road, **Phódele** lies a short distance inland amid orange groves. There are pleasant shady kapheneíons beside a stream where water runs for most of the year, and paths around the village offer escape from the ubiquitous souvenir shops, though not always from the black-shrouded grandmother offering her macramé or crochet work.

Traditionally Phódele was accepted as the birthplace of the painter El Greco (Doménikos Theotokópoulos, c 1541– 1614), but scholars now believe that he was born in Herákleion (see the Historical Museum for recent acquisition). However, in 1934, the University of Valladolid in Spain erected, under the plane and chestnut trees at the top of the village, a bilingual inscription in his honour carved on slate from Toledo.

On the drive into the village the domed Byzantine church of the Panayía, Loubiniés (dedicated to the birth of the Virgin) can be seen across the valley to the right. There are paths leading to it through the orange groves, stunning at blossom time around Easter, or a track that starts across the larger bridge in the village.

The cross-in-square pillared church, with the dome supported on a drum lit by 11 narrow windows, is built into the central nave of a 8C (pre-Arab) basilica; traces of the basilica apses can be seen. Remains of several layers of frescoes have been uncovered, in contrasting styles. The older paintings date back to the early years of the Venetian occupation (13C); those in the south cross-arm include a donor inscription of 1323. The ruins of the medieval village lie round about the church.

44km from Herákleion on the highway there is an exit (left) for *Balí* (Μπαλί). Set in a particularly beautiful bay, with coves at the western end sheltered from the prevailing summer wind or 'meltémi', the tiny village of Balí, frequented until recent times only by fishermen, is growing each year to accommodate holiday visitors. There is a modern Class B hotel and a considerable choice of rent rooms and tavernas.

In Classical times this was the site of Astále, sea-port of Axós, and the 'sheltered harbour' of Venetian maps keeps that name. (The modern name is derived from the Turkish word for honey.)

At 45km, just above the highway, and with a fine view of the coastline below, lies the *Monastery of Ayios Ioánnis*, dedicated to St. John the Baptist. Feast Days are celebrated on 24 June (birth) and 29 August (beheading). Tradition associates the monastery's foundation with a hermit from across the valley to the east, and circumstantial evidence suggests a date in the first half of the 17C.

In an isolated position for most of its existence (before the building of the New Road) the monastery commanded the route through the Kouloúkonas hills to the Milopótamos valley, on the kalderími between the remote and sheltered landing-place below and the stronghold of the Ida range. This lifeline to and from the out-side world played its part in the struggle for freedom during these centuries of Tur-kish rule, particularly after mainland Greece achieved independence; there are stories of loss of life on many occasions from bombardment of the bay by enemy ships.
    The monastery was attacked during the 1866 Revolt but escaped complete destruction. The Italian scholar G. Gerola came here at the turn of the century and noted the Venetian architectural detail on the two rows of rooms separated by arches, and also the roofed main entrance with a 1635 inscription. But the monastery fell into decline (deserted in 1941) and stood empty until 1983 when Abbot Anthimos and his monks started to bring it to life again.
    Necessary restoration has not in general added to the romance of the place; how-ever wall-paintings (dated to the first half of the 17C) have been uncovered in the two-aisled church. 400m up the mule track inland (the kalderími to Melidóni) which starts through the gate behind the church, is a much-admired fountain dating from 1791. On the terrace in front of the church a fine bell was cast in Trieste in 1884. (*View.)

10km beyond Balí you arrive at the turning for Pérama which lies inland on the Old Road to Réthymnon; the side road soon joins the Ieropótamos river valley.
    At the junction the highway bypasses *Pánormos* on the coast. (Tavernas and a small hotel.) This is now a relatively unspoilt backwater for most of the year, but traces of substantial buildings where the village meets the sea bear witness to its former importance from Venetian times till the turn of the century as a port and trading centre for the surround-ing area. As road communication developed between Herákleion and Réthymnon, commercial traffic moved to these two ports and inland to Pérama on the road between them.

The ancient site of Pánormos, of which very little is known, extends over the low ridge to the south west, inland of the highway and above the narrow coastal plain. Coins from here in the Herákleion Museum date from 1C BC–9C AD. On the crest of the ridge, with extensive views to the south across the island, are the excavated foundations of the Early Christian *basilica* of Ayía Sophía. (Approach signed left on the way into the village—10 minutes walk, possible by car. At a fork keep to the left or upper road which soon passes under the highway and the site is straight ahead, 150m uphill. Or slip off the main road on to a dirt track (left), 400m west of the turning for Pérama, and proceed uphill.)

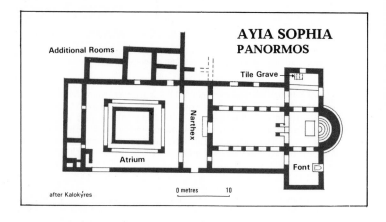

The *basilica*, dated to the early 6C, was excavated by K. Kalokýris and N. Pláton in 1948. The three-aisled church ended in a triple transept and single apse (see plan), and the nave was divided by stylobates of four Ionic columns. Under the chancel floor was a small container filled with bones, presumably a foundation offering. There are no mosaics, and the floors are of slabs or pebbles, but architectural fragments such as capitals and details from the screen were of high quality. West of the narthex there is an *atrium* which originally had a Corinthian colonnade around the central cistern. The function of the rooms along two sides of the atrium is uncertain but the one nearest the narthex may have been the original baptistry, before a horseshoe-shaped font was installed in the south pastophorion. The tile grave in the north pastophorion is known from inscription as the tomb of a minor cleric, Theodoros.

60km. Just before the highway bridge over the Ieropótamos the White Mountains come into view. The Bay of Réthymnon opens out ahead, a coastal plain with a long sandy beach attracting a number of large hotels. (There are also well-established camping facilities.)

The airstrip here (just beyond the bridge) was one of the major objectives of the German airborne invasion which in 1941 launched the Battle of Crete. The sector was successfully defended by Australian forces, with skill and bravery in the face of great odds against them in men and equipment. During the first wave of attack over this beach, 161 German transport planes were counted in the sky at one time.

5km beyond the Ieropótamos bridge, near Stavroménos (and the main Australian war memorial), the highway is raised to cross the Old Road, visible immediately below on the right. There are slip-roads on both sides. To visit the monastery of Arkádi you can leave the highway here, and take the parallel coast road to Plataniás (p 242). (There is also a more direct route now signed to cut across to the Arkádi road at Loútra or Piyí. Or continue on the highway to a turn-off, also signed, 1km before the T-junction below.)

At 73.5km this stretch of the New Road has until recently ended at a T-junction, but since 1987 work has been in progress on the planned Réthymnon bypass which will continue straight ahead. Left at this point leads up into the beautiful Amári valley. (This junction is the start of Rte 12A, c 35km to Amári.) Turning right, and soon joined from the right by the Old Road (alternative approach from the west to Plataniás and Arkádi), you proceed through the extensive outskirts to the centre of Réthymnon (see p 243).

B.   The Old Road

The road leaves Herákleion by the Khaniá gate, and at 3km passes the junction for the north coast highway (New Road) as well as for Phaistós and the Mesará plain. The next section of the Old Road (with short excursions into the hills) is described in detail in Route 3A to Týlissos and Anóyia. You continue through *Gázi* and under the highway, following signs for Réthymnon.

At 11km on this Old Road to Réthymnon, you pass the left fork for Týlissos and Anóyia to climb high round the seaward flank of the conical Mount Stroúmboulas (800m). The domed building (Koumbédes) in ruins on the right of the road was in Turkish times an inn for travellers unable to reach the city before the gates were closed at nightfall; it probably succeeded a similar Venetian establishment. It is recorded that in 1670 this hillside was covered with cypress trees. Viewed from here, the shape of Júktas (the isolated peak behind Knossós which can be seen as a reclining bearded god) goes some way to explaining the tradition that the mountain was the burial place of the Cretan Zeus.

On a left-handed hairpin bend, you pass (on the right) the so-called Voulisméno Alóni, or sunken threshing floor; the best view over this curious geological feature is round the next corner.

Near the 15km post, a cleft (right) between two outcrops of rock briefly affords a dramatic view back over of the Bay of Herákleion. The landscape is wild and strewn with boulders.

A little way beyond (20km) *Márathos*, just at the 21.5km post, a rough road to the right runs downhill to *Phódele*, offering an opportunity for a middle-distance walk.

Arrange to take a bus on the Old Road route to Réthymnon, and alight at this turning. On the gradual 7km descent to Phódele (see p 234) you pass (left) the abandoned monastery of Ayios Pandeleímon dating from the Venetian period. Some of its finest icons are now in Herákleion's Historical Museum.

The afternoon bus from Phódele may leave inconveniently early, but a further 3km on a minor road through orange groves brings you to the highway, and a choice of Khaniá and Réthymnon buses for the return to Herákleion. The bus stop is 500m east of the junction, at the other end of the bay.

Past the Phódele turn, the Old Road continues through the Ida foothills and a number of small villages, where memorial stones are a reminder of the sufferings of the population during the 1940–45 war. At 30km you enter the nome (province) of Réthymnon, and descend gradually amid vineyards. *Drosiá* is a pleasant shady village, one of many along the twisting road. After (45.5km) the junction with the road from Axós and Anóyia (Rte 3A), you follow the east–west Mylopótamos valley.

At 55km in the middle of *Pérama* (pop. c 1000) is the turning for the road down the valley of the Ieropótamos to (7km) Pánormos and the north coast highway.

Immediately across the river bridge a branch from the Pánormos road keeps straight on for (4km) Melidóni. In summer charcoal-burners are often at work in this region. Keeping left through the unspoilt village, the road climbs 2km to the *Melidóni cave* which has been frequented intermittently since Neolithic times (including during the Minoan period) and was the site of a Classical sanctuary dedicated to Hermes Tallaios. It is now revered, and a place of pilgrimage for Cretans, because of an atrocity in 1824, when 370 Christians, most of them women and children, who had taken refuge in the cave, were trapped by a Turkish force under the ruling Pasha of the time. When the Christians refused to surrender, the entrance was blocked up and a great fire lit to suffocate them.

There is easy access just above the church (and for illumination a light switch just inside the church door). The cave has some fine stalactites. From the church platform there is a good view south across the Mylopótamos valley to the Psilorítis (Ida) mountain range.

2km on the Réthymnon side of Pérama, on the Old Road, is the turning left for a recommended detour to (5km) Margarítes, and on to the site of the ancient city of Eléftherna. *Margarítes* is a village of potters and (despite the fact that it is now established as a regular tourist attraction) a pleasant place with extensive views, and cafés from which to enjoy them. The ruins across the valley are the deserted village of Káto Tripódos.

At the far end of the village on the left (back from the road where it has been slightly realigned) is a workshop specialising in the traditional large undecorated storage jars or pitharia. These have altered little since Minoan times, and during the summer months all stages of their manufacture can be studied here.

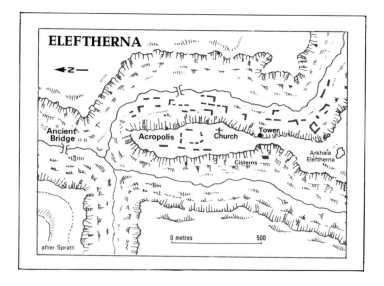

From Margarítes the asphalt road continues through Kinigianá to *Arkhaía Eléftherna* (formerly Prinés). At the top of the village street, opposite a fountain, the lane to the right leads in 200m to the taverna (exokhikó kéntro) which now dominates the approach to ancient **ʹEléftherna**.

Ελεύθερνα, one of the most important of the Dorian city-states, flourished at least from the 10C BC to medieval times; there is now also evidence of Minoan occupation. The city put up strong resistance before being overrun by Quintus Metellus during the Roman campaign of 67 BC, but nevertheless thrived again under Roman rule.

Captain T.A.B. Spratt visited the site in the mid 19C; he described a number of features (see plan based on his sketch) and drew attention especially to the defended approach to the acropolis and to two ancient bridges. The British archaeologist H. Payne excavated here (briefly in 1929), and noted massive walls from the Classical period repaired in Roman times, but after that little was done in the way of archaeological investigation until 1984 when the Faculty of Archaeology and History of the University of Crete (based at Réthymnon) began a number of independent excavations which have uncovered remains of great interest from various different periods in the long history of the site.

The *acropolis* of Eléftherna occupied a near impregnable promontory between two streams. The approach to the neck of the promontory (followed by the modern path) is along a rock-cut road to a saddle which forms a natural causeway only 3.6m wide at its narrowest point. The surface of the road was worked, perhaps to imitate paving stones, and equipped with drains at the side. (Part of this feature has recently been covered with gravel.) At the acropolis end of the saddle are the ruins of a massive *tower* still standing to a height of 8m, dating either from the late Roman or early medieval period.

The city apparently spread down both the east and west slopes of the acropolis and across the western valley to the hill beyond the stream where the village of Néa Eléftherna is today. An ancient *bridge*, one of the two described by Spratt, still spans this stream bed.

The old path (some sections of it still a paved kalderími) keeps to the left (west) of the acropolis, under the little chapel of Ayía Eiríne (probably on the site of an earlier church), and then bends sharply round left to a remarkable complex of rock-cut *cisterns* supplied by an aqueduct thought to be Roman, though the cisterns are probably earlier. The aqueduct brings water from springs on the other side of the hill.

On the bend before the cisterns a well-trodden branch of the path continues north along the hillside. It will eventually take you down in a steep descent from the north-west tip of the acropolis to a little above the stream-bed where you turn right to find the *Hellenistic bridge* (refer to sketch-plan for a sense of direction and allow at least 30 minutes). In spring the hillside offers an undisturbed habitat for wild flowers and the stream-bed is carpeted with cyclamen.

The path along the flank of the acropolis first passes below one of the recent excavations on the summit. You notice a short but distinct descent on the way before you need to watch right, up the hillside, for a makeshift gate from which a terraced path leads out on to the top of the ridge. The excavation fence encloses the quatrefoil plan of a large structure of the Early Christian period. This was built on the site of a *sanctuary* of the Archaic and Hellenistic periods; from the quantity of inscriptions found the sanctuary is believed to have been of central importance to the city.

Perhaps the most remarkable archaeological discoveries from Eléftherna have been associated with a *cemetery* of the Early Iron Age which has been studied by N. Stamboulídes and his team from Réthymnon University. The excavation took place in the area known as Orthí Pétra on the heavily cultivated valley floor, more or less directly below the highest point on the acropolis and c 100m in from the western stream.

The site was damaged by cultivation and by a paved Roman road winding across it, and it was necessary to disentangle the disturbance created by superimposed and continuous use at least from the 10C–6C BC, to arrive at a detailed picture of the funerary enclosure in successive periods.

Hellenistic bridge near Eléftherna (from Spratt, Travels and Researches in Crete, *1865)*

Apart from simple inhumations (usually of children) in a pithos or amphora, there were rectangular stone enclosures with a complex mixture of burial practices associated with both inhumation and cremation probably reflecting family, clan or even class traditions. There were opportunities for detailed study of pyre construction which will allow the archaeological record to add a further dimension to events (such as the cremation of Patroclus) described by Homer or painted on Greek vases.

The pyre might be built in a rectangular trench up to a metre deep, on a layer of stones to provide draught. In a grid-iron pattern of tree trunks and branches, pine, cypress and olive wood have been identified. The body, sometimes elaborately clothed, was laid on the pyre with personal belongings, jewellery, perfume jars or weapons. It is estimated that the fire reached a temperature of 900°C and lasted a considerable time. It was eventually quenched with water, presumably from the nearby stream, and a mound of stones might be piled over the spot, though sometimes the bones were first retrieved, cleaned and interred in an amphora.

During the 1990 season intriguing discoveries, with further cross-references between this Early Iron Age material and the legends of Homer, concerned the suggestion that human sacrifice had been part of the ritual associated with one of these pyres. The evidence assembled included a 30cm iron knife found near the neck of the victim (whose head was missing), a whetstone presumably used to sharpen the knife and a jar which could have held water to moisten the whetstone.

Study of the grave gifts and of the evidence of ritual feasting on the site is throwing light on the connections of Eléftherna with other communities on the island but also abroad (the Greek mainland, Cyprus, the Phoenician coast and Egypt). Among the many exquisite finds in gold, crystal, faience, bronze and glass, as well as pottery, outstanding are four tiny (5cm) ivory heads which demonstrate carving of exceptional quality; they may have come from figures of gold-covered wood. (Material from the site is on display in the Réthymnon Museum.)

An important Archaic statue from Eléftherna (a female torso in the Daidalic style) is a long-established exhibit in Herákleion Museum, Gallery XIX. Recent discoveries at Orthí Pétra, such as the lower part of a Kore with well-preserved painted decoration and (in the foundations of a large burial monument) the fragments of an early 6C Kouros executed in local limestone are also of great interest, seen in the light of the Cretan contribution to the development of large-scale Greek sculpture.

A longer visit should include the eastern side of the acropolis hill. The easiest approach is from the Margarítes end of the village street where a good dirt track drops down into the valley to (1km) a curious double church. The 10C (Second Byzantine period) domed, cross-in-square Sótiros Khristós (12C frescoes preserved only in the dome) was built over, and re-used material from, the foundations of a 6C basilica, believed to have been the episcopal church of ancient Eléftherna during the First Byzantine period. Then towards the end of Venetian rule (16C), the 10C Byzantine church had joined on to it (probably to accommodate the Latin rite) the barrel-vaulted, pitched-roof structure of Ayios Ioánnis.

The track continues north along this eastern flank of the acropolis until (after c 1km) a makeshift barrier indicates below (right) the excavated remains of a Roman villa (2C–4C AD) also another basilica of the Early Christian (First Byzantine) period. These were built on the massive artificial terraces (dating back to the Hellenistic period) noted as a 'fine Hellenic platform' by Captain Spratt. A kalderími still leads down to a cistern where foundations of pillars are all that remains of his second ancient bridge.

From Arkhaía Eléftherna you can continue (3km) to Néa Eléftherna and on, either to the Monastery of Arkádi (p 242) or to rejoin (after 14km) the Herákleion–Réthymnon Old Road. This route soon affords a fine retrospective view across the valley to the ancient site marked by the ruined tower and chapel on the acropolis. An open-air sanctuary was uncovered in Néa Eléftherna with large quantities of terracottas of human figures and animals, and also features of architectural interest from the Classical period (nothing remains to visit). 3km beyond the village of Eléftherna, you pass a turn (left) for a reasonable dirt road to Arkádi (see below). If you continue ahead towards the coast, you keep left in *Skouloúphia* to reach the Old Road in *Virán Episkopí*.

Medieval (Ano) Virán Episkopí lies 1km south of the main road, and is approached from the modern village by the side-road down from Eléftherna. From the village street you would take the second dirt road right. Ayía Eiríne, partly hidden (left) by old houses (and a few ugly modern additions), is built into the ruins of a 10C/11C basilica. There was another earlier church on the site which replaced a temple thought to be dedicated to the goddess Díktynna, because an associated milestone records road repairs paid for under her aegis. The basilica may have succeeded Sýbrita (modern Thrónos) as the seat of the bishopric of Agrion after Sýbrita was destroyed by the Saracens. The medieval village was surrounded by a wall, part of which is still standing, as are many contemporary dwellings now often used for livestock. Continue through the village down the hill to a T-junction and turn left. After 1km you come to a bridge over a stream and the romantic ruined church of

Ayios Demétrios. Note the re-used (early Roman) Ionic capital. Returning in the reverse direction by the same track, you can keep straight on along it, to rejoin the main road.

The Old Road nears the coast at *Stavroménos*, passing (left) the Australian war memorial. There is a slip-road to join the Herákleion–Réthymnon New Road. For the monastery of Arkádi it is better to remain on the Old Road, which for 300m runs parallel to the highway on the side away from the sea, and then passes under the highway bridge. Keeping close to the shore it is 7km from the bridge to the main Arkádi turn in Plataniás on the Old Road. (New short cuts are signed along the way.)

From the *Plataniás* junction (4km outside Réthymnon, see also bus services from town to monastery—three a day) the Arkádi road leads inland through great groves of ancient olive trees. After 4km you pass through *Piyí* and soon a short detour is offered to a Byzantine church noted for its elegant architecture.

1km beyond the village, and round a sharp bend, watch for a by-road signed (1km) for Ayios Demétrios. Follow the signs to the edge of the village of the same name and then proceed on foot. The path hugs the whitewashed village church (right) and keeps on downhill c 200m to the restored Byzantine church.

The cross-in-square domed building is tentatively dated to the 12C/13C. Four columns are completed by Corinthian capitals re-used from the First Byzantine period. From the (14C) wall-paintings only one full-length figure of a female saint is preserved, though there is also evidence for earlier fresco decoration. Externally, decorative arches echoing the barrel-vaulting of the cross-arms are emphasised by patterns executed in tiling, and similar patterns are repeated on the domed drum (restored 1971) which is lit by eight arched windows separated by slender columns.

From Piyí the road continues inland to *Loútra* and *Amnátos*, and up a gorge to (17km from the coast) the handsome *Moní Arkadíou, venerated in Crete as a symbol of freedom. This stems from a heroic episode during the 1866–69 revolt against the Turks. Besieged by overwhelming Turkish forces, the defenders of the monastery, under the leadership of the Abbot Gabriel and together with many women and children, chose death rather than capture or surrender. They waited till the enemy broke in, and then blew up the gunpowder magazine, killing themselves and at the same time many hundreds of Turks.

In the little museum, where a guidebook is on sale, relics of this holocaust are preserved. 60m to the west outside the main gate is the cemetery of those who died, with the customary display of skulls. (Annual festival of commemoration 9 November.)

There is also a small tourist pavilion café (erratic summer opening only).

Much of the monastery that you see today dates from the 17C, though the main *gateway* into the courtyard was rebuilt to the original design after the 1866 destruction.

The chief architectural interest lies in the ornate 16C *west façade* of the double-nave church (dedicated to the Transfiguration of Christ and to Sts Constantine and Helen.) This two-aisled design is reflected in the twin pediments of the façade, which are unified by a tall bell-cote (with an inscription dated 1587). In the colonnade below, the pairs of Corinthian columns are evenly spaced, forming three equal bays in which the two doors serve the aisles, and the conventional central doorway is converted into a niche. Thus the Corinthian order was adapted to the double-naved Orthodox church.

On the north side of the courtyard the *Old Refectory*, pitted with bullet holes, and the roofless *gunpowder storeroom*, scene of the historic explosion, are melancholy places. There is a fine view from the adjacent east gate, and to the south towards the peaks of Ida from the walls above.

300m below the monastery, beside the modern road up from Réthymnon, is a well-preserved ancient *bridge* (1685).

The dirt road north east from Arkádi starts near the café and leads (c 6km) to the road between Virán Episkopí and Eléftherna (see above). This is good walking country—Arkádi to Eléftherna c 2 hours.

For Réthymnon direct, retrace the route from the monastery to Plataniás and turn left to follow the Old Road 6km into the centre of town.

RETHYMNON (PEΘYMNON), a pleasant town (pop. 20,000) and capital of its nome as it formerly was of a Venetian province, is widely considered to be the intellectual capital of the island. It houses two departments of the University of Crete with a lively student population drawn from all over Greece. In the old part of the town the relics of its medieval past have begun to be appreciated and restored.

The town stands behind a long sandy beach dominated at the western end by the massive walls of a great fort on the hill above. Below the fort is the picturesque little Venetian harbour and a splendid lighthouse; the harbour, crowded with caiques, is lined by popular tavernas. A new quay now accommodates a regular *ferry service* from Piraeus (the port of Athens).

As an important market centre, the town is connected by bus with most of the villages of the province which reaches to the south coast. In a car it is within easy reach of the wilder regions of both Ida and the White Mountains. Herákleion (for the Archaeological Museum and the Palace of Knossós) is only an hour away by the New Road. For excursions to Eléftherna and the monastery of Arkádi see Route 11B.

Réthymnon offers a wide variety of hotel accommodation, as well as rooms for rent, many self-catering holiday apartments and a youth hostel, and the town's comparatively relaxed environment contributes to an attractive as well as comfortable base for exploring this part of the island. The excellent *Rethymno: a guide to the town* by A. Malagári and H. Stratidákis, translated into English and regularly updated, is strongly recommended. It is widely available from bookshops, craft centres and kiosks as well as at the entrance to the fort.

The *Municipal Information Office* is centrally placed on the road along the beach. Activities designed to appeal to visitors, such as sea cruises from Réthymnon and organised walks in the hinterland, are steadily expanding, and enquiries should start here.

The main *bus station* for the north coast (New Road) routes to Herákleion and Khaniá is one block inland of the through road (Odós Koundourióti) and east of the public garden (see plan). South coast routes leave from the opposite side of the same road. There is a third bus station in Plateía Iróon (behind the beach at its eastern end) for services to the Amári and Mylopótamos valleys. If necessary consult Municipal Information. Where schedules are awkward for the return journey a local village taxi (Agoraíon) can sometimes be of use to connect with a more frequent service.

Town buses serve the hotels and extensive beaches in both directions along the coast. All routes pass along Odós Koundourióti.

Wine Festival in the Public Gardens during the last week of July.

History. Minoan occupation is attested by LMIII tombs at Mastambás, now a residential area at the back of the town. There is little doubt that Réthymnon occupies the site of Greco-Roman Rhíthymna, well known from ancient texts and inscriptions and from its coinage, but the physical remains must lie hidden under later buildings, most probably under the castle hill. Despite the many harsh privations of Venetian rule, the town flourished during that time, a period of artistic and literary distinction. The Venetians surrounded their sea-port with walls and built the great fortress above the harbour, but in 1645, after a siege of 23 days, Réthymnon surrendered to the Turks and became one of the three seats of government set up under Turkish rule.

The City Park or municipal garden, which was laid out over the former Turkish cemetery, is a convenient landmark for the start of a walk through the old part of town. It stands on the main thoroughfare, ΛΕΩΦ. ΚΟΥΝΤΟΥΡΙΩΤΗ (Leophóros Koundourióti), at the junction with the road south across the island (signposted for Ayía Galíni). This is the venue of the annual Wine Festival.

From the north-east corner of the public gardens (see plan), cross the main road and walk downhill under the arch of the Venetian 'Porta Guora' into an atmosphere far removed from modern commercial Réthymnon. Charming Venetian house façades and doorways are preserved, while the minarets and overhanging wooden balconies with iron supports are a reminder of Turkish times. The street, crowded with colourful shops, eventually curves left and widens into ΠΛΑΤΕΙΑ ΤΙΤΟΥ ΠΕΤΙΧΑΚΗ (Plateía Títou Petikháki).

On the left the 'Odeion', or concert hall, has a 17C *doorway* in the style of Sebastiano Serlio from its Venetian days as the Latin church (Santa Maria) of a religious house. The Turks converted the church into a mosque, replacing the timber roof with cupolas and the bell-tower with a *minaret*, but the original doorway remains. It has an arched entrance flanked by pairs of Corinthian half-columns on tall pedestal bases; each pair of columns is separated by a moulded impost with two levels of rounded niches. The Italian architect Serlio (1475–1554) was renowned for his treatise, 'Archittetura' (Venice, 1527), and this doorway has been shown to follow very closely one of his designs.

In summer the plateía is a pleasant open-air café. At the far end of it, just ahead on the left, is the *Rimóndi fountain* (1629), with Corinthian columns and lion-head waterspouts. A Venetian engineer, assessing the city's defences against the Turks, expressed more confidence in Réthymnon's water supply through this fountain than in its fortifications or harbour.

From the plateía a street right, ΟΔΟΣ ΠΑΛΑΙΟΛΟΓΟΥ (Odós Palaiológou) leads past the 16C Venetian *loggia* (which used to house the city's museum collection) to the Venetian harbour, the ferry quay and the bustle of cafés and tavernas along the town beach. Parallel one street inland ΟΔΟΣ ΑΡΚΑΔΙΟΥ (Odós Arkadíou) retains a number of elegant buildings but also offers some high-quality shops for books, prints, leather goods and other souvenirs.

To reach the fort (and the museum) continue from Plateía Petikháki (above) along the street behind the fountain and then left uphill (signed). To the left of the approach ramp is the formidable *main gate* into the enceinte, and to the right, freestanding, is the pentagonal *bastion* built by the Turks as additional defence for the gate, and now housing the Archaeological Museum.

The **Venetian Fort**, known as the Phroúrion (stronghold) or Fortétsa is open 08.00–20.00 (winter 10.00–16.00). Small admission fee. It is well worth visiting both for the imposing fortifications and for the vantage point they afford for views over this part of the island.

Begun in 1573, the fort was a response both to damaging pirate raids which had pillaged the town a number of times during the middle years of the century, and to the growing threat of Turkish intervention in the seas around Crete. The architect was the Venetian engineer Pallavicini. The building took ten years to complete and the cost was enormous, with islanders from a wide surrounding area being dragooned into forced labour. The immense ramparts still stand, with their intriguing loopholed battlements and six great bastions. But in imagination we can fill the area within the walls with the governor's palatial quarters, with buildings of the administration, barracks, a hospital, churches, storerooms, cisterns, with artillery and perhaps squadrons of Albanian and Croatian cavalry, as well as with the mixed Cretan and Venetian population that all this implies.

Visible now in the *lower ward* (left near the main entrance) is a deep well reached by a sloping subterranean passage. In the main *enceinte* are a small church, and a *mosque* with a huge dome, which is thought to have been converted from a Venetian building; nearby there is a lone date palm. The Venetian *governor's quarters*, partially restored, stand near the main gate.

As the Turkish menace increased in the 17C, there were misgivings that the ramparts should have been surrounded by a moat and fears lest the limitations of the harbour below would prevent reinforcement in times of emergency. In 1645, after the town had been overrun by a large Turkish force, the great fort held out for only 23 days.

The **Archaeological Museum** was rehoused in 1990 in the bastion opposite the main gate of the Fortétsa (see above). The move to this beautifully restored building has allowed a new design for the display which can now include elements of the museum collection on view to the public for the first time.

Opening hours: 08.30–15.00. Closed Mondays. Entrance charge, but Sundays and holidays free.

The exhibits, from sites all over the province of Réthymnon, are arranged chronologically, clockwise, from the Neolithic to the Roman periods. A large number of the objects on display speak for themselves as examples of artistic imagination or of craftsmanship, but the intention is clearly also to inform and educate the visitor about the context in which the objects were found, and their significance in understanding the ancient people and places of the region. Thus the excellent labelling in both Greek and English gives a definitive framework of dates, and the introduction to each section, assuming no previous knowledge, supplies maps which helpfully subdivide the sites into categories: cemeteries, peak sanctuaries, caves, other cult areas, city-states and so on, as relevant to the period.

On the left wall as you enter is the start of the *prehistoric* section with Neolithic material from the Yeráni and Ellénes caves; this is one of the most comprehensive exhibits of finds from that period in any of Crete's museums, and includes clay and stone idols, obsidian and bone *tools. Then comes the transition to the Early Bronze Age.

Material from the Protopalatial settlement at Monasteráki (up in the Amári valley) is deservedly allocated two cases. Note the clay model of a sanctuary and an incised stone kernos. Study of the large numbers of clay sealings discovered at this site, recently excavated by the University of Crete, has contributed to a better understanding of administrative aspects of the Minoan economy during the early years of the palaces.

The peak sanctuary of Mount Vrýsinas overlooking Réthymnon was excavated in 1972 but examples of the large quantity of figurines—votive offerings, chiefly of worshippers and cattle, found in rock clefts on the summit—were not on public view until the opening of this new museum. Note the Linear A script incised on a stone vase.

Before the next groups of material excavated from tombs (from Stavroménos on the coast, Apostolí in the Amári valley, the Mastabás cemetery on the outskirts of Réthymnon, among many other sites) there is an instructive outline of Minoan tomb architecture and burial practices. A collection of clay sarcophagi (larnakes) from all over the province illustrates a rich variety of decoration, and excavation photographs add a further dimension. The motifs in the decoration include the octopus, bulls, birds, 'agrímia' in a hunting scene, with the double axe, horns of consecration and 'tree of life'.

The LMIII (1400–1200 BC) cemetery at Arméni just inland of Réthymnon produced a remarkable series of larnakes (burial chests). Some of these have been on show in the Khaniá Museum, but there is now an outstanding display here of grave gifts which accompanied the Arméni burials. Note the reconstruction of the boar's tusk helmet and the evidence for the Linear B script.

Material from the LMIII periods, and the succeeding (transitional) Subminoan, includes figurines of the 'psi' and 'phi' types, so-called because their stylised shapes recall these letters of the Greek alphabet; widely scattered at this period across the eastern Mediterranean, these idols indicate a Mycenaean presence. In the same case are two tall bell- skirted goddess figurines, with characteristically raised arms.

The section of the display dealing with sites dating to the *historical period* in the province begins with an outline of the important new excavations by the University of Crete at the city-state of Eléftherna in the foothills of Mount Ida. From the Geometric and Archaic cemetery known as Orthí Pétra is displayed pottery, including an important series of miniatures, also human and animal figurines, exquisite ivory artefacts and a tripod table for offerings.

The following cases contain artefacts from other regional sites flourishing at various times in the Archaic, Classical, Hellenistic and Roman periods. There is one group from the tomb of an athlete (at Stavroménos), another from a shipwreck off Ayía Galíni. There is an outstanding exhibit of silver and bronze coins, Classical to very late Imperial, from various mints both on Crete and the mainland.

The terracottas on display include Archaic heads and animal figurines, notably from Axós, and shows moulds used in the manufacturing process. The Daidalic style is well represented. One section of wall is devoted to inscriptions of historical significance. There are grave steles from Eléftherna and Stavroménos (athlete's tomb). The cases conclude with 4C red-figure pottery, both imported and from local workshops, and some early (Hellenistic and Roman) glass, including a mould-blown flask and superb core-formed amphoriskoi. On a metal rod the glassmaker shaped a core (of clay or sand with an organic binder) to fit the inside of the body of a vessel, and then wound a trail of glass around this core; sometimes the core may have been dipped in molten glass.

The museum has room for a considerable number of pieces of large-scale sculpture, most of them of Roman date, all clearly labelled. A 1C AD relief of Aphrodite from the city-state of Láppa (Argyroúpolis) is composed of joining fragments discovered during excavations in 1910 and 1964.

12 Réthymnon to the South Coast

A. Via the Amári Valley

65km (40 miles) to Ayía Galíni on the south coast. Recommended round-trip excursion (c 120km; 75 miles) from Réthymnon: 25km Apóstoli at the head of the Amári valley; then a circuit of the valley, down the main road to (48km) Apodoúlou, returning north by the minor road along the western slopes to (92km) Apóstoli, and thence back to Réthymnon. This beautiful area between the Ida massif and Mount Kédros has many frescoed Byzantine churches within easy reach of the road.

There are bus services to the villages of the valley, but the expedition needs careful planning.

On a touring holiday there is the alternative of turning east at Apodoúlou to (c 60km) Kamáres, to link up with Rte 4 to (c 120km) Herákleion.

This route sets off to the south from the junction on the eastern outskirts of Réthymnon (3km east of the centre) where the stretch of the north coast highway from Herákleion meets the Réthymnon bypass—currently under construction (see Rte 11, p 237). The road inland is signed (36km) for Amári.

Immediately there is a right turn for a detour to (7km) *Khromonastíri*, and the church of Ayios Eftíkhios; the abandoned church, dating to the Second Byzantine period is architecturally interesting and preserves remains of 11C frescoes that are among the earliest yet uncovered on the island.

After 4.5km, the deserted village of *Milí* clings to the wall of a narrow valley down on the left. As you approach *Khromonastíri* the road runs straight with the village and its modern church in view ahead; 50m beyond a concrete culvert is the track (signed, left) to Ayios Eftíkhios. It is possible to drive (rough and very narrow) down into the valley, but many will prefer the walk—less than 2km. There is no problem about access to the church which lies below the track (right) with a small-holding close by it.

Inside, a magnificent Pantokrátor looks down on a building strongly evoking former glories. The long nave consists of five bays (no parallel on the island) with the central one raised to form a cross-arm and surmounted by the dome. The 11C frescoes, preserved only in the bema, are in the flat linear style still influenced by the conservative artistic traditions of the Macedonian dynasty in Constantinople. The Christ of the deesis composition was flanked by the Virgin and St. John the Baptist; the extant apostles include St. Peter. Very few examples of frescoes from the Second Byzantine period (961–1204) have survived on Crete.

From the highway junction the Amári valley road soon begins to climb into the hills through groves of huge, aged olive trees. At 6km there is a fine view (right) of Ayios Eftíkhios (see above) on the wooded hillside across the valley. In the distance to the south west, the highest peak, with a white chapel on its summit, is Mount Vrýsinas (860m), site of one of the richest Minoan peak sanctuaries. Finds are now on view in the Réthym-

non Museum. At 8km *Prasés* is attractively situated, and some buildings
are preserved from its Venetian past. On the through road, the cemetery
church of the Panayía (Virgin Mary) has remains of 14C frescoes (key at
kapheneíon near turning into the village centre).

Above the village the road crosses a ridge, and a wide valley opens out
ahead. The rare Bonelli's eagle is sometimes sighted in these hills.

At 11.5km is a turning for (3km) Mýrthios on a cross-country road which joins (in
c 11km, near Arméni) the main road to the south coast from Réthymnon (Rte 12B).
4km beyond Mýrthios is *Gouledianá*, and above the village on an isolated upland
plateau the excavated remains of a 5/6C basilica (p 253).

At 14.5km you cross a tributary stream and enter the eparchy, or district,
of Amári, and, with the valley closing in, the road runs alongside the
main river, the Stavromána.

17km. A good (surfaced) road sets off to the right through beautiful country for (9km)
Patsós and on to Lambíni, near Spíli on Rte 12B. The cave of Ayios Antónios west of
Patsós was intermittently an important sanctuary from the Middle Minoan period
to Roman times, with a cult of Hermes Kranaíos.

At 26.5km *Apóstoli*, with a 14/15C church, stands at the head of the
Amári valley which lies between the Psilorítis range on the east and
Mount Kédros to the west. Steps (right) lead to the church terrace, with
magnificent views of Ida and (further left, marked by a telecommunications mast) the site of the Greco-Roman city-state of Sýbrita. At a
T-junction, less than 1km further on, there is a full view of the valley from
the hamlet of *Ayía Photiní*; the circuit (as recommended in the introductory notes above) will bring you back to this point.

This valley is one of the natural routes between the north and south
coasts of the island, and yet historically it has often served as a remote
refuge, especially after the Venetian conquest and during the Nazi occupation, though the number of war memorials shows that the refuge was
not always secure. It is still a region of unspoilt natural beauty, and there
is a strong sense of community among the 40 villages of the eparchy of
Amári.

The major road keeps left at the Ayía Photiní fork. At the first bend a
left turn uphill is signposted for (1km) *Thrónos* (ancient Sýbrita). In the
middle of the village the frescoed church of the Panayía (dedicated to the
Assumption of the Virgin) is built into the foundations of an Early Christian basilica, with remnants of mosaic floor (possibly 4C and if so re-used
from a previous building). The frescoes (very dark, torch useful) are of
two periods, dated stylistically to the early 14C and the late 14C or early
15C. The paintings of the first period survive only in the bema. An
interesting comparison is possible because the scene of the Presentation
of the Virgin has survived from both periods: on the north wall of the
bema, and on the north side of the vault of the nave (west bay, lower
register). The Transfiguration (south side of the vault) has a graffito date
1491.

The village occupies part of the site of Greco-Roman Sýbrita, which flourished at
least from the 5C BC into the first Byzantine period. The city spread over this hill
with a cemetery at Yéna in the valley below; probably the basilica site was always
one of its focal areas.

An easy 10-minute walk leads up the acropolis above the village, a strongly recommended climb which at suitable seasons will reward wild-flower enthusiasts.

Continue (east) down the main street from the church, and after 50m a ridged concrete slope (left) leads up to an ancient stone path (kalderími) visible from the village street. The path starts to climb, and then briefly levels out along the flank of the hill before it forks left to climb again. On the right of the level path (at the turn and with a dirt track in view ahead) a stretch of the ancient *city wall* is quite well preserved. From here the built path leads to the summit.

There are traces of Classical or Hellenistic walls along the crest, and of a gateway on the east ascent, but little archaeological investigation has yet been undertaken. Among the portrayals on the notably fine coinage are Dionysos and Hermes; dedications to the latter reinforce the suggestion of an undiscovered temple here, perhaps related to the cult of Hermes Kranaíos at the cave sanctuary near Patsós (see above).

The climb is worthwhile for the *view alone. Sýbrita commanded all this fertile, wooded and well-watered Amári valley, and must have owed its prosperity at least in part to its apparently unchallenged position on this important trade route. The city's harbour was at Soulía, the modern Ayía Galíni.

The next recommended objective is *Ayios Ioánnis Theológos (St. John the Evangelist), a little frescoed church below a hermit's cave near *Kalógeros*, but best reached by a footpath (10 minutes) from the main valley road.

Less than 1km after the Thrónos turning you pass a left turn to Kalógeros. Continue 800m on the main road, watching carefully for a well-trodden but narrow path that climbs the bank to the left. The path ascends (5 minutes) to a gate, in front of which you turn uphill left. The way levels out along the hillside, with a wall on your left, and as you pass the hermit's grotto, the church comes into view ahead. An inscription dates the frescoes to 1347. In the bema Christ is flanked by the Virgin Mary and St. John, and this composition honouring the church's patron saint was repeated on the south wall of the nave.

500m further along the road, you will notice in a field (right) the tiny 15C domed and cruciform church of Ayía Paraskeví.

At 31.5km the former *Moní Asomáton* has since 1931 housed an agricultural school. This wealthy monastery had a long tradition of Greek learning and education—the Abbot ran a neighbourhood school during the Turkish occupation—and also a stirring history of support for the Cretan cause. Buildings from the monastery's Venetian past stand alongside those of the modern farming complex, and a huge ancient plane tree provides summer shade. A considerable range of rich liturgical furnishings from the former monastery chapel is preserved in the Historical Museum in Herákleion.

The monastery stands in the angle of two roads. The branch to the right leads through Monastiráki to (4.5km) the village of Amári. In April the fields are colourful with wild tulips and lupins.

On the slopes below *Monastiráki* excavations since 1980 by the University of Crete (directed by A. Kánta) have uncovered an important Minoan settlement. (The site is in view under a blue roof on the approach to the village.) Evidence for monumental architecture during the Middle Minoan period—contemporary with the Old Palaces—as well as the extensive workshop and storage blocks point to the palatial character of the complex, but the most significant finds of that time were two separate archives of seals which are contributing to a fuller understanding of the administrative and economic organisation of Protopalatial society. The more recent work has brought to light a Neopalatial complex of large buildings with wall paintings. At the end of both these periods of use the settlement seems to have been destroyed by earthquake and fire.

Downhill (bell in view) from the memorial in the village plateía is the
Venetian period church of the Arkhistrátigos (St. Michael the Archangel).
Only one frescoed scene remains (the Assumption of the Virgin), but it is
of high quality as is the elaborate carving of the doorway. In the apse of
the church of Ayios Yeóryios, at the top of the village, there is a well-
preserved 'Platytéra' (Virgin with Child, symbolising the Incarnation)
which is said to have been influenced by the art of portable icons.

Outside *Amári*, the little 'capital' of the district, the church of Ayía
Anna preserves the earliest frescoes dated by inscription yet known on
Crete (1225). The paintings are worn and perhaps of interest only to
specialists, but the chapel occupies a fine position in wooded countryside.

Through the hamlet of Opsigiás, just before Amári, there is a solitary church (right)
and 150m beyond this on the left the District Police Station. Opposite, at an acute
angle, a good track leads in less than 1km to Ayía Anna. Originally (as a monastery
church) Ayía Anna had two naves, which explains the walled-up arches along the
south side.

On the way back to the valley road, in Monastiráki, a narrow turning right leads
(3.5km) to *Lambiótes*; at the far end of the village a path (left) will bring you in less
than 1km to the chapel of the Panayía, with elegant frescoes dated to the second
half of the 14C, good examples of the stylistic influences of the Palaiologan Revival.
(Enquire for the key at the houses by the start of the path.)

The main valley road continues south from the Asómatos monastery
through *Aphratés* to (37.5km from Herákleion) *Vizári*. Here, 1km west of
the village, on the site of a large Roman town, are the ruins of an Early
Christian basilica, one of the best preserved on the island.

Opposite the post office in the middle of the village take the side road
right. Out in the country this bends sharply right then left and levels out
between stony remains of the ancient town. 250m from the second bend
an inconspicuous path, right, crosses the ditch and soon runs between
two walls—5 minutes to the basilica site.

The church, excavated by K. Kalokýris, is tentatively dated to the late 8C, not long
before the Arab conquest. Two Saracen coins were found in the destruction debris.
The plan is unusual in that the side aisles end in small apses of their own. In the
south aisle in front of the apse is a stepped font built of tile and cement. The church
floors are also tiled. Not many architectural fragments were found, but there is evidence for a screen mounted between columns dividing the central aisle into a spacious chancel and nave. In spring the site is overgrown and exploration may be
difficult.
The building of this large church reflects the wealth of the Amári valley at the
end of the First Byzantine period, at a troubled time in the eastern Mediterranean
when the island's coastline was frequently harassed by foreign raiders.

40km *Phourphourás* is a starting point for walking in the Ida range. By a
fountain at the entrance to the village is a left turn for detour to (4km)
Plátania. The church of the Panayía, with remains (lowest register only)
of 14/15C frescoes, lies on the right of the main street near the middle of
the village. (Ask for key at kapheneíon opposite church gate.)

Soon after Phourphourás at a crest the Libyan sea comes into view,
with distant views of the Mesará plain and the Asteroúsia mountains.
Through *Kouroutés* and *Níthavris* you reach (51km) *Apodoúlou*.

On the last bend before the village is a LMIII tholos tomb (sign on the left, beside
steps up the bank). A dromos, or passage, cut into the hillside leads to the entrance,

with the lintel still in situ. The tomb, excavated by C. Daváras, had been plundered, but four (disturbed) clay larnakes remained; one with a scene of lamenting figures is now in the Khaniá Museum.

Across the road, just before the tomb, is a sign for the footpath (10 minutes) to the abandoned church of Ayios Yeóryios (mid 14C frescoes by Ieréas Anastásios). There is also a driveable track (concrete surface) starting awkwardly downhill opposite a fine Venetian building in the middle of the village. Keep right at the fork as the broad valley opens out ahead.

On the far side of Apodoúlou the road divides. The left fork follows the southern slopes of Ida to (63km) Kamáres, and on to Zarós, Ayía Varvára and Herákleion (see Rte 4, p 156). The right fork runs down to the south coast at (65km) Ayía Galíni (Rte 12B).

For the circuit of the valley, follow this road south for 5km to the meeting of the two Amári valley roads, where you turn sharp right and begin to climb north again. There are fine tall olive trees as far as the eye can see. After 4.5km, in *Ayía Paraskeví*, the old church of the Panayía stands on a rise (right) in the centre of the village just before the large modern church. (Key at kapheneíon back down the street.) Elegant frescoes dated by inscription 1516.

After *Ayios Ioánnis* (c 60km on the circular route) the scenery becomes grander. You cross the River Plátys which runs into the sea near Ayía Galíni. The old bridge is preserved to the right of the modern one. Now the road climbs above the olive-tree zone to a series of high villages along the slopes of Mount Kédros: *Khordáki, Ano Méros, Drigiés, Vrýses.* Between the first two there are fine retrospective views of the southern coastline, and across the valley the dramatic wall of the Psilo-rítis mountains. The memorials are a reminder that these villages suf-fered severe reprisals for the activities of the Cretan Resistance during the 1940–45 war.

At 82km *Kardáki*. Less than 1km beyond this village, opposite a spreading oak tree, you pass the ruined monastery church of *Ayios Ioán-nis Theológos, Phóti.* The unusual architectural scheme can still be appreciated, though the building is open to the elements and the frescoes have suffered accordingly. A rare feature is the domed narthex. Remains of frescoes: late 13C in the chapel, 14/15C in the narthex. The old stone road on which the monastery lay still runs behind the church.

Through *Yerakári*, which was razed to the ground in 1944, you come to (88.5km) *Méronas*, where the church of the Panayía lies on the right of the road towards the end of the village. The soft pink, three-aisled church shows Venetian influence in its architecture. Some of the frescoes have been uncovered; they are known to have been painted between 1339 and 1341. In the bema, the Hierarchs officiate appropriately, but the portrayal of the Christ child lying on the altar, representing the elements of the Eucharist, is very rare on Crete. In addition, the icon of the Panayía (late 14C) is one of the earliest known on the island. (Key with the village priest—enquire across the road.)

A further 3km brings you back to the T-junction at Ayía Photiní, where you turn left for the last 30km back to Réthymnon.

B.   Réthymnon to the South Coast via Spíli

62km (38m) direct to Ayía Galíni. Convenient bus service.
    A branch road right to Selliá, for (36km) the resort of Plakiás, links up with Rte 15 along the south coast to Sphakiá. A second branch leads to the Préveli monastery near the sea, 35km from Réthymnon.

This itinerary starts from the crossroads by the public gardens in the centre of Réthymnon. The road, signposted for Ayía Galíni, climbs inland (and under the new bridge carrying the bypass) with the town spread out below. *View of the fort.

At 8km, the LMIII *cemetery of Arméni. Immediately over the crest of a long hill, a turning is signed right for Somatá, and the cemetery lies in the grove of Valonia oaks 100m back from the main road. The eminent Greek archaeologist Y. Tzedákis has been excavating here since the early 1970s and has uncovered a remarkable series of approximately 200 rock-cut tombs. There is a fence round the cemetery (though some tombs remain outside).

The official opening hours are 09.00–15.00 except Saturdays and Sundays closed.

Visitors can appreciate the great variety of tomb architecture found here, ranging from chambers little larger than niches to elaborate chamber tombs with a bench round the wall and approached by a stepped or sloping dromos. In a few cases, only the dromos seems to have been completed.

Similarly the burials ranged from a single inhumation without grave gifts to examples of multiple use with successive burials on the floor and also in clay chests or larnakes. The richness of the grave goods which accompanied these burials has been known by repute but with the opening of the new Réthymnon Museum some of the outstanding finds are now on display. They include decorated vases, bronze weapons, tools and ornaments, sealstones and beads. Cult associations were presumed for a quantity of broken pots (both fine and cooking wares) noted on a small paved area linked to a dromos by a channel. One remarkable find, uncommon on Crete, consisted of 60 boar's tusk plates from the covering of a helmet of a type described by Homer. A similar helmet is displayed in Herákleion Museum, Gallery VI.

The tombs yielded an important series of decorated clay larnakes (some in the museum in Khaniá).

The broad main road continues through a forest conservation area of pine, cypress and oak. 2km beyond the cemetery is the pleasant village of Arméni. At 12km, a cross-country road (signed, left, for Karé) leads over gentle and wooded hills to join (after 11km) the Réthymnon–Amári valley route (12A). On the way, high above the village of Goulediá is the probable site of the city-state of Phálanna; two houses investigated by N. Pláton were found to belong to the Archaic period. On the same plateau are the excavated remains of an Early Christian basilica, one of the most remotely situated in the whole island.

2.5km from the main road Karé; 4.5km Goulediá. At the far end of the village take a dirt road right (at an acute angle) which climbs behind the houses, and gains height up a fertile and well-watered valley. After 1km you pass a fountain, and 500m further on, emerge on the rocky upland plateau at the ruins of the village of

Onythé—an increasingly rare glimpse of the old vernacular architecture of the island. In the middle of the little plateau turn left and follow the track north, past a sheep-fold. It is less than 1km to the basilica; keep right where the track forks, and then follow it as it curves left (gate) to end at the site. The mountain to the north is Vrýsinas; on the summit the Minoans established an important peak sanctuary (see finds in Réthymnon Museum).

The basilica, excavated by N. Pláton in the 1950s but not yet fully published, is built on a downward slope from south to north. The narthex, entered down three steps from a porch, has rooms at its north end, probably for a baptistry, and at the south (uphill) end there may have been an atrium. Three doors lead into the aisles; one needs a step because of the slope, and the two side-aisles are of unequal width. Polychrome mosaics (no longer visible) of elaborate geometric designs in the apse, chancel, nave and narthex helped to date the building to the late 5C or early 6C. Much of the chancel and apse had been destroyed by a later chapel, but a collection of small bones deposited in a pit sunk into the chancel floor is interpreted as a foundation offering, similar to that found at Pánormos (Rte 11A).

The main road to the south coast climbs gently into a broad valley growing cereal crops which are harvested in June.

At 18.5km a secondary road diverges right beside a modern cemetery with chapel. This is the turn for Plakiás and also for Selliá (14km from this junction) where you link up with Rte 15 in the direction of Rodákino, Frangokástello and the district of Sphakiá. (This section of Rte 15 is described in the reverse direction from Khóra Sphakíon—see p 278.)

This minor road at first follows a valley running west through a landscape of meandering streams lined with plane trees. There are several small villages, including *Ayios Vasílios*, before (26.5km) *Ayios Ioánnis*; then the road turns south through the Kotsiphós gorge, to emerge above the wide Pláka Bay.

At 29km the road forks. Ahead (c 2km) is Selliá (see above). For Plakiás keep left downhill, continue a kilometre or so through Mýrthios (tavernas with view) and just beyond the village turn right, signposted 3km to Plakiás. (You pass a turning left for a road along the coast to Levkóyia and the Préveli monastery.)

Until not much more than a decade ago **Plakiás** was only a cluster of houses around the tiny quay at one end of a long tamarisk-shaded beach, but it has grown rapidly into a small resort. (A dozen or so hotels heavily booked from abroad, many rooms to rent and a number of tavernas.) This is still an especially fine beach and there is also good swimming from coves along the coast to the east. The walk to the Préveli monastery (see below) is highly recommended (c 2 hours), and the country inland is beautiful and unspoilt.

The main Réthymnon–Ayía Galíni road continues in a south-easterly direction. 20km from Réthymnon (1.5km beyond the cemetery chapel and the turning for the first detour above) a second branch road to the right leads to Moní Préveli, signposted from the Ayía Galíni direction for Plakiás. Beyond Koxaré this road enters the Kourtaliótis gorge of the Megapótomos which flows into the sea near Préveli.

7km from the main road is *Asómatos* where for Préveli you turn left (downhill beside a kapheneíon) towards Levkóyia. (Ahead would lead to Mýrthios and Plakiás.) After 1.5km, just short of Levkóyia, you turn left again on to a dirt road signposted (5.5km) to the monastery.

Walkers from Plakiás can make use of coastal tracks which shorten the distance. The dirt road from Plakiás to Levkóyia passes a number of rocky coves and the occasional beach taverna.

From Levkóyia the Préveli road drops down to the Megapótomos (literally the great river), one of the few rivers on Crete which flows all the year round. After 2km you pass a steeply arched early 19C bridge, and

500m further on are the deserted ruins of the original 16C monastery, Káto (lower) Préveli, set on a slope above the river; its church was dedicated to St. John the Baptist.

In the 17C the Abbot Prévelis built a second monastery, hidden in relative safety in the hills nearby, to which he moved the monastery's valuable library. He dedicated the new church to Ayios Ioánnis Theológos, St. John the Evangelist, and for a time this new foundation was referred to as Píso Moní Préveli (píso meaning behind). The road climbs up to this second monastery.

Round the last corner the splendid buildings, now always known simply as **Moní Préveli**, come suddenly into view. The 19C traveller Captain Spratt enthused over 'this paradise of Crete, in one of the most happily chosen spots for a retreat from the cares and responsibilities of life!' Today the monastery is no longer allowed to accommodate overnight visitors looking for such a retreat.

Open: 08.00–13.00 and 17.00–20.00. The rules on decorous clothing are strictly observed. Only the abbot and two or three monks are now in residence at Préveli, but there is a guardian who opens the church and the small museum (guidebook on sale). If you intend to visit the frescoed church of Ayía Photiní (see below) enquire whether you will need a key.

After the Battle of Crete (1941) the abbot and monks of Préveli organised an escape route for Allied soldiers stranded after the evacuation; there is a commemorative plaque in the courtyard, and a gift of silver candlesticks from Britain is exhibited in the museum.

The present relatively modern church (1836) is surrounded on three sides by picturesque buildings which include the original bakery with a huge oven capable of turning out 800 loaves a day. The terrace commands an extensive ˙view down to the Libyan Sea. In the lower courtyard the fountain has an inscription dated 1701. On either side of it are a long stable and a workshop for making beeswax candles, and behind is an underground chamber, a naturally insulated cold store.

Early in the period of Turkish occupation (1669–1898) Abbot Prévelis's monastery was granted a privileged position subject directly to the Patriarchate in Constantinople. It acquired great wealth for Cretan money was thereby protected from seizure by the Turks. It became a focus of Greek learning and education, and the monks ran many secret schools. The monastery became known as a strong ally of Cretan nationalism. During the 1866 Rebellion the fast steamship, the 'Arkádi' (purchased in Liverpool) made several sorties from the free Greek mainland along the south coast of the island, running in guns and ammunition (and boot-leather, among other necessities) for the insurgents, and taking off to safety women and children, as well as the Cretan wounded. J.E. Hilary Skinner, a reporter for the London *Daily News*, sailed in the 'Arkádi', and gave a fascinating account of the experience in his book 'Roughing it in Crete'. Préveli was an important link in this chain of relief operations.

The tradition of support for Cretan independence persisted through the 1940–45 war and then, as before, the monastic community suffered because of its involvement.

To walk to the palm-fringed Préveli beach, return 1.5km along the approach road. The broad path can be clearly seen starting across a flat expanse of clifftop towards the sea (15 minutes from the road). You can also drive to the sea down the river valley (see below).

For the frescoed chapel of Ayía Photiní continue 1km further. The road bends left and right, and (at 2km from the monastery) crosses a culvert.

100m beyond this the little church is in view among olive trees in the valley below, but for the easiest path continue 300m (across a second culvert) to a left bend where there is room to park. From here (10 minutes to the chapel) first follow the water pipe south, and then at the ridge strike downhill. The path is making for the river, so it is necessary to branch right just above the chapel.

The frescoes date from the late 14C/early 15C. Ayía Photiní is among the female saints (named as Paraskeví, Marína, Kyriakí and Eiríne) who, with the Archangel, line the south wall.

To drive to the sea (5.5km detour) at the mouth of the Megapótamos near Préveli beach (see above), you cross the river at the 19C bridge near the ruined monastery, and immediately turn right along the river. Soon you recross it by another picturesque and earlier bridge and continue the descent down the valley. There has been a taverna at the cove in recent years. A walk (scramble) of 10 minutes west along the rocks brings you to the palm-fringed beach.

From the Koxaré junction (see above) the main Réthymnon– Ayía Galíni road continues south east in the direction of Spíli. After 3km, in the middle of *Mixórrouma*, a side-road left signed Karínes leads (1km) to the former episcopal church of the Panayía at *Lambíni*, a large domed church of cruciform three-aisled type looking out over the valley. An unusual feature is that the east cross-arm is longer than the west one. Externally the transerse vaults are emphasised by decorative recessed arches, while the dome rests on a blind-arcaded drum. A plaque left of the doorway commemorates a Turkish atrocity in 1827 when the congregation was burnt to death in the church.

Fragments of two layers of frescoes (14C– early 15C) have been uncovered. The key is held at one of the houses nearby.

The minor road (now surfaced all the way) continues east through beautiful hillcountry to Patsós and on to join (after c 25km) the main road up to the Amári valley (Rte 12A).

On the main road south from Lambíni *Spíli*, 30km from Réthymnon, lies on a steep hillside that is well-watered and fertile all the year round. In the plateía, one of the most delightful on the island, a picturesque tree-shaded fountain has a long row of 19 lions' head spouts. (Tavernas and a small hotel.)

Beyond Spíli you follow a valley between Mount Kédros (1777m) to the north and Sidérotas (1136m) to the south. Great efforts have been made to improve this road and stretches have been realigned, but the terrain is liable to subsidence, and it is wise to anticipate potholes and broken road edges. Beside the broad river bed of the Plátys the road nears the coast. The Amári valley, Timbáki and Phaistós are to the left. Turn right to run down (3km) into *Ayía Galíni*.

Around a tiny harbour this village has developed into the principal resort on the south coast. It caters particularly for the inexpensive end of the package holiday market, and in summer its charms attract more people than it can comfortably absorb. The rocky beach at the mouth of the Plátys has a long-established camping site.

13   Réthymnon to Khaniá

Direct route 59km (37 miles) by north coast highway (New Road): 21.5km
Yeoryioúpolis; 26km Vrýses; c 50km Aptéra above Soúda Bay. The Old
Road (superseded as a through route) meanders into the hills through (c
20km) Episkopí and returns to the coast at (30km) Yeoryioúpolis. All along
the way to Khaniá there are side-roads to the south for recommended
excursions into the eastern and northern foothills of the White
Mountains—to the monastery of Prophítis Ilías at Roústika, to
Argyroúpolis and the frescoed church at Myrioképhala, from Aptéra to
Stýlos and Kyriakoséllia. The relatively unspoilt Vámos peninsula lies to
the north of the highway route.

Frequent bus service by the New Road, twice-daily by the the Old Road
through Episkopí and Vámos.

The main road through Réthymnon continues westward from the centre
of town. After c 3km (at the junction with the planned bypass) the Old
Road diverges inland, and the highway or New Road keeps close to the
shore; the kilometre posts give distances from Khaniá.

A popular (and recommended) excursion from Réthymnon (c 20km) is to the monas-
tery of Prophítis Ilías at *Roústika*, founded towards the end of the Venetian period
(Feast Day 20 July). Take the Old Road here and after 12km turn left off it (signed).
The monastery is on the south-east edge of the village with superb views back to
the coast. Two 17C bells hang in the bell-cote of the domed three-aisled church.
   In the picturesque village the double-naved church of the Panayía and Sotíros
Khristós (the Virgin and Christ the Saviour) has frescoes in the north aisle (Panayía)
which are dated by donor inscription 1381–82. Some of the iconography reflects
western influence but the scenes from the Hymns to Mary recall the almost complete series at Valsamónero (Rte 4).

At 6.5km on the New Road, below the *Yeráni bridge*, is a cave (not open
to the public) only discovered in 1967 during the construction work for
this road. The Yeráni cave was in use as a sanctuary during the Neolithic
period, and a series of finely worked Late Neolithic bone and obsidian
tools from it is exhibited in Réthymnon Museum. Also of interest from the
excavation was a find in pleistocene levels of bones of the curiously
named dwarf giant deer.
   Now the Levká Ori (White Mountains) are in view ahead. The road
runs for 10km parallel to a fine sandy shore; there are frequent access
points, and though development is beginning at several places most of
the beach is relatively deserted. Midway along it there is a long-
established camping site. The bay is not always as innocent as it appears
in calm weather, and even strong swimmers should be wary of unexpected currents. Early in the year the stream beds which the road crosses
may be of interest to birdwatchers.

13.5km. A recently improved side-road sweeps up (3km) to Episkopí. This can be
used as a short-cut to the detour from Yeoryioúpolis (see below), and may particularly help those using buses.

At 21.5km *Yeoryioúpolis*, at the end of the bay, is just off the highway
where a bridge carries the Episkopí road inland from the coast.
(Approaching from the west leave the highway at the main Vrýes junction and take the very pretty minor road which follows the river valley

through the marshy approach to the village known as the *almyró*, from the Greek word for saline.) Egrets, on migration in April, are among the many birds which appreciate this terrain.

Yeoryioúpolis is named after Prince George, High Commissioner of Crete (1898–1906), who had a shooting lodge here. During the last ten years this village at the mouth of the Vrýsanos river has developed rapidly from a beguilingly peaceful place shaded by eucalyptus trees, with a quay for one or two fishing boats at the end of the long beach. However it has still managed to retain some of the original character. It now has several Class C hotels, one right on the beach, and a wide choice of rooms for rent and tavernas. Freshwater springs back from the stretch of beach immediately to the east of the harbour produce unexpectedly cold patches of sea which may have a particular appeal in the summer heat.

The village makes a good base for exploring the Vámos peninsula which is still relatively undisturbed by tourist development.

Yeoryioúpolis stands on the site of Amphímalla, port of ancient Láppa, one of the more powerful Greco-Roman cities of western Crete. The Dorian city of Láppa was destroyed during the Roman invasion in 67 BC but later flourished again until the Arab occupation.

A recommended detour inland leads to (16km) Argyroúpolis built on the site of Láppa (of which little is therefore preserved); however the village retains strong hints of its more recent (medieval) past, and occupies a fine position above the Mouséllas river valley, looking back to the sea from the wooded eastern foothills of the White Mountains. The road continues a further 12km into the hills to the Second Byzantine period frescoed church at Myrioképhala. The return route drops down to the only freshwater lake on the island.

From Yeoryioúpolis take the road south (signposted Kournás) to cross the highway by a bridge. After 2km keep straight ahead when the Kournás road leads off to the right. At 8km there is a second turn for Kournás, the way to the lake on the return journey. After 10km you reach *Episkopí*, and towards the end of the village fork right to *Argyroúpolis*. On the approach to the village (c 14.5km, at the sign for Así Goniá, right) keep straight ahead to arrive by the upper road at a plateía in front of a large church and a war memorial; the dates 1912–18 are a reminder of Greece's Balkan War. The plateía gives a bird's eye view of the the the pitched roofs typical of the mountain villages of western Crete. From the plateía you can explore downhill on foot. The architecture of one or two of the old buildings reflects the style of the Cretan aristocracy who made this an important centre during the period of Venetian rule.

The country around Argyroúpolis is a little-known part of Crete, but it repays exploration. The road continues (south) from the war memorial, 12km to *Myrioképhala* (at a height of 500m) where the former monastery church of the Panayía, a foundation of the 10/11C evangelist Ayios Ioánnis Xénos, has Second Byzantine period frescoes that are among the earliest on the island. When you reach the village keep on downhill till the street widens under spreading trees. The church is in view standing in a courtyard below the road left. Fragments of frescoes (early 11C) are preserved in the dome, bema and south cross-arm, as well as four scenes from the Passion of Christ in the west cross-arm which are later (end of 12C) but still predate Venetian rule on the island.

From the turning on the way into Argyroúpolis (on the approach from the coast, see above) a beautiful road climbs 6km to the west into the foothills of the White Mountains to *Así Goniá* (at 400m) home village of the author of *The Cretan Runner* (see Bibliography). A great festival, the blessing of the sheep, is celebrated here on St. George's Day (23 April unless this falls in Holy Week).

To return to the coast by way of *Lake Kournás*, at first retrace the route from Argyroúpolis. Before Episkopí, across the valley (left) the ruins of another medieval village, Arkhontikí, can be seen rising above the modern houses. 2km beyond Episkopí, turn left on a good dirt road to (4km) *Kournás*. The surface is asphalt from there on. After the village you descend steeply to the hamlet of Kástellos with a *view as you approach the only freshwater lake on Crete (160 acres, 65 hectares). There is holiday activity in summer but out-of-season a footpath round the shore (leisurely circuit, c 1 hour) is little frequented.

Passing the lake, continue until you meet (3km) the direct road from Episkopí to the coast. At the north coast highway turn left for Yeoryioú-polis.

After 4km on the New Road you arrive (26km direct from Réthymnon) at the junction for Vrýses (Rte 15).

The highway, beautifully planted with cypress, tamarisk, mimosa and oleander, cuts across the peninsula of Vámos, and beyond the Kiliáres river nears the sea at the entrance to *Soúda Bay*.

Before this, at 40.5km, a detour right leads (1km) to *Kalýves*. This pleasantly old-fashioned village resort is strung out along the waterfront at the eastern end of a sandy beach looking across Soúda Bay to the hills of the Akrotíri. 4km east along the north coast of the Vámos peninsula the hamlet of *Almirída* has several recommended fish tavernas on the beach and is growing to accommodate visitors. From Kalýves the coast road continues west towards Khaniá, 5km to Kalámi where it rejoins the highway. You cross the mouth of the Kiliáres, often a rewarding area for bird-watchers.

On the promontory above Kalámi the New Road passes a massive Venetian fort, now a prison known by its Turkish name, 'Itzedin'. A little way beyond it there is a *view of the entrance to the superb natural harbour of Soúda, one of the largest in the Mediterranean, and sheltered by the hills of the Akrotíri peninsula. The Venetian fortress, on the island of Soúda towards the far shore, was built to guard the narrows, and did not surrender to the Turks till 1715, 46 years after the fall of Candia (Herákleion). In 1941 the anchorage played an important role, first during the evacuation of the Allied Expeditionary Force from the mainland of Greece, and then in supplying the garrison during preparations for the Battle of Crete, though by this time all shipping was at the mercy of the Luftwaffe which had undisputed command of the air. Now the area is a Greek and NATO naval base, so photography is strictly forbidden.

At 46.5km is a left turn for a detour to (3km) the site of ancient **Aptéra**, which is said to take its name (Wingless Ones) from the Sirens who, defeated in a musical contest by the Muses, plucked off their wings and, drowning in the bay below, formed the islets there.

From its vantage point at the mouth of the island's safest harbour, Aptéra, already flourishing by the 7C BC, was one of the largest and most powerful of the Greco-Roman city-states of western Crete. The impressive Early Hellenistic city walls and the huge Roman cisterns indicate the scale and strength of the city at those times. Aptéra was destroyed by the Arabs, but flourished again in the Second Byzantine period when it was the seat of a bishop.

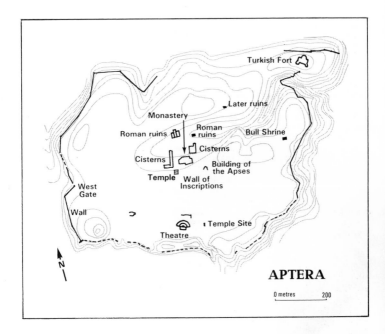

From the turning off the main road you ascend to the site, keeping left in (1km) *Megála Khoráphia*. 1km beyond this village, where the road bends left, there is (right) a fine stretch of defensive *wall* in polygonal masonry. Ahead in the ruins of the overlapping walls are traces of the main *west gate* with towers (see plan). At the top of the hill the road divides: left for a deserted Turkish fort (*view), and right for the partly restored monastery of Ayios Ioánnis Theológos. Scattered excavations have taken place since 1987; the centre of the site is fenced but not always locked. If restricted hours apply, the site will not open on Mondays.

Aptéra is a vast site, with remains scattered on a plateau surrounded by 4km of defensive walls still standing to 3m high in places. The rare Eleonora's falcon sometimes hunts across this upland, perhaps from breeding grounds on the off-shore islands further west.

In the angle of the paths in front of the monastery a small *double-cella temple* (2C BC) built of clamped ashlar blocks was excavated by German archaeologists in 1942. The temple, without central communicating door, would have been dedicated to a pair of divinities. Across the path to the east a *Wall of Inscriptions*, probably part of an important public building, was seen by the English scholar R. Pashley (1834); excavated in the mid 19C, it no longer survives.

The large L-shaped building, of concrete faced with brick, is one of two Roman *cistern complexes*. The remains of a small theatre are now little more than a hollow in the ground with traces of seating preserved. Two further temples are recorded from this site; one, excavated, is known as the *Bull Shrine* from figurines found nearby, and one has been identified only by its preserved Doric column fragments.

In spring the undergrowth may make exploration of the outlying parts of the site difficult or impossible.

From Megála Khoráphia, a minor road leads inland (south) 6km to *Stýlos*, and on into the wooded foothills of the White Mountains to Ayios Nikólaos at Kyriakosélia which is comprehensively decorated with early 13C wall-paintings. It is also one of the most romantically situated Byzantine churches on the island.

After 2km you pass (left) a sign for the Minoan settlement of Stýlos just above the road. A well-preserved LMIII tholos tomb was excavated with stone-lined dromos and vaulted chamber; evidence for a settlement was found nearby also a kiln now under a protective roof.

As the road descends the long hill before the village of Stýlos you catch a glimpse of a solitary Byzantine church (domed and cruciform) in the the cultivated valley ahead. (A turning right is signed 8km back to Maláxa on a bluff looking out over the Bay of Soúda—see below.)

The partly-ruined church of the Panayía Serviótissa is all that remains of a monastery founded in 1088 by monks from the monastery of St. John the Evangelist on Patmos. For the easiest path, continue to the bridge across the river (Kiliáres) where a track runs back to the church through the orange groves (15 minutes on foot).

At the end of the village of Stýlos fork right uphill to climb (with fine retrospective views of the north coast) 5km to Samonás. The key for Ayios Nikólaos is held at a house on the left of the road at the far end of the village just before the road turns left to leave it. The guardian or his wife will accompany you the further 3km (last 1km on a good dirt road) to the church now isolated in a remote valley at *Kyriakosélia*, wooded with cypress, plane trees, olives and figs.

Ayios Nikólaos is a single-naved church of three bays (11/12C with later addition at the west end); the central bay is raised to take the dome supported on an elegant drum lit by eight slender arcaded windows. A highly important set of frescoes is dated 1230–36. At this time the Venetians were already introducing colonial rule and their western church in the city of Candia, but these wall-paintings in this remote part of the island are apparently entirely unaffected. They continue in the strictest traditions of Byzantine style and iconography, under the influence of the aristocratic Komnenian style which emanated from Constantinople during the previous century.

The road continues (soon surfaced again) climbing into the White Mountains, 3km to a T-junction on the edge of Ramní (left for the return to the coast through Néo Khorió). At the junction you can turn right to (a further 3km) Karés at a height of 500m. Beside a war memorial shaded by a huge plane tree in the plateía of the Revolutionary Assemblies 1821–66 the road ends, but the old stone-paved kalderími leads on enticingly into the mountains.

The north coast highway (New Road) continues west from the Aptéra turning, high above Soúda Bay, with splendid views across to the *Akrotíri peninsula*. At 51.5km a road diverges right signed for the Soúda ferry.

You can turn off here to visit the *Commonwealth War Cemetery* at the head of the bay. Past the naval installations you come down to the waterfront in Soúda at a plateía with cafés (by the Piraeus ferry quay). Continue towards Khaniá (alternative approach), and in less than 1km turn right (signed for the airport); the road follows the shore for c 2km.

The cemetery, beautifully planted and tended, occupies a superb position at the head of the bay. It contains the graves of 1527 men (862 British, 446 New Zealanders, 197 Australians, 22 from other Commonwealth countries) who were killed in the last ten days of May 1941 during the Battle of Crete. There is a brief account of the campaign just inside the cemetery gate (see also p 30).

In 1963, 19 First World War graves were transferred here from the Consular Cemetery, as were 51 others dating back to 1897.

Among the graves (10E) is that of John Pendlebury, the English archaeologist shot by the Germans on 22 May 1941 as a member of British Intelligence. From 1929 Pendlebury continued the work of Sir Arthur Evans at the Palace of Knossós. He is remembered for a legendary series of travels on foot throughout even the wildest parts of the island, winning the friendship and respect of very many Cretans and searching for hidden evidence of Crete's past; he published the results in 'The Archaeology of Crete', still in print. At the outbreak of war Pendlebury joined the army and was sent back to Crete to coordinate preparations for its defence. He was captured and killed during the German attack on Herákleion. After the war the people of Herákleion held a memorial service for him; an address given by the eminent Greek archaeologist Dr N. Pláton included the eulogy: 'Dear friend, Crete will preserve your memory among her most sacred treasures. The soil which you excavated with the archaeologist's pick and enriched with a warrior's blood will shelter you with eternal gratitude.'

Staying on the New Road you come to the beginning of the Khaniá bypass, where the slip-road right is signposted for (3km) Soúda. Despite the signs for Khaniá ahead (8km) the city centre is more easily negotiated if you leave the highway here. The bypass is completed only as far as (5km) the Mourniés junction (left 1.5km into the village which is much visited as the birthplace of Elefthérios Venizélos). Engineering has however begun for the next stretch, which will eventually join the coast road west of Khaniá.

At Nerokoúrou, on the hillside just south of the bypass, a joint Greek–Italian excavation (1977–80) investigated the foundations of a MMIII–LMI villa, including a large rectangular room with access between two columns to a small closed courtyard. The discovery was of particular interest because comparatively little is known about the western part of the island during the Bronze Age. The site is just north of a partly ruined Venetian farmhouse visible from near the start of the bypass (slip-road after 2km); unfortunately it is not possible to view it properly from outside the protective fence. Finds are on display in the Khaniá Museum (Case 7).

For Khaniá leave the highway at the start of the bypass, and at the end of the slip road (joined from the right by the old road from Soúda) turn left and continue along an avenue of eucalyptus trees.

After 5km, Maláxa is signed left (14km) and a well-engineered road climbs the escarpment which has played a part in the defence of the anchorage at the head of Soúda Bay during many periods of its history. The views are stunning. The drive up to the village at a height of 500m (tavernas and kapheneíons) is a recommended evening excursion from Khaniá.

To complete the present route you continue west on the road from Soúda until you are compelled to fork right down a one-way street system. This leads (signed *kéntro* high up on lamp posts) straight ahead through a suburb of faded elegance to Odós Stratigoú Tzanakáki, at the bottom of which is the bustle of the east–west road in front of the cruciform covered market in the centre of Khaniá.

14 Khaniá and Excursions in the Locality

KHANIA (XANIA), officially plural, Ta Khaniá (pop. 50,000), is the administrative capital of its 'nome' or province, and the second city of Crete. The old town preserves many features of its Venetian and Turkish past. Khaniá makes an agreeable base for exploring western Crete, and as a tourist centre is still geared more to the independent visitor rather than to the mass market. The Archaeological Museum housed in a restored Venetian church is an added attraction.

Travellers at the planning stage are urged elsewhere in this Guide to consider the possiblity of starting their holiday in Khaniá, to enjoy the leisurely pace of this end of the island before embarking on the bustle of Herákleion, and the demands of the major Minoan sites.

Tourist Information: the NTOG works from fourth floor premises in the Pantheon, a new corner block in Plateía 1866, with an entrance round the corner at 40 Odós Kriári. The office is open 08.00–14.00, weekdays only; tel. (821) 26 426.

In recent years there has been a municipal information bureau in the more convenient location of the Janissaries Mosque on the Outer Harbour; this was a model of its kind—in the range of useful information easily accessible on notice boards, in the extended opening hours and in the provision of exchange facilities. However in 1992 the mosque was closed for major restoration work and future plans are uncertain.

Tourist Police: Odós Karaiskáki, tel. 24 447, open all day.

Airport at Sternés, 13km east of the city on the Akrotíri peninsula. Olympic Airways summer schedule: four flights a day from Athens (and daily connection with London Heathrow). Airport bus to and from Khaniá Olympic Terminal opposite the public gardens in Odós Tzanakáki and in high season also to Réthymnon. Many charter companies now operate direct to Khaniá (see Practical Information: Getting to Crete).

Directions for leaving the airport in a hired car: bear left round the end of the runway, and (1km) turn right on to the main Sternés–Khaniá road. 5km along this road, a fork left to Soúda is the route to (c 7km) the north coast highway for destinations east of Khaniá. The main road continues straight ahead, and descends, with views over Khaniá Bay, to a T-junction with the coast road. Here turn left, almost in front of the Dóma hotel, and soon cross a main dual-carriageway into the suburb known as Koúm Kapí, to arrive (13km) in the centre of Khaniá in front of the covered market. For destinations further west keep on the main road through town. Khaniá is carefully signed; look for directions high up on lamp standards or electricity pylons. (Town plan at end of Guide.)

Car ferry services from Athens (Piraeus) dock at Soúda (6.5km to the east). Year-round nightly service by ANEK and sailings three nights a week by Minoan Lines. ANEK office: Plateía Soph. Venizélou, opposite the covered market, almost next to the National Bank, tel. 23 636. Minoan Lines: 8 Odós Khálidon, near the harbour, tel. 24 352. Buses (frequent) to Soúda stop on the main road in front of the market.

For car ferry service to the Peloponnese (Greek mainland) see Kastélli Kisámou (Rte 19).

Hotel accommodation, provided at all price levels, is most desirable with harbour views, but the seafront is now very noisy at night. Khaniá offers a great number of rent rooms and pensions; the Kastélli and Topaná quarters around the harbour (see below) are suggested as good places to start enquiries, but the Koúm Kapí Bay to the east of the inner harbour may be quieter. Advance booking of hotel rooms is advisable in the high season and essential during Battle of Crete Week.

An invaluable leaflet (widely available in recent years) is entitled 'Plan your inexpensive accommodation in Canea district'. It is the result of a co-operative effort by owners and landlords to list (with telephone numbers) and advertise their NTOG-approved rent rooms and self-catering apartments; it covers both the city and the whole nome or province of Khaniá.

Commemoration of the Battle of Crete, with many organised festivities, takes place during the last week of May.

Youth Hostel: 33 Odós Drakonianoú (not on plan; Ayios Ioánnis bus from in front of the covered market).

Tavernas on or near the Outer Harbour.

Post Offices: the main post office is at the market end of Odós Tzanakáki. A subsidiary (caravan), for both mailing and currency exchange, operates in Plateía Mitrópolis, in front of the cathedral.

OTE (Telephone Company headquarters) next door to main post office. Khaniá area code 0821. Open 07.00–23.00.

Bus station for out-of-town services at the south-west corner of Plateía 1866; these buses are green. Town buses are blue; their stops are on the main through road opposite the market, and in Plateía 1866.

Swimming: 20 minutes west on foot from centre to Néa Khóra beach. Buses (blue) from Plateía 1866, marked Kalamáki or Galatás (ΚΑΛΑΜΑΚΗ or ΓΑΛΑΤΑΣ). Kastélli Kisámou buses (green; four a day) will stop further along this coast (see Rte 19). On the Akrotíri peninsula, Stavrós and Kalathás are popular (also convenient bus service).

Guided tours. A great number of agencies operate successfully in this field; the following are well-established and can be contacted by telephone if necessary: Canea Travel, 28 Tzanakáki, near the main post office (tel. 24 780); Kydonia Travel, 10 Karaiskáki, inland of the market and east of Plateía 1866 (tel. 57 412); Aptera Travel, 11 Ktistáki, near the municipal gardens (tel. 52 666). Diktynna Travel at 103 Odó Khálidon (the uphill end of the street, just out of Plateía 1866) is a small family business offering a friendly service (tel. 41 458).

Car parking near the waterfront is not easy. The harbour quays are closed to cars from the end of March till October (except from 07.00–11.00), and strict controls are enforced, under threat of the removal of number plates and a substantial fine. Tourist status does not provide immunity. There are meter bays in Plateía 1866 opposite the main taxi rank, and on the east side of the covered market. There the street beside the minaret (Odós Daskaloyiánni, signed at the junction with the main road 'to the Old Town') leads to an area centred on Odós Kaneváro where unrestricted parking may be found in the side streets. On the road in from the airport (see above and town plan) the area around the stadium, within 5–10 minutes walk from the market, has also to date been free of restrictions, and is a little removed from the traffic hassle usually encountered in the centre.

Mountain climbing: contact the Secretary of the Alpine Club at 90 Odós Tzanakáki (tel. 24 647). The premises are staffed by volunteers and are usually open only 19.00–22.00. In case of difficulty consult the NTOG. The club maintains the Kallérgis and Volikás refuge huts in the Levká Ori (White Mountains).

RC Church on Odós Khálidon near the Archaeological Museum.

Hospital: Οδός Δραγούμι (Odós Dragoúmi).

History. Khaniá lies on the site of ancient Kydonía, founded according to legend by Kydon, a grandson of King Minos; the place-name (ku-do-ni-ja) occurs in the Linear B tablets of Knossós, and is familiar from many ancient literary sources. Since the 1960s, extensive excavations on the Kastélli hill above the harbour have confirmed the existence of a Bronze Age settlement from EMII–LMIIIB (c 3000–1200 BC). Despite partial destruction by fire in LMI, this site continued to flourish after the destruction of Knossós, and it seems likely that the centre of Mycenaean power was transferred here. Modern occupation makes it difficult to prove the existence of the presumed palace, but the architecture so far uncovered, and the range and quality of the finds, demonstrate that the culture was undoubtedly Palatial in style.

There was Geometric period occupation on the Kastélli, and Kydonía was prominent in the politics of the Classical and Hellenistic city-states. It minted coinage from the 5C BC, and by the 2C was the leading city in western Crete. It fell to the Roman commander Metellus early in the campaign of 69 BC but went on to flourish throughout the period of Roman rule, and in the first Byzantine period became the seat of a bishop.

The etymology of the name Khaniá is uncertain, but it may have derived from the place-name Alkania, known from an ancient inscription. During the Venetian occupation it was rendered as La Canea. In 1266, the Genoese, frustrated in their ambi-

Khaniá in the early years of Turkish rule, by (?Claude) Aubriet

tion to control the whole island, took the city from the Venetians and held it till 1290. When Venetian rule was restored, the new buildings included a cathedral, a rector's palace and a theatre on the Kastélli hill, which, as the Venetians' Castel Vecchio, had a wall around it by the mid 14C, partly on the line of earlier Byzantine fortifications. La Canea prospered both materially and culturally at this time. But in 1537 the threat of raids by Turkish corsairs such as the notorious Khaireddin Barbarossa compelled Venice to fortify the whole town. The wall had four bastions and a great moat nearly 50m wide, which ran along the line of what are now the streets Skalídi and Khátzi Mikháli Yiánnari. The architect of the fortifications was the Italian Michele Sanmicheli who was also responsible for the great walls of Candia (Herákleion), but these at La Canea were less successful for in 1645 the city held out against the Turks for only two months. It became the seat of a Pashalik and in the 19C the island was governed from the Kastélli hill. The English scholar Robert Pashley landed at Khaniá in 1834 and was impressed by its peaceable nature for by this time over three-quarters of its population professed the Moslem faith. However, from the viewpoint of the movement for Cretan independence, it was from this city that the heroic uprisings originating in the mountainous hinterland were ruthlessly repressed.

The Turkish occupation ended in 1898. The Great Powers (Britain, France, Italy and Russia) installed the Greek Prince George as High Commissioner, and Khaniá was made the capital of an independent Crete. It remained the capital city after 1913 when Crete became part of Greece, until in 1971 this title was transferred to Herákleion, the geographical centre of the island. Khaniá retains the island's highest judicial authority, the Court of Appeal, and houses the Art and Architecture departments of the new University of Crete.

A useful starting point on the town plan is the cruciform *covered market* constructed in 1911 and now one of the landmarks of Khaniá. On the south (inland) side a paved open space borders the busy main road and traffic junctions, but looking up (east) from here a graceful *minaret* is conspicuous as the relic of a Turkish mosque. With your back to the market, ahead (broadly speaking) is modern commercial Khaniá, and behind you the old crowded city of Venetians and Turks ending at the harbour.

The busy main road (Khátzi Mikháli Yiánari, a famous name in the district of Kydonía during the struggle for independence) leads west past a little plateía commemorating the Battle of Crete to the central Plateía 1866, green with trees and shrubs. (Main taxi rank and some metered car parking.) On the east side is the NTOG office (see above), and south of this big square is the regional *bus station*.

Immediately across the dual-carriageway main road from the covered market is the National Bank, and just into ΟΔΟΣ ΤΖΑΝΑΚΑΚΗ (Odós Tzanakáki), leading away from you, the post office is next door to the telephone and telegraph office (OTE). Along this busy commercial street are tour agencies, car-hire firms and Olympic Airways, but also the *municipal gardens* with a pleasantly shaded café.

One block beyond the gardens turn left for the **Historical Museum and Archives** (open Monday–Friday only: 08.00–13.00, admission free) at 20 Odós Sphakianáki in an area of 19C villas and fashionable apartments. The collection of historical records held here is considered second in importance in all Greece only to those of Athens. Translation of the labels is a little haphazard; a pocket dictionary might be useful.

The museum exhibits are arranged on two floors. The first room to the right of the entrance is devoted to the politician and statesman Eleuthérios Venizélos (1864–1936), Khaniá's most distinguished citizen of modern times; here and in the hall are exhibits connected with the penultimate stage (1896–98) of the struggle for independence in which he played a leading part. A Greek force was sent to support the Cretan Revolutionary Assembly, and despite the initial ambivalence of the Great Powers, the Turks were finally compelled to withdraw from the island. But not until 1913 did the flag of Greece at last fly from the Firkás overlooking the harbour of Khaniá.

At the foot of the staircase is a 16C cupboard elaborately carved with hunting scenes; its three sets of doors conceal drawers. It is rare for Venetian furniture of this quality to have survived on the island to the present day. Upstairs there is an outstanding collection of Venetian maps and topographical engravings, with several of contemporary Khaniá but also including a view of Herákleion which shows the great Latin church of the Franciscans dominating the city skyline from the hill where the archaeological museum now stands.

However the majority of the exhibits in the museum are related to the long struggle against the Turks for Cretan independence, and they illuminate the spirit of those engaged in it, as much as the events themselves. Chronologically they begin with a portrait of Daskaloyiánnis, leader of the 1770 Sphakiot rebellion, which hangs in the upstairs corridor. There is a series of portraits of the 19C regional commanders; their proud bearing as well as examples of their formidable weaponry proclaim their deadly earnest. An imposing collection of bishops is a reminder of the close involvement of the Orthodox church. The British Consul in Crete from 1870–85, Thomas Backhurst Sandwith, was an observer known to have been sympathetic to the Cretan cause.

On the landing at the top of the stairs, the theme of resistance to invaders is extended to resistance to the Germans during the Second World War. The New Zealander General Bernard Freyberg VC was Supreme Commander of the Allied forces defending the island in 1941 during the Battle of Crete.

The museum's folklore collection includes traditional costume (already well illustrated in the many 19C portraits), Cretan weaving and embroideries (some outstanding pieces in silk, as well as gold embroidery and metalwork.

Most visitors will now retrace their steps to the municipal gardens (see above) but beyond the Historical Museum on the eastern edge of the town is the faded elegance (increasingly encroached upon by modern buildings) of the Khalépa quarter, where at the turn of the century social and political life revolved around the villa of the High Commissioner, Prince George.

A minor road along the waterfront starts at the junction just to the east of the Dóma hotel where the main road from the airport (see above) and the Akrotíri comes down to the coast. (The hotel building housed in 1912 the British Embassy to independent Crete and after the fall of Crete in 1941 served as the residence of the German Commandant.) The coastal road leads east to a picturesque waterside village with tanneries.

The old *walled city* of the Venetians lies north of the main through road. From the seaward (main road) end of the big Plateía 1866 ΟΔΟΣ ΧΑΛΗΔΩΝ (Odós Khálidon) leads down to the waterfront. Dedicated shoppers will notice on the right the two narrow side-streets concentrating on the local leather goods; these streets run in the direction of the covered market. But if you continue downhill towards the sea you will pass (right) the modern cathedral of Ayía Triáda. (In the cathedral square is one of the useful post office caravans—with currency exchange.) A multi-domed building on the next corner was once a Turkish bath. Across the street is the restored Venetian church of St. Francis, now housing the *Archaeological Museum* (see below) which displays the antiquities of this western province of Crete.

Odós Khálidon reaches the waterfront at Plateía Santriváni (also known as Plateía Venizélou). The *Outer Harbour* has been deserted by shipping, but its quays, lined with picturesque houses and tavernas, are now the focus of social life, especially for the evening 'volta'. To the right is the Plaza hotel, where an external staircase and canvas awnings conceal the Venetian *Santrivani fountain*, and beyond is the *Mosque of the Janissaries* constructed in 1645, the year in which the Turks captured the town. The mosque, severely damaged by bombing during the last war, was partially reconstructed soon afterwards (and for some years housed an excellent information bureau) but recently further work has become necessary. Above the mosque, the *Kastélli hill*, site of the earliest settlement, overlooks both harbour basins.

Walking round the foot of the Kastélli, where the Venetian wall is still formidable on the hillside above, you come to the *Inner Harbour* protected by a Venetian mole, with a ruined fort (in process of restoration) half way along it. The mole is probably built on the foundations of an earlier one. The original Venetian *lighthouse* was restored by the Egyptians during their brief occupation in support of the Turkish administration (1832–40); it offers a fine viewpoint. On the east and south sides of the inner harbour a number of *arsenals* remain from the Venetian dockyard. Here the galleys were built or repaired, each vaulted structure holding one ship. Nine survive, in two groups, comparable with those at Herákleion but better preserved. Beside the first group, a street running inland offers a view of the unconventional twin towers of the big Venetian church of Ayios Nikólaos (see below).

Guarding the harbour from the north east (on the edge of the sea) is the *Sabbionara Bastion*. If you follow the eastern stretch of the wall along the Koúm Kapí shore from the bastion and then make your way in the direction of Ayios Nikólaos (see plan), you will discover the maze of narrow streets which is one of the most picturesque corners of Khaniá.

Ayios Nikólaos, a Dominican church of the Venetians, was transformed by the Turks into the Imperial Mosque of Sultan Ibrahim, and still retains both bell-tower and minaret; it did not become an Orthodox church until 1918. The tall galleried nave has a fine coffered ceiling.

In front of the church is Plateía 1821 with convenient pavement cafés. (Excavations here have been examining the levels of the Venetian and Turkish periods of the city.) The plaque in the middle of the square records that an Orthodox bishop was executed by hanging from the plane tree during the 1821 revolt. At the west end of the square the little Venetian church of San Rocco, no longer in use, has a bold Latin inscription of 1630. A block further south, 16C Ayii Anárgyri (the Holy Poor) contrived to remain an Orthodox church under both Venetians and Turks.

Stretches of the *Inner Wall* are best seen on the way back to the harbour along ΟΔΟΣ ΣΗΦΑΚΑ (Odós Síphaka), where the Venetians incorporated into their 14C rampart numerous column drums from earlier Greco-Roman buildings. The Kastélli suffered much damage during the last war, and modern houses are often built into the remains of old structures. ΟΔΟΣ ΚΑΝΕΒΑΡΟ (Odós Kaneváro, parallel to Síphaka) was the Venetian 'Corso', with the Arcade of St. Mark at its eastern end. Across the top of ΟΔΟΣ ΛΙΘΙΝΩΝ (Odós Lithínon, at the harbour end of Kaneváro) the doorway of the Venetian Archives (No. 45) has an inscription of 1623.

There are signs of archaeological activity all over this area. Half way along Odós Kaneváro, on the left walking up from Plateía Venizélou, the largest and most important excavation can be seen. This is Plateía Ayía Aikateríni, a site which helped to establish the chronological sequence of Minoan Kydonía. Many of the finest exhibits in the museum come from here.

Parallel to the south quay of the Outer Harbour is ΟΔΟΣ ΖΑΜΠΕΛΙΟΥ (Odós Zambelíou), which leads to the Topaná area, well worth exploring. Past the first crossroads, walking away from the Kastélli, is the shell of a Venetian palazzo with, high up on the façade, a crest and Latin inscription. Just as this street starts to climb some steps, a right turn leads to the *Renieri Gate*, with the family coat of arms and a 1608 inscription. Through the gate is an elegant little Venetian chapel, overdue for restoration; it is now locked. Beyond it, on the left, the vaults of the Venetian armoury have been restored and put to use. The steps in Odós Zambelíou lead to the attractive ΟΔΟΣ ΘΕΟΤΟΚΟΠΟΥΛΟΥ (Odós Theotokopoúlou). Visitors looking for higher quality, specifically Khaniot, souvenirs will enjoy this area which has become a marketplace for local craftsmen. When you reach the waterfront, the Xenía hotel is to the left, and above it there is a good view of the outer fortifications and moat. The athletically inclined can follow the western wall to the bastions of San Demetrio and Schiavo-Lando (mid 16C).

On the harbour point is the Bastion of San Salvatore, reached through a passage beside the newly restored Venetian church of the same name. Below, in the Venetian fort known as the Firkás, is the *Naval Museum of Crete* (open daily: 10.00–14.00, Tuesday, Thursday, Saturday 19.00–21.00, closed Monday; small entrance charge). Episodes of Greek naval history are illustrated by ship models and photographs. There is an open-air theatre here for summer drama productions, and exhibitions of Cretan dancing are a weekly event. At the Firkás the Greek flag was for the first time officially hoisted on the island in 1913 to celebrate Crete's long-awaited union with Greece; the ceremony is repeated on Sundays and festivals to this day.

The *Archaeological Museum* is in Odós Khálidon, opposite the modern cathedral. Opening hours: Monday 12.00–19.00, Tuesday–Friday 08.00–19.00, Saturday, Sunday and holidays 08.30–15.00; entrance charge. The museum is housed in one of the largest Venetian churches on the island, once part of the Latin monastery of St. Francis. The building is crudely constructed with a vaulted nave and narrow side-aisles; a peculiarity is its reverse ecclesiastical orientation, the additional side-chapels being off the north aisle. In the adjoining garden a Turkish fountain and the base of a minaret survive from the church's days as the Mosque of Yusuf Pasha.

The exhibits, from sites all over western Crete, are displayed in chronological order, beginning to the left of the entrance with finds of the Late Neolithic period from the cave of Platyvolá. The labels (Greek and English) in the show-cases are clear and informative; they date the exhibits and give details of their provenance, sometimes with photographs of the site. There is comment where appropriate on the most important objects, and these are comparable to items starred in this Guide at other museums. The display is regularly brought up to date, and cases may be rearranged as the results of recent work become available. It has been considered superfluous to repeat the museum's information.

The collection falls into five broad categories: artefacts of the Neolithic, Bronze and Early Iron Ages, in cases along the left wall as you enter, and continued in the side-chapel behind the ticket desk; the larnakes (coffins) prominent in the centre; the later material (Archaic–Roman, associated with the city-states of western Crete) in cases in the rear side-chapels; statuary and stelai; Roman mosaics.

Case 7 has material from a Minoan site at Nerokoúrou on the rising ground south of Soúda Bay; this is the first excavation in this part of Crete of a Minoan villa or country house of the type familiar further east on the island. Case 11 displays vases from the local Khaniá workshops; Plateía Ayía Aikateríni, from which many of the exhibits come, is on the Kastélli hill above the harbour. The discovery of inscriptions in Linear B, hitherto confined to the Palace of Knossós, is of major archaeological significance. Note also the remarkable seal impression of a Minoan god or king on a great building topped by horns of consecration. Case 12 builds up a picture of relations between Kydonía and other parts of the Aegean world. The LMIIIA–B cases (1420–1200 BC) are particularly important as pottery of this quality from this period has not been found in the centre and east of the island.

The material in the side-chapel to the right of the entrance is from cemeteries of this period in and around Khaniá; outstanding is the extraordinary pyxis (mus. no. 2308), which portrays a man playing a lyre to birds; it is from a tomb at Kalámi below Aptéra on Soúda Bay.

The collection of Minoan clay *larnakes includes magnificent polychrome examples from the cemetery near Arméni, south of Réthymnon; among the animal and plant decorative motifs are the religious symbols of the double axe and horns of consecration. Further remarkable material from this cemetery is now on display in the new museum at Réthymnon.

Among the statuary (at the far end from the entrance): the 'Philosopher of Elyros', a heroic Roman copy of a Greek orator; from Lissós, an Asklepios, a head of Hygieia, and a youth with delicate features; from the Diktýnnaion sanctuary on Cape Spátha, Díktynna with hound (head missing).

To the Akrotíri

This is a round trip of c 40km to the limestone peninsula to the north east of Khaniá which protects the anchorage of Soúda Bay. The recommended excursion includes two important monasteries (closed 14.00–17.00), with the possibility of a walk to a cave near the superbly sited ruins of one of the earliest monastic foundations on the island.

The bus service to Khordáki (ΧΩΡΔΑΚΙ) passes close to the Monastery of Ayía Triáda, but the recent timetable has not been very convenient for visitors. It is worth noting that a 2km walk from the monastery brings you to the village of Khoraphákia with four buses a day on the route up the west coast of the peninsula to Stavrós. This coast also offers excellent swimming, at Kalathás and especially at Stavrós.

Leave Khaniá on Odós Elef. Venizélou, signposted for the airport and Akrotíri. After 4.5km a left turn leads to the hill of *Prophítis Ilías* and the graves of the eminent Cretan-born statesman Elefthérios Venizélos and his son Sophoklés. The tomb is impressive in its simplicity.

Born in Khaniá in 1864, Elefthérios Venizélos was prominent in European politics for nearly four decades (see p 28), and is honoured as one of the architects of the modern Greek state.

On this hill in 1897, while the Turks were nominally still in control of the island, the Greek flag was raised by Cretan insurgents in the teeth of an international naval bombardment ostensibly designed to defuse a tense situation between the Greek and Turkish nations.

There are popular summer tavernas on the hill, with a fine view over the Bay of Khaniá to the distant Cape Spátha where in ancient times the marble columns round the temple of the Diktýnnaion sanctuary would have gleamed in the sun.

The monastery of Ayía Triáda can be reached directly by the main road to the airport, c 15km from Khaniá by this route. However, a relatively peaceful minor road across the Akrotíri peninsula is very little longer, and is especially recommended in spring to wild-flower enthusiasts.

For the direct route, keep on the main road. Soon Soúda Bay comes into view ahead. Both here, around *Korakiés* and Moní Kalograión, and on the road along the shore of the bay, are good areas to explore for tavernas on summer evenings, or for live Cretan music. After 2km you pass the main turning, right, for Soúda (4.5km from this junction to the Commonwealth War Cemetery, see Rte 13). Continue, following signs for the airport (and with military installations increasingly conspicuous) until you pass (right) the end of the runway. Then turn left at the T-junction within sight of the terminal buildings, and almost immediately right and left again, signed by now for the monastery.

For the cross-country route turn left off the main road at the Venizélos graves—signed to (1km) Kounoupidianá. Branch right at a fork (leaving Ayios Ounoúphrios left), and keep left at the fork in the middle of *Kounoupidianá* (where there is a popular psitariá or rotisserie in the angle of the two roads). On the far side of the village you pass the left turn for the road up the west side of the peninsula to *Stavrós*.

The last part of the road to Stavrós is indiscriminately dotted with summer bungalows but it ends at an enclosed bay overlooked by a dramatic cliff. There are tavernas close to the fishing boat quay with a relatively unspoilt view, and the swimming (outside the crowded high season) is recommended. The final scenes of the film 'Zorba the Greek' were shot at the foot of this cliff.

The spectacular cave of Lerá half-way up the cliff was frequented in Neolithic times and there is evidence for a cave sanctuary from the end of the Bronze Age through to the Hellenistic period.

From Kounoupidianá on the road to the monastery continue straight on through *Kambáni*. The uncultivated areas along the way shelter many species of wild flowers. After another (winding) 2km bear left, guided by signs for Ayía Triáda. Almost immediately after the junction with the road from the airport, turn left again. (This corner is the most convenient bus stop on the Khordáki route.) In 1km a long tree-lined avenue marks the approach to the monastery.

*Moní Ayías Triádas** (the Holy Trinity) was founded in the first years of the 17C by two brothers, Venetians from the Zangaróli family who had adopted the Orthodox faith. The monastery is still sometimes known by their name. The massive multi-domed church (1632), its façade reinforced by Doric columns, reflects the Venetian influence as do the elaborate entrance and the mid 17C campanile. There was a religious college here in the 19C, and the monastery is still a rich and influential foundation with a fine library. On Trinity Sunday it is a place of pilgrimage from far around.

From Ayía Tríada it is 4km further to the second, more isolated, Venetian monastery, the **Gouvernéto**. The track (with hard-packed dirt surface) sets off to the north at a right-angle to the end of the cypress avenue. At a crossroads (after 1km) turn right and from the point where you start to climb into the wild north-eastern corner of the Akrotíri the track surface is concrete.

The monastery is thought to date back at least to the first years of the Venetian occupation, and perhaps to the 11C when pirates were ravaging the coast of Crete and an inland position offered relative safety. The history of the Gouvernéto is bound up with that of its predecessor in this region, the monastery of Ayios Ioánnis Xénos known as the Katholikó, certainly one of the earliest religious foundations on the island; its ruins are hidden in a ravine to the north east, near the sea (see below).

The plain exterior wall of the Gouvernéto quadrangle, with towers at the four corners, hides the richly decorated façade of the church dedicated to the Presentation of the Virgin, Η Κυρία των Αγγέλων (Our Lady of the Angels), which was started in 1548 (but not at that time completed), and reconstructed after damage during the 1821 Revolt.

The relief carving of the bases of the six columns set into the church façade is highly unusual for Crete, as is the ground-plan of the church. One of the side-chapels is dedicated to the Ayii Déka (Crete's ten martyrs under the Persecution of Decius in 250), and the other to the renowned (11C) local saint, Ayios Ioánnis Xénos, St. John the Stranger, who died a hermit in the cave down at the Katholikó.

The ruins of the **Katholikó** are the objective of a recommended walk (40 minutes) which starts from the Gouvernéto. The well-built path drops away over the right-hand side of the rise beyond the monastery.

After ten minutes you pass a first cave with a chapel at its entrance, and inside a stalagmite said to resemble a bear. The cave, excavated by C. Daváras, was originally sacred to Artemis, venerated here in the form of a bear (Αρκούδα in Greek). The chapel is dedicated to the Panayía (Our Lady) Arkoudiótissa.

The ancient path continues downhill and becomes a long flight of rock-cut steps; on a bend the Katholikó is suddenly in view. The ruined buildings lie on either side of a wide bridge across the bed of a dried-up stream, between cliffs from which the unmistakable notes of the blue rock thrush can often be heard.

St. John's Feast Day is 7 October, and the vigil, beginning here on the previous evening, is one of the great religious festivals of western Crete. Although known in the last years of his life as 'Ermítis', the hermit, St. John was an influential evangelist in the early 11C, devoted to the task of re-establishing the Christian faith after the Byzantine Empire had recovered the island from the Saracens. His grave is at the end of a spectacular

The Katholikó monastery on the Akrotíri near Khaniá (from Pashley, Travels in Crete, 1837)

cave on the left at the bottom of the rock staircase, at the level of the bridge. (The cave is perilously slippery underfoot and is considered unsafe in places.)

A 10-minute walk down the river-bed leads to the rocky shore. It is possible to swim from an ancient rock-cut slipway.

To the Gorge of Thériso. This is a short excursion, 17km from the centre of Khaniá. Leave on the main road west to Kastélli Kisámou. Two blocks beyond the end of the one-way traffic system (2km from Plateía 1866) watch for a sign on the wall left to Thériso. Then follow signs through the suburbs to Perivólia now on the edge of Khaniá. At 4km, and 200m into Perivólia, fork left where a board on a tree points to Thériso. From then on the road follows the stream-bed, passing a curious church, and winds up the valley crossing and re-crossing the tree- shaded stream until it enters the wild and dramatic gorge to emerge at Thériso. The village is proud of its connections with the great Cretan statesman Elefthérios Venizélos (see p 28). There are family ties because this was his mother's home village, but he also established his headquarters here during the revolution of 1905 which preceded the resignation of the island's High Commissioner, Prince George.

From the double-naved church at the top of the village a kalderími sets off south into the Levká Ori (White Mountains). A very rough dirt road to the west loops round to Mesklá (Rte 16).

15 Khaniá or Réthymnon to Khóra Sphakíon and the South Coast

About 70km (43 miles) to Khóra Sphakíon, one of the principal harbours
for the south coast boat service, and also a base for exploring the
mountainous hinterland of Sphakiá. The road crosses the island from
Vrýses which is roughly equidistant (c 30km) from Khaniá and
Réthymnon. For motorists a full petrol tank is a wise precaution.

The south coast road is described east as far as Selliá where it joins
Route 12B across the island from Réthymnon.

Buses to Khóra Sphakíon from Khaniá, and from Réthymnon, about three
a day, with guaranteed connections at Vrýses. Daily bus along the south
coast in summer (usually Easter to mid October).

The first part of this route uses the north coast highway (Rte 13). At 30km
from Khaniá, immediately after a bridge over the road, an insignificant
turning leads (right, across the stream, and then left) into Vrýses from the
west. The main highway junction is 3km further east, 26km from Réthymnon. Distances on the road across the island are calculated from Vrýses.

Vrýses has a reputation as one of the more beguiling villages on Crete.
Two rivers, the Vrysanós and the Boútakas, meet (winter snowfall permitting) at a shallow cascade frequented by ducks, where a monument
commemorates the Constitutional Commission set up in the wake of the
1897 Revolt which was to lead to autonomy for Crete. Local yoghurt with
honey is a speciality of the tavernas under the plane trees beside the
stream. Nowadays the village's popularity as a staging-post for coach
tours is much in evidence, and many independent travellers will not stop
for long before the dramatic climb through the district of Apokóronas to
Sphakiá.

5km out of Vrýses is a left turn for *Alíkambos*. The *church of the
Panayía (Virgin Mary) is one of the most delightful of the frescoed churches of Crete.

1km along the narrow lane, on a wide hairpin bend right, you see ahead
a Venetian fountain, still used to water flocks. Below left, an old path
leads past the church, hidden in a graveyard shaded by an oak and a bay
tree and looking out over orange groves in the valley. The interior is dark
but the church is well cared for and the frescoes are in a good state of
preservation. The paintings in the nave are the work of Ioánnis Pagoménos (see Rte 18, p 290), dated by inscription to 1315.

On the north wall next to the iconostasis the Virgin with Child (Odiyítria), with the
Baptism above. Ayios Demétrios, mounted left of Ayios Yeóryios. Opposite: Ayios
Konstantínos. Rather indistinct on the upper register of the vault (south side) is a
fine Nativity.

The frescoes in the bema, by a different artist, date from the later 14C.

The main road climbs steadily into the increasingly rocky scrub of these
eastern ranges of the Levká Ori (White Mountains). It gains height up a
valley, often crossing the older more direct track, and reaches at 10km
the little upland plain of Krápi. (Lekanopédio on the sign is literally a
basin plain.) The only natural route into Sphakiá from this direction ran
through the ravine of Katré, which opens out of this plain, and Cretan
folk-memory enshrines many heroic ambushes and rearguard actions
against Turkish armies here at the frontier of the Sphakiot stronghold.
3km beyond Krápi the pass of Katré is noted on signposts.

16km At a ridge, the *plain of Askýphou* (730m) comes into view. The villages occupy the raised ground around the patchwork field-system dominated by a ruined Turkish fort on a conical hill. On this plain one of the major pitched battles of the 1821 Cretan insurrection was fought between the Turks and bands of mountain warriors; it resulted in a resounding and bloody victory for the Sphakiot forces which is still related in poetry and song. The 19C traveller Robert Pashley described the plain as 'so surrounded by lofty mountain-summits that it has somewhat the appearance of a large amphitheatre'. The traditional mule-paths out of the Askýphou plain climbed west into the Levká Ori, south west to Anópolis and east over to Asi Goniá (see Rte 13); the present-day tracks (used by shepherds) can be spotted from the plain as scars on the hillsides, and are recommended to walkers, bird-watchers and naturalists in search of the wild solitude of Cretan mountains.

The main road follows the western edge of the plain, and then climbs again.

At the top of the pass (22km) a narrow side-road turns left, signed (8km) to *Asphéndou*, for local traffic through the hills to Kallikrátis and on to Asi Goniá. It is not yet suitable all the way for normal hire cars, but the first stretch offers a chance to turn off the beaten track; very soon there is a glimpse (right) of the Libyan Sea.

For Khóra Sphakíon the main road continues south to (23km) *Imbros*, and the descent begins. The traditional route kept to the eastern wall of the spectacular *Nímbros gorge*, the ravine running down to Komitádes, and this well-worn track is now a popular walk using the bus from the south coast up to this starting point (signed at the southern edge of the village). The modern road twists high (to the west) above the gorge.

Along this route, during four days and nights at the end of May 1941, 12,000 exhausted troops, survivors of the Battle of Crete (see p 30), withdrew to the coast under constant attack, the majority to be embarked by the Royal Navy for Egypt.

The road emerges high above the Libyan Sea, with superb views of the coast. The large island directly south is Gávdos, the most southerly inhabited point in Europe (see Rte 18). To the east you can make out the Venetian fortress of Frangokástello down by the shore, and beyond it are the Paximádia islands in the Bay of Mesará, backed by the Asteroúsia range of mountains. At the foot of the vertiginous (850m) descent, 36km from Vrýses, the road divides; to the left it is 11km along the coast to Frangokástello but the right branch leads in 4km to *Khóra Sphakíon*.

In the 18C this was a substantial town defended by a castle (ruins on the hill as you descend to the harbour), and an important centre, as its name implies, for the fiercely independent district of Sphakiá, which had a coastline sheltering a fleet of 40 merchant ships. The traditional Sphakiot costume of black shirt and trousers or breeches with tall leather boots is still habitually worn at least by the older generation of men of this region. After the 1770 rebellion under Daskaloyiánnis, Sphakiá was savagely repressed by the Turks, and although its people took a leading part in the struggle for freedom all through the 19C, the area never regained its former economic strength.

Today the tiny harbour's prosperity is closely related to the great number of foreign tourists brought here by the renowned attractions of the walk down the Gorge of Samariá, an hour away by sea to the west. From late afternoon on, the boats put in from Ayiá Rouméli at the bottom of the gorge, and from May–October (the months when the walk is permitted) the village is sometimes overwhelmed by people and coaches. However it is still possible to spend time in Khóra Sphakíon provided you do not insist on complete tranquillity. In the evening the coaches leave for the northern coast resorts, and then the diminutive harbour regains its charm. The waterfront is packed with the tables of prosperous fish tavernas. There is a small hotel (pleasantly situated though rather ambitiously listed as Class B) but visitors often prefer the well-equipped rooms for rent above these tavernas. There are also pleasant and quieter rooms in the village behind, some with views to the west along the rocky coast.

South Coast Boat Service. Khóra Sphakíon is at one end of the route for boats which now operate from their base at Palaiókhora (Rte 18) in the district of Sélinos near the south-west corner of the island. The service grew up as a rather haphazard affair using the traditional fishing boats or caiques, but Samariá I, a larger type of ferry able to carry vehicles, came into operation in 1987 and the schedule is now thoroughly reliable, subject always of course to weather conditions.

The primary function is the service to and from Ayiá Rouméli at the bottom of the Samariá Gorge, but the boats also put in to Loutró and Soúyia, and at least once a day it should be possible to travel the whole route between Khóra Sphakíon and Palaiókhora in either direction. All the ferries run more frequently during the high season (mid June to mid September), and there is a schedule of day-trips to the island of Gávdos, 2 hours away (otherwise, outside the high season, from Palaiókhora—see Rte 18). The new timetable is issued every March and should be available at all tourist information offices on the island.

Suggested excursions from Khóra Sphakíon

A. To Ayiá Rouméli. The boat journey (see above) along the coast to *Ayiá Rouméli* via *Loutró* takes c one hour, and the timetable should allow four or five hours for exploring the lower part of the Gorge of Samariá. (On a day trip book for the return journey when you arrive.) Ayiá Rouméli lies on the site of ancient Tárra, known for the manufacture of Roman period glass. The excursion into the Gorge of Samariá from this southern end (advertised as Samariá the Lazy Way) gives no idea at all of the magnificent scenery surrounding the first descent from the Omalós (see Rte 16) but you can walk up the stony river valley of the Tarraíos to (c one hour) the narrow pass known as the 'Iron Gates', in the relative peace before, in the high season, the worst crowds begin to arrive from the top. Before you reach the entrance to the designated National Park (which posts a number of regulations which it is wise to observe) you pass through the deserted village of old Ayiá Rouméli where the little church of the Panayía is built into the remains of a 5C/6C basilica with walls still standing up to 3m in places. Some evidence suggests that there may have been a sacred building here before the basilica, in the shape of a Hellenistic temple to Apollo.

The modern settlement of Ayiá Rouméli has grown, without any great charm, to meet tourist needs and is well provided with tavernas and rooms for rent. The main beach is crowded after midday.

There are organised tours from the north coast centres to Khóra Sphakíon and Ayiá Rouméli, known as 'Samariá the Lazy Way', though it should be said that there is nothing especially lazy about a stiff 2-hour climb up the gorge. If you are staying locally and have any choice, you might like to make enquiries to try to avoid these tour days.

A different and recommended expedition from Ayiá Rouméli follows one section of the well-marked path which is an attractive feature of this coastline. This particular walk sets off along the coast to the east and in a little over an hour you come upon Ayios Pávlos, a domed, cruciform chapel of the Second Byzantine period; its 10/11C origins are associated with Ayios Ioánnis Xénos, a revered evangelist of western Crete. Remains of frescoes are tentatively dated to the 13C. Tradition links the sweet-water spring beside the church with baptisms administered by St. Paul who sailed along this coast on his way to Rome.

From Ayios Pávlos the coastal path continues east, but the old kalderími into the mountains ascends the river gorge, c 3 hours to the village of Ayios Ioánnis (at a height of 750m) to join up with excursion C. for Arádena and Anópolis described below. Allow about 6 hours in all to Anópolis where taxis are available if required for the last leg down to the coast—ask at any kapheneíon. It used to be possible for long-distance walkers, properly equipped, to take the early boat to Ayiá Rouméli from Khóra Sphakíon and walk back in the day over this southern flank of the Levká Ori, but with the first boat rescheduled to mid-morning the expedition may now require an overnight stay in Ayiá Rouméli.

B.   To Loutró. This walk of c 2 hours may be combined with the boat trip to or from Loutró. The footpath along the cliffs follows the route of an 'ancient way'; nowadays it is well maintained, and marked with splashes of red paint, but they not infrequently indicate a diversion after a rock fall and this is an expedition for reasonably agile walkers which should not be attempted in bad weather.

Set out along the road to Anópolis. At 3km on the first hairpin bend (easy parking if required) the path drops down from the road and leads west along the coast. The second chapel in sight marks your destination. The first beach (less than half an hour) has always offered especially fine swimming; here the cliffs are perpendicular, creating a narrow coastal strip sheltered and calm in all weathers except a strong southerly wind. You pass a number of caves, one reputedly a refuge for the legendary 18C Sphakiot leader Daskaloyiánnis who came from Anópolis. (A new café-bar on a moored pontoon has diluted the former romantic isolation of this beach.)

Loutró, in the shelter of a promontory and an island, is the only natural year-round harbour on Crete's south coast. The location has been appreciated for many centuries for on the promontory between two anchorages are scanty remains of the ancient city of Phoínix, the harbour town in Greco-Roman times of Anópolis in the hills above. St. Paul's vessel was making for safety here before sudden unfavourable winds carried it south of Gávdos and on to shipwreck on Malta (see Kalí Liménes, Rte 4). More recently this was the winter harbour of Sphakiá, and the home port of craft large enough to trade as far as Smyrna and Alexandria. The only route inland is a near-vertical ascent, on a well-built footpath, up more than 700m to Anópolis, and perhaps for this reason the importance of Loutró gradually declined in favour of Khóra Sphakíon.

Less than two decades ago Loutró was virtually deserted, but then came a move to reinvigorate the harbour. Thanks to the benefits derived from tourism in this region, the quay could be rebuilt and the mono-chrome houses behind the shingle beach began to be resettled. The word got about, and this exceptionally beautiful bay, still accessible only by boat or on foot, gained a well-deserved reputation as an escapist para-dise, with rent rooms and tavernas attempting to meet the demand. Now,

in a further escalation of tourist development, many new villas and apartments have been inserted, canoes are for hire to reach isolated beaches,
and the village is transformed by a ubiquitous coat of white paint
uncharacteristic of the traditional Cretan coastal settlement. The modern
ferry drops its bow ramp on the shingle beach.

C. To Anópolis. Daily bus, but in the late afternoon with early morning
return. A fine asphalt road sweeps up from Khóra Sphakíon to (12km)
Anópolis in a high valley running east–west under the White Mountains;
this and the plain of Askýphou are the traditional heartlands of Sphakiá.
The straggling modern village has kapheneíons and a number of rooms
to rent. Above it, to seaward, are the unexcavated remains of one of the
foremost Greco-Roman city-states of the area. As you enter the village
you can distinguish on the skyline the church of Ayía Aikateríni, which,
with the adjacent tower, is at the centre of the site.

Anópolis was the birthplace of Ioánnis Daskaloyiánnis who was
martyred by the Turks for his part as leader of the 1770 rebellion; his
statue stands in the plateía at the end of the village, and this is the
starting-point for the walk (20 minutes) to the ancient site. The lane south
from the plateía leads to the start of the old stone-built path or kalderími
for the climb up over the hill, but now the bulldozer has carved out a
(rough) track so that vehicles can reach Ayía Aikateríni. The church is at
the crest, and immediately to the west is the large but still unexplored
site. Great quantities of stones mark collapsed buildings and strong fortification walls can be made out in places. The city commanded the route
between the upland plain and its harbour of Phoínix, modern Loutró; the
descent to the coast, stepped in places and still a well-worn path, zigzags
down the near-vertical slope to the sea below. Clearly this is a very stiff
climb uphill, but in the downhill direction it is a highly recommended (c
30 minutes) walk with stunning coastal views. For the return to Khóra
Sphakíon see the alternatives (of coast path or boat) in excursion B.
above.

From the plateía in the centre of Anópolis, an improved dirt-road continues across the plain to (3.5km) Arádena and on to Ayios Ioánnis. Leave
the statue of Daskaloyiánnis to the left, and just out of the plateía fork left
in front of a kapheneíon.

The right fork leads c 14km into the Levká Ori. The surface is not for long suitable
for ordinary hire cars, but this is a route into the mountains for serious walkers.
Anópolis is one of the established starting-points for the climb to the summit of
Pákhnes (2452m); the climb takes 8 hours and as there is no refuge hut on the way it
involves a night camping out on the mountain. Anyone planning this expedition
should consult the Greek Alpine Club—see introductory information for Khaniá
(Rte 14).

About 2km after you leave Anópolis, *Arádena* comes into view, with the
mellow Byzantine church of Mikhaíl Arkhángelos tranquil on the edge of
one of Crete's most dramatic gorges. At this point for many centuries
travellers have descended by the steep path into the ravine to arrive at
the church on the far side, but in 1986 the gorge was spanned by a great
steel bridge, financed by the internationally successful Vardinoyiannís
family. The bridge was built as a gift to the village of Ayios Ioánnis from
which the family came, and is welcomed locally as a move towards
economic viability for these isolated communities.

Romantics may like to take the old path down into the gorge to savour the obsolete road system of Sphakiá. Strike off the modern road 600m short of the bridge to pick up the old track before the stepped descent. This detour should also be rewarding for botanists.

Modern Arádena occupies the site of the Greco-Roman city-state of Aradén, and the domed, cruciform church of Mikhaíl Arkhángelos is built into the central nave and apse of an Early Christian basilica. The 14C frescoes include scenes from the Christ cycle in the vaulting, and the donors with the archangel in the north crossarm, but unfortunately the church is usually locked (enquire in Anópolis).

The road continues on the far side of the bridge, climbing gradually across wooded slopes with intermittent rewarding views, to *Ayios Ioánnis*. (Recommended as a peaceful walk, c 1 hour 15 minutes).

In 1823 Egyptian troops, called in to reinforce the Turks, were pursuing along this route a band of the women and children of patriots of the region who had taken refuge in the Gorge of Samariá. At Ayios Ioánnis, in a heroic stand, the army's path was blocked by a mere 32 Cretan rebels; all perished, but they gained enough time for the women and children to reach the safety of Samariá.

On the approach to the village (below the road left, within sight of an outlying taverna) there are two frescoed churches, Ayios Ioánnis and the Panayía, both painted in the 14C. (Ask for the keys at the taverna.)

Serious walkers can cover the distance between Anópolis and Ayiá Rouméli in one day—see excursion A. above.

The south coast road to Frangokástello, and on to (38km) Selliá to link up (c 50km) with the Réthymnon–Ayía Galíni route (Rte 12B).

There has for many years been one daily bus each way from Khóra Sphakíon to Ayía Galíni during the summer season only (mid April to mid October). Check beforehand in Réthymnon or Khaniá if plans depend on it.

The road has been widened and its surface greatly improved in recent years; only short stretches may still not be surfaced with asphalt. Care is always needed, especially after bad weather, as the edges of the road tend to be unstable in places, but this is now a highly recommended scenic drive.

Return from Khóra Sphakíon to the start of the road inland for the Nímbros gorge and Askýphou, but continue east along the coast. Just past the junction the church of the Panayía (below the road to the right) all that remains of the Thymianí monastery, is important in Cretan history because here on the 29 May 1821 1500 Sphakiots met to proclaim the revolt against the Turks in sympathy with the struggle for freedom on the Greek mainland. That struggle resulted in independence (1831) but the Cretan revolt was crushed with the aid of Egyptian forces, and the island remained under Turkish rule until the end of the century.

The next village (5km from Khóra Sphakíon) is *Komitádes*, where the chapel of Ayios Yeóryios has the earliest known frescoes (1313) by Ioánnis Pagoménos.

The road bends left in front of the village church. To find Ayios Yeóryios (10 minutes below the village, route marked by red paint) unaided, start down the path from the church which bends left round the church wall and then keeps straight ahead downhill. Three or four minutes from the main street you pass (right) a small white chapel. Thirty paces further turn left through a break in the wall on to a side path, and follow it as it bends right downhill towards the sea. Continue until the path seems as if it must plunge into the ravine below, but persevere, and there half hidden to the left is the arched doorway of the ruined narthex in front of Ayios Yeóryios. The chapel has been sadly neglected, but the frescoes are sufficiently preserved to reward the enthusiast.

At the end of Komitádes a track (signed from this direction) emerges from the bottom of the Nímbros gorge (see p 274). The way is marked by blue arrows, and the point where the walls of the ravine begin to close in is reached in about 15 minutes.

The road links a series of villages on the lower slopes along the edge of the coastal plain. At 11km a turning right is signed to (3km) **Frangokástello**. (There is a second, eastern, approach road, 4km on through *Patsianós* and *Kapsodásos*—the choice if travelling this road in the opposite direction.)

On this western approach a broad asphalt road sweeps down to the sea, and, at the time of writing, to a beach. (The movement of sand between one year and the next is disconcertingly unpredictable along this coast.) This approach to the fort is not visually improved by new concrete buildings, but they do offer agreeable tavernas and rooms for rent, some right on the shore.

The Venetian fort of Frangokástello dominates a small marshy bay with a fishing boat haven and a picturesque lighthouse tower at the western end of a popular beach. The sea here is shallow for a long way out, giving noticeably higher sea temperatures early in the season, and making this one of the best beaches on Crete for children, but there is also deeper water where the harbour channel runs out to sea. Another more secluded bay lies 1.5km east along the coastal dirt-track above the shore, just past the ruined double-naved church, a relic of the monastery on the point.

In the mid 14C a petition urged Venice to protect this coast from pirate raids. Frangokástello was built in 1371 and appears always to have been an isolated fort without nearby settlement. It must have served a dual purpose, also strengthening the Venetian hand against the rebellious stronghold of Sphakiá. The fortress is rectangular, with square towers at the corners; the south-west tower is larger than the rest and forms a guardhouse for the main gate facing the sea, watched over by the Lion of St. Mark. The interior now preserves only the skeleton of the original plan.

The fortress was at first called by the name of the nearby Venetian church of Ayios Nikítas, but it became known to the Cretans as Frangokástello. ('Frankish' is still used as a generic term for all West Europeans.) In 1770 the Sphakiot leader, Ioánnis Daskaloyiánnis, gave himself up to the Turks here, and was later brutally executed in Herákleion. In 1828 the adventurer Khátzi Mikhális Daliánis made a heroic last stand at the fort with 385 men against vastly superior Turkish forces. The Cretans were massacred, but it is claimed that in the dawn mist on the anniversary (17 May) each year, a phantom army known locally as the 'drossoulites', the 'dew shades', returns to dance on the plain.

400m north east of the fort, on the alternative way direct from it back to the main coast road, you pass the chapel of Ayios Nikítas; it is built on the bema of the smallest Early Christian basilica yet known on the island. There are remains of a polychrome mosaic.

The route continues east towards *Skalotí*, 18km from Khóra Sphakíon. The coastal plain peters out, and the road runs high above the sea, with narrow strips of cultivated land and the occasional glimpse of a beach far below. Beyond the village a stretch of rough road may still require a slower speed but it should last for no more than 2km.

At 27km *Rodákino* is a delightful village still relatively little affected by organised tourism. There are a few simple rooms for rent. A turning in the village leads down the river valley (recommended to bird enthusiasts in spring) c 2km to the shore and access to swimming from isolated beaches or rocks; there is a car track west as far as some tavernas.

The main road climbs out of Rodákino. Tracks into the hills offer opportunities for walking. At the watershed (32.5km), on a bend where the road is still high above the sea, the view extends east to the Mesará and Mount Ida, and the White Mountains are left behind. In the foreground is the holiday resort of Plakiás at the far end of the beautiful Pláka Bay.

38km *Selliá*. 2km further along the road (some time after the coves and beaches have come into view enticingly spread out below like a large-scale map) you reach an oblique T-junction where Plakiás and the Préveli monastery are to the right. To the left the main Ayía Galíni–Réthymnon road is reached (in c 12km) through the *Kotsiphós Gorge* and the village of *Ayios Ioánnis*. On this main road you are then 18.5km from Réthymnon. For these alternatives turn to Rte 12B, p 254.

16 Khaniá to Omalós and the Gorge of Samariá

This can be treated as a simple excursion, 44km (27 miles) by car or bus to the Omalós plateau to spend a day among Crete's most impressive mountain range, the Levká Ori (White Mountains).

Alternatively the trek to the south coast through the Gorge of Samariá, which can also be undertaken as part of a day's round-trip from the north coast centres, is a major expedition that needs careful planning (see below, and also Samariá the Lazy Way, Rte 15).

Mesklá, in the foothills, is a short drive (20km from Khaniá). A recommended 5km walk up the valley to this attractively situated village uses the Omalós bus service as far as Phournés.

There are several buses a day on the Omalós route, including one in the early morning. One bus a day to Mesklá.

The road leaves Khaniá along the coast to the west in the direction of Kastélli, but after 1.5km turns left for Omalós up an avenue of eucalyptus trees. These soon give way to groves of orange trees behind reed windbreaks; in spring the scent of orange blossom is overpowering.

This broad, fertile valley is watered by the Kerítis and its tributaries. The area was nicknamed 'prison valley' during the Battle of Crete, on account of the Ayiá prison which still exists. German paratroops were landed here in strength as part of a pincer movement in the planned attack on Khaniá, then the capital of the island; they met with fierce resistance, not least from the local population.

At c 9km a flash of water (right) is a glimpse of the Ayiá reservoir, which, with the adjacent reed-beds, has proved consistently rewarding for bird-watchers, especially during the spring migration. The open water is best viewed from the dam at the southern end.

At the beginning of the village of *Ayiá* (9.5km from Khaniá), there is a possible detour to the ruins of an episcopal church of the Second Byzantine period built over the one dating from Early Christian times. The church is dedicated to the Panayía (Virgin Mary) though there is an old tradition of association with Konstantínos and Eléni, the first Christian Emperor and his mother. In the Second Byzantine period and throughout the Venetian rule this was the seat of the Orthodox bishop of Kydonía (Khaniá).

Turn off the main road at the sign for Kyrtomádos, but after 100m fork left. After a further 300m turn right, and 150m along this narrow track the ivy-clad walls are in view ahead to the right, opposite well-tended orange groves. The area is known locally as Episkopí.

When the Arabs were driven from the island (in 961) by the forces of Byzantium under Nikephóros Phokás, a great building programme was required to replace the churches which had been destroyed during more than a century of Saracen occupation, and for the new episcopal churches the sites of the pre-Arab ones were naturally, as in this case, favoured.

The Early Christian church here has not been excavated, but it seems to have been a substantial structure with narthex and atrium. The 10C/11C episcopal church is in ruins but the walls, which incorporate material from its predecessor (see lower courses of the north wall), still stand to above window height in places, preserving some of the brickwork round the arches. It can be seen from the remains that this was a three-aisled basilica divided by two colonnades, each of three columns—the pair to the west marble, the others granite. The tall (50cm) column bases may have facilitated the re-use of the columns of the Early Christian basilica for its loftier successor.

At 12km on the main road, opposite a memorial to partisans killed by the Germans, the Soúyia road (Rte 17) diverges right; it crosses the river into Alikianós—see p 285 for a short (c 2km) detour to Ayios Ioánnis near Kouphós, another Second Byzantine period church with frescoes as well as interesting historical and architectural features.

The Omalós road continues ahead past the memorial until at 15.5km, in the middle of the village of *Phournés*, it swings right. Here a left fork offers a recommended detour to (5km) *Mesklá*, lying in the fertile tree-lined Kerítis valley and surrounded by orange groves. On foot it is more pleasant to follow the old track which keeps to the river-bed; fork right downhill 100m after leaving the main road.

On the edge of Mesklá, just across a bridge and on a long right-hand bend, a track on the left leads uphill (100m) to the frescoed church of the Metamórphosis Sotírou (Transfiguration of the Saviour); its gate is overhung by a mimosa tree. The frescoes, very worn in the bema, are well-preserved in the nave, and include a fine Transfiguration in the arch on the south wall. Right of this is the donor inscription dated 1303; the artists are named as Theódoros Daniél and his nephew Mikhaíl Venéris. Below the inscription is Leontios, as the patron saint of the donor, the monk Leontios Khossákis. (The paintings in the narthex are by a different hand—graffito 1471 on the south wall.)

The houses of Mesklá are strung out up one side of the street beside the river. The war memorial of this small village carries a long list of names, including those of a group of about 30 described as 'missing' in Germany during the Second World War.

It is known that there was a city on the slopes above the valley in the Greco-Roman period, but its name is still disputed. At the top of the village stands the big modern church of the Panayía, and beside it the old 14C chapel with the same dedication (the Assumption of the Virgin) is built into the foundations of a 5/6C basilica, from which fragments of a mosaic floor were only recently removed to greater safety. It is thought that there was an earlier building on the site, a temple of Aphrodite.

The terrace below these churches overhangs a meeting of streams and there is the constant sound of running water, a rare delight during the Cretan summer. The track beside the stream (not recommended for vehicles) leads on invitingly into the hills, over to Thériso (p 272).

To the west there is a steep footpath (less than 1 hour) up to Lákki (see below). Ask for the kalderími 'stous Lákkous'.

The Omalós road crosses the Kerítis and leaves the valley, climbing in great zigzags. The land is terraced for olives and the view increases in grandeur. At 24.5km *Lákki*, a superbly sited mountain village, has trim red-roofed houses widely dispersed over the hillside. The climb continues across bleak stony uplands and the air is scented by aromatic rock-plants. For a while the Levká Ori appear in the distance to the left. Then, across a saddle, the road turns towards them, and (33km) reaches a pass.

Less than 1km further on, a plaque 'from your comrades in the National Resistance 1941–45' records the death in a German ambush on 28 February 1944 of the New Zealander, Sergeant Dudley Perkins, and a Cretan companion. Perkins (known variously in the Resistance movement as 'Vasilí' and 'Kiwi') had escaped from a prison camp and then from the island in 1942 and the following year returned from the Middle East as an undercover agent. He operated with a small band of guerilla fighters based on the Sélinos district in the south west of the island. Their exploits and his personal bravery in support of his comrades have become part of Cretan folklore.

The road climbs yet higher. The fir trees are stunted, but in season they shelter a profusion of mountain flowers. At the crest the **Omalós** plateau comes into view.

The mountain plain (average height 1100m) is roughly triangular, with the distance along each side about an hour's walk. At each of its three corners a pass leads out of the plain, which thus forms a focal point of the traditional routes through the White Mountains. Snow lies till March, leaving behind as it recedes a cloud of the crocus (*C. sieberi*), tulips (*T. cretica*) and other rareties. The land drains slowly by a swallow hole, and remains green during the early part of the summer. It is too high for the olive, but cereals and potatoes are cultivated by the villagers from Lákki and from Ayía Eiríne (Rte 17).

Cretan leaders met here on the Omalós in May 1866, and protested to the ruling Sultan against new taxation; their approaches to foreign consuls and the declaration by Sphakiá of union with independent Greece, precipitated the ill-fated 1866–67 Cretan revolt.

Where the road comes down to the plain you notice a chapel on a knoll to the left; beside it is the house and grave of Khátzi Mikhális Yiánnaris, one of the great rebel leaders of 19C Crete. He survived to become president of the Cretan Assembly which in 1912 at last achieved for the island the long-desired union with Greece, and he built the chapel of Ayios Pandeleímon as an act of gratitude after his deliverance from a Turkish prison where he had prayed to the saint for help.

At the edge of the plain the hamlet of Omalós, inhabited only during the summer months, has several tavernas and comfortable rooms to rent. The constantly improving accommodation is useful as a base for exploring these mountains, or for an early start on the walk through the gorge.

Leaving the tavernas you straightaway join the road around the plain. The main route keeps left. As you near the rising ground on the far side, you pass, left, a track to (5km; c 75 minutes on foot) the Kallérgis mountain refuge (1680m, 30 beds); from the hut it is a climb of 7 hours to the summit of Pákhnes, (2452m). Psilorítis (Mount Ida) is higher at 2456m, but the Levká Ori are a formidable range, with ten peaks over 2000m. The Kallérgis hut is run by the Greek Alpine Club (see Khaniá information, Rte 14).

Almost opposite the turning to the refuge, a dirt road branches off to encircle the plain (clockwise back to the tavernas) and to reach the western pass out of the Omalós. Through wild and beautiful country this eventually connects (c 15km) with the asphalted Khaniá–Soúyia road (Rte 17).

At 44km on the main route you reach the pass of *Xylóskalo* where a Tourist Pavilion (café refreshments; overnight accommodation closed in recent years but worth an enquiry) is dramatically sited, 1227m above sea level, at the head of the Samariá Gorge. The area is now a national park, well cared for and strictly regulated, with protection for animals and plants. In the afternoon (15.00–sunset) you are allowed to descend into the gorge for the first (very steep) 2km or so—to the Neroutsikó spring. Alternatively, to avoid the crowds in the gorge, there is a recommended path (starting beside the Tourist Pavilion) which climbs west on the slopes of Mount Gíngilos.

The **Gorge of Samariá

Though many tens of thousands make the 17km trek each year from the Omalós plain to Ayiá Rouméli on the Libyan Sea, this ought to be treated as an expedition for experienced and fit walkers. Fatal casualties are not unknown, usually caused by unpreparedness or foolish disregard for regulations, and many tourists ruin several days of their holiday by walking down the gorge in unsuitable footwear or insufficiently protected from the sun.

The gorge is closed until the beginning of May. The exact date depends on the volume of water coming down from the mountains and is at the discretion of the rangers (enquire at Municipal Information or NTOG in Khaniá, also for admission time which varies slightly according to season, also if necessary for last boat sailings from Ayiá Rouméli). It is forbidden to spend the night in the park. You will be issued with a (free) ticket at the entrance and this should be retained for surrender on leaving, for it is seen as part of the rangers' safety checks. It is foolhardy to embark on this walk when the river at the bottom of the gorge, which has to be crossed many times, may be above knee height and affected by sudden flash floods or rock falls. The gorge is closed again at the end of October and the regular boat service from Ayiá Rouméli ceases then too.

This said, the expedition properly planned and prepared for is one of the major tourist adventures that Crete has to offer. There are a number of ways of tackling it, and where there is a choice the advantages of starting at first light to avoid the crowds, as well as the midday heat, cannot be too strongly emphasised. The all-inclusive round-trip conducted coach tour from places as far afield as Ayios Nikólaos will suit many people. The guides iron out all logistic problems. For those who prefer an independent, less regimented approach, a car is no help unless a party happens to include a willing 'chauffeur'. A taxi (Khaniá to Omalós) is one possibility to be considered; a fare might be arranged (in advance) in the region of £20 and this allows arrival in the mountains at 06.00, when the park usually opens. The ordinary bus service offers an early start from Khaniá but does not reach the plain until 07.30. (There are guaranteed connections with this bus service from Herákleion and Kastélli Kisámou, and many places between, all along the north coast; enquire locally.) Some readers may choose to arrive on the Omalós the previous evening, as is suggested in the route description above. The last bus gets you up to the plain in the late afternoon. Advance telephone bookings for rooms are accepted; ask for a recommendation and number at the tourist information offices in Khaniá (see above). In the early morning there is no organised transport across the plain; to be ahead of the buses you must be prepared to walk (5km) though you may be able to get a lift locally or from the first taxis up from the coast.

You should allow between five and seven hours to enjoy the walk, depending on fitness and personal preference about pauses to absorb the surroundings. In most places when you are actually walking this trail you have to pay attention to the terrain underfoot. There are springs and toilets at three points on the way down. Ayiá Rouméli has tavernas and many rooms for rent, and also a good pebble beach (usually crowded after midday). Most people leave by boat for Khóra Sphakíon (Rte 15), some for Palaiókhora. The service is efficient, but it is advisable to buy tickets as soon as you arrive at Ayiá Rouméli. The latest departure times vary slightly according to season. The practice (during the main season) has been for the 17.00 boat to connect with the 18.00 bus from Khóra Sphakíon to Khaniá; guaranteed connection at Vrýses for Réthymnon.

Sideróportes, the 'Iron Gates' pass, the narrowest point in the Gorge of Samariá (from Pashley, Travels in Crete, *1837)*

Everyone who undertakes this formidable walk remembers the excitement of the first precipitous descent (from 1200m) down the Xylóskalo (the 'Wooden Staircase', originally constructed of tree trunks) and the drama of the scenery dominated by the rock face of Gíngilos. There is an overpowering smell of pine. For early starters the rising sun strikes the peaks with the chance of eagles or vultures (including the rare bearded vulture or lammergeier) soaring above. More predictable is the nesting colony of crag martins before the Neroutsikó spring. The White Mountains are the last region where the 'agrími' (Cretan ibex) is still to be found in its natural habitat, but these wild creatures usually take care to keep well away from the frequented trail.

The 900m descent continues, in sweeping bends, from pines into deciduous trees. Far down at the bottom, the path joins the river-bed of the Tarraíos, running to the sea at Ayiá Rouméli, the site of the city-state of Tárrha in Greco-Roman times. First you notice the course of a dried-up torrent, then a spectacular waterfall where a tributary from the east, from the region of the Kallérgis mountain refuge (see above), joins the Tar-raíos. Near by is a second spring, Ríza Sykiás, and then, right of the path, the chapel of Ayios Nikólaos overshadowed by some of the tallest cypresses on the island. The sound of running water increases as a back-ground to birdsong. The rare peony *P. clusii* survives in damp areas beside this path; indigenous to Crete it flowers a creamy-white in late May and early June. After another spring you climb briefly to a high path along the contour, in dappled shade, before at the 6km mark rejoining the widening river-bed. The walls of the gorge are less hospitable as you reach the deserted village of Samariá.

The broad valley floor makes a popular half-way stopping place. (A helicopter pad is a reminder of rescue operations.) But you can also cross into the village now partly restored as a base for the park rangers (toilets). After many centuries as a naturally defended refuge at the heart of the Sphakiá region, Samariá at last saw its inhabitants rehoused at the coast soon after the park was established in 1962.

Five minutes beyond the village (to the east across the stream-bed) the little church of Osía (Blessed) María, with the date 1379 above the door and remains of frescoes, is romantically situated at the foot of a steep cliff. The church's dedication was corrupted to the name for village and gorge.

At first the path is shaded and a breeze may be blowing up from the south coast. The deepest and narrowest part of the gorge is ahead, with stepping stones for the many crossings of the stream. You pass the 10km mark and in about half an hour the chapel of Aphéndis Khristós (Christ the Lord) on the left of the path signals the approach to the Sideróportes or 'Iron Gates', the narrow (3–4km) pass out of the gorge between vertical cliffs towering to a height of 600m.

Leaving the park you continue through the original (now deserted) vil-lage of Ayiá Rouméli (see also Rte 15—Samariá the Lazy Way) to the wel-come of the modern village on the Libyan Sea.

17 Khaniá to Soúyia

A scenic road, 70km (42 miles) through the western foothills of the White Mountains to a remote village on the Libyan Sea. The itinerary includes a suggested expedition on foot or by boat to the site of the Greco-Roman city-state of Lissós.

The bus service to Soúyia enforces an overnight stay.

Leave Khaniá following Rte 16. After 12km, opposite the war memorial, the Soúyia road diverges right, signed for (1km) Alikianós, to cross the Kerítis river with the distant wall of the Levká Ori (the White Mountains) upstream left. It skirts *Alikianós* and, passing the turn into the village, makes a left bend, and heads for the mountains.

To visit the 14C church of Ayios Ioánnis (1.5km off the road) it is neces-sary to detour into the village. Almost immediately keep right at a fork following the sign for Kouphós. 300m from the fork you pass, right, the tiny cruciform chapel of Ayios Yeóryios, dating from the early part of the Venetian period. The chapel has been restored after war damage which destroyed its admired frescoes.

Continue on this road 1.3km and you will find the church of *Ayios Ioánnis* hidden in an orange grove (right) 50m back from the road. Despite partial restoration in 1951 the church is abandoned (and has lost its dome).

In the First Byzantine period there was a basilica here, dated to the 6C; there are records of a mosaic floor depicting deer, peacocks and vases similar to that of the basilica at Soúyia (see below). Ayios Ioánnis replaced a church probably destroyed in the severe earthquake of 1303; that church, dedicated to the Panayía (Zoodókhos Piyí, the Virgin as the source of life) is thought to have been founded in 1004 by the evangelist Ayios Ioánnis Xénos, and the tradition survives in the name given to the existing early 14C building.

Ayios Ioánnis is cross-in-square in plan with the west cross-arm wider than that of the east end (the narthex is later); the design of the apse is most unusual for Crete, and is said to show the influence of Constantinople. The dome was supported on three columns (the south-west one now restored) and a single square unadorned pillar. The capitals of the two northern columns are of an early 6C type, probably re-used from the Early Christian basilica.

The surviving frescoes, tentatively dated to the 15C, are valued as illustrations of an early phase of the Cretan School of painting. The best-preserved scenes are: in the apse the Platytéra with the Ascension and Pentecost; in the south cross-arm (west wall) Ayios Pandeleímon, and in the same position in the north cross-arm Demétrios; opposite, in a niche, Ayía Paraskeví. Left of the main west door is a worn portrayal of the Archangel Michael.

The main Soúyia road continues south to (16km) *Skinés*, a pleasant village along a wide street, and one of the main centres for the citrus trade of the region. Soon after (17km) *Khliaró* the orange groves come to an end, and the road begins to gain height following a narrow river valley into the well-watered and wooded foothills of the White Mountains. It crosses the river at 21.5km, and at 24km you reach a watershed. Through (26.5km) *Néa Roúmata* and (30km) *Prasés*, and on past *Sémbronas* (at 620m), the long climb continues. The afforested hillsides are particularly beautiful in the autumn as their colours change to red and gold.

Finally at 37.5km the road reaches the pass, with extensive views ahead as well as back to Khaniá and the north coast.

A turning to the left, along the spine of the island, is signposted to Omalós (10km). This dramatic road, still rough in places, runs through wild country to the western pass out of the Omalós plain, and then down to join the main road across it (Rte 16). The pass is marked by a white church. At the fork near houses down on the plain, keep right for the head of the Gorge of Samariá, left for the hamlet of Omalós (tavernas and rooms) and the return to Khaniá—also for the swallow-hole draining this high plateau, which is a worthwhile stop for bird-watchers.

The Soúyia road follows the Ayía Eiríne valley, high above the ravine. For centuries the people of *Ayía Eiríne* have spent the winters in their village here, and during the summer months cultivated their land on the Omalós plain, or pastured their flocks above it.

The descent to the south coast begins. At 45km, by a chapel on a ridge above *Epanokhóri*, comes the first sight of the Libyan Sea. The road drops through *Prinés* and *Tsiskianá* to (52km) *Kambanós*. There is evidence of malachite mining in antiquity in this region. *Marália* clings to the hillside in tiered rows hidden below the road. 1km beyond this, after a long bend, a big modern church with clerestory is conspicuous on a saddle far ahead. This marks the site of Elyros, one of the largest and most powerful Greco-Roman city-states of south-west Crete.

57km At a T-junction just below the church the Soúyia road turns left.

The right turn at this junction leads into the village of *Rodováni* and then through Teménia to Anisaráki and (c 17.5km) Kándanos on the main Khaniá–Palaiókhora road. This cross-country road (see Rte 18) has been widened and where necessary realigned, to open up this remote area of the Sélinos hills. With the last stretches scheduled for an asphalt surface it also offers an alternative, and shorter, main route between Khaniá and Palaiókhora.

The site of *Elyros* was rediscovered in the early 19C by the English scholar and traveller, Robert Pashley. The modern church of the Panayía is built on the site of a 6C basilica near the centre of the ancient city, which controlled the valley running down to one of its harbours at Syía (modern Soúyia); the other was at Lissós. In the First Byzantine period the basilica was the seat of a bishop, and the city flourished until the Saracen invasion. The site has not been excavated and scant traces of walls remain above ground, but a detour to the church is recommended for the *view.

A large Roman statue of 'the Philosopher of Elyros' is prominent in the museum at Khaniá.

From the junction the new broad road sweeps down the river valley, 10km to Soúyia.

Halfway to the coast, outside (62km) *Moní*, is the church of Ayios Nikólaos with remains of frescoes by Ioánnis Pagoménos (see Rte 18), dated by the donor inscription to 1315; they include (south wall) an unusually large portrayal of the patron saint.

At the entrance to the village the house just beyond a fountain on the left keeps the church key. There is a driveable track from the turn-off 800m back along the road, but the footpath starting from below the house is recommended (15 minutes). The main church has at its west end a later addition that is not a conventional narthex, because originally it could only be entered from the church nave. Unique on Crete is the free-standing campanile adjacent to the south east, which is thought to be contemporary with the main church.

2km beyond Moní a good dirt road crosses the river and climbs east, 8km into the mountains to *Koustoyérako*.

Here in 1943 a German platoon was preparing to execute the women and children of the village for concealing the whereabouts of their menfolk of the Resistance, suspected of involvement with an arms drop and a British wireless transmitter. A German machine gun threatened the women huddled in the plateía. But the men of the village were concealed on the slope above, their rifles trained on the platoon, and from 400m their leader shot dead the machine gunner at the start of a stirring rescue. The episode is vividly described in George Psychoundákis's *The Cretan Runner* (see Bibliography—also for *Crete* by A. Beevor which elaborates on the exploits of the Sélinos guerilla bands). Thereafter the abandoned village suffered accordingly, but was later rebuilt.

From the top of the plateía a paved path, or kalderími, leads east into the White Mountains (c 2 hours) to the village's summer pastures on Mount Akhláda.

The improved road has brought visitors to Soúyia, for centuries no more than a haven for the fishing boats of the people of Koustoyérako, and has lessened the isolation of its remote position tucked away under the southwest flank of the White Mountains. Until fairly recently it used to be a tiny cluster of houses sought out for its back-of-beyond air, but, inevitably, prosperity (and the consequent building boom) has removed this particular charm, without apparently any very clear idea of what might replace it.

Soúyia has one of the best beaches on the south coast (which attracts a fairly constant population living outdoors) and the country inland is superb for walkers and entirely unspoilt. There is a small hotel, many rooms to rent, and tavernas on the tamarisk-shaded beach. The tiny harbour at the extreme western end of the bay is a regular port of call for the south coast boat service (see Rte 18) for excursions to the Samariá Gorge and the island of Gávdos.

The modern village is on the site of ancient Syía, the port of Elyros. The sea level was higher in antiquity, and the harbour lay to the west of the river mouth, protected by a mole. On the east side of the stream-bed, traces of tile- or stone-faced concrete remains of the Roman city can be made out. On the raised beach at the west end of the village, a modern church stands on the site of a 6C basilica. The basilica's polychrome mosaics, which until 1986 could be seen both inside and outside the modern chapel, have been removed to the safety of the Khaniá Museum. They are considered the finest of this date yet known on the island; the design includes kanthoroi, tendrils of ivy leaves, deer and peacocks, these birds being symbols of immortality.

An expedition to ancient **Lissós** is a highly recommended walk of one and a half hours (or 15 minutes by boat to the west of Soúyia). Lissós had a temple of Asklepios, the god of healing, and in antiquity the sanctuary was visited from afar by pilgrims in search of cures. The city-state was prominent in the 3C BC in the League of the Oreíi (the People of the Mountains) and flourished until it was abandoned during the 9C Saracen occupation.

The path to Lissós (well marked all the way with paint splashes) strikes inland from the harbour, 500m west of Soúyia, where a narrow gorge leads into the mountains. At first you pick your own way up the stream-bed, but after c 20 minutes keep to the left side and watch for a cairn and arrows indicating the path which, built at first and afterwards where necessary, snakes straight up the cliff, and then continues to climb through trees on the pine-scented hillside. From the crest you cross a broad stony upland, from the far side of which the little bay of Ayios Kýrkos is visible far below, with back from the shore a roughly triangular valley in which the ancient city lay. There remains a precipitous descent on a skilfully built path with an increasingly detailed view of the site.

There are two chapels: the Panayía near the shore, and, inland, towards the apex of the triangle, Ayios Kýrkos (built into the remains of an Early Christian basilica) which is a useful landmark near the centre of the site. The outline of the theatre can be distinguished, just on the seaward side of it.

The marked path leads down the steep hillside on the north-east side of the site to the temple of Asklepios built against the cliff at the place where the required sacred spring flows out of the rock. The sanctuary is fenced and locked, but a guardian or phýlax lives near by, along the path into the valley. If he is not available to unlock the sanctuary site it can be viewed fairly well from a vantage point on the slope to the south east.

The remains of a small Doric temple of the Hellenistic period (4/3C BC) have been excavated; it is built of ashlar blocks except for the east wall where the rougher masonry may be earlier, or may be designed for added strength against the thrust of the hillside. The cella has a doorway from the south, with two steps up to it, and on the opposite wall is a marble podium for the cult statue. In the north-west angle a stepped bench with a hole in it could be a libation channel, or a pit for the sacred snake. A low bench or kerb surrounds the remains of a good-quality mosaic floor of later date (1C AD); panels of black and white geometric designs include the remains of a large maze inlaid with polychrome birds, one a quail. The excavation uncovered a pit, dug through the mosaic, which contained about 20 fragmentary statues, including the (headless) Asklepios now on display in the Khaniá Museum; probably this damage was the work of the fanatical Christians who destroyed the temple and defaced its walls with their symbols.

There was a stoa on the west (downhill) side of the temple, from which a flight of steps leads past the sturdily constructed fountain of the medicinal spring.

Less than 100m west of the sanctuary is Ayios Kýrkos and to the south of the church the indistinct outline of the theatre. On the terraces up the western slopes of the valley are a great number of built, barrel-vaulted tombs, a type so far known on Crete only from three sites in this locality—the other two being Lasaía and Soúyia. There are traces of Roman ruins among the cultivated plots on the way down to the Panayía on the shore; built into the church wall is a fragment of an Asiatic sarcophagus with Medusa head.

18   Khaniá to Palaiókhora

This route (77km; 48 miles) follows the north coast road west to (c 20km) Tavronítis, then climbs into the hills to (59km) Kándanos, before descending to the south coast at Palaiókhora. The district of Sélinos, south of Kándanos, is a part of the island particularly rich in churches with Byzantine frescoes.

Improvements to the Khaniá–Soúyia road (Rte 17), including the branch west to Kándanos, have meant that Khaniá–Palaiókhora via Alikianós and Rodováni offers an alternative return route.

Palaiókhora is a convenient base for exploring this extreme south-western corner of the island, and its harbour is now the home base for the ferries of the south coast boat service which operates a schedule to the Gorge of Samariá and Khora Sphakíon, and also out to the island of Gávdos.

Buses three times daily, duration of trip 2 hours.

The coast road (see Rte 19) runs west from Khaniá to (20.5km) *Tavronítis*. In the middle of the village you turn inland for Kándanos and follow the west bank of the broad river-bed up a fertile valley. At 26km *Voukoliés* is a market centre with a large plateía around plane trees. The road climbs out of the valley, for a while running along a ridge with views on either side and back to the sea near *Máleme*. In the vicinity of *Kakópetros* (c 40km) the hillsides are densely wooded, but soon the landscape becomes wilder. Above the village is a monument to a patriot hanged by the Germans in 1944, and beyond there is a final glimpse (right) of the north coast near Kastélli. Passing through a cut, the road continues above a deep narrow valley and climbs to a pass before the descent to Kándanos.

A stretch of the old road leads down (left) into a gorge, scene of a heroic delaying action, in May 1941, by the local population against a German force pushing south after the capture of the Máleme airfield. Motor-cycle detachments armed with Spandau machine guns mounted on their side-cars had been instructed to prevent Allied reinforcements landing at Palaiókhora. The force was held up for two days by the Cretan resistance, and in retribution for the death of 25 German soldiers, Kándanos was utterly destroyed. On the outskirts of the town (left) are the waterworks given by a German group after the war, as an act of atonement.

58km. *Kándanos* is the administrative centre of the 'eparchy', or district of Sélinos.

A detour here to (2km) *Anisaráki* offers a chance to visit a group of easily accessible frescoed churches.

Before the big plateía, the Teménia road turns left. (It is 14.5km across country to the Rodováni junction below Elyros on the direct Khaniá–Soúyia road (Rte 17).) This

cross-country route, realigned and partly resurfaced, has opened up this still relatively unspoilt region of the south coast, and also links Palaiókhora to Khaniá on an
improved road through Rodováni.

For Anisaráki turn at the sign for Teménia (11km). On the outskirts of
Kándanos you pass through the hamlet of *Kouphalotós* and 300m further
on is Ayios Mikhaíl Arkhángelos, Kavalarianá. The landmark here is a
square house with a flat roof, on the left below the level of the road. On
the bend just before it a track descends (5 minutes) to the cemetery
church visible across a stream. Frescoes of 1327–28 (unfortunately somewhat clouded by chalky film) by Ioánnis Pagoménos. Work of this artist
dated by inscription between 1315 and 1347 can be found in several areas
of western Crete; outstanding examples include the church of Ayios Yeóryios, Anýdri (near Palaiókhora, see below), Ayios Nikólaos, Moní, near
Soúyia (Rte 17), and the Panayía, Alíkambos (Rte 15). His style is said to
show the influence of the Palaiologan revival while retaining conservative elements.

Anisaráki has four churches with well-preserved frescoes. At the
entrance to the village the first of these, *Ayía Anna (signposted left in
an olive grove below the road), is built over an earlier church, probably of
the First Byzantine period (see column fragments outside). The frescoes,
dated 1462, depict scenes from the life of St. Anne, the mother of the
Virgin; the donor is depicted on the south wall (west end), with the
donor inscription opposite. A very rare feature is the iconostasis in
stone; it is fully decorated, with the two main scenes depicting Christ
Pantokrátor and Ayía Anna with the infant Mary (see below, Mikhaíl
Arkhángelos, Sarakína).

These small Byzantine churches very often lie along the medieval road network of
the Cretan countryside, which the modern realigned roads have only partially
superseded. The paved tracks and paths, terraced and stepped where the gradient
demands it, are still known by the Turkish word *kalderími*. Children on their way
to school, villagers going to work in their fields, women gathering herbs, as well as
shepherds with donkeys and goats use these traditional roads as the most direct
route across the countryside.

200m further along the modern road, a track for *Ayios Yeóryios* leads left
past a group of houses set at an oblique angle to both road and track. It is
5 minutes on foot to the chapel, keeping left at the fork beyond the
houses. Late 13C–early 14C frescoes: scenes from the life of St. George on
the south side of the vault (martyrdom on the north side) and on the south
wall (west) the saint mounted on his horse, between the Virgin (left) and
Ayía Marína.

At the top of the village the street bends right and just after this,
signposted left, the church of the *Panayía* (Virgin Mary) is visible on a
terrace immediately above the road. The architecture of this church
shows strong Venetian influence. The original doorway was in the south
wall, and the graffito 1614 may be associated with the alterations. The
late 14C *frescoes are particularly well preserved, with the Communion
of the Apostles below the Platytéra in the bema, and the barrel-vaulting
densely painted with scenes from the life of Christ.

On the adjacent higher terrace is the church of *Ayía Paraskeví* which
has frescoes dated stylistically to the first half of the 14C. The saint is
depicted on the north wall, with Ayía Varvára.

The road turns south, with a wide view over Kándanos, and climbs
steadily through (6.5km) *Vamvakádes*, and then a further 2km to the

crest. At 11km *Teménia* is delightfully situated at 700m in a sheltered valley. It is worth enquiring about rooms for rent as an alternative, in the heat of summer, to the crowded coastal villages.

Above Teménia is the site of the city-state of Hyrtakína, which flourished in the Hellenistic period. There are traces of walls in polygonal masonry, probably of a late-Classical or early-Hellenistic date, and Hellenistic houses have been excavated, as well as a 4/3C sanctuary of Pan. A 1C AD statue of the god is in Khaniá Museum.

Just outside the village keep left for the Khaniá–Soúyia road; right at this fork would take you back to Palaiókhora (c 15km) via Anýdri (Ayios Yeóryios, with Pagoménos frescoes, see p 293). Continue through *Máza* to (16km) *Rodováni* and, just out of the village, the junction with the main Khaniá road (Rte 17). (Site of ancient Elyros above right; turn to p 286.) You are 10km from Soúyia.

From Kándanos the main Palaiókhora road continues south, and in less than 2km crosses at *Plemenianáthe* little river Kandanós which runs for most of the year. Immediately before the bridge (right of the road) is the path (5 minutes) to the frescoed church of Ayios Yeóryios; walk under a pergola to the right of the last house to pick up the paved path. The frescoes here are dated by inscription 1409–10. On the north wall one of the archangels is shown mounted on a horse, a rare scene although there is a similar one in the Astrátigos church (below).

Just beyond the bridge is a turning for (10km) Strovlés, near the head of the Yíphlos valley; this turning leads across country to the improved roads described in Route 20, and makes possible a circular drive from Palaiókhora with the return through Sklavopoúla (see below).

There are two interesting frescoed churches above *Kakodíki*. Continue 8km along the main road from the junction for Strovlés. At 64.5km from Khaniá, on a bend towards the end of the long village, there is a sharp turn left on to a track signposted Ay. Triás (kapheneíon above the turn). The track leads steeply uphill and then through olive groves, 1km to the large modern church (Ayía Triáda, at *Astratigós*) and beside it the old frescoed •church of Mikhaíl Arkhángelos.

The key is held by the priest (papás) whose house is 250m further up the hill. Pass the church gate (leave a car at the fork just beyond) and the left track uphill ends at the papás's house. He or his wife will open the church. (Short-cut on foot: from the fork, follow the concrete water channel straight uphill to the spring, where the path veers left out on to the last stretch of the track.)

Mikhaíl Arkhángelos, with frescoes from the first half of the 14C and a beautiful old wooden iconostasis, is a single-naved church, but the nave is divided by pilasters into four bays (rather than the usual two or three). The original Byzantine chapel was altered and elaborated by the Venetians; a new door and window have damaged the frescoes on the south wall. Scenes preserved include the Apostle Communion below the Pantokrátor in the apse, and on the north wall, next to the iconostasis, a rare portrayal of the Archangel mounted on a horse (see Plemeniána, above).

A little further south, at *Tselenianá*, is the church of Ayios Isídoros, with elegant frescoes dated by inscription 1420–21. From Astratigós, keep right at the fork by the houses (see above), and less than 1km along the hillside, just across a stream-bed—in spring a ford—the keyholder's house is in view down a track to the right; he will accompany you (700m further along the road) to the church.

These are the only frescoes on Crete dealing with themes from the life of St. Isídoros, who was martyred for his faith on the island of Chios during the reign of the Emperor Decius, notorious for his persecution of the Christians. The upper registers of the vault are devoted to the Christ cycle, but in the lower registers are: on the south side scenes of the baptism, imprisonment behind a grill and beheading of Isídoros, and opposite, the saint's avowal of his faith before Numerius, commander of the Roman fleet, and in consequence the punishment of being dragged behind two Arab horses.

The dirt road continues (less than 2km) to the church of the Panayía, Kádros, which can also be approached from the main valley road (see below). Using the Khaniá bus service from Palaiókhora, it is possible to spend a day walking on this peaceful hillside; the tracks connecting the hamlets are high above the valley with wide views across it.

On the main road, continue 1km south from Kakodíki and then (at 68km from Khaniá) turn left for *Kádros*. Nearly at the top of the village (more than 1km from the turn), 80m beyond the last shop-cum-kapheneíon, a path leads downhill right (5 minutes) to the church of the Panayía dedicated to the Nativity of the Virgin (Feast Day, 8 September). The key is kept at the nearby house (over a stile beside a gate). This church has a

Castel Selino, the Venetian fort at Palaiókhora (from Gerola,
Monumenti Veneti nell'Isola di Creta, *1905–32)*

well-preserved and complete set of *frescoes dated to the second half of
the 14C; in the apse is the Panayía Eléousa (the Virgin of Mercy).

Less than 10 minutes on foot above the village enthusiasts can find the frescoed
Ayios Ioánnis Theológos (the Evangelist). Keep right where the road forks; the little
church is hidden below a group of old houses downhill to the right.

77km Palaiókhora is the 'Castel Selino' of the Venetians who in 1279
built a fort on the promontory here. The modern village, which owes its
popularity more to its idyllic setting than to any intrinsic charm, now
straddles the base of the peninsula, with to the west a fine long sandy
beach backed by tamarisk trees. Small boats moor at a quay on the east
beach in front of the village, but the main harbour is out on the point,
500m beyond the fort.

Palaiókhora seems set on resort development that is in general geared
to the cheaper end of the tourist market. It is often extremely crowded in
high summer and has become popular with young foreigners who live
here all the year round. However there is not a great choice of places to
stay in this corner of the island, and this big village, with shops, pensions
(heavily pre-booked Easter–September) and numerous rooms for rent, as
well as a good variety of taverna food, can be a useful base for exploring
the many Sélinos churches, or the unspoilt hill country back from the
coast (for example, see Kakodíki and Kádros described above, and the
Sklavopoúla region below). It is certainly a logical stop on a journey
using the scheduled south coast boats—for details see end of this chapter.

The entrance to the 'Phroúrion' or fort is near the church; the enceinte
provides good mountain views to the east but a better idea of the walls is
obtained from the beach below.

Palaiókhora to (5km) **Anýdri**, where the church of Ayios Yeóryios has
*frescoes (1323) by Ioánnis Pagoménos (see p 290). The road runs east
along the coast before climbing in a wooded valley; the double-naved
church is in the middle of the village. The north aisle is densely painted
by Pagoménos with scenes from the Christ cycle and of the miraculous
deeds and martyrdom of St. George. (Some chalky film.) The patron saint
is one of the supplicant figures beside Christ in the vaulting of the apse,
and the portrayal on a white horse is found on the north wall of the cross-
vaulted bay. (The frescoes in the south nave, which is dedicated to Ayios
Nikólaos, are by a different painter and of inferior quality.)

Palaiókhora to (20km) **Sklavopoúla**, on newly-improved roads which
have opened up this remote south-west corner of the island. Leave
Palaiókhora on the road running parallel with the village's west beach,
and after 1km watch for a turning right, signed for Voutás. The first 3km
stretch may still be rough, but it is worth persevering.

At 9km, by a bridge below the village of Kondokinígi, there is a short detour, right,
to (3km) the little frescoed church of Mikhaíl Arkhángelos at Sarakína. The side-
road climbs beside the stream-bed, passing a monument (erected in 1986) to com-
memorate a battle in 1897, the last year of the Turkish occupation, in which 150
Turks were killed by Christian forces. After 3km, at the meeting of two streams, the
church is hidden in undergrowth at the end of a paved path, ahead right. The frescoes are dated stylistically to the second half of the 14C; the stone iconostasis (a
rare feature, cf. Ayía Anna, Anisaráki above) is painted with icons of Christ and the
Panayía Eléousa (The Virgin of Mercy).

The church of Ayios Ioánnis, ahead in the village, has remains of frescoes
(1341–49).

For Sklavopoúla the road continues to (13.5km) *Voutás* where you keep left. Just out of the village the old bridge still remains, to the right of the modern one. The road, narrow but surfaced for most of the way, starts to climb and the valley opens out. At 17.5km, still climbing, you pass Kalamiós, and at 20.5km reach *Sklavopoúla* looking out from a height of 640m across cultivated hillsides to the distant sea. The name reflects the origins of the village, which was settled by Slav mercenaries of the army of the Byzantine Emperor Nikephóros Phokás who remained on Crete after the reconquest of the island for Christendom in 961.

There are three much-admired frescoed churches in the village. Left of the road on the way in is *Ayios Yeóryios*, an unusually tall church beside a school playground. Remains of frescoes in two different styles; the earlier work, chiefly in the apse, has an inscription of 1290–91 above the window. The key is kept at the house down the slope beside the playground—or enquire at the café-bar in the plateía, opposite the big modern domed church.

The other two frescoed churches are close together below the village. From the plateía, continue downhill 400m and take a rough track (left) which leads to the lower village. Walk straight on into the village street, up some steps and through a roofed passage, past a partly-ruined tower of the Venetian period (key, see below). Where the houses stop, the kalderími runs on ahead but the two chapels are above the path (left). The first you come to (recently not locked) is dedicated to Sotíros Khristós, Our Saviour Christ. The remains of 14C frescoes include the portrait (defaced) of the donor, Partzális, on the north wall, with trees and the chapel in the background. (On the south wall with the military saints are graffiti of 1422 and 1514; on the north wall some scraps of earlier painting.)

Immediately (30m) above on the hillside is the chapel of the Panayía (Virgin Mary); the key is held at one of the village houses near the old tower. Densely painted, and well-preserved, set of gospel scenes, and on the north wall the donor with a model of his church. The frescoes are dated stylistically to the late 14C–early 15C (graffito 1518); art-historians value them as an important link in the development of the Cretan School of painting.

South Coast Boat Service. Palaiókhora is at the west end of the route to Soúyia, Ayiá Rouméli and Khóra Sphakíon. (See also Rtes 15 and 16.) In recent years the reliability of the schedule has greatly improved, as has the frequency though this varies according to season. The timetable is published each spring, before Easter, and should be available from all tourist information offices on the island. During the high season (May–September) there is at least a daily service from Palaiókhora to Ayiá Rouméli at the bottom of the Samariá Gorge (duration of trip c 2 hours), with a connection on to Khóra Sphakíon if required. In April and October the service is reduced.

Ferries designed to lower a bow ramp for loading and unloading can operate to beaches that were previously inaccessible by boat, and such day-trips (e.g. to Elaphonísi—see Rte 20) are increasingly popular. Enquire locally.

Boats run twice a week in summer to the almost deserted island of **Gávdos**, 24 nautical miles south of Khóra Sphakíon, and the most southerly point of Europe.

With archaeological evidence for occupation dating back to the Neolithic period, the island was in Greco-Roman times a dependency of the city of Górtyn. The ship carrying St. Paul from Kalí Liménes (p 154) on his voyage to Rome was driven past the island, then known as Clauda, during a storm caused by the fierce north wind, Euroclydon (Acts 27, 12). The storm prevented the intended landfall in the safe winter harbour of Phoínix (modern Loutró on the mainland directly to the north) and caused the voyage to end instead in shipwreck on Malta. Gávdos seems to have flourished as the seat of a bishop during the last years before the Arab conquest, but then became known as a pirate lair. Now it has four small settlements and less than 100 inhabitants, mostly sheep farmers.

The boat trip, with a call at Soúyia, allows only about four hours on the island. From the little harbour (with a few rent roms for the adventurous—also at the main village of Kastrí) it is a half-hour walk to swim off the beautiful sandy bay of Sarakíniko (tavernas). There are now high-season day-trips to Gávdos from Khóra Sphakíon (Rte 15), and the shorter journey time (2 hours) may allow longer on the island.

19 Khaniá to Kastélli Kisámou

43km (27 miles) to Kastélli Kisámou (officially renamed Kísamos but still known locally as Kastélli), which may be used as a base for exploring the extreme west of the island. 24km Kolymbári for the Goniá monastery and the Rodopós peninsula. Excursion from Kastélli: 7km to site of ancient Polyrrhénia.

Until recently this road west of Khaniá was a main route, but not of highway standard. However the Kolymbári–Kastélli section of the New Road is making steady progress; it is realigned to the north (seaward) of the old route, and it is to be expected that newly completed stretches, perhaps with provisional roadsigns, will be opened from time to time.
There is a good bus service from Khaniá to Kastélli.

The road leaves Khaniá to the west, and passes at 1.5km the turning for Omalós and the Gorge of Samariá. Ahead is the stretch of coast which in 1941 was the scene of the German airborne invasion from bases in Attica which launched what came to be known as the Battle of Crete. Left of the road (2.5km) on the outskirts of town, the German monument to their 2nd Parachute Regiment takes the aggressive form of a diving eagle.

At 3km a beach convenient for Khaniá is signed by EOT. (Town buses to Kalamáki and Galatás, see practical information in Rte 14.) A turning (at 4km) leads to Galatás where New Zealand troops fought a heroic rear-guard action in 1941 (now also site of the New Zealand War Memorial).

The road runs close to the shore along the Bay of Khaniá. The beach here is not wide, but long stretches of good sand alternate with rocky outcrops. The prominent off-shore island of *Ayii Theódori* is one of several reserves for the Cretan ibex, the 'agrími'.

As far as Plataniás there is continuous and apparently haphazard ribbon development on a modest scale, offering accommodation and beach taverna meals, but also bars and discotheques. Self-catering apartments and 'studios' are here replacing the traditional 'rent rooms' and there is the occasional larger hotel geared to package holidays. On foot there is (on many stretches) no choice but to take to the road, and groups of pedestrians crowd along it especially during the evening stroll in search of entertainment. This is not a road to drive in a hurry.

11km *Plataniás* is a large village which has spread from its flat-topped hill to cater for tourism along the shore. Beyond, the scene remains more rural, with much less coastal development.

At 13km the road crosses a river, here the Plataniás, fed from the White Mountains (through Mesklá and Alikianós) by the Kerítis. A minor road inland along the west bank cuts across to Ayiá (Rte 16); the signs are for Vrýses, but keep left at a fork to follow the river. The area is recommended to bird-watchers—the rare Eleonora's falcon nests not far away.

The main coast road winds through groves of orange and tangerine trees, which are sheltered by the windbreaks of growing bamboo sometimes laced together for greater strength. Around Easter the scent of blossom is overpowering. You are approaching (16km) *Máleme*; the airfield here (right of road beyond the village) played a decisive part in the German airborne attack in 1941. Before the airfield, now a military base, there is a left turn (at 17.5km) for the German war cemetery, which signposted in Greek and German lies 1.5km inland on the rising ground. A schematic wall map illustrates the sombre facts of the Battle of Crete, 20 May–1 June 1941. 6580 Germans were killed, including those missing at sea, and there are 4465 well-tended graves on the hillside here. (Of the total Commonwealth force on the island some 2000 were killed; 1527 are buried in the cemetery at the head of Soúda Bay—see Rte 13).

The Máleme cemetery lies at the end of a north–south ridge running out from the White Mountains. This was the notorious Hill 107, a vital tactical position in the battle for the airfield that in pre-war days had been the aerodrome for Khaniá, then the capital of the island. The bird's-eye view of the coast from here is the best-possible illustration of accounts of the battle (see bibliography and p 30).

The Goniá monastery (from Pashley, Travels in Crete, *1837)*

The Late Minoan (LMIIIB) chamber-tomb of Máleme is just below the military cemetery. Return 200m down the road to the first left bend, and walk 100m east along the terraced hillside; the tomb lies on the right of the path.

An exceptionally long (13.8m) lined dromos leads to a rectangular chamber with corbelled roof; the doorway is designed with a relieving triangle behind the upright slab above the heavy lintel. The tomb, which had been robbed, was excavated in 1966 by the Greek archaeologist, C. Daváras. Two interesting seals are recorded; one in bronze, perhaps originally covered with gold leaf (a rare find), showed a cow suckling her calf, and the other in agate was carved with agrímia.

The main road continues past the airfield to (19km) the bridge over the broad stony river-bed of the Tavronítis; on the right are the remains of the wartime Bailey bridge which continued in use for some 30 years.

You can walk or drive (1km) out to the estuary down the west bank (first skirting the works buildings); when the river is fed by the melting snows there is enough water to form a small lagoon which often shelters wading birds on migration.

In the village of *Tavronítis*, a centre for melon-growing, Rte 18 diverges left to Kándanos and (c 55km) Palaiókhora on the south coast. As you approach the Rodopós peninsula which forms the western limit of Khaniá Bay, the red-painted dome of the *Moní Kerá Goniás* (Γωνία meaning corner) stands out ahead just above the shore.

24km. At the Kolymbári crossroads the main road bears half-left uphill for Kastélli, but a 1km detour to the right leads to *Kolymbári* and the monastery just beyond. The village only recently began to develop its tourist potential, and the atmosphere is correspondingly agreeable. The tamarisk-lined main street backs on to the diminutive harbour, at the end of a long pebble beach sheltered from the summer wind, the meltémi. There are good fish tavernas (popular for an evening outing from Khaniá in the height of summer), a new small hotel that is heavily booked from abroad in the season, and many pleasant rooms for rent, the best overlooking the harbour.

The existing monastery of the Panayía Goniás (Feast Day, 15 August) also known as the Odiyítria, Our Lady Guide, was founded in 1618 by the monk Blaise (who came from Cyprus) with the help of the Zangaróli family, Venetians who had adopted the Orthodox faith. The first (1634) cruciform church was severely damaged by the Turks, whose forces disembarked nearby in the Bay of Khaniá at the start of their assault on Crete (1645). However the monastery managed to obtain a charter which put it under the direct authority and protection of the Patriarch in Constantinople, and the church was rebuilt (1662); the side-chapels and narthex are 19C additions. Although the monastery escaped relatively unscathed during the Turkish rule, its rich library was burned at the time of the 1866 Rebellion; certain treasures including a 17C codex were saved.

Tradition links the origins of the monastery, at least by the early years of the Second Byzantine period if not before, with the church of Ayios Yeóryios, Meniés, which is close to the site of the Greco-Roman sanctuary of Díktynna, north along the coast near Cape Spátha (ancient Tityros) at the tip of the Rodopós peninsula. The monks are thought to have moved from that remote spot to the greater safety of Kolymbári, and the ruins of a monastery dating from the 13C survive on the hillside above the main buildings.

The Odiyítria possesses one of the most important collections of icons on Crete. A monk is on duty to open the church and museum (both closed 13.30–15.30); he may point out the more important works in the church or he may offer a leaflet which identifies them. In the north side-chapel an icon of Ayios Nikólaos (1637), by the greatly admired Cretan painter Konstantínos Palaiókapas, adheres strictly to the artistic conventions of the painters of the Cretan School.

The small museum (south-east corner of the quadrangle) displays vestments and ecclesiastical valuables, some interesting historical documents, and a number of precious icons. These include a superb Crucifixion by Palaiókapas, and in contrast to his Ayios Nikólaos in the church, this painting shows the influence of Italian art in the background buildings and landscape, and in the realistic anatomical treatment.

The refectory, at the north-east corner of the quadrangle, is entered through a classical doorway embellished with baroque volutes. From the terrace at the east end of the church there is a *view of Khaniá Bay and the White Mountains; the cannonball preserved in the wall of the south apse is a memento of the Turkish bombardment.

Outside the handsome west gate is a fountain (1708). Its inscription translated reads: Most delicious Spring of water bubbling up for me; Water, for all creation, the sweetest element in life.

Steps beside the fountain lead to a steep path up the herb-scented hillside and in 5 minutes to ruins of the monastery's predecessor. The 13C church has remains of frescoes.

The modern building above the shore just beyond the monastery is the Orthodox Academy of Crete. The road continues only a short distance north along this coast of the peninsula; after 1.5km you pass a turn for a Cretan war memorial, and in a further 3km reach *Aphráta*. For the beach (1.5km) keep right in the village; the track may still be rough for the last stretch through a ravine before the narrow rocky bay. (After 600m a fork left leads out on to wild scrubby hillside, the typical maquis or phrýgana of much of the Cretan terrain.)

To the Diktýnnaion. Boats may be hired from Kolymbári for the excursion to the north-eastern tip of the Rodopós peninsula, near Cape Spátha, to a cove that was the site of the ancient sanctuary of Díktynna; ask at the kapheneíon next to the OTE in the narrow part of the main street. Private hire is not cheap but in high season the larger caiques make the trip with parties of tourists. (Journey time variable according to size of boat— between one and two hours.) Almost nothing remains of the great temple to Díktynna (see reconstruction) which was visible for a great distance from sea and land, but the site is evocative. There is excellent swimming at the (uninhabited) cove.

On the way up the coast the boat passes a cave known as Ellinóspilios, an important Neolithic habitation and burial site, where sherds were found at the back of the 100m-deep chamber.

The alternative is to drive (taxis available at Kolymbári crossroads) to the village of Rodopós on the spine of the peninsula and then walk—a whole day's expedition. The village can be reached from the main Kastélli road, but from the Goniá monastery take the coast road to *Aphráta* (described above). Turn left for (7km) *Astrátigos* and climb (good dirt surface) across the peninsula, with views ever deeper into the Levká Ori. 9km from Kolymbári you join the asphalt road from Khaniá, and turn right for (11km) *Rodopós*.

Beyond the long village the newly improved road climbs again, higher on to the spine of the peninsula. (Until very recently only a mule-track, this is the route of an annual pilgrimage on 29 August to the church of Ayios Ioánnis, Yioní, for the baptism of babies with the name John who are brought from all over western Crete.) There is now a vehicle track of sorts, roughly levelled by bulldozer, all the way to the Diktýnnaion (17km from Rodopós to the sanctuary site), but as a dirt road of hard-packed red earth interrupted by sections of dangerously uneven rock it has not been suitable for the normal hired car. However the track is highly recommended to long-distance walkers. If a car is available it may be taken at least 3km beyond Rodopós, and after that there is always the chance of a lift from a pick-up truck. It is also possible that in due course the surface for the rest of the way will be improved. About 6km from Rodopós there is a branch left for Ayios Ioánnis, a further hour on foot.

At c 12km the main track runs for some distance along a flat valley floor; at the end of this stretch it veers left, and shows up as a scar on the rock wall. At this point raised stretches of the ancient paved road continue straight ahead. The new track continues north until, nearing the sanctuary, it makes a long bend right to come down to the east shore of the cape. You can see, in a hollow (right), the old church of Ayios Yeóryios, Meniés, beside a medieval tower which was perhaps part of the monastery traditionally associated with the Goniá foundation (see above). The track comes to an end just above the bay and the sanctuary site.

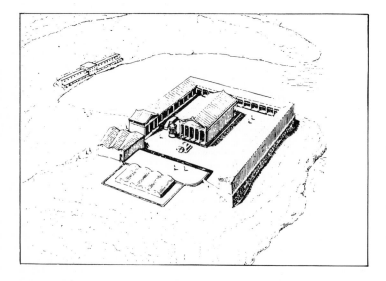

A reconstruction of the Temple of Diktynna on Cape Spátha

The *Diktýnnaion*, mentioned with admiration by many writers in antiquity, was the most important religious sanctuary in western Crete during the Greco-Roman period. The prestige derived from control over it is well documented, and was fiercely contested among the powerful city-states of the region, in particular Kydonía and Polyrrhénia. The accumulated wealth of the sanctuary was sometimes used to finance public works programmes.

The cult of the Cretan goddess Díktynna, closely related to that of Britomártis (an old Minoan name known to mean 'sweet maiden'), was to some extent a survival of the worship of the Minoan mother goddess. Although there were cult centres in Athens and the Peloponnese, and as far away as Marseilles, Díktynna seems to have been especially venerated in the west of Crete. The name may perhaps be related to Mount Díkte or (the Greek historian Strabo's version) to the word δίκτυον (díktyon), the fishermen's net which is supposed to have saved the goddess when, in flight from the unwelcome attentions of Mínos, she leapt into the sea. Díktynna had many of the attributes of the Greek goddess Artemis; she was a huntress, and the deity of nature, the wild countryside and mountains, and her sanctuary on Cape Spátha was guarded by hounds which the Cretans claimed to be as strong as bears.

The sanctuary site occupied the sheltered (south-east facing) cove where the boats now land, and lay on either side of the water-course. There are remains of Roman buildings on the north side of the beach (the statue of Hadrian now in Khaniá Museum came from one of them), and traces on the south side of the stream-bed of the bridge which crossed it; this may have served also as an aqueduct. The temple, no doubt visible from a great distance, stood on the high promontory to the south of the cove. The foundations of the Roman cisterns are preserved, but of the courtyard temple, unique on Crete, only some ashlar blocks of the terrace and a few architectural fragments survive.

The temple was excavated by German archaeologists in 1942, but uncertainties remain because it had been systematically looted and robbed. The temple terrace measured 55m by 50m. The peripteral temple (the only such design known on Crete) was built of limestone, with marble paving; Ionic columns on its east side were in blue marble, and the remainder white marble of the Corinthian order. The temple stood in a paved court surrounded on three sides by stoas. South of the terrace were four cisterns; their total capacity has been estimated at 400 cubic metres. Between the temple and the cisterns stood a stepped altar of white marble. At the south-west corner of the temple there was a small circular building which may perhaps have been a treasury; the statue of Díktynna with hound, now in Khaniá Museum, was found here.

The excavated temple is tentatively dated to the 2C AD. There was certainly an earlier building on the site, and there were also suggestions of a Doric predecessor to the west of the Roman temple.

To Spiliá and Episkopí. From the Kolymbári crossroads on the Khaniá–Kastélli route, take the minor road south. Pass the turn for Marathokephála and continue to (3km) *Spiliá*, one of the most delightful villages in this part of the island. The frescoed church of the Panayía lies on the far side of the village (signed, right) but it is agreeable to walk (5 minutes) from the prominent modern church (bearing left at the bottom of the flight of steps up to it and following clear signs), past a fountain and out to the edge of the village, to the tree-shaded old church dedicated to the Presentation and Assumption of the Virgin. The frescoes (torch useful), dated stylistically to the 14C, with graffito of 1401, are cited as an early example on the island of the style of painting which is referred to as 'Cretan', though it was not confined to and probably did not originate on Crete.

Above Spiliá is a cave which is a popular place for Cretan outings. It can be reached through Marathokephála (see above), or from the centre of the village—signed from the modern church. A church in the cave is dedicated to Ayios Ioánnis Xénos, the 10/11C evangelist principally associated with the monastery of the Katholikó on the Akrotíri near Khaniá (Feast Day 7 October).

The minor road continues south from Spiliá towards Episkopí. After 2km Ayios Stéphanos (frescoed) is signed right. A path (5 minutes) follows a bank, that in spring is smothered in cyclamen, to the tiny chapel, dating (10C) from the time of the restoration of the Christian faith after the Arab occupation.

1km further, turn right for *Mikhaíl Arkhángelos, Episkopí,* a church of particular architectural interest, beautifully situated on the slopes of a wooded valley. This became the seat of the bishopric of Kísamos during the Second Byzantine period.

Essentially the church is a rotunda provided with a U-shaped bema and enclosed in a (more or less) rectangular building; the rotunda rises to a curious stepped dome consisting of five concentric rings. The design is unique on Crete and has few exact parallels in Byzantine architecture. (The only comparable building on the Greek mainland is Ayios Yeóryios at Thessaloníki.)

There have been various theories about the architectural development of Mikhaíl Arkhángelos. Remains of a mosaic floor apparently dating back to the 6C (Crete's First Byzantine period) suggested that the present church was built over the foundations of an Early Christian basilica. However a thorough investigation by the Service for Byzantine Antiquities (under M. Andrianákis and a team from Khaniá) has been underway since the mid 1980s, and the results seem to support the view that the rotunda itself dates to the First Byzantine period and was the original church on the site, with later (post-Arab) adaptations. Frescoes have been uncovered from three periods. The earliest detected fragments date back to the 10C, with evidence for two phases of wall-painting during the 12C.

Restoration continues and access to the church may be limited, but the guardian (phýlakas) who holds the key lives in the village 500m further on the road continuing up the hillside (ask at the first houses on the right).

Continuing towards Kastélli on the main road from the Kolymbári crossroads, you pass (right) the turning for Rodopós. The old road is narrow and winding as it crosses the neck of the peninsula, but radical work is in progress to realign it (nearer the coast) and to upgrade it to highway standard.

Following the old road through a natural gap in the hills, the Bay of Kísamos (sheltered by the two long capes, Voúxa and Spátha) and the plain of Kastélli are suddenly in view below. The road descends steeply in a series of bends. To the south, craggy dolomitic mountains fill the sky, and ahead is the Gramboúsa promontory, the extreme north-western tip of Crete; the plain is densely planted with olive trees.

The New Road cuts across the neck of the Rodopós peninsula and down to the shore of the bay. On the coast there is a long-established camping site.

At c 40km a minor road sets off inland from *Kaloudianá* and follows the broad Yíphlos valley towards (8km) the attractive village of Topólia, and the south-west corner of the island (see Rte 20).

43km. **Kastélli Kisámou** was so named because of the castle built here by the Genoese freebooter Enrico Pescatore as part of his attempt (after 1206) to challenge Venice's claim to the island. In recent times (1966) to avoid confusion, in particular with Kastélli in the Pediáda district, the town officially reverted to Kísamos, after the Greco-Roman city-state at this place. However, locally, the traditional name persists.

Kastélli is a convenient stop on a touring holiday. The plateía and one main shopping street are inland of a straggle of buildings along a fine sandy beach (tavernas). The little town (pop. 2800) is not much affected by international tourism, and has an air of preoccupation with regional business rather than with visiting foreigners, but a road-building programme opening up the west coast, and a regular car-ferry service (via the island of Kýthera) from the nearby Greek mainland (Peloponnese) have increased its popularity with tourists, and the highway from Khaniá is expected to continue the trend. There are several small hotels, also many simple rooms for rent.

The *ferry quay* is 3km west of the town (see Rte 20). On the way along the coast road you pass the small harbour for fishing-boats (tavernas).

Agent for the ferry service to the Peloponnese (and on to Piraeus): M. Kheroukhákis in the main plateía; tel: (0822) 22 655. In the high season there may be day-trips by caique to the Venetian fortress of Gramboúsa (Rte 20).

The *bus station* is on the main thoroughfare or ring-road on the inland side of the town, 100m south of the central plateía.

Ancient Kísamos, one of the two harbours of the inland city-state of Polyrrhénia, became an independent city itself only in the 3C AD, but then gradually superseded Polyrrhénia. It was the seat of a bishop till the Saracen occupation (9C), and later a thriving Venetian settlement, fortified in the 16C. There are eye-witness accounts from early travellers of ancient remains, but, as at Khaniá, the existence of the modern town impedes archaeological investigation of the site. New building work sometimes makes it possible to excavate on a limited scale, and gradually details of the Roman city are being pieced together to improve knowledge of public buildings and individual houses. The small archaeological museum in the main plateía functions as a storeroom for local finds but unfortunately, in recent years, it has not been open to the public.

A new *folklore museum* opened in 1990 and is dedicated to preserving the fast disappearing material remains of the traditional Cretan way of life.

To Polyrrhénia, 7km inland where the city-state occupied a hilltop stronghold from the Iron Age to Venetian times. This is a recommended excursion offering spectacular views; the site is renowned for its spring flowers.

The bus leaves Kastélli for the once-a-day return journey in the early afternoon, so without private transport a taxi may be useful (taxi rank in the plateía.)

By car or on foot find the main ring-road inland of the town. At the Khaniá end of it there is a junction with central triangle planted with oleanders. 250m along the ring-road, travelling west, take the first turn left, signed for many years only in Greek (ΠΡΟΣ ΠΟΛΥΡΡΗΝΙΑ). The road climbs inland through olive groves with a view of dramatic rock formations ahead, and ends, near a ruined tower, at the foot of the village formerly known as Ano Palaiókastro.

Both cobbled streets ahead lead to the ancient site (10 minutes). To the left (steep only briefly), after 150 paces at a meeting of tracks take the upper one to the left. At the top of the village turn left on to a dirt track which winds round right to the landmark of a church.

Here on a relatively level shoulder of the hill, the church of the Ninety-nine Martyrs is built over the foundations of a large Hellenistic building, probably a temple. The lower courses of massive walling now support the cemetery. A clear Roman inscription is built into the wall of the church.

The ancient city of *Polyrrhénia* lay on the slopes around the church and down to the village, with the acropolis and its secondary spur above to the north east. Sherds indicate occupation from the Archaic (6C) to the Roman periods. The site was reoccupied in the late 10C and became a Venetian stronghold. Although its position was almost impregnable, on a steep hill surrounded by ravines, the city was also walled. The remains of the fortifications, including the towers, date from the Second Byzantine and the Venetian periods (best preserved on the northern spur), but lie in part on earlier foundations, probably of Hellenistic walls repaired in Roman times. Water was supplied by rock-cut aqueducts.

There are few remains within the acropolis walls, but the walk (c 30 minutes) to the top is highly recommended. There is a steep path up the western (left) side of the hill, but the easier way sets off from the church, and (marked occasionally with splashes of red paint) gains height round the right flank, with views spectacular even by Cretan standards, including from the summit both north and south coasts of the island. In spring the hillsides of Polyrrhénia are carpeted with wild flowers.

For the walk to the tip of the Gramboúsa peninsula, see Rte 20.

20   Kastélli to the West Coast

A circuit of c 100km (60 miles); 16km ancient Phalásarna; 34km Sphinári; 54km Kepháli; 62km monastery of Khrysoskalítissa (and a further 5km to the Elaphonísi islands) with the return to the north coast from Kepháli by the Yiphlós valley.

An alternative is to turn south after Kepháli and Elos, towards the coast at Palaiókhora, on the newly improved roads of this south-western corner of the island.

There is a limited bus service from Kastélli to Phalásarna and Sphinári on the west coast, and also a daily service from Khaniá (with connections from Kastélli) to Khrysoskalítissa and Elaphonísi.

From Kastélli the road runs west along the coast past a small fishing harbour (tavernas), to (3km) the quay for the car-ferry to the Peloponnese—see p 301. (Café-bar on the quay, and taxis meet the ferries.)

Soon the road turns inland to cross the base of the *Gramboúsa peninsula* that stretches away to the north sheltering the Kísamos Bay. Off its north-western tip is a rock on which, in 1579, the Venetians built a fortress that held out against the Turks till 1692, 23 years after the surrender of Herákleion. Gramboúsa later became a stronghold of piracy. In the 19C the Turks exploited its position to harass the short sea-crossing between rebellious Crete and the island of Antikýthera, by then a part of independent Greece. (Attempts have been made to run boat trips to Gramboúsa, both from Kastélli and from Khaniá, but arrangements still vary from year to year. Enquire at shipping agency—see under Rte 19, or at Tourist Information Office—Rte 14.)

At 5km an insignificant right turning leads to (c 2km) Kalyvianí. From a little beyond the village there is the opportunity of a long walk on the peninsula, 2–3 hours out to the cape where (opposite the Gramboúsa fortress) Tigáni Bay, the name signifying its frying pan shape, is a surprising beach of white sand.

The unmarked turning is beside a cement works, and immediately (after 100m) you fork left. In Kalyvianí the road bends left, but at this corner keep straight ahead to the end of the village street where at a kapheneíon (left, opposite a tree) a broad track branches off downhill to the right; the track is rough but driveable with care for c 3km. From this point allow about 2½ hours for the walk to Tigáni Bay.

The path is marked spasmodically with paint splashes; it keeps to the eastern side of the spine of the peninsula, and gains height gradually to pass the head of several small water-courses. Long stretches of this walk are across bare hillside, but at a little over half way a large clump of oleanders marks a welcome spring, and conceals the weathered blocks and pointed arch of the old Ayía Eiríni fountain. A long slow climb brings you up on to a plateau; bear left across it, cutting off the narrow tip of the peninsula. Before the path begins the steep descent to the bay on the west coast, you can walk out to the edge of the perpendicular cliff; one little island is linked to the beach by a sandy spit, but just to the north is the island of Gramboúsa. The rock is flat-topped except for a knob at its seaward end on which the Venetians built their fortress; the turreted walls of this isolated outpost still stand.

On the main road west from Kastélli you pass at 6km the turn for the village of Gramboúsa at the base of the peninsula, and at 10km reach a fork at the beginning of *Plátanos*. To visit the Greco-Roman harbour site of Phalásarna keep right at the fork on the new road which avoids the village centre. After 200m take a narrow turning right, and in 1km keep to the right round a red-roofed church.

From the church the well-made road drops downhill 6km to Phalásarna. The panoramic view of the Bay of Livádi includes a dense olive grove, and plastic-sheeted greenhouses glinting behind a long sandy beach; the Gramboúsa peninsula stretches away to the north. Halfway down the hillside, at a junction, follow a hairpin bend right (signed) to head towards the archaeological site which is below Cape Koutrí at the northern end of the bay.

The asphalt ends 5km from the church at some scattered blocks of rent rooms behind two or three tavernas looking out over the sea. You can get down to the shore from the tavernas but the long sandy beach 500m to the south is one of the finest on Crete.

The last stretch of track ahead runs across the site, past the so-called 'rock-cut throne' which has been the subject of much speculation. It remains an enigma. Keep on towards the chapel of Ayios Yeóryios on the headland until the track curves away to the right to the cove beyond it, and then strike left (on a footpath) to the relatively level area distinguished by evidence of recent archaeologiical activity.

Phalásarna, the most westerly city-state of Crete, was at the height of its power in the Hellenistic period (4–3C BC), though sherds from the 6C testify to earlier occupation, and for a time it was the west coast port of Polyrrhénia (Rte 19). The city was mentioned by ancient geographers especially for its 'enclosed harbour'. The Englishman Captain T.A.B. Spratt, on a Royal Naval survey expedition in the mid 19C, was the first to realise that owing to an alteration in the sea-level, this enclosed harbour was high and dry c 100m inland. Recent excavations have been able to demonstrate that tectonic displacement took place in the late 5C AD, raising this coast 6–9m above the present sea level; the movement of the island is said to be caused by the subduction of the African plate under the Aegean in an area just to the west of Crete.

Spratt left an invaluable record of the upstanding remains of the city walls which he supposed had surrounded the 'ancient port'. In 1986 a geophysical survey carried out by scientists from the University of Patrás provided confirmation of the existence of an artificial harbour with surrounding defence walls very much as they had been planned in 1860.

The *acropolis* of the city-state lay to the north of the harbour on the headland of Cape Koutrí which drops sheer into the sea; there is a rough path up from the east, above the chapel of Ayios Yeóryios. Remains on the higher summit may belong to a temple, perhaps to Diktynnaion Artemis; the other known temple (to Apollo) was probably down by the harbour. The city spread on to the slope below the headland. The north east–south west orientated promontory was crossed in the Hellenistic period by a fortification wall which can still be traced in places.

The city's cemeteries were on the rising ground inland, with at least 32 cist graves (4C) on the south-east side of the town. From 6C tombs came imported black-figure Corinthian pottery now on display in Khaniá Museum.

The archaeological investigation of the harbour works at Phalásarna (see sketch plan) has proceeded under the joint auspices of E. Hadjidáki of Khaniá Museum (with support from the municipality) and F. Frost of California University.

The artificially excavated *harbour basin*, measuring 100m by 75m, had been connected to the sea by a natural opening in the rock enlarged to form an entrance channel 10–12m wide. At some point in antiquity passage had been deliberately obstructed with large blocks of stone. A secondary, shallower, channel diverged from the main one to reach the sea 100m further north; it may have had a desilting function or served as a dock for small boats. The roughly rectangular basin is now a flat area filled with earth, and the courses of both channels can still be traced. It is estimated that the harbour could take vessels of at least 1.2m draught.

The approximately rectangular harbour was defended by stretches of the city wall, and by four towers and a mole. The South Tower (excavated 1986–87) turned out to be a formidable fortification built in the second half of the 4C BC, circular in plan (not square as Spratt had supposed), with massive foundations built of ashlar sandstone blocks in isodomic style, without mortar, and strengthened by an internal arrangement of quadrants deliberately filled with rubble. At one place eight courses of its external wall are preserved, to a height of 4.5m. The excavators draw attention to the design of the base of the tower by which the diameter decreases above a rounded moulding three courses from ground level. This structural feature is common in Greek military architecture but not on harbour towers, and had not previously been uncovered on Crete. To the west of the tower two parallel walls with moat between are interpreted as a protective sea wall. Another unusual feature is the cistern which was bonded into the north-west side of the tower and, intriguingly, had its plastered interior treated with a black paint. This cistern would have provided a secure water supply for defending forces but may also have facilitated the swift resupplying of ships.

The rectangular North Tower dating back to the 4C BC was reconstructed in late Hellenistic times. In antiquity there was a second basin to the north of this tower which might have been a small inner harbour, but it is awkwardly limited by walls and anyway turns out to have had no connection with the sea. Probably it was a brackish lagoon but any function remains uncertain.

In Hellenistic times the menace of piracy from vessels based in Cretan waters is well documented. Faced with the lack of evidence for commercial harbour activities, and with the obviously defensive works and hints of military structures around this 'enclosed port' the excavators have put forward the hypothesis that the city-state of Phalásarna sheltered a pirates' lair. When the Romans invaded Crete in 67 BC one of their main aims was to reduce the menace of piracy from bases on Crete, and the blocking of the entrance channel into the harbour here may have been an effective episode in their campaign.

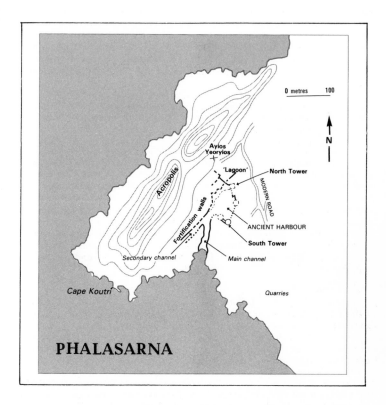

Back in the village of Plátanos turn right to continue south towards (8km) Sphinári. After 2km you pass (left) a turn for Lusakiés, climbing to a fine retrospective view over the bay to Phalásarna and Cape Koutrí. The road was newly engineered more than ten years ago to open up this stretch of the west coast, and in some places there has been work on a second phase of widening, but (at the time of writing) the asphalt surface has not been completed and you should expect to take the journey slowly and with care. The rewards are considerable. The road winds high above the sea, with the (as yet) undeveloped coastline spread out below and many tracks down to it clearly visible, while others point invitingly into the hills. Oleanders are beginning to hide the scars left by the roadworks.

At 34km *Sphinári*, a small village 800m inland of a pebble beach, has a few rooms for rent. The track to the shore starts at the far end of the village. The road turns inland climbing to Ano Sphinári, and on through lightly wooded country, past the turning to (2km) Melissiá in the hills. You emerge on to a corniche road with stunning views back along the coast and at 42km reach *Kámbos*, strung out along a wooded stream; here also there are rooms for rent and the chance of a taverna, also a new track (c 2km) to the coast. A kaldẽrími following the stream into the hills leads over the watershed in the direction of Sirikári. In spring all this region is highly recommended for its profusion of wild flowers, but the climate is much cooler than across the rest of the island, and the season usually at least two weeks behind it. Soon there is a fine view ahead from the road down the coast to the south-western corner of Crete, over the narrow plain behind Stómio Bay, with Moní Khrysoskalítissa perched on a rock; the roof of its church, when not camouflaged by heat haze or dust, gleams a brilliant blue.

At 47km a dirt road descends (c 2km to the coast, 15km to Khrysoskalítissa) to join at Akti Livásia the (driveable) track that follows the shore from below Kámbos to Stómio and the monastery.

You continue past (48km) *Keramotí* and (50km) *Amigdalokephálı*. The road turns inland through Pappadianá to (56km) *Kepháli*, a flourishing village with many simple tavernas and some rooms to rent. This remote region of Crete remains quite isolated and secondary schooling still involves weekly boarding with family or friends in Kastélli or Khaniá but there are welcome signs of a new prosperity associated with the benefits of tourism. Kepháli is beautifully situated high above a wooded valley, looking down to the distant sea at Stómio. A church on the southern edge of the village, Metamórphosis tou Sotírou (the Transfiguration of the Saviour) has frescoes dated to 1320. Ask for directions and key at the kapheneíon.

At the end of the village there is an acute right turn on to a minor road, widened and improved but not yet surfaced, to (11km) **Moní Khrysoska-lítissa** on the coast. 2km down the hill you come to *Váthi* (formerly Koúneni). There are two frescoed churches here for enthusiasts; both are locked, and the village priest holds the keys—his house is 100m south of the plateía, straight ahead where the road bends left. In case of difficulty ask at the kapheneíon.

The church of Ayios Yeóryios (in the village, to the right of the road at the plateía) has frescoes dated by inscription 1284. (Some of the scenes in the upper register of the vault were inexpertly reassembled during repairs to the roof.) The original sketches in the apse form an interesting comparison with the frescoes themselves.

In the fields immediately below the road, a few minutes south of the village (path left) the church of Mikhaíl Arkhángelos has early 14C frescoes, notably the Fall of Jericho and the Presentation in the Temple. The paintings in the bema are later 14C work.

The road continues beside a stream overhung by sweet chestnut trees; chestnuts are a commercially important crop in this part of the island. Walkers will enjoy exploring the tracks off the road to the unspoilt villages of this valley. About 7km from the turn in Kepháli there is a new bridge over the stream, and when there is much water coming down from the hills it is advisable to cross to the other bank here. Otherwise you can keep straight ahead (signed for Stómio) to emerge on the bay. To the right are the ruins of the village of Stómio and a gypsum quarry.

Turn left towards the blue roofs of the monastery, nowadays a convent though few nuns remain. The first church here was built inside a grotto. The double-naved church is dedicated to the Panayía Khrysoskalítissa (Our Lady of the Golden Stair—χρυσός means gold, plus σκαλί, a stair). Ninety steps lead down to the sheltered cove to the south of the pinnacle on which the church is built, and it is said that only those without sin can tell which is the stair that is made of gold. The present buildings are of no great age, but the panoramic *view from the terrace is worth the climb. The gates are closed 12.00–15.00.

MM and LM sherds in the area of the monastery indicate a Minoan coastal settlement.

Scattered concrete buildings (tavernas and bars with rooms to rent) have not increased the romance of this remote spot. You are strongly recommended to continue 5km further south along a flat dirt road, for the *Elaphonísi* islands just off-shore protect a long tree-shaded sandy beach coloured pink by fragments of coral, one of the most idyllic spots on Crete for a lazy afternoon. The main island (with deep water swimming) is reached by wading thigh-deep across a lagoon. Up to 1991 there was neither mains electricity nor telephone, though the ferry ran day-trips from Palaiókhora, but there are strong rumours of future development so the sense of isolation and extraordinary natural beauty may not last for much longer.

On the return journey retrace the route only as far as Kepháli and there turn right (signpost for Khaniá). After 5km you pass through the long tree-shaded village of *Elos*, one of the most attractive in the region; there is a Chestnut Festival held here every October. 4km beyond this, just before Milí, is the junction for a cross-country route (right) on newly-improved roads to Kándanos and Palaiókhora (Rte 18).

The road, signed for Strovlés, sets off up the Yiphlós valley following the stream. After 2km, in *Strovlés*, turn left at a T-junction. At 3.5km you can turn left again to cut across (7km) to Plemenianá, just south of Kándanos, on the main Khaniá–Palaiókhora road. Ahead the broad new road (well-engineered though not asphalted all the way and still rough in places) climbs into the wild and unspoilt hill country of the south-western corner of the island, to Voutás and Sklavopoúla (described as part of an excursion from Palaiókhora, see p 293). After 2km a dirt road branches left down into the valley 7km to Sarakína (see Rte 18), but the major road continues to climb to the watershed (6.5km from Strovlés) before a gradual descent of 10km, with extensive views, to a fertile valley of orange groves, and *Voutás*.

Continuing through *Míli* on the circular itinerary, the road runs back towards the north coast through chestnut woods along the valley of the Yiphlós. At c 90km, above the dramatic *Gorge of Topólia*, the cave of Ayía Sophía has a chapel at its entrance; the cave (with remarkable stalactites) was frequented from Neolithic to Roman times. *Topólia* is a particularly pleasant village in a fine setting. The road continues down the river valley to the coast where you turn left for the last 5km to Kastélli-Kisámou.

INDEX

Topographical names are printed in **bold** type, personal names in *italics*, other entries in Roman type. Churches are indexed alphabetically by the name of their Saint.

ATLAS SECTION

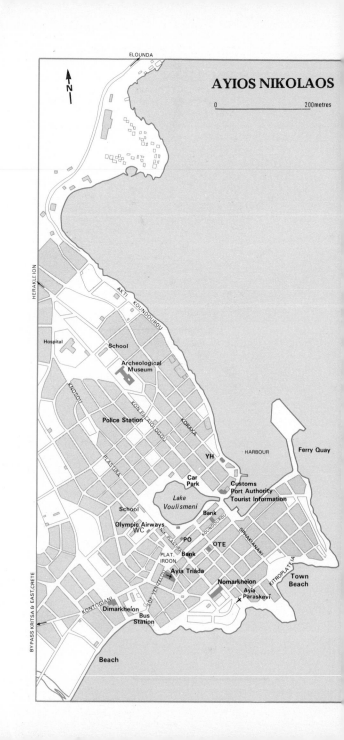

AYIOS NIKOLAOS

ELOUNDA

N

0   200metres

HERAKLEION

AKTI KOUNDOUROU

Hospital

School

Archeological Museum

KNOSOU

KON. PALAIOLOGOU

Police Station

KORAKA

PLASTIRA

YH

HARBOUR

Ferry Quay

Car Park

Lake Voulismeni

Customs
Port Authority
Tourist Information

School

Bank

KOUNDOUROU

Olympic Airways
WC

PO

OTE

SFAKIANAKI

Bank

PLAT. IROON

KIT. PLASTIRA

Ayia Triáda

Nomarkheíon

KITROPLATIA

Town Beach

Ayía Paraskeví

KONTOGIANI

SOF. VENIZELOU

Dimarkheíon

Bus Station

BYPASS KRITSA & EAST CRETE

Beach

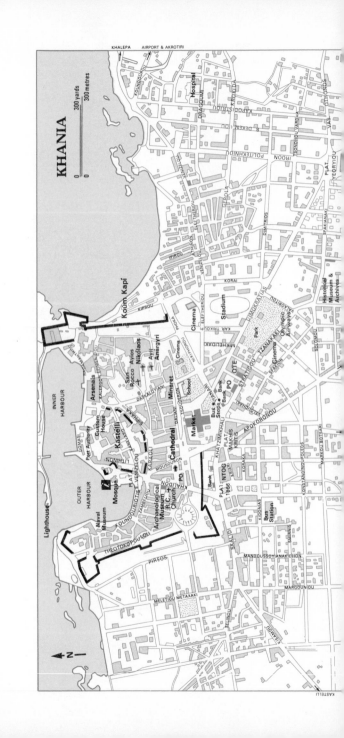

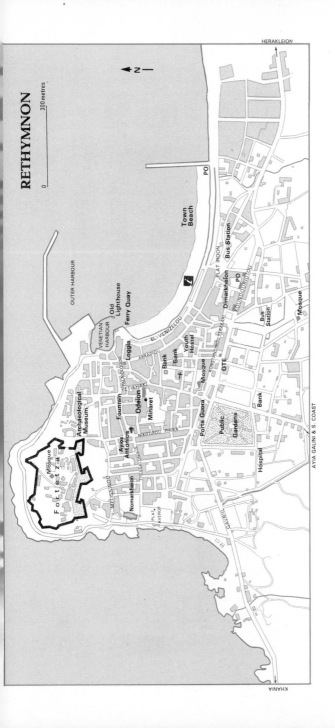

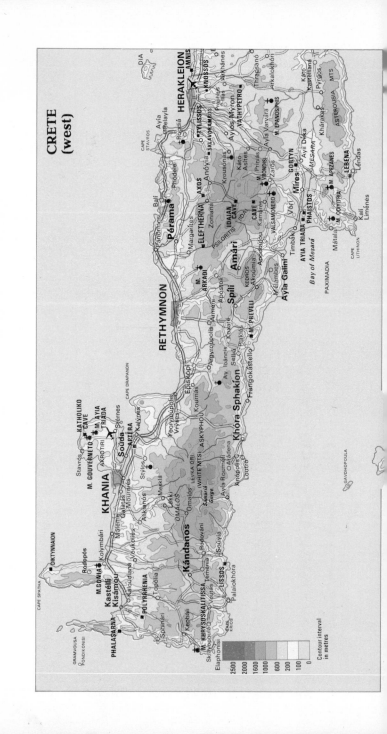

CRETE
(west)

GRAMVOUSA
PONDIKONISI

CAPE SPATHA

DIKTYNNAION

Rádopos
Kolymbári

PHALASÁRNA

M.GONIA

Kastélli
Kisámou

Koutoúli
Kaloúdiana

Topólia

POLYRRHENIA

Kepháli

ST. KHRYSOSKALITISSA
Stavropoúla

Elaphonísi

Sphinári

Palaiókhóra

Voútas

Kándanos

Temenía

LISSÓS

Anópolis

Ayía Rouméli

Loutró

Khóra Sphakíon

Frangokástello

GAVDHOPOULA

GAVDHOPOULA

Máleme
Galatás
Moúrnies

KHANIA

Stylos

Mesklá
Lákki

Anikiános

Omalós

OMALÓS

LEVKA ÓRI
(WHITE MTS)

Samariá
Gorge

ASKYPHOÚ

Askýphou

O Aradena

Anópolis

Soúgia

Rodováni

Stavrós

M. GOUVERNETO
CAVE

KATHOLIKÓ
CAVE

M. AYIA
TRIÁDA

AKROTÍRI

APTÉRA

Kalýdes

Soúda

Sýrnes

Vrýses

Kournás

Yeoryioúpolis

EPISKOPÍ

CAPE DRÁPANON

Ay. Ioánnis
Sellía

Prasés

Koxaré

Argyroúpolis

Armení

M. PREVELI

Plakiás

RETHYMNON

M.
ARKADI

Apóstoli

KEDROS

Spíli

Amári

Méronas

Mé2ámbes

Apodoúlou

Timbáki

AYIA
TRIÁDA

PHAISTÓS

M. ODHITRIA

Mátala

Kalí
Liménes

CAPE
LÍTHINON

Bay of Mesará

PAXIMÁDIA

Ayía Galíni

VALSAMÓNERO

KÁMARES

CAVE

Kamáres

Zarós

Vorí

GORTYN

Míres

MESARÁ

M. APEZANES

LEBENA

Léndas

Kató
Deká

VRÓNDISI

M. EPANOSÍPHIS

Ayía Varvára

Priniás

Ayios Myron

Kró́usónas

Kató
Astes

Anóyia

AXÓS

ELEFTHERNA

Zoniana

Margarítes

IDAIAN
CAVE
(IDA)

PSILORÍTIS M.

M. EPANOSÍPHIS

Péráma

Pánormos

Balí

Pródromos

CAPE
STAVROS

Ayía
Pelayía

Rogdiá

VATHÝPETRO

SKLAVOKAMBOS

TYLISSOS

Arkhánes

Proftitis Ilías

Fódele

HERAKLEION

KNOSSÓS

Kalokorío

Thrápsano

Arkalokhóri

Kató
Kasteliana

Pyrgos

ASTEROÚSIA
MTS

AMNISÓS

DIA

Contour interval
in metres

2500
2000
1600
1000
600
200
100
0

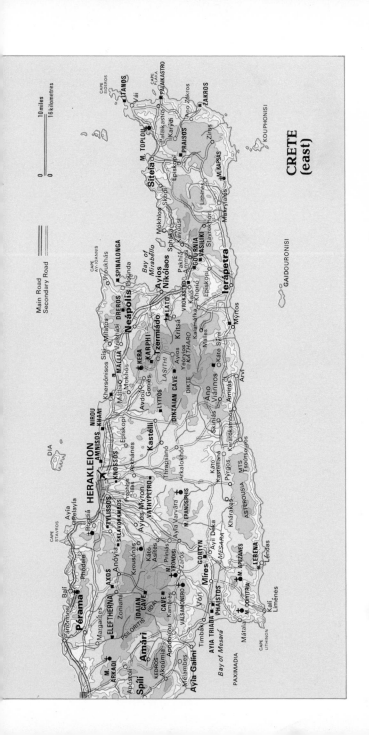

CRETE
(east)

Main Road
Secondary Road

0   10 miles
0   16 kilometres

HERAKLEION

Pérama
Spili
Amári
M. ARKADI
Ayía Galíni
AYIA TRIADA
PHAISTOS
M. ODIYITRIA
LEBENA
GORTYN
Míres
M. APEZANES
VRONDISI
CAVE
IDAIAN CAVE
ELEFTHERNA
AXOS
TYLISSOS
KNOSSOS
AMNISOS
NIROU
HANI
Kastélli
EPANOSIPHS
VATHYPETRO
Ayios Myron
LYTTOS
DREROS
Neápolis
MALLIA
KARPHI
KERA
Tzermiádo
LASÍTHI
DIKTAIAN CAVE
DIKTE
Ayios Nikólaos
LATO
VROKASTRO
KRITHARO
GOURNIA
VASILIKI
Ierápetra
Sitela
PRAISOS
M. TOPLOU
PALAIKASTRO
ZAKROS
ITANOS
M. KAPSAS

DIA
Ayía
Pelayía
CAPE
STAVROS
Rogdiá
Phódele
Margarites
Bali
Pánormos
Apóstoli
Akoúmia
Mélambes
Koxaré
KEDROS
Zoniana
Anóyia
Kroussónas
Káto
Asítes
Prinás
Ayíos
Vasílios
Arkhánes
Episkopí
Khersónisos
Sísi
Milatos
Vrákhasi
Mókhlos
Mílatos
Eloúnda
Bay of
Mirabéllo
CAPE
AYIOANNIS
Vrioukhás
SPINALONGA
Kritsá
Yéoryios
Ayios
Goniés
Avdoú
Krási
Ano
Viánnos
Kató Sými
Myrtos
Arví
Arvi
Skiniás
Amiras
Karávados
Pýrgos
Kastellianá
Asimi
Pýrgos
Káto
Thrapsanó
Arkalokhóri
MTS
ASTEROUSIA
Khárakas
Tsoútsouros
PAXIMADIA
Bay of Mesara
Mátala
CAPE
LITHINON
Kalí
Limènes
Léndas
Timbáki
Váli
Vóri
Kamáres
K. Kamáres
VALSAMONERO
TSILORITIS
(IDA)
M. Varvára
Ayía
Varvára
Zarós
Apodoúlou
Kournia
Platanos
Thrónos
M. Varvára
Maláxa
Thrapsanó
Avdoú
Gonés
Kalamáfka
Pakhiá
Ammos
Kaló
Chorió
Vasilikí
Kalamáfka
Stavrós
Máles
Kavoúsi
Sphaká
Makryialos
Lithines
Episkopí
Skópi
Zíros
Áno Zákros
Páno Zákros
Palaíkastro
Karýdi
Váï
CAPE
PLAKA
CAPE
SIDEROS
KOUPHONISI
GAIDOURONISI